Energy

THE ENERGY EFFICIENT HOME 101 MONEY SAVING IDEAS

Other TAB books by the author:

No. 1068 *Successful Sandy Soil Gardening*
No. 1302 *All About Greenhouses–with 15
build-your-own plans*

No. 1415
$19.95

THE ENERGY EFFICIENT HOME
101 MONEY
SAVING IDEAS

BY BETTE GALMAN WAHLFELDT

TAB BOOKS Inc.

BLUE RIDGE SUMMIT, PA. 17214

FIRST EDITION

FIRST PRINTING

Copyright © 1982 by TAB BOOKS Inc.

Printed in the United States of America

Library of Congress Cataloging in Publication Data

Wahlfeldt, Bette G. (Bette Galman)
    The energy efficient home—101 money saving ideas.

    Includes index.
    1. Dwellings—Energy conservation. I. Title.
II. Title: Energy efficient home—one hundred one money
saving ideas.   III. Title: Energy efficient home—one
hundred and one money saving ideas.
TJ163.5.D86W34   1982   644   82-5851
ISBN 0-8306-2415-5   AACR2
ISBN 0-8306-1415-X (pbk.)

Cover courtesy of U.S. Department of Housing and Urban Development.

Contents

Dedication vii

Epigraph vii

Acknowledgments viii

Introduction ix

1 **Understanding Energy** 1
Major Energy Supplies—Alternate Energy Sources—Saving Energy Saves Money—You and Your Electric Service—Costs and Savings—Air-Conditioning Savings—Heating and Air-Conditioning Savings—Your Energy Budget—Thermostat Control—Your Heating Bill—Heating and Cooling Factors Energy Conservation List

2 **Energy-Efficient Home Planning** 16
Siting a New Home—Sun and Wind—Glazing—Design Tips—Mobile Homes and Energy—Solar Energy—Solar Questions and Answers—Some Solar Ideas—The Standard Practice House—House Designs—Exterior Features—Flexible Ceiling Partitions—Putting Some Ideas Together—A Solar Water Heater—A Two-Tank Concept for Solar-Heated Water

3 **Insulation** 40
Types of Insulation—Buying Insulation—Insulate an Unfinished Attic—Insulate a Finished Attic—Insulate Your Walls—Insulate Your Floors—Insulate Your Basement Walls—How-to Insulation Procedures

4 **Heating and Cooling** 71
Choosing an Air Conditioner—Reducing Energy Usage of Window Units—Mobile Home Cooling—Checklist for Cooling Systems—Heating Systems—Forced-Hot-Water Heating Systems—Electric Heating—Mobile Home Heating—Heat Pumps—Hot-Water Systems—Chimney Inspection and Cleaning—Fuels and Burners—Automatic Controls—Room Ventilation—Fan Belts—Thermostats and Humidistats—Air Leaks—Common Areas for Leaks—Heating- and Cooling-System Maintenance—General Guidelines—Seasonal House Checks

5 Condensation and Ventilation **94**
Condensation—Moisture—Vapor Barriers—Concrete Slabs—Crawl Spaces—Finished Basement Rooms—Walls—Vapor Barrier in a Two-Story House—Knee Walls—Ceilings and Attics—Ventilation—Snow Belt Protection—Protection at Unheated Areas—Protection at Outlet Boxes—Minimizing Exiting Condensation Problems

6 Windows and Doors **123**
Insulated Glass—Storm Windows—Plastic Covers for Doors and Windows—Storm Doors—Making Selections—Avoiding Moisture Problems—Caulk and Weather Stripping—Window Installation—Storm Doors—A Colorful Idea—Installing Decorative Panels—How to Install Sliding Screens—Patio Doors

7 Plywood **178**
Plywood Characteristics—Species Groups—Plywood Grades—Plyform—Selecting an Engineered Panel—Specifying and Buying Plywood—Plywood Floor Construction—Plywood Underlayment—Finishing Plywood for Exterior Exposure—Staining—For a Lasting Finish

8 Lumber **200**
Grading—Familiarity—Installing Wood Siding—The House and Moisture—Treatment for Siding—House Paints—Staining—Maintenance of Finishes—Eliminating Paint Troubles

9 Fireplaces **211**
Chimneys—Flue Size—Height—Support—Flue Lining—Walls—Soot Pocket and Cleanout—Mortar—Smoke-Pipe Connection—Smoke Test—Insulation—Connection with Roof-Top Construction—Maintenance of Chimneys—Fireplace Design—Fireplace Construction—Footings—Hearth—A Do-It-Yourself Fireplace—Cast-Iron Stove—Why Your Stove Might Smoke

10 Appliance Care and Repair **241**
Home Tool Kit—Refrigerators—General Refrigeration Care—Electric Ranges—General Electric-Stove Care—Gas Ranges—General Care of Gas Ranges

11 Appliance Management **246**
Purchasing a Water Heater—How a Water Heater Works—Solving Water-Heating Problems—Change Your Habits and Lower Your Bills—Laundry Techniques for Saving Energy—Energy and the Kitchen—Estimated Home Energy Costs—Energy-Saving Tips

12 Landscaping for Energy Conservation **260**
Using Trees in Landscaping—Espaliered Plants and Vines—Dead-Air Space—Windbreak Design and Composition—Planting for Shade—Movement of the Sun—Low-Maintenance Landscapes—Selecting Shade Trees—Avoid Common Problems—When to Transplant

Glossary **271**

Index **274**

To
Dorothy (Dot) Brown
Staff Writer — Pensacola *News Journal*
and
My Mentor

FORTUNE SMILES ON THE STOUT-HEARTED
AND THE SELF PRESERVING . . .
Hindu Proverb

HAPPINESS IS THAT PLEASURE
WHICH FLOWS FROM THE SENSE OF VIRTUE
AND FROM THE CONSCIOUSNESS OF
RIGHT DEEDS . . . .
Henry Moore

Acknowledgments

HEARTFELT THANKS ARE DUE THE many people and organizations who contributed so generously with facts, figures, illustrations, and photography in order to provide a work designed for energy-conscious homeowners.

A special thank you to Mort Miller, Hunter Morin, Cabell Eanes Advertising, for their client, General Products, and Daniel J. Korman, Mary Sue Baron, and Cabell Eanes. All were kind and generous with their time in order to make the section on doors complete.

Larry Kelleher, All Nighter Stove Works, Inc.; Tom Zug, George Eisenhuth, and Mike Bruening, Heatilator Fireplaces; and Donald W. Minton, Keller Crescent Company for the Majestic Fireplace Company, for their help with the chapter on fireplaces, and their beautiful photography.

Raymond W. Moholt, Western Wood Products Association; Maryan Ezell, project coordinator American Plywood Association; Harold L. Keith, Department of Housing and Urban Development, D.G. Jedele, University of Illinois, Wayne Lovett and Henry Fuller, county agents, Escambia County, Florida who are always on hand with helpful answers to thousands of questions; John Shear and Scott Harrington of Gulf Power Pensacola, Florida, who were so kind to me when I needed help locating the right research material for my insulating section, and the numerous people I interviewed and who provided information found throughout this book.

Information on building solar passive homes was provided by the National Solar Heating and Cooling Center. They work tirelessly in their research to provide us with better living for the future.

In the year it has taken to complete this book, I have become telephonically close to all of those named and many unnamed. Our readers, along with me, say thank you!

Introduction

WHY INSULATE? WHY USE STORM windows or caulk doors and windows? Why do the hundreds of things to our homes that we have not seen fit to do to such extent in the past? The answer is simple. The energy crisis that began in the late 1960s has not gone away—it is still with us.

With today's inflation, energy savings also mean financial savings. Having and operating an energy-efficient home is one way individuals can alleviate some energy problems. In its many facets—from insulating to simple repair and care of household appliances, to the essentials of how to care for specific areas in the home that are large energy users—this book has been written to help you make your home a tight, efficient, energy-saving, money-saving place in which to live.

The energy we use for our homes and automobiles—gas, oil, electricity—draws on all of our energy resources. Cutting back on these uses is the simplest, most effective way to make our resources last longer. Each individual conservation effort, multiplied by millions, will help balance our energy accounts.

We can cut energy use and living costs by making our homes energy efficient, even if we have to spend some money to do it. The money we spend now will be returned through lower utility bills month after month. And then the savings are all ours and as good as tax-free raises in income.

We can conserve if we make energy thrift a way of life and adopt common sense energy habits. Learn about energy savings and do it yourself. Learn about your heating and air conditioning systems, about how to make better use of doors and fireplaces, and how to install them. Learn how landscaping helps conserve energy while you enjoy the aesthetics of good landscape design.

Whatever the reasons for our energy dilemma, past or present, they will be with us for a long time to come. As homeowners, we must learn to operate energy-efficient homes in order to maintain the standard of living to which we in the United States have become accustomed. There is little need to give up anything as long as we learn how to live with the problems at hand.

Having an energy efficient home is one way. Operating an energy-efficient home with energy consciousness in the entire family is the way that each of us can help maintain the standard of living we now have.

For just one day, try to imagine what your life would be like without abundant energy. As you eat your breakfast, get ready for work or school, and drive or ride to your destination, think about how much fuel is used for what you are doing. Then try to decide how you can reduce your consumption by at least 10 per-cent in the coming year.

In order to have energy for the future and to make it less costly today, let's find new ways to use energy more efficiently. Keep in step . . . save energy. You'll have good sense plus extra cents!

Chapter 1

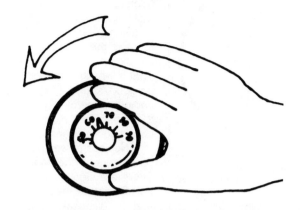

Understanding Energy

S O MUCH HAS BEEN WRITTEN ABOUT energy since the 1970 oil crisis and the Arab Oil embargo, many of us have been thrown into confusion. The conservation of energy, and proper more efficient uses of it is the key to an energy-efficient future.

It took 5 million years to form the oil supplies buried in the Earth, and we have depleted a major portion of these supplies in just 50 years. There is no way to replenish these fossil fuel supplies when they are gone. Statistics indicate that, while the United States has worked diligently to tap newly found oil reserves in Alaska and off-shore, those projected reserves have already been considered in calculating the total reserves.

By 1990 these new reserves will be the major domestic oil supplies because Texas, Oklahoma and California, which have been the major domestic supplies of oil for the United States, will be almost depleted.

The Mideast countries, Venezuela and Russia have larger supplies of oil. Even with these larger supplies, however, it is projected that the world supply of oil will be practically exhausted in 50 years. Government statistics show that in the United States we double our energy uses every 20 years. Even as our

production of oil and natural gas decline, energy consumption in the United States has been rising at 4 percent annually. The alarming prediction is that by the year 1990 we will use twice as much energy as was used in 1970.

The energy problem is complex. It is also closely tied to political policies, economics, scientific and technological achievement, and limitations. The United States consumes one-third of the total energy that is used in the world. Where do we get the energy we use? How much energy reserves exist? How do we use energy? And how can we stretch our energy supplies?

MAJOR ENERGY SUPPLIES

Of the energy used in the United States, three-fourths of it comes from oil and natural gas (Fig. 1-1). The remaining supplies come mainly from coal, and from smaller contributions by hydroelectric, nuclear and geothermal sources.

United States' use of energy in 1970 was distributed approximately as follows: Industry used about 42 percent of the total, private homes used approximately 19 percent and 24 percent of total was used in transportation (Fig. 1-2). Due to high energy costs,

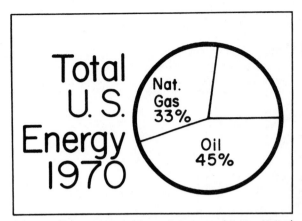

Fig. 1-1. Three-quarters of the energy used in the United States comes from Natural Gas and Oil (courtesy USDA).

some conservation by industry in heating, cooling, and lighting practices have already been put into effect.

About one-fifth of the energy used in the United States is in private homes. The largest uses in the home are for heating, air conditioning, and heating water. Proper insulation, along with weather stripping, can reduce the cost of heating in a home by as much as 30 percent to 50 percent.

Commercial buildings use about 14 percent of the nation's energy; most of it goes for lighting, space heating, and cooling. Although agriculture accounts for just 3 percent of the country's total energy use, about 7 billion gallons of gasoline, diesel fuel, and LP gas are used on the nation's farms yearly. This fuel is used to power machinery, to dry crops, irrigate, pump, and for other farm purposes. As little as 5 percent reduction through conservation on the nation's farms would save 350 million gallons of fuel yearly. While conservation in these major areas of energy use is crucial until new sources of energy are found.

The Organization of Petroleum Exporting Countries (OPEC) has shown that foreign oil supplies can control the price of the oil they sell. In 1973, the OPEC countries raised world oil prices more than three times what it had been. By now we are all aware that imported oil is an expensive, unreliable source of energy. Because it is unlikely that domestic production of oil and natural gas will increase significantly, we must find ways to conserve energy in our homes.

ALTERNATE ENERGY SOURCES

Research is steadily going forward for alternate energy sources. Solar energy is being used in many sections of the country by both industry and individu-

als. Because energy from the sun is inexhaustible and universally available, many homeowners have already begun using solar energy for domestic water heating. In many sections of the country, commercial buildings such as schools and some industry have installed solar heating systems.

For the most part, however, solar energy is still too expensive for the average homeowner to install. That is why in this book so much emphasis is placed on good, sound, easy, do-it-yourself home insulation and other energy-saving steps. There remains a need to develop less expensive systems for installing and collecting solar energy.

Nuclear power plants account for only a small percentage of the energy used in the United States. There are significant problems related to the use of nuclear power; these include limited uranium supplies and the disposal of radioactive waste. There is also concern that atomic materials might fall into the wrong hands if nuclear plants become more common.

Other sources of energy such as wind, geothermal energy, and methane from biological waste products are possibilities. These sources will require much more research and technological development if they are to become useful energy alternatives.

Conservation of our present energy reserves is essential in order to buy the time needed for the development of energy sources for practical, long-term solutions to our energy problems.

SAVING ENERGY SAVES MONEY

Attempting to conserve electricity sometimes means giving up comforts and convenience that have been taken for granted and become a way of life. It is not uncommon to hear one say that they have resorted to turning their air conditioning and early winter heating off completely and putting on appropriate clothing.

Electric companies throughout the country have made studies and experimented with varieties of conservation methods. Results have shown many ways of conserving energy in the home, short of turning off the electricity completely, but some methods are much more effective than others. When you are trying to reduce electrical use in *your* home it is important to keep the entire problem in perspective.

To discard an electric toothbrush or a clock, for instance, would only save 25 cents worth of energy per year. It makes more sense to conserve in areas that consume the most electricity—heating and cooling.

In many areas of the country, heating and air conditioning constitute approximately 52 percent of the energy used in residences. Heat moves from warm to cold; in winter, it goes from the inside of the house to the outside. This is known as *heat loss*. In summer, heat comes in and this is known as *heat gain*. Either way, too much movement of heat results in higher energy costs.

YOU AND YOUR ELECTRIC SERVICE

The electrical requirements of each appliance in the home—*watts*—and the length of time they are used— *hours*—determine the size of your electric bill. Your electric bill is calculated in kilowatt hours; the product of watts and hours. A 100-watt bulb burned for 10 hours will register on your meter as 1000 watt hours, or 1 kilowatt-hour (100 × 10 = 1000 watt hours or 1 kwh).

Reducing either the wattage or the hours used on each of your appliances is a simple way to reduce the amount of *watt-hours* you use them. Because the wattage of most appliances is controlled in the factory where they are produced, the easiest way to reduce the individual bill is to reduce the hours you use your appliances and learn ways to use them more efficiently.

It is not difficult to calculate exactly what it costs to operate a specific appliance. All electrical appliances have the wattage listed on them. Using this information, you can call your local electric supplier to determine the average cost per kilowatt-hour (KWH). Keeping a record of the hours used on each individual appliance provides you the information to calculate how much it costs to operate each appliance. Table 1-1 provides a simple formula to use.

There are things that affect the size of your electric bill beyond your control. A prolonged cold spell causes higher bills during the winter simply because your heating system operates more often. The following list indicates common causes of bill fluctuations.

Conditions Beyond Your Control

Seasons of the year.
Sunlight and weather.
Five weekend months.
Long billing periods.
Defective wiring.

Changes in Living Conditions

Size of family.
Average age of family members.
People visiting.
Children or new babies.
Changes in living habits.
Hired help.
Illness.
Special diet.
Guests and entertainment.
Watching long-lasting events on television.
Spring cleaning.
Vacations.

Appliances

New appliances.
Additional use of older appliances.
Larger refrigerators.
Defective appliances (shortage of refrigerant).

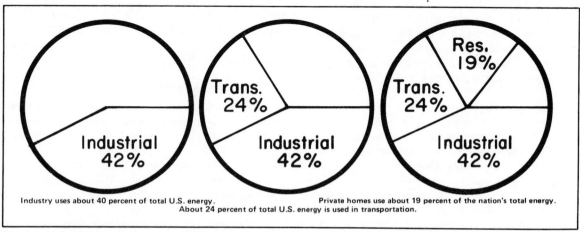

Industry uses about 40 percent of total U.S. energy.
Private homes use about 19 percent of the nation's total energy.
About 24 percent of total U.S. energy is used in transportation.

Fig. 1-2. United States Energy use in 1970 (courtesy of USDA).

Wattage	Hours	Average Cost Per KWH		Operating Cost

$$\frac{\text{(per appliance)}}{1,000} \times \text{(used per month)} \times \text{PER KWH} = \text{(Per month)}$$

for example:

$$\frac{1,200 \text{ (fry pan)} \times 12 \text{ hrs}}{1,000} = \frac{14,400}{1,000} = 14.4$$

$$14.4 \times .033 \text{ (cost per KWH)} = 47\cancel{c}$$

Table 1-1. Appliance Operating Costs.

Inefficient use (other than for house heating).
Excessive use of hot water.
Leaking hot water faucet.
Exposure of hot water pipes to air and lack of maintenance (clogged air filters or frost in the refrigerator).
Expensive cooling and heating (thermostat control setting).

New Home or Apartment

Larger than former home.
Windier or hotter location.
More leakage of air through windows.
Inadequate insulation.
Larger air conditioner.
Larger electric heating or water heater.
Further from kitchen or more appliances.

Most of the 40 million owner-occupied houses in the United States could use additional insulation to offset sharply rising energy prices. This is especially true for houses built prior to the 1960s and those with air conditioning units added after the house was completed.

Currently, electricity is usually more costly than fuel oil, and fuel oil is more costly than natural gas. Even in the same climate, houses heated and cooled by different energy sources require different levels of investment. Also, family lifestyles differ and affect energy budgets.

Balancing your energy budget means striking a happy medium between dollars spent on energy consumption and energy conservation improvements as they apply to the individual household. A balanced budget provides you the greatest possible long-run net savings on heating and cooling expenses—your most costly expense.

How much should be spent in energy conservation improvements varies according to individual homes and the climate in your area. For example, insulation is a good investment no matter where you live. It aids in keeping your fuel/energy bills down in the winter when the heat is on and it keeps the cool in during the summer months. Storm doors and windows are beneficial in hot climates and cold climates. They also keep the cool air in during the summer in extremely hot climates and keep the heat in during the winter in extremely cold climates.

Balancing your "energy budget" also means using a balanced combination of energy conservation techniques. If you invest only in attic insulation and neglect the use of storm windows or insulation in floors over unheated areas where these are economical, you will not be making the best use of your energy conservation money.

COSTS AND SAVINGS

There are ranges of costs and savings for the energy-savings improvements that appear in the following chapters. For comparison with your home, an example would be a single-story, 1250-square-foot house in Washington, D.C., paying 45 cents per gallon of oil, 16 cents per hundred cubic feet of gas, or 3 percent per kilowatt of electricity. Substitute your rates in order to compare costs.

You can save significantly on heating if you live practically anywhere in the United States (see Fig.

Fig. 1-3. A heating savings map guide.

1-3). If you live in the part of the country represented by the shaded portion of the map (the major portion of the continental United States falls into this category).

Two packages of energy-saving measures are shown in Fig. 1-4. Package 1 is inexpensive and easy. And it pays for itself every year. Package 2 saves even more year after year. It can cut your heating bills by as much as one-half. It will pay for itself within 5 years. Table 1-2 gives an idea of the costs and savings in a typical home. If you already have storm windows, or if you don't have an oil furnace, you need to consider Package 2.

AIR-CONDITIONING SAVINGS

Package 3 (Fig. 1-5) can save you money on your air-conditioning bills if you live in the part of the country represented by the shaded portion of the map. See Table 1-2 for an idea of what Package 3 costs and saves in a typical home. If you live in the part of the country represented by the shaded area on both maps, these cooling savings are in addition to what you save on heating.

HEATING AND
AIR-CONDITIONING SAVINGS

If you have whole-house air conditioning and if you live in the part of the country represented by the shaded area on both of the maps, some of the energy-saving steps apply to both heating and cooling. But you only have to pay for them once. See Table 1-3.

YOUR ENERGY BUDGET

In how many ways does electricity help you live better, and what does each of these benefits cost you? Knowing how to save means knowing how much electricity you're spending on a variety of electrically operated activities. Figure 1-6 lists examples of most of the most-used appliances in use in the home today. Go down the list and note the ones you do use. Copy the monthly dollar cost into the right hand column. This will get you started on the road to keeping energy-savings records. Make this a perpetual record-keeping system.

If you find that you are using an overabundance of energy in operating some of your appliances, it will show up in your records after several months or a year. By keeping a perpetuating recording keeping system, you and your family will be able to cut back in areas where you find you are expending an excessive amount of energy.

Figure 1-7 provides 50 energy conservation options costing less than $50. Mark the box that applies to you and keep this as part of your permanent energy-savings records. Table 1-4 shows you how to prepare energy-saver cards. Record what you did today to use more or less electricity than on any other day. Fill these in as often as you can and maintain them with your permanent energy-saving records.

1. Turn down thermostat 6° in winter from your usual setting.

2. Put on plastic storm windows.

Fig. 1-4. Heat savings (courtesy of HUD, Office of Policy Development and Research).

5

Table 1-2. Energy-Savings Comparisons.

PACKAGE 1

	Yearly Cost	Yearly Savings
1. Turn down thermostat	$0	$27.87
2. Put on plastic storm in winter	$7-9	27.73
3. Service oil furnace	$25	33.87
Total	$32-34	$87-247

If you already have storm windows or if you don't have an oil furnace, take a look at Package 2.

PACKAGE 2

	1st Year Cost	Yearly Savings
1. Turn down thermostat	$0	$12-53
2. Put on plastic storms	$7-9	20-60
3. Service oil furnace	$25	20-53
4. Caulk and weatherstrip	$75-105*	40-100
5. Insulate your attic	$300-450*	50-75
Total	$407-589	$143-341

*These are do-it-yourself costs. If you call a contractor these items could cost twice as much.

PACKAGE 3

	1st Year Cost	Yearly Savings
1. Turn up thermostat	$0	$7.20
2. Insulate your attic	$300-450*	33.67
3. Caulk and weatherstrip	$75-105*	27-67
Total	$375-555	$67-154

*These are do-it-yourself costs. If you call a contractor, these items could cost twice as much.

THERMOSTAT CONTROL

Table 1-5 shows what percentage of your heating bill you will save by turning down your thermostat. Refer to the map shown in Fig. 1-8 to see which zone you live in. Read the column in Table 1-5 for that zone.

Circle either the top or bottom number in that column; you'll need it after you figure out your heating bill. Circle the top number if you want to see what you'll save with a 5-degree turn-down from your usual setting. Circle the bottom number if you want to see what you'll save with an 8-degree turn-down from your usual setting.

If you have whole-house air conditioning, you can save about 3 percent of your air conditioning bill for each degree you turn up your thermostat. Usually, about a 4 degree turn-up will still be comfortable. Above that the air-conditioning system will have trouble keeping the house cool during the hot part of the day. Figure out how many degrees you can turn up your thermostat, and then multiply the number of de-

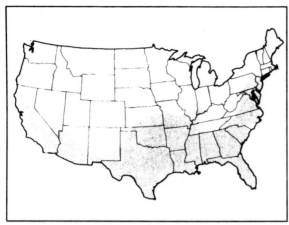

Fig. 1-5. Air Conditioning Savings Map (courtesy of HUD, Office of Policy Development and Research.

grees by 3 to get your percent of savings:

$$\text{degree turn-up} \times -3 = \% \text{ savings}$$

YOUR HEATING BILL

The method for figuring out your heating bill depends on what kind of fuel you use. Pick the method below that applies to you. Note: You might be heating with two fuels. For example, most of your house might be heated with oil or gas, while some newer rooms might have electric heat. In such a case, do this section once for each fuel and add the results.

Oil or Coal Heat

If you have an oil furnace or coal furnace that heats your house, but not your hot water, all of your oil

Table 1-3. Heat- and Air-Conditioning Savings.

PACKAGE 1 PLUS TURNING UP THE THERMOSTAT IN SUMMER

	Year Cost	Yearly Savings
Turn down thermostat in winter	$0	$27-87
Turn up thermostat in summer	$0	$7-20
Put on plastic storms	$7-9	$27-73
Service oil furnace	$25	$33-87
Total	$32-34	$94-267

PACKAGE 2 AND PACKAGE 3 TOGETHER

	1st Year Cost	Yearly Savings
Turn down thermostat in winter	$0	$27-87
Turn up thermostat in summer	$0	$7-20
Put on plastic storms	$7-9	$20-73
Service oil furnace	$25	$20-53
Caulk and weather strip	$75-105*	$67-167
Insulate attic	$300-450*	$80-227
Total	$407-589	$221-626

*These are do-it-yourself costs. If you have a contractor do it, these items could cost about twice as much.

ELECTRIC PRODUCT	EST. KWH USED MONTHLY*	MONTHLY OPERATING COST	
Air Cleaner	36	$ 1.80	______
Blender	Less than 1	Less than $ .01	______
Broiler	7	$ .35	______
Clock	1	$ .05	______
Clothes Dryer, 1 Load/Day	90	$ 4.50	______
Coffee Maker	7	$ .35	______
Deep Fryer	3	$ .15	______
Dehumidifier	12	$ .60	______
Dishwasher, 1 Load/Day	30	$ 1.50	______
Electric Blanket	9	$ .45	______
Floor Polisher	1	$ .05	______
Freezer (15 cu. ft.)	99	$ 4.95	______
Freezer (frostless, 15 cu. ft.)	160	$ 8.00	______
Frying Pan	8	$ .40	______
Hair Dryer	3	$ .15	______
Heater (1600 watt portable)	18	$ .90	______
Heating Pad	Less than 1	$ .05	______
Hot Plate (1257 watts)	8	$ .40	______
Humidifier	13	$ .65	______
Iron (hand)	5	$ .25	______
Total Lighting	95	$ 4.75	______
Microwave Oven	19	$ .95	______
Mixer	Less than 1	Less than $ .01	______
Radio (3 hrs./day)	7	$ .35	______
Radio/Record Player (3 hrs./day)	11	$ .55	______
Range with Oven	85	$ 4.25	______

ELECTRIC PRODUCT	EST. KWH USED MONTHLY*	MONTHLY OPERATING COST	
Range with Self-Cleaning Oven	59	$ 2.95	______
Refrigerator (12 cu. ft.)	52	$ 2.60	______
Refrigerator (frostless, 12 cu. ft.)	90	$ 4.50	______
Refrigerator/Freezer (17 cu. ft.)	79	$ 3.95	______
Refrigerator/Freezer (frostless, 17 cu. ft.)	152	$ 7.60	______
Roaster	5	$ .25	______
Sewing Machine	Less than 1	Less than $ .05	______
Shaver	Less than 1	Less than $ .01	______
Television (black & white) (6 hrs./day)	29	$ 1.45	______
Television (color) (6 hrs./day)	54	$ 2.70	______
Toaster	3	$ .15	______
Tooth Brush	Less than 1	Less than $ .05	______
Trash Compactor	4	$ .20	______
Vacuum Cleaner	4	$ .20	______
Waffle Iron	2	$ .10	______
Washing Machine, 1 Load/Day	9	$ .45	______
Waste Disposer	3	$ .15	______
Water Heating (bathing, clothes washing, dish washing, misc.)	470	$23.50	______
Total Monthly Cost			

Fig. 1-6. An energy budget guide.

have done	will do	**Air Conditioning/Space Heating**
☐	☐	1. Set the thermostat for cooling equipment at 78°F (26°C) or higher in the summer months. 85°F (29°C) if you plan to be away from home for more than two hours during the day or over a weekend.
☐	☐	2. Set the thermostat for heating equipment at 68°F (20°C) or lower in the winter months, 55°F (13°C) at night in the winter, and 50°F (10°C) when you are away from home for an extended period of time.
☐	☐	3. Keep windows and doors tightly closed when heating or air conditioning is operating.
☐	☐	4. Turn off air conditioning and heating equipment in unused rooms. Close off vents to unused rooms.
☐	☐	5. Use thermostat with automatic setback time controls for regulating heating and air conditioning equipment.
☐	☐	6. Inspect and clean cooling and heating system, and replace or clean dirty filters.
☐	☐	7. Open and close outside doors quickly.
☐	☐	8. Use cross ventilation instead of air conditioning when possible.
☐	☐	9. Close the fireplace damper when not being used.
☐	☐	10. Apply caulking and weatherstripping to make house as tight as possible.

have done	will do	**Water Heating**
☐	☐	1. Set hot water temperature controls below 120°F (49°C) if the home does not have an automatic dishwasher. 140°F (60°C) if it does.
☐	☐	2. Turn off the water heater if it will not be used for an extended period of time.
☐	☐	3. Take short showers instead of baths, and use as little hot water as possible.
☐	☐	4. Use a flow restrictor showerhead—reduces volume not pressure.
☐	☐	5. Repair leaky faucets promptly.
☐	☐	6. Drain the bottom water of hot water tank twice a year to remove sediment.

have done	will do	**Transportation**
☐	☐	1. Plan activities to reduce trips and mileage.
☐	☐	2. Walk, ride bikes, car pool, or use public transportation when possible.
☐	☐	3. Avoid rapid starts and stops when driving.
☐	☐	4. When possible, avoid purchasing these vehicle options that reduce efficiency: air conditioning, power steering, power brakes, and power windows.
☐	☐	5. Drive at 55 m.p.h. or at recommended lower speeds.
☐	☐	6. Turn off your engine when it must idle for more than 30 seconds.
☐	☐	7. Do not ride the brake or pump the accelerator of the car when you drive.
☐	☐	8. Keep engine properly tuned.

have done	will do	**Lighting**
☐	☐	1. Turn out all unnecessary lights.
☐	☐	2. Keep shades up in winter and down in summer in a room when it is exposed to direct sunlight.
☐	☐	3. Keep all lighting fixtures clean.
☐	☐	4. Replace high wattage bulbs with the same number of low wattage bulbs where possible.
☐	☐	5. Paint indoor walls light colors.
☐	☐	6. Use energy saving light bulbs. Flourescent uses less energy than incandescent.

have done	will do	**Laundry**
☐	☐	1. Wash only full loads of clothes.
☐	☐	2. Dry clothes outside on a clothesline.
☐	☐	3. If you must use the dryer, dry clothes in consecutive loads and keep the lint filter clean.
☐	☐	4. Use cold water laundry detergents.

have done	will do	**Other**
☐	☐	1. Turn power tools and appliances off when they are not in use.
☐	☐	2. Use organic compost for fertilizer when possible.
☐	☐	3. Keep power tools clean and properly maintained.
☐	☐	4. Consider the energy efficiency ratio (EER) when purchasing appliances.
☐	☐	5. Buy tools with the lowest required hp for the job intended.

have done	will do	**In the Kitchen**
☐	☐	1. Use small appliances instead of the oven for cooking small amounts of food.
☐	☐	2. Disconnect and empty the refrigerator when you plan to be away for a long period of time.
☐	☐	3. Turn off surface units and oven of electric range just before you are finished using them. If gas range, immediately after you are finished.
☐	☐	4. Limit oven preheating to five minutes if necessary at all.
☐	☐	5. Use exhaust fans to remove odors and waste heat only when necessary.
☐	☐	6. Defrost foods before cooking.
☐	☐	7. Keep reflector pans below range surface units clean.
☐	☐	8. Fit pots and pans to surface unit size.
☐	☐	9. Open the refrigerator, freezer and oven doors only when necessary.
☐	☐	10. Keep refrigerator and freezer door gaskets in good condition.
☐	☐	11. Keep dust off refrigerator and freezer coils.

Fig. 1-7. Energy conservation options.

Table 1-4. Energy Saver Score Card.

Date	Day of Week	Meter Reading	Kilowatt-hours used	Month August Reason for increase or decrease
3	Sun.	3260		
4	Mon.	3280		
5	Tues.	3304	20	
6	Wed.	3332	28	did some washing
7	Thurs.	3353	21	ironing - some washing
8	Fri.	3369	16	nothing unusual
9	Sat.	3383	14	away part of day, lowered thermostat

Weekly Total = $123 \times 0.05 = \$\underline{\hspace{3cm}}$

or coal bill goes to heating. Simply add up your fuel bills for last year and write down the total.

If your furnace also heats your hot water, add up your fuel bills for the last year and multiply the total by 8.

Your Dollar Savings

Now that you have found your approximate heating and air-conditioning bills, you are ready to find out how much you can save each year on these measures. Multiply your heating bill by the percent you circled in Table 1-5 and divide by 100. Total your thermostat savings for heating and air conditioning.

If you have an oil or coal furnace that hasn't been serviced recently, multiply your heating bill by 0.1 if you immediately have the furnace serviced. If you have a central air conditioner that has not been serviced recently, multiply your air conditioning bill by 0.1 if you immediately have that unit serviced.

HEATING AND COOLING FACTORS

There's one *heating factor* and one *cooling factor* for your house. They are based on where you live and how much you pay for the fuel you use for heating and/or cooling. Table 1-6 lists heating and cooling factors. There are two ways to use such figures:

Table 1-5. Percentage of Savings.

	Zone 1	Zone 2	Zone 3
5° turn down	14%	17%	25%
8° turn down	19%	24%	35%

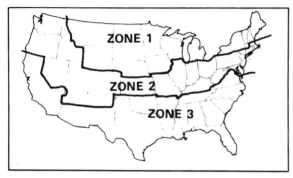

Fig. 1-8. A thermostat zone map.

Building Shell	Yes	No	NA
1. Are window panes and frames properly caulked?			
2. Are exterior doors weatherstripped? Are door frames caulked?			
3. Are walls insulated to a minimum level of R-11?			
4. Are ceilings insulated to a minimum level of R-26?			
5. Does the home have a vapor barrier in the walls to prevent water vapor from passing through and condensing in the insulation?			
6. Is the floor above the crawl space insulated?			
7. Have you considered 6″ walls with studs on 24″ centers to allow maximum space for insulation?			
8. Has a clock thermostat been installed making it possible to reduce evening temperatures automatically?			
9. Is window space on the north side of the house at a minimum?			
10. Is the home efficiently shaped to limit heat loss, avoiding such configurations as L-, T-, and H-shaped dwellings?			
11. Does the house have an overhang for the south wall which will protect it from summer sun, but allow exposure to winter sun?			
12. Does the fireplace have a heat exchanger to collect and distribute unused heat?			
13. Is the fireplace a high-efficiency type with a tight damper?			
14. Is fluorescent rather than incandescent lighting used in the kitchen and bathroom?			
15. In rooms such as bedrooms, living and dining areas, are fluorescent tubes used as the main source of light with well-designed architectural lighting (lighted soffit or cove around the perimeter of the room)?			
Appliances			
1. Were appliances with the highest Energy Efficiency Ratio (EER) chosen?			
2. Is the temperature setting on the hot water heater at a reasonably low level such as 120°?			
Heating, Ventilating, and Air Conditioning			
1. Are hot water pipes and ductwork insulated?			
2. Are air leaks in ductwork sealed?			
3. Are exposed hot water pipes and hot water storage insulated to reduce heat loss?			
4. Have you considered a heat-recovery system which preheats outside air with exhaust air from the ventilation system?			
5. If home has air-conditioning units, are they placed on the shady side of the house or are units shaded from the sun?			
6. Does cooling equipment have the highest Energy Efficiency Ratio?			
7. Is cooling equipment the smallest size to do the job most efficiently?			
8. Is the air-conditioning compressor located where it will receive afternoon shade, and consequently increase compressor efficiency and reduce energy use?			
9. Is the heating system the most efficient? Is it the appropriate size? Oversized systems waste a great deal of energy.			
10. Do heating and cooling systems provide for continuous fan operation, which often provides comfort without using the full system capacity?			
11. Does the attic have one square foot of ventilation (louvers and ridge vents) for each 300 square feet of ceiling area?			
12. Have local fuel costs and supplies been evaluated to select equipment and fuel on a cost / efficiency /availability basis?			

Fig. 1-9. Energy conservation checklist.

Table 1-6. Heating/Cooling Cost Factors (courtesy of HUD, Office of Policy Development and Research.

State	City	Heating Factors Gas (A)	Oil (B)	Elec (C)	Coal (D)	Cooling Factor (E)	Fuel costs Gas ¢/100 cu. ft. (F)	Oil ¢/gal. (G)	Elec ¢/Kwh (H)	Coal ¢/lb. (I)	Heating Multipliers Gas (J)	Oil (K)	Elec (L)	Coal (M)	Cooling Multiplier (N)
ALABAMA	Montgomery	.13	.28	.34	–	.13	12.00	38.88	1.50	–	.0105	.0071	.2260	.0987	.0859
ALASKA	Anchorage	.33	.86	1.21	–	.00	12.00	53.82	2.03	–	.0275	.0160	.5956	–	.0001
ARIZONA	Flagstaff	.48	.61	.72	–	.01	20.71	37.78	1.43	–	.0233	.0162	.5040	–	.0056
	Phoenix	.07	.23	.23	–	.20	8.20	37.78	1.43	4.55	.0081	.0062	.1741	–	.1430
ARKANSAS	Little Rock	.12	.40	.45	–	.11	8.40	39.22	1.40	–	.0147	.0102	.3176	–	.0769
CALIFORNIA	Bishop	.29	–	.59	–	.67	17.69	–	1.69	–	.0163	–	.3515	–	.0414
	Eureka	.35	–	.84	–	.00	16.51	–	1.84	–	.0212	–	.4580	–	.0001
	Los Angeles	.09	–	.28	–	.06	12.17	–	1.69	–	.0078	–	.1682	–	.0367
	Bakersfield	.12	–	.39	–	.17	12.17	–	1.84	–	.0097	–	.2093	–	.0941
	San Francisco	.22	–	.55	–	.01	15.70	–	1.84	–	.0137	–	.2967	–	.0059
COLORADO	Alamosa	.28	.58	1.18	–	.01	10.15	38.16	1.96	–	.0278	.0153	.6010	–	.0023
	Denver	.19	.56	.71	–	.05	11.03	39.90	1.96	–	.0168	.0140	.3640	–	.0231
CONNECTICUT	New Haven	.58	.67	1.77	–	.13	30.09	46.87	4.26	–	.0192	.0143	.4155	–	.0312
DELAWARE	Dover	.28	.64	.65	–	.07	15.30	45.55	1.60	–	.0188	.0140	.4054	.1770	.0447
D.C.	Washington	.41	.55	1.12	.69	.18	25.26	45.92	3.22	4.55	.0161	.0120	.3473	.1517	.0559
FLORIDA	Miami	.10	.04	.07	–	.49	10.00	52.96	3.07	–	.0010	.0007	.0211	–	.1589
	Tallahassee	.09	.25	.37	–	.23	13.90	48.78	2.49	–	.0068	.0051	.1465	–	.0941
GEORGIA	Atlanta	.14	.40	–	.49	–	12.50	43.50	–	4.63	.0113	.0092	.2435	.1063	.0612
	Savannah	.10	.23	–	–	–	12.50	37.81	–	–	.0083	.0062	.1794	–	.0892
IDAHO	Boise	.39	.52	.36	–	.03	23.62	42.06	1.01	–	.0166	.0124	.3582	–	.0330
ILLINOIS	Chicago	.35	.60	.54	.54	.05	19.25	44.19	1.38	3.12	.0182	.0136	.3944	.1722	.0373
	Springfield	.26	.44	.77	.33	.12	19.16	42.79	2.59	2.52	.0138	.0103	.2976	.1300	.0453
	Cairo	.22	.40	.82	.24	.20	17.85	42.79	3.04	2.00	.0125	.0093	.2692	.1176	.0663
INDIANA	Indianapolis	.30	.50	.48	.50	.05	18.27	41.60	1.33	3.25	.0168	.0124	.3514	.1534	.0398
IOWA	Des Moines	.28	.58	–	–	–	14.92	41.32	–	–	.0188	.0140	.4062	–	.0406
	Dubuque	.24	.65	–	–	–	11.24	41.32	–	–	.0210	.0151	.4548	–	.0257
KANSAS	Wichita	.15	.41	.49	–	.09	9.70	36.42	1.49	–	.0151	.0112	.3255	–	.0603
	Goodland	.14	.48	.38	–	.03	8.16	36.42	1.00	–	.0175	.0133	.3780	–	.0337
KENTUCKY	Lexington	.26	.50	.63	–	.08	17.26	43.75	1.90	–	.0153	.0114	.3300	.1441	.0423
LOUISIANA	Baton Rouge	.05	–	.28	–	.19	7.10	–	1.82	–	.0071	–	.1539	–	.1046
	Shreveport	.08	–	.38	–	.16	7.50	–	1.77	–	.0100	–	.2155	–	.0914
MAINE	Portland	.65	.72	1.04	–	.03	28.00	44.70	2.25	–	.0231	.0161	.4631	–	.0138
MARYLAND	Baltimore	.45	.58	.98	.51	.12	27.12	46.74	2.71	3.25	.0167	.0124	.3603	.1573	.0461
MASSACHUSETTS	Worcester	.73	.77	1.09	–	.06	32.14	45.78	3.02	–	.0227	.0169	.4911	–	.0185
MICHIGAN	Lansing	.56	.65	1.10	–	.05	28.47	43.86	2.60	3.75	.0197	.0147	.4260	.1860	.0200
MINNESOTA	Duluth	.60	.76	–	–	–	23.80	43.09	–	–	.0254	.0177	.5482	–	.0073
	Minneapolis	.33	.72	–	–	–	15.59	46.18	–	–	.0213	.0156	.4595	–	.0268
MISSISSIPPI	Jackson	.11	–	.57	–	.24	10.50	–	2.58	–	.0102	–	.2209	.0904	.0918
MISSOURI	St. Louis	.21	.76	.39	–	.06	14.12	45.63	1.18	–	.0153	.0167	.3306	–	.0540
	Springfield	.17	.49	.45	–	.07	10.50	41.37	1.30	–	.0160	.0119	.3453	–	.0518

State	City														
MONTANA	Helena	.26	—	.69	—	.01	12.45	—	1.55	—	.0206	—	4456	—	.0093
NEBRASKA	Omaha	.33	.58	.73	—	.08	17.65	40.90	1.80	—	.0189	.0141	4077	—	.0446
	Scottsbluff	.25	.52	.68	—	.04	14.00	41.35	1.87	—	.0169	.0126	3658	—	.0232
NEVADA	Elko	.33	.63	.71	—	.02	17.75	44.34	1.75	—	.0188	.0141	4075	—	.0128
	Las Vegas	.14	.34	.46	—	.23	13.90	44.34	2.08	—	.0103	.0077	2228	—	.1114
NEW HAMPSHIRE	Concord	.70	.73	1.05	.56	.04	33.29	46.38	2.30	—	.0211	.0157	4552	—	.0170
NEW JERSEY	Atlantic City	.62	.62	1.20	—	.09	33.84	45.32	3.02	3.25	.0183	.0137	3957	.1728	.0312
NEW MEXICO	Raton	.17	—	1.03	—	.09	8.60	—	2.35	—	.0203	—	4388	—	.0391
	Silver City	.09	—	.69	—	.10	7.05	—	2.63	—	.0121	—	2611	—	.0391
NEW YORK	New York City	.65	.68	1.72	.76	.19	35.28	49.46	4.34	4.40	.0183	.0137	3959	.1729	.0434
	Rochester	.53	.76	1.36	.82	.07	24.05	46.53	2.85	3.95	.0220	.0164	4755	.2076	.0259
NORTH CAROLINA	Raleigh	.30	.52	.95	.64	.12	19.41	45.10	2.35	4.40	.0155	.0115	3347	.1462	.0500
	Wilmington	.17	.35	.54	.70	.17	15.46	43.43	2.35	4.76	.0107	.0080	2315	.1011	.0730
NORTH DAKOTA	Bismarck	.59	—	1.21	—	.04	26.50	—	2.49	—	.0224	—	4852	—	.0171
OHIO	Youngstown	.19	.69	1.18	.36	.05	8.88	43.95	2.62	1.80	.0209	.0156	4522	.1974	.0204
	Cincinnati	.18	.47	.52	.53	.07	12.79	43.95	1.68	3.90	.0144	.0107	3107	.1357	.0439
OKLAHOMA	Oklahoma City	.21	—	.74	—	.20	17.45	—	2.80	—	.0121	—	2625	—	.0705
OREGON	Salem	.57	.72	1.02	—	.02	26.41	44.20	2.17	—	.0217	.0162	4690	—	.0101
	Medford	.58	.75	1.05	—	.06	25.11	44.20	2.13	—	.0229	.0170	4440	—	.0283
PENNSYLVANIA	Philadelphia	.49	.63	1.08	.61	.12	26.87	46.10	2.73	3.55	.0183	.0137	3959	.1729	.0448
	Pittsburgh	.35	.60	1.04	.44	.03	19.25	44.75	2.68	2.60	.0180	.0134	3890	.1698	.0120
RHODE ISLAND	Providence	.45	.68	1.37	—	.09	23.03	47.20	3.26	—	.0194	.0145	4195	—	.0285
SOUTH CAROLINA	Charleston	.19	.27	.44	—	.20	21.58	42.17	2.34	—	.0087	.0065	1888	—	.0869
	Greenville-Spartanburg	.18	.36	.56	—	.13	16.23	42.17	2.28	—	.0113	.0085	2450	—	.0561
SOUTH DAKOTA	Rapid City	.22	.58	.79	—	.04	11.88	41.76	1.95	—	.0186	.0139	4027	—	.0209
TENNESSEE	Knoxville	.19	.44	.61	.31	.12	14.20	44.20	2.13	2.50	.0133	.0099	2873	.1255	.0557
	Memphis	.11	.38	.55	.31	.17	9.25	42.36	2.13	2.80	.0119	.0089	2569	.1122	.0780
TEXAS	Austin	.07	—	.51	—	.32	8.60	—	3.00	—	.0078	—	1688	—	.1071
	Dallas	.07	—	.29	—	.16	7.90	—	1.49	—	.0090	—	1943	—	.1049
	Houston	.05	—	.21	—	.16	9.00	—	1.62	—	.0061	—	1319	—	.1000
	Lubbock	.15	—	.53	—	.13	12.46	—	2.11	—	.0117	—	2529	—	.0617
UTAH	Salt Lake City	.23	.58	.87	—	.08	11.56	39.60	2.05	—	.0197	.0147	4264	—	.0371
	Milford	.28	—	.90	—	.05	13.39	—	1.97	—	.0212	—	4578	—	.0267
VERMONT	Burlington	.63	.84	1.20	—	.04	27.81	47.58	2.36	—	.0222	.0176	5098	—	.0178
VIRGINIA	Richmond	.24	.50	.72	.61	.12	16.64	45.58	2.25	—	.0147	.0110	3178	.1388	.0537
WASHINGTON	Olympia	.75	.80	.79	—	.01	32.19	44.72	1.52	4.40	.0239	.0178	5165	—	.0035
	Walla Walla	.21	.46	.45	—	.05	15.40	44.72	1.51	—	.0137	.0102	2963	—	.0357
WEST VIRGINIA	Charleston	.32	.50	.79	.13	.10	21.92	45.73	2.50	.96	.0146	.0109	3154	.1377	.0388
	Elkins	.44	.63	1.10	.18	.06	23.82	45.73	2.76	1.05	.0185	.0138	3999	.1746	.0208
WISCONSIN	Milwaukee	.44	.75	—	.79	—	20.29	46.10	—	3.85	.0218	.0162	4707	.2055	.0216
WYOMING	Casper	.32	—	.81	—	.03	16.90	—	2.00	—	.0188	—	4062	—	.0151

See how your house scores on this FEA energy quiz. Answers will pinpoint strengths and weaknesses. The total score will rate your home's energy efficiency.

INSULATION. Score 30 points for R-26 or higher in the ceiling, 25 points for R-11 through R-13 in the walls and 20 points between R-9 R-11 in the floor. _____

If there is unheated space beneath your house, add 5 points for an insulated floor. Score 5 points for no space. _____

THERMOSTAT. If you set the thermostat at 68° F. or less during the day in winter, score 5 points, 4 to 69°, 3 for 70°, 2 for 71° and 1 for 72°. _____

In winter if you set the thermostat at 60° or less overnight, score 10 points, 9 points for 61°, 8 for 62° and so forth. _____

If you set the air-conditioning unit at 80°, score 5 points; 4 for 79°; 3 for 78°; and 1 for 76°. Score 5 points for no air-conditioning system. _____

AIR LEAKAGE. If no air leaks around windows, score 10 points. If no air enters around doors, score an additional 2 points. _____

If you keep the fireplace damper closed or block air flow when not in use, score 3 points. Score 3 points if you don't have a fireplace. _____

If the outside temperature often falls below 30° and you have storm windows, score 3 points. If the temperature rarely or never falls to 30°, score 1 point. _____

MISCELLANEOUS. If you close the curtains and shades to sunlight in summer and open them during the day in winter, score 5 points. _____

If the water heater is adjusted to 120°, score 5 points, for 140°, score 2 points. _____

If you run the dishwasher, clothes washer and dryer only with full loads, score 1 point. _____

If you open the dishwasher to let the dishes air-dry, score 1 point. If you have no dishwasher, score 1 point. _____

If the hot water faucets don't drip, score 1 point. _____

total _____

A score of 90 or above shows your house is in good shape to conserve energy. A score between 75 and 90 suggests definite room areas for improvement, below 75 indicates you are wasting a substantial amount of energy and money.

Fig. 1-10. Rating energy efficiency checklist.

☐ A quick approximate way.
☐ A slower but more accurate way that uses your fuel bill to set your own factors.

The Quick Way. Find the row in Table 1-6 that's for the city nearest you. Look at the first four columns in that row (A,B,C,D). Circle the number for your fuel. It's your heating factor. If you have whole-house air conditioning, also circle the number in column E of the same row. That's your cooling factor.

Check the fuel prices given in columns F through I. They were collected in mid-1977 and were used to figure the Heating and Cooling Factors given in columns A through E. Compare them with the price you pay for fuel. If you find a significant difference, figure your heating and cooling factors using your own bill.

Using Your Own Bill. You can calculate your heating factor and your cooling factor if you have whole-house air conditioning. Use figures from your own utility bills. To figure your exact heating factor, find the *heating multiplier* for your city and your fuel in Table 1-6 (columns J through M), and multiply it by the price you pay for heating fuel today. Make sure that you use the right units:

gas = ¢/100 Cu. Ft., oil = ¢/gal., electricity = ¢/kwh, coal = ¢/lb. Your fuel price times your heating multiplier equals the heating factor.

To determine your exact cooling factor, find the cooling multiplier in column N of Table 1-6 for your city, and multiply it by the price you pay for electricity in *cents* per kilowatt hour. Electricity price times your cooling multiplier equals the cooling factor.

Note. Your true cost for 100 cubic feet of gas, a kilowatt of electricity, etc., is sometimes well hidden in your bill. Call your utility company and ask them for the true cost (including all "fuel adjustment" factors and taxes) of the *last* unit of fuel that you buy every month. Use this cost to figure your heating and cooling factor.

ENERGY CONSERVATION LIST

To get you started on conserving energy in your home, fill out the questionnaire shown in Fig. 1-10. Rate your house on energy efficiency by filling in the blanks in Fig. 1-10. The energy crisis is made up of extremely complex issues. You must make your own choices based on how you interpret those issues. The chapters ahead will provide you with the how-to's for making your home more energy efficient. The choices you make affect not only you, but those around you and those who will come after you.

Chapter 2

Energy-Efficient Home Planning

THE BIGGEST SINGLE INVESTMENT most families will make is the purchase or the building of a home. During the planning phase of home selection, one of the most important factors that arises is obtaining the proper heating and cooling systems.

Central? Window? Solar? Which is best for you? The answers are varied and complex whichever your choice. Federal and state regulatory agencies recommend heat pumps because of efficiency. The heat pump is a solar energy machine powered by electricity. Even in cold weather, a certain amount of warmth is present in outside air. The heat pump blows this warmth into your house when it is needed during cold weather. During hot weather, it reverses and pumps heat out of your house. Efficient, year-around climate control is possible.

SITING A NEW HOME

Homes can be tucked into valleys, built on hilltops, put on protected sides of hills, built on the south or southwest (sunny) sides of slopes, or built partly into hills for natural insulation (Fig. 2-1).

Positioning of a house should be selected with climate, wind, and sun in mind. If possible, locate the main roof of the house about parallel to the east/west axis to allow for more south-facing windows for better winter heating. This orientation also provides a desirable location for a solar heat collector.

Because winter winds prevail from the north, northern walls should face north. If your home has extensive glass areas, face them south so that the low winter sun will shine into them during much of the winter daylight hours and so that they will be shaded by an overhang from summer sun. This is equally important in warm climates where cooling is the primary concern. When properly designed (wide) roof overhangs or awnings, little or no sunlight will come in during the summer. By contrast, east or west windows pick up heat almost half the day and put an extra load on the cooling system (Fig. 2-2).

If your new homesite is in a rural area, or other open space, it will be easier to orient your house to save on energy. In any event, use the natural features of the site to best advantage.

SUN AND WIND

A home with a westward orientation will have a smaller heat gain than one with a north-south orienta-

Fig. 2-1. Hillside location aids insulation.

tion. In order to obtain maximum warmth from sunlight in the winter and maximum coolness during the summer, it is best to have your home's principle facade (front) facing south. In cool regions, the direction of the long side of the house should face 12 degrees east of south. In hot, humid regions, 50 degrees east of south is desirable. In hot, arid regions, direct southern exposure to 35 degrees east of south is acceptable. In temperate zones, 17 degrees east of south provides a balanced heat distribution.

A westerly orientation is most troublesome. During the summer, walls and windows facing west receive direct afternoon sunlight. This greatly taxes the cooling load at a time when the home has already been overheated by solar radiation and the warmth of the outside air. In many areas, cold winter winds also prevail upon the west walls and windows to increase the home's heating load.

By using natural and man-made shadings, stopping the sunlight prior to its entrance through the windows is often as effective in keeping your home cool as blinds and curtains on the inside. The most common

method of architectural heating for south walls are roof overhangs (eaves). The sun's arc is low in the winter and high in the summer. Therefore, the overhang should have a projection that shades the south wall from the high summer sun yet permits the sun to warm it during the winter. See Fig. 2-3.

While large overhanging eaves are desirable as shading for a house, they do have a disadvantage for those who enjoy raising house plants. Other shading devices that offer aesthetic value, energy conservation, and admit the maximum amount of light (especially during the winter) are louvred overhangs, wooden trellises, canvas awnings and panels, horizontal or vertical louvred panels, adjustable shutters for windows and doors, masonry grilles, and extended porches.

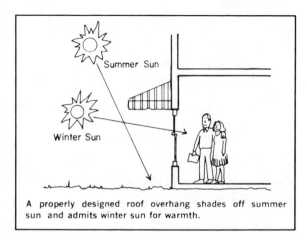

A properly designed roof overhang shades off summer sun and admits winter sun for warmth.

Fig. 2-3. Roof overhangs and the sun.

GLAZING

The amount of glazed area has a great effect on the total amount of energy consumption. The use of glassed area on the east and west walls is an effective way to reduce a home's summer heat and decrease air-conditioning costs. For heating considerations, double glazing, instead of single glazing, can substantially reduce heat and cooling costs. Combination storm windows are a *must* regardless of where you live. They will more than pay for themselves by reducing the consumption of heat and air conditioning.

Careful consideration should be given in selecting heating and cooling equipment. Take into consideration the capacity needed for the particular type home being built. Oversized equipment results in short periods of operation, poor comfort conditions, lower

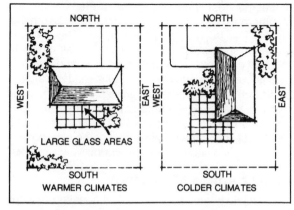

Fig. 2-2. Orient houses with climate in mind.

17

seasonal efficiency, and more energy consumption. Undersized equipment will be over-taxed and it will give poor temperature and humidity control. The amounts of insulation, the number of appliances, the size of windows, the size and shape of the house, and its orientation, enables you to fairly accurately determine the heat loss and heat gain requirements of the dwelling.

When you are building a new home, position your furnace centrally. Locate the thermostat in the room most frequently occupied unless you have multiple heating controls. Do not locate thermostats in interior corridors, in areas that receive direct sunlight, beside doors or windows, in the kitchen, in the bathroom, or near fireplaces.

DESIGN TIPS

If you are building a new home, here are a few tips:

☐ Use light-colored roofing material. It reflects some sunlight; this puts less strain on cooling equipment.

☐ Do not have any large west-facing windows unshaded, or unprotected from the wind.

☐ Main entrances should be located where they will be protected from winter wind.

☐ Locate "hot" rooms, such as the kitchen and laundry, in the cooler sections of the house away from the westerly sunlight.

Garages, Carports, and Porches

Position garages, carports, and porches to reduce energy loads. In cold climates, garages should be located on north, northeast, or northwest exposures. Keep the doors of any attached garages closed when not in use. In hot climates, build the attached garages or carports on the east or west walls of the house to shade east or west glass. This will reduce heat gain. Attached porches also shade walls and windows from direct sunlight.

Home Design Versus Energy

Consideration must be given to local climatic conditions. A home design that is practical in a warm climate might look just as good in a colder zone, but a sprawling layout and large glass expanses will make it expensive to heat and cool.

Choose house shapes that are practical to heat and cool. The key is the amount of wall area compared with the floor area. Reducing the amount of exterior wall area relative to floor area will reduce the energy demand. A round house is the most efficient, but that shape is difficult to build. A square house is the second best choice. The third best choice is a rectangular shape. Homes with an L, H, U, or T shape will use more energy.

The roof of your dwelling should be designed with the climate in mind. Even with a well-insulated ceiling, the color of the roof makes a difference in heat gain. Light-colored roofing materials reflect rather than absorb sunlight. This reduces the load on cooling equipment in warm climates. Nevertheless, a dark-colored roof would be better in cold climates.

Window/Glass Planning

Glass is the single largest source of heat loss from a structure (even with storm glass or double glazing). When reducing the window area, it is better to do it by raising the sill height. This has two advantages:

☐ It keeps the upper portion of the window. This provides better natural illumination.

☐ It helps to reduce heat gain in the summer. The upper portion of the window is more easily shaded by the overhang.

When you are planning your window placement, keep more than just the view in mind; also consider wind and sun direction. Keep the number of east and west windows to a minimum unless they can be shaded by trees, tall shrubs, fences, awnings, or tinted glass. Panoramic windows might not be advisable on the east or west side of the house even if the most scenic view is there. Wherever practical, locate large glass expanses on the more temperate southern side.

To reduce heat gain during the summer without impairing heat gain during the winter, shade the southern exposed glass with a retractable overhang, an awning, or with operable shutters. This will also provide wind protection at all times. If half of the 10 percent glass area is operable windows and the other half is fixed-glass (inoperable insulated, double-glass windows), this will help the ventilation (operable) and reduce heat loss (inoperable). Operable windows should be located so that cool air can travel through the house in summer and escape at the high point of interior space such as an upstairs hallway window.

MOBILE HOMES AND ENERGY

Mobile homes present special heating and cooling problems because they have more outside wall surface for heat loss or gain. Mobile homes should be oriented to take advantage of the shade in summer and the sun's warmth in the winter. And it must be set in a location to protect it from strong winds.

☐ Position your mobile home so that the long sides face north and south. Otherwise, the home will be warmed unevenly and heat coming through east and west windows will create a problem.

☐ Shade the south side in summer by using awnings or porches.

☐ Plant deciduous trees on the east, west, and south sides of the house.

☐ Windbreaks can be effective when located along the north and west sides. Some windbreaks are:
—a semi-enclosed carport.
—large evergreen shrubs.
—evergreen trees that hold their lower limbs.
—a tall fence (Fig. 2-4).

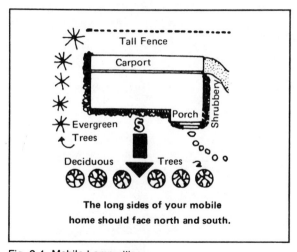

The long sides of your mobile home should face north and south.

Fig. 2-4. Mobile home siting.

Skirting for Mobile Homes

Proper skirting of your mobile home will provide added insulation and help reduce the cost of heating and cooling. It also keeps high winds from producing an uplift effect on the home. Corrugated metal or plastic, as well as concrete blocks or brick, can be used.

Skirting requires ventilation by (approximately) 8-×-16 inch vents. These should be placed one on each end, two along the front, and two along the back. Place one vent as near as possible to the air intake of the furnace. Install a panel to provide access to equipment underneath the mobile home. Exposed water pipes—especially hot water pipes—should be wrapped with pipe insulation that is fitted and taped carefully over the full length of the exposed pipe.

Mobile Home Weather Stripping and Caulking

Air leakage increases the cost of heating and cooling. Cracks and leaks also allow moisture to enter and this can damage both the interior and exterior of your mobile home. Weatherstrip around all windows and outside doors. Check the threshold of outside doors regularly. Wear can cause cracks to develop. Caulk all cracks and openings—regardless of how small—around the moldings, joints, nails, splash panels, windows, top seams, doors, roof vents, and wheel housings.

SOLAR ENERGY

What does solar power have to offer the new homeowner? Should you build a solar house in lieu of a "conventional" home? Can you afford it? How does it operate?

Solar energy is not new, but until several years ago it was considered far too expensive for the average homeowner. The use of solar energy in housing actually dates back many thousands of years. Experiments in the 1940s proved that solar energy could heat contemporary homes.

Although these systems worked well, they did not compete economically with the conventional methods of heating (oil, gas, or electricity). But with energy costs consistently on the rise, solar energy is once again becoming increasingly attractive. It provides a competitive alternate source for heating houses and domestic water. The following questions and answers will help you make a decision on whether or not to use solar energy.

SOLAR QUESTIONS AND ANSWERS

Why should you consider a solar-heating system for your home? There are four reasons:

☐ You will have long-term savings.

☐ Your home will have a higher resale value as conventional energy prices increase.

☐ You will conserve energy.

☐ Your system will be economical, safe, and clean.

Depending upon your location, about 55 percent of the energy needed to run your home will be used for space heating. About 15 percent will be needed for hot water. Some of the nonrenewable fossil fuels used to generate energy can be put to other uses. Our oil and gas supplies will last longer and provide more time for other energy sources to be developed.

Radiation (heat) is absorbed by a *collector,* placed in *storage* with or without the assistance of a *transfer medium,* and distributed to the point of use—your living area. The performance of each operation is maintained and monitored by either automatic or manual controls. An auxiliary heater provides back-up for times when the solar system (lack of sunlight) is not working.

What kind of solar heating systems are there?

There are two basic types: *active* and *passive.* Active systems are divided into liquid systems and air systems. They use pumps and pipes or fans and ducts to carry heat from the collectors to storage, and from storage to the living space of the house. Some passive systems use a wall of the residence or a separate station wall as both the collector and storage medium. In a passive house system, movable wall panels, or *flaps*, are often used to direct the heat throughout the living area. Another approach is the collection and storage of heat in water bags on the roof. This system can also provide cooling in the summer months. See Fig. 2-5.

Where are active and/or passive systems used?

Active systems can be used in new or existing construction. They can be very useful for older homes if remodeling is planned, if you are upgrading your present heating system, if you are adding additional insulation to an existing structure, or if you are adding weather stripping or any other energy-conserving feature. Your property must have good southern exposure to take full advantage of the sunlight.

A passive system for space heating should be considered when you are designing a new home. The design of a passive system solar home requires careful consideration of siting, north-south orientation, protective landscaping and high-quality construction. The use of movable curtains and awnings on large picture windows can be effective in collecting and retaining heat. See Fig. 2-6.

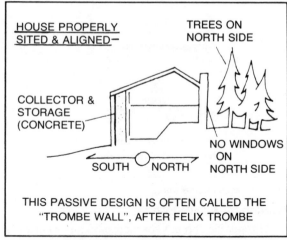

Fig. 2-6. Suggested house siting for a passive solar system.

What if you already have a home?

You will probably have to make some alterations and modifications in order to install a solar energy system. If your home is older it undoubtedly is insufficiently insulated. The first step is to add insulation along with weather stripping, storm windows and storm doors. Solar collectors are usually placed on the roof, but they can be erected in your back yard or attached to a wall. If you add solar equipment to your

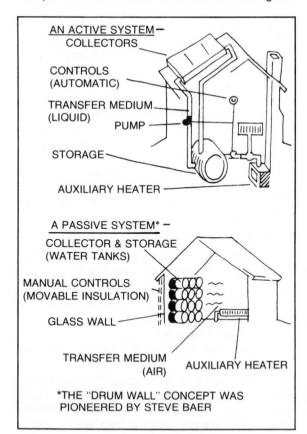

Fig. 2-5. Active and passive solar systems.

20

existing heating system, you will have to allow for piping or duct work connections. Storage tanks or bins are usually in basements, but they can be placed underground or outside the house. This would certainly be the case in locations in warmer climates where basements are not common. See Fig. 2-7.

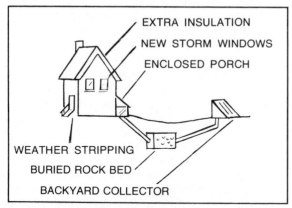

Fig. 2-7. Some suggested alterations for solar heat.

How does the heat get distributed?

There are basically two ways that the heat from the collector or storage medium reaches the rooms of your house. It can circulate through a forced-air duct system that distributes the warm air. Or it can be circulated as hot water in radiators or baseboard units. The water would be preheated by solar heat and brought up to the high temperature needed by the back-up system. In many cases, this means your present heating system can be adapted to distribute solar heat.

How is the house heated at night?

During the day, the heat generated in the collectors is transferred to the storage system (Fig. 2-8). A

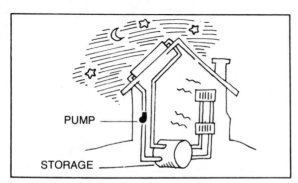

Fig. 2-8. Heating at night.

second set of pipes (for liquid) or ducts (for air) is used to circulate heat from storage to the rooms of your house.

What happens on several cloudy or very cold days in a row?

After the heat in storage is depleted, an auxiliary heater takes over. There should be enough heat in the storage medium to last one or more days. For your system to keep you warm much longer than that, it would have to be larger than the average homeowner could afford (thus too expensive to operate). Most systems are designed to provide 50 to 75 percent of your total heating needs. See Fig. 2-9.

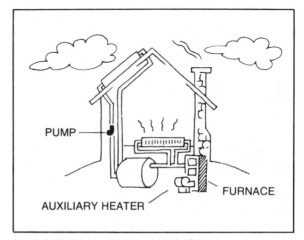

Fig. 2-9. Solar operations on cloudy days.

What is a auxiliary heating system?

They are the standard furnaces fueled by electricity, oil, coal, or gas. It is necessary to have a full-sized backup heater because it will be used when the weather is at its worst. It can also be used when maintenance of the solar heating system requires shutting down the system.

How is heat stored in a solar system?

In space heating systems using liquid heat transfer mediums, the storage system is usually a large tank of water—about 600 to 1000 gallons or more. For systems that use air as a heat transfer medium, the storage system is usually a bin of large gravel. Hot air flows through the space between the 1 to 2-inch gravel and heats it. The bin must be about 2½ times as large as the tank used in a water storage system. Another way of putting this is that there should be one-half cubic foot of rock for every square foot of collector. See Fig. 2-10.

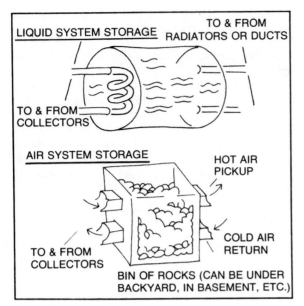

Fig. 2-10. Auxiliary system.

How is hot water produced for home use?

Fluid drawn from the solar collector is run through a coil in a tank of water and the tank is heated. Water is circulated through a second coil in the tank, heated, and drawn off for domestic uses. If you have a solar domestic hot water system, your system must be so constructed that any anti-freeze solution used cannot leak into your hot water supply. See Fig. 2-11.

Can you use solar energy systems just to provide hot water for domestic use?

Yes. Domestic hot water systems are small and easy to install. They can be connected to your present hot water system and many commercial systems are available.

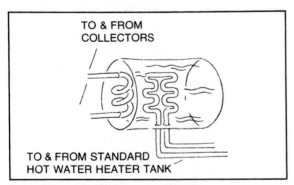

Fig. 2-11. Limited domestic use production of solar-heated water.

Can a solar energy system produce air conditioning?

Yes. The heat from a solar energy system can be used to drive an absorption air conditioner, but solar air conditioning systems are presently very expensive compared to conventional systems. Passive air cooling systems are available. They are inexpensive and efficient, but they work best in climates with low humidity and cool nights.

How about operating costs?

This is a very complex question. Much depends upon the individual usage, location, property and income taxes. There is, as yet, no definite answer to this all important phase in regard solar versus "regular" energy cost.

What should you consider?

Before a decision is made to install any type of solar energy system, the economics of solar power for your home should be carefully considered. Consult with an expert such as your local electrical supplier with regard to installation and equipment. Make comparisons with your regular energy supply. See Fig. 2-12.

Will a solar system affect value of my home?

Probably! Here again individual needs and requirements play a major role in answering this question. With the ever-rising costs of and shortages of conventional fuels, in the next 10 years solar homes could be selling at a premium.

Because a home is a prime user of energy, its consumption and conservation features are of special

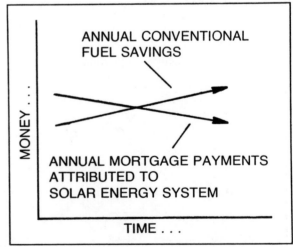

Fig. 2-12. Consider before deciding to invest in solar.

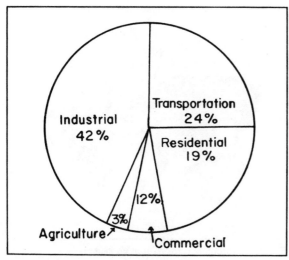

Fig. 2-13. Prime energy consumers.

importance (Fig. 2-13). Besides being more comfortable and economical for the homeowner, energy conserving columns decrease energy demands and contribute greatly to an increase in savings.

In selecting a new home, or remodeling your present home, its orientation affects the amount of energy required to heat and cool it. Topography, noise reduction, scenic views, privacy, regional climate, climatic differences, seasonal changes, solar radiation, and wind are a few of the factors involved (Fig. 2-14).

Fig. 2-14. Home orientation.

SOME SOLAR IDEAS

Many people have decided that energy consciousness for the home goes beyond conventional energy-conserving methods such as insulation, double-glazing and weather stripping. They have de-

cided to "go solar." But what is really meant by *passive design.* The basic ideas are:

☐ Using solar energy efficiently.
☐ Using little mechanical hardware.
☐ Requiring little or no energy to operate the solar equipment.
☐ Costs tend to be low.

It is easiest to understand passive ideas by contrasting them to with *active design* examples. For instance, furnaces, boilers, electric water heaters and air conditioners all fall into the active category. They require complex, expensive, and energy-consuming equipment. An active approach to solar heating and cooling uses a carefully designed, complex and sophisticated solar collector with fans, pumps, storage or heat exchange units and sophisticated controls. In contrast, one passive approach to solar heating or cooling is a regular window (of the right size) with the right orientation to the sun, designed to capture natural breezes, with insulated window shutters and sufficient heat storage mass. Passive options are readily available to the home owner.

Energy savings estimates given in the following sections were derived by comparing the heating energy used in the design shown with a more conventional design of 1600-square-foot "standard practice home" located in an area with a fairly cold climate. The standard practice home already incorporates good current practice (insulation, etc., with a 65° winter thermostat setting).

You might be tempted to select a number of these ideas and then add the percentage savings. That should *not* be done because of all the facts involved in determining the energy required in a given home. It's not possible to add the energy savings shown and assume that the cumulative savings will result. The passive design ideas presented here are a diverse group. Many might not apply to your situation. Some make more sense in either cold or warm climates. Some ideas can be incorporated into existing homes. Other ideas are applicable only in new construction. Energy-conscious, solar design begins by choosing a site offering opportunities to conserve energy as well as to capture it from the sun.

South-Facing Glass Facade

To capture solar energy, face your main living areas to the south and provide sufficient glass area to allow the solar radiation to enter. Once the solar radiation enters, it has to be stored or prevented from being

23

lost through the walls. There are numerous ways of storing and retaining this solar energy. The building's walls, floors, and ceilings and furniture can act as storage devices. Special heat-storage components can be used (Fig. 2-15).

Fig. 2-15. South-facing glass facade design.

Orientation

Orientation for natural ventilation is important. You can use prevailing summer breezes to cool your home. The ideal orientation of the side of the house through which the breezes should enter is an oblique angle of 20° to 70° between the wall and wind direction. This maximizes the natural ventilation in the interior.

Positioning the house is usually a compromise between south-facing windows for heating in the winter and capturing the breezes for cooling in the summer. To protect your facades from winter winds, place evergreens, fences, and earth berms on the north and west side of your home. If you are located on a hill or near a lake, remember these points:

☐ Near a body of water, breezes move from the water to the land during the day, and flow in reverse at night.

☐ On a south-facing hill, breezes tend to move up the hill during the day, and downhill at night.

Regardless of how your home is sited, you can increase natural ventilation and cooling by using casement-type windows, or partially opened shutters on the windward side of the house. These projections create minipressure zones in front of the window openings and increase the velocity of the breeze passing into the openings. See Fig. 2-16.

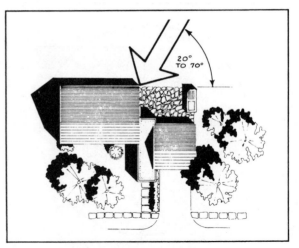

Fig. 2-16. Orientation for natural ventilation.

Basic Rules in Solar Home Design

When designing with these concepts in mind, there are some general guidelines you should use in making appropriate decisions. How you use the site relates to several factors.

South-facing glass. To capture a sufficient amount of solar radiation, it is necessary to provide a minimum amount of south-facing glass. The minimal is ¼ to 1/5 of the floor area in temperate climates, and it is 1/3 to 1/4 of the floor area in colder climates. Combined with proper heat-storage mass and insulating shutters, these glass areas can provide 50 percent or more of the building's space heating needs in warmer climates (Fig. 2-17).

Heat Storage. Heat can be stored in containers filled with water, masonry walls and floors, flower boxes, rock or sand beds, and even furniture. The storage capacity required depends on the amount of radiation captured and the building's use characteristics. In temperate climates, it is necessary to provide 30 pounds of water or 150 pounds of rock storage for each square foot of south-facing glass. If the storage medium cannot be directly exposed to the sun, this number will have to be increased by as much as four times. The ratios of floor area and heat storage surface area should be a minimum of 1:1 to gain the maximum benefit of passive solar heating.

Shading. To prevent excess heat gain in the summer, provide window shading such as overhangs, grilles, and awnings. These devices should shade the total glass area at noon during the hottest months. Careful attention to orientation and the sun's path

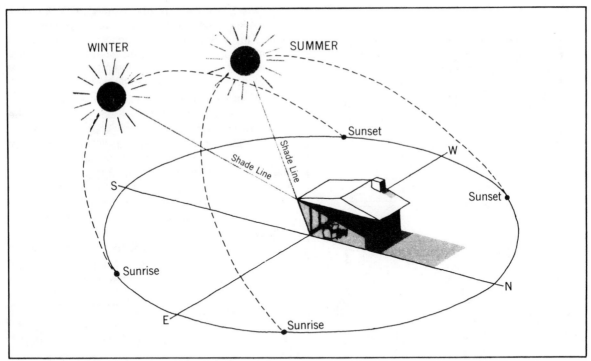

Fig. 2-17. Sun position at noon for latitude 40° north.

through the sky will be required during design. For additional shading, use deciduous trees on the south side of the house; they block the summer sun while allowing the winter sun to penetrate.

Shutters. To prevent heat loss at night, insulated shutters should be closed over the glass areas. During the summer, the process can be reversed to gain some cooling. Close the shutters during the day. Open them at night to expose the glass areas to the cool air.

Window Protection. Add an extra degree of winter protection to windows by installing a layer of 4-6-mil polyethylene. Use pressure sensitive masking tape or duct tape to hold the plastic in place over the window.

THE STANDARD PRACTICE HOUSE

The shape and overall volume of your house can contribute to savings—or excesses—when it comes to energy consumption. Shape and volume can also maximize the use of solar energy through passive means. To provide some basis for comparison use the basic Standard Practice House shown in Fig. 2-18. It is similar to many single-family dwellings today.

The Standard Practice House has approximately

1600 square feet of living space on two floors and a full basement. It already includes conventional energy-saving features such as insulation, storm windows, and weather stripping.

To illustrate the energy savings *possible* for some passive design ideas, it is necessary to first modify the Standard Practice House without changing its floor area or complement of rooms. Then calculate the amount of heating, and sometimes cooling, energy required. Compare the energy required in the modified Standard Practice House to that required before the modification was introduced to arrive at the percentage of energy savings. This figure is included with each passive design idea. For these examples, the location of the passive design houses discussed in this chapter are based on the assumption that they are in a cold-weather region of the United States.

HOUSE DESIGNS

The following house designs provide comparisons for those who are contemplating passive solar construction. The percentage figures noted in each indicates the reduction in energy consumption compared to the Standard Practice House. See Fig. 2-19.

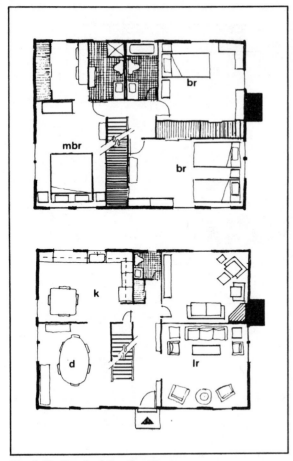

Fig. 2-18. Standard Practice House.

Fig. 2-19. Standard Practice House (1600 square feet).

One-Story Rectangular House (4%). See Fig. 2-20. A large amount of the total heat loss in a home during the winter occurs through exterior walls, and particularly through and around windows and doors in those walls. Reconfiguring the Standard Practice House into a one-story rectangle does the following:

☐ The total exterior wall area is reduced.

☐ The interior rooms have less exposure to the outside, and window area is also reduced somewhat.

☐ Roof area is increased. With conventional construction, it is possible to include more insulation in the roof than in the walls. This further reduces heat loss. This is not to suggest that all one-story homes are more energy efficient than two-story homes. Trading wall area for roof area, however, can save heating energy.

Reducing wall area saves energy. Minimizing the perimeter of the house is also an energy saving design (as shown by the next two approaches).

Fig. 2-20. One-story rectangular house.

Circular Floor Plan (9%). See Fig. 2-21. The smallest perimeter for a given area is a circle. This provides the minimum exterior surface area (and the savings as indicated of 9%).

Square Floor Plan (5%). Round houses are considered by most people to be ultracontemporary. The next best alternative is the square floor plan. It saves energy, but not as much as the round plan. See Fig. 2-22.

Square Plan with Atrium (21%). See Fig. 2-23. Windows can contribute between 15 percent to 35 percent of the total heating energy lost in a house. Therefore, placing them strategically makes a significant difference in reducing heat loss and maximiz-

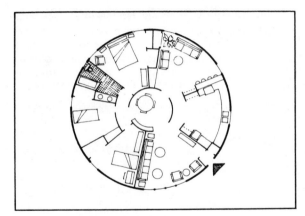

Fig. 2-21. Circular floor plan.

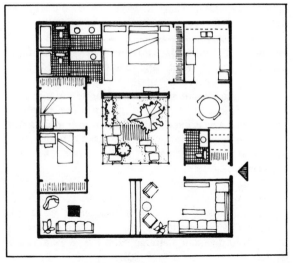

Fig. 2-23. Square plan with atrium.

ing solar gain. Use the square configuration and face the windows into an atrium that is covered with a skylight, and have the windows exposed to the inner atrium instead of to the exterior (as shown in Fig. 2-22). The atrium is unheated, but because of the skylight its winter temperature is not as low as that outside.

The energy savings shown results only from the reduction in heat loss through the windows and walls. The savings can be doubled or tripled if the atrium is also used (with insulated shutters) as a passive solar collector. The atrium design shown in Fig. 2-23 can also be used to reduce heat gain in warm weather if proper sun control and shading devices are used.

Many architects throughout the country have been designing solar homes using the earth to save energy. They are constructed homes that are *below grade*. Earth, like most other materials, does provide some thermal resistance. But in principle earth is not a good insulator. The benefit of earth sheltering is derived from its capacity to moderate temperature variations between interior and exterior. And it provides protection from cold winter winds. It can contribute a great deal to reducing a building's heat loss.

If you do build a house below grade, insulation must be used just as with a standard home. In this case, however, the insulation is placed between the earth cover and the exterior of the structure. This arrangement gives the walls, roofs, and ceilings the heat-storage capacity previously described.

To help illustrate the impact of working with earth sheltering, refer again to the Standard Practice House. All the bedrooms were on the second floor. Figure 2-24 shows the Standard Practice Home with bedrooms below finished grade. They have been relo-

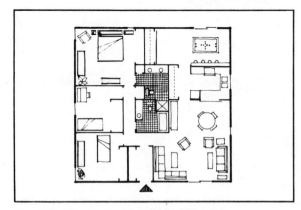

Fig. 2-22. One-story square floor plan.

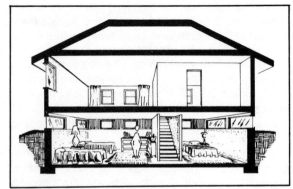

Fig. 2-24. Bedrooms below grade level.

cated below the first floor in what was to be the basement.

By so doing, the amount of excavation is not increased, but the first floor is raised slightly to maintain a 7'6" ceiling height and to accommodate 2' high clerestory windows in the under-the-ground floor level.

This makes the space much more liveable and saves considerable energy (23%) because much of the exterior wall is exposed to earth rather than to the outside. In the summertime, or in warm climates, this approach also reduces heat gain (requiring less cooling energy).

Another approach to using earth is to berm it against the walls of the house. When conventional windows (for example, with 3' high sills) are used, earth can be bermed to the first-floor sills as shown in the Standard Practice House. See Fig. 2-19 and the Square Plan House (Fig. 2-23).

Fig. 2-26. Earth berming to window sill in a Square Plan House.

Fig. 2-25. Earth berming to windowsill in the Standard Practice House.

Figure 2-25 shows earth berming to the window sill in Standard Practice House. Figure 2-26 shows earth berming to the window sill in the Square Plan. Figure 2-27 indicates that earth berming to the roof eaves provides a 32-percent savings.

If clerestory windows can be used, and earth bermed to their sills, additional savings are possible. The temperature 4' to 5' below grade is relatively constant at around 55° F, and a duct located in the berm, with a small fan, provides a simple passive cooling system. See Fig. 2-27.

Earth-berming and the introduction of below-grade spaces in houses require careful attention to waterproofing, foundation drainage, means of egress, and humidity control. Further, earth berming existing

buildings requires special design and technical expertise for the many varied facets they involve such as protection from moisture, rodents, and insects. An expert *must* be consulted for these applications. Nevertheless, the prospects for energy savings with underground houses are becoming well known.

EXTERIOR FEATURES

Floor plans, configuration, window placement and earth sheltering can contribute to energy savings through passive design. Figures 2-28 and 2-29 show other features that can produce energy savings. Doors are the most important openings in exterior walls. Where they open directly into the interior of the house, large amounts of heated or cooled air can escape

Fig. 2-27. Earth berming to roof.

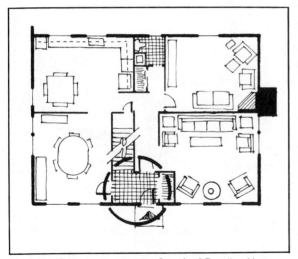

Fig. 2-28. Entry lock within the Standard Practice House.

Fig. 2-29. Entry lock added to the Standard Practice House.

each time they are opened. An entry lock designed into the interior of the house or added to the exterior, reduces energy loss by providing two doors (only one of which is normally open at any moment) separated by a small unheated or uncooled air space.

Additional savings can be obtained by turning an entry lock into a greenhouse (Fig. 2-30) providing a heat-loss of 8 percent and gain of 7 percent. The *greenhouse* effect is well known. Solar radiation through large glass areas will keep temperatures at reasonable levels (even without supplementary heating) in the winter. By adding plants and other insulating/shading devices, the effects of high heat gain in warm weather can be mitigated.

Adding a greenhouse to a home increases the

thermal resistance of the outside envelope in two ways:

☐ The "outside" temperature of the main exterior wall is increased in cold weather and decreased in warm weather.

☐ Infiltration losses around doors and windows are reduced because the main wall no longer is directly exposed to the elements. The energy savings result only from the increased thermal resistance of the envelope. Using a greenhouse as a passive solar collector provides additional savings if it is oriented properly and if heat storage capability is included in its design.

Window shutters (Fig. 2-31) with a heat loss of 28 percent and heat gain of 34 percent provide a more

Fig. 2-30. Entry Lock turned into a greenhouse.

Fig. 2-31. Window shutters.

conventional approach to "adjusting" the thermal resistance of windows *if* they have genuine insulating value. The shutters shown in Fig. 2-31 have a wood face and an insulating core. Once applied to the windows of the Standard Practice House, the savings shown result if they are opened on the following schedule:

☐ East wall: opened from 8 A.M. to 11 A.M. in the winter, and 1 P.M. to 4 P.M. in the summer.

☐ South wall: opened from 8 A.M. to 4 P.M. in the winter and 7 to 9 A.M. and 3 to 5 P.M. in the summer.

☐ North wall: opened from any three hours in the winter and 8 A.M. to 7 P.M. in the summer.

The solar window shutter shown in Fig. 2-32 produces a room savings of 54 percent and an overall house savings of 6 percent. The hinged solar window shutter can be inclined to respond to the appropriate radiation angle and it can be closed against the window frame. The shutter retains the heat generated by solar radiation. When closed, operable vents facilitate heat transfer into the room.

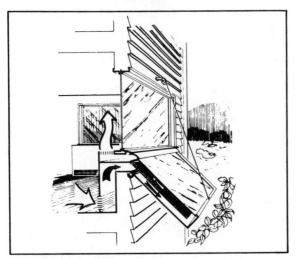

Fig. 2-32. Solar window shutters.

The calculation assumes the use of such shutters in one of the bedrooms of the Standard Practice House (Figs. 2-18 and 2-19) where one window faces east and another faces south. The second figure given indicates the impact of the example on the total energy consumption of the house.

Another approach to passive solar systems is to integrate a solar collector with the window assembly. The collector incorporates collection, storage and di-

Fig. 2-33. Solar window unit.

rect venting into the interior room. To produce the savings as indicated, the collector windows are used in the southeast bedroom of the Standard Practice House. See Figs. 2-18 and 2-19.\ The solar window unit, shown in Fig. 2-33, has a 62 percent savings.

One approach is to integrate collectors into earth berming. The berm angle should be the same as the average solar radiation angle for the locale. The collector unit is self-contained, and heat is transferred into the building by convection and by control of manually operated vents. See Fig. 2-34.

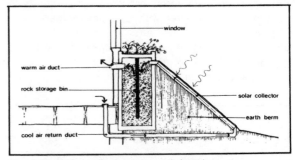

Fig. 2-34. Solar collectors on earth berm.

The importance of south-facing glass in capturing solar radiation has been noted. In Fig. 2-35, showing vertical solar collector and heat storage wall, the entire south-facing facade is treated as a *solar collector wall.* It depicts the principles behind the solar collector wall. Sunlight penetrating the glass strikes the blackened surface of the masonry or concrete wall. This simultaneously heats both the wall and the air space between the glass and the wall. The air enters at the

Fig. 2-35. Vertical solar collector and heat storage wall.

bottom of the wall and is heated in a continuous cycle. This principle is called *thermosyphoning*. In addition, the heat in the masonry wall migrates to the inside and, when sunlight is absent the wall acts as a radiator. Careful use of insulation also allows use of the wall for cooling at night in the summer.

A solar collector wall (Fig. 2-37), with a savings of 27 percent, illustrates the conversion of the south facade of the Standard Practice Home (Figs. 2-18 and 2-19) to a solar collector wall. All of the doors and operable windows have been retained.

Fig. 2-36. Solar collector wall.

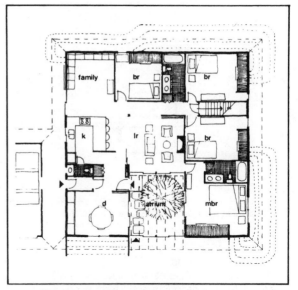

Fig. 2-37. Energy-Conscious House Plan.

FLEXIBLE CEILING PARTITIONS

High ceilings and cathedral ceilings in homes provide spaciousness even in the smallest modern home. These expansive areas can keep rooms cool during the summer, but they are liabilities during winter. A flexible moving ceiling panel, that makes it possible to reduce the ceiling height to 8' in the winter, allows considerable energy savings. Figure 2-38 shows a typical living room with hinged ceiling panels to produce a savings of 10 percent.

PUTTING SOME IDEAS TOGETHER

Each house presents its own situation and requires its own energy consumption calculations. To illustrate, take a number of the passive energy savings ideas as outlined and incorporate them into an energy conscious house. An Energy Conscious House Floor Plan (Fig. 2-38) has a heat-loss of 32 percent, a heat-gain of 23 percent and a hot water use of 36 percent. It contains 1600 square feet (excluding the atrium) and is analyzed under the same conditions as the Standard Practice House (Figs. 2-18 and 2-19). The Energy Conscious House Section and Energy Conscious House Perspective illustrate that the following features have been used:

☐ One-story configuration.
☐ Minimum perimeter distance.
☐ Window shutters.

Fig. 2-38. Energy-Conscious House perspective.

☐ Atrium and entry locks.
☐ Earth berming.
☐ Maximum insulation in roof and walls.
☐ Weather stripping and storm windows.

The Energy Conscious design can provide significant energy savings in homes. It begins with choosing the right site and properly locating the house to take advantage of the sun and wind as well as other natural forces. The house's configuration plan, exterior features, and interior characteristics all contribute.

Most of the ideas presented for the passive designs are now being used in many parts of the country. A few are still in the prototype stage. In new construction, all can be considered and many can also be incorporated into existing homes. See Table 2-1.

A SOLAR WATER HEATER

The components of a solar water heater includes three basic parts:

—The solar heat collector.
—The hot water storage tank.
—The circulation system.

The solar heat collector acts as the water heating element. Flat plate collectors are the most practical for homeowners and are comprised of:

☐ Metal tubing solidly connected to a metal sheet, both painted flat black to absorb heat.
☐ An insulated, weather-resistant box to retain heat.
☐ A transparent cover of glass or plastic.

Two of the 3′-×-8′ solar collectors described will heat approximately 80 gallons of water per day. This should be sufficient for the average family of four. Additional collectors can be constructed for hot water needs exceeding the 80-gallons-per-day average.

Placement of the Collector

Mount the solar heat collector in a sunny spot—preferably facing south. To make the best use of the sun's rays, mount the collector at an angle equal to the latitude at your particular location, plus 10 degrees. For example, in Northern Florida, where the latitude is approximately 30 degrees, a tilt of 40 degrees will give the best year-around performance. Deviating from prescribed angles will reduce efficiency only slightly. For example, reducing an angle from 40 degrees to 25 degrees to correspond to the pitch of your roof reduces efficiency approximately 10 percent.

Solar collectors are usually mounted on the roof, but they can be placed on the ground or installed as an awning. A collector box is heavy and it must be securely anchored to beams, trusses, rafters, or some secure part of the building framework. In storms or hurricanes, an insecurely mounted collector box can be very dangerous.

Storage Tank Size

Use a hot water storage tank that is large enough to store the amount of hot water required by a family during a period of 24 hours or longer. The average family of four requires a storage tank of at least 80 gallons. A larger tank, 100 to 120 gallons, does not cost much more and it will store extra hot water for use when demand is unusually high or when the weather is bad.

Table 2-1. Application and Availability Summary.

	Can be Used in Existing home	Consult Architect or builder	Only a prototype	Only a prototype
South-Facing Glass Facade		*		
Orientation for Natural Ventil		*		
One-Story Rectangular House		*		
Circular Floor Plan		*		
One-Story Square House		*		
Square Plan with Atrium		*		
Bedrooms below Finished grade	*	*		
Earth Berming to Window Sill	*	*		
Earth Berming to Roof Eaves		*		
Entry Locks	*			
The Greenhouse	*			
The Bead-Window		*		
Window Shutters	*			
Solar Window Shutters	*			*
Solar Window Units	*			*
Solar Collector Walls		*		
Solar Collector on Earth Berm	*		*	
Drum Wall		*		
Flexible Ceiling Partitions	*	*		
Foldaway & Built-in Furniture	*			
Zoned Heating	*	*		
Individual Domestic Water Heaters	*	*		

Because of rust and other residues, only a glass-lined tank should be used. Some solar storage tanks will already be insulated. If your tank is not well insulated you should insulate it with at least 4 inches of foil-backed fiberglass wool. If the tank is exposed to the weather, it must be protected with a waterproof structure.

To gain the most savings and to make the best use of solar energy, the solar water heating system should be used without any type of conventional heat source such as an electric booster. This saves 100 percent of your water heating costs, but you must be willing to use warm or cool water occasionally. Using an electrical heating element continuously as a backup could reduce your savings as much as 50 percent. Much depends upon your particular conditions and hot-water usage habits.

An alternative to this plan is to use an electrical heating element in the storage tank and keep the breaker switch turned off or the electric power cord disconnected except when all the solar heated water has been used and there is a need for hot water. The larger your tank, the greater the use of solar energy.

You can connect a solar collector to an existing conventional hot-water tank. However, most conventional tanks do not have the 20-gallon-per-person a day capacity necessary to make the best use of solar energy. The savings in electricity would probably not be worth the trouble and expense of installing a solar-heat collector. If you have a relatively large conventional heater (50-gallon), and you want to try it, it is necessary to use only one of the 3'-×-8' collectors.

Heated water can be circulated through tubing from the collector to the tank by thermosyphon circula-

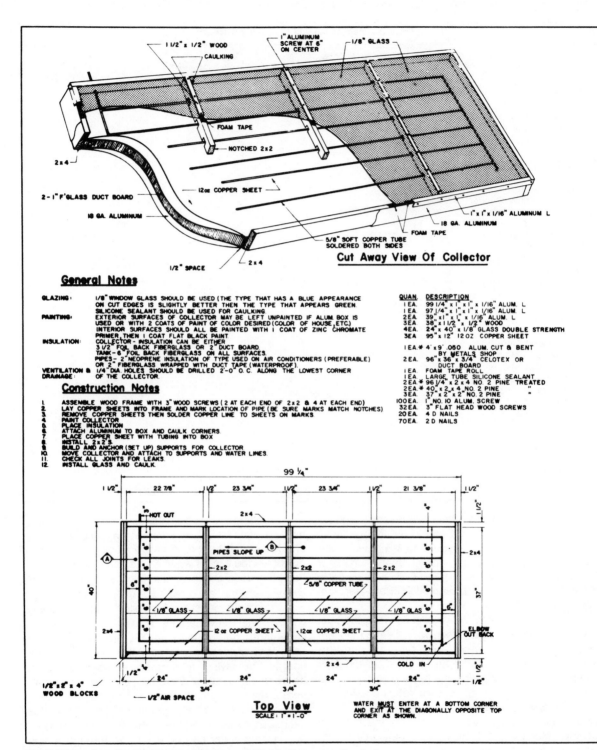

Fig. 2-39. Basic solar water heater (courtesy of Florida Extension Service).

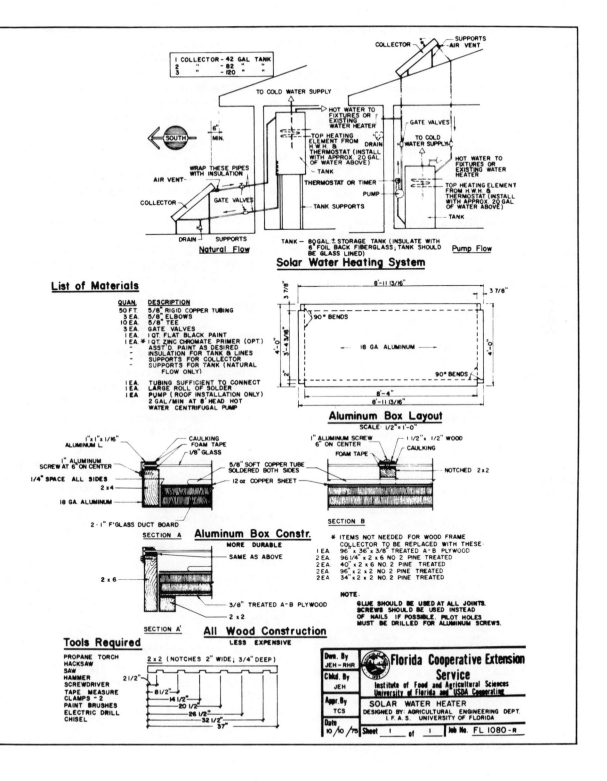

Solar Water Heating System

COLLECTOR	- 42 GAL TANK
2 "	- 82 " "
3 "	- 120 " "

TO COLD WATER SUPPLY

HOT WATER TO FIXTURES OR EXISTING WATER HEATER

TOP HEATING ELEMENT FROM H.W.H. & THERMOSTAT (INSTALL WITH APPROX. 20 GAL OF WATER ABOVE)

THERMOSTAT OR TIMER

PUMP

TANK SUPPORTS

WRAP THESE PIPES WITH INSULATION

AIR VENT

COLLECTOR

GATE VALVES

DRAIN   SUPPORTS

TANK — 80 GAL ± STORAGE TANK (INSULATE WITH 6" FOIL BACK FIBERGLASS; TANK SHOULD BE GLASS LINED)

Natural Flow

SUPPORTS
AIR VENT
COLLECTOR

GATE VALVES

TO COLD WATER SUPPLY

HOT WATER TO FIXTURES OR EXISTING WATER HEATER

TOP HEATING ELEMENT FROM H.W.H. & THERMOSTAT (INSTALL WITH APPROX. 20 GAL OF WATER ABOVE)

TANK

Pump Flow

SOUTH
6" MIN.

List of Materials

QUAN.	DESCRIPTION
50 FT	5/8" RIGID COPPER TUBING
3 EA.	5/8" ELBOWS
10 EA.	5/8" TEE
3 EA.	GATE VALVES
1 EA.	1 QT. FLAT BLACK PAINT
1 EA. *	1 QT. ZINC CHROMATE PRIMER (OPT.)
-	ASST'D. PAINT AS DESIRED
-	INSULATION FOR TANK & LINES
-	SUPPORTS FOR COLLECTOR
-	SUPPORTS FOR TANK (NATURAL FLOW ONLY)
1 EA.	TUBING SUFFICIENT TO CONNECT
1 EA.	LARGE ROLL OF SOLDER
1 EA.	PUMP (ROOF INSTALLATION ONLY) 2 GAL/MIN AT 8' HEAD HOT WATER CENTRIFUGAL PUMP

Aluminum Box Layout
SCALE: 1/2" = 1'-0"

8'-11 13/16"
3 7/8"
3 7/8"
90° BENDS
4'-0"
3'-4 3/16"
18 GA. ALUMINUM
4'-0"
2"
90° BENDS
8'-4"
8'-11 13/16"

Aluminum Box Constr.
MORE DURABLE

1"x 1"x 1/16" ALUMINUM L
CAULKING
FOAM TAPE
1/8" GLASS
1" ALUMINUM SCREW AT 6" ON CENTER
1/4" SPACE ALL SIDES
2 x 4
18 GA. ALUMINUM
2 - 1" F'GLASS DUCT BOARD

SECTION A

SAME AS ABOVE
2 x 6
3/8" TREATED A-B PLYWOOD
2 x 2

SECTION A'

All Wood Construction
LESS EXPENSIVE

1" ALUMINUM SCREW 6" ON CENTER
1 1/2" x 1/2" WOOD
CAULKING
FOAM TAPE
NOTCHED 2 x 2

5/8" SOFT COPPER TUBE SOLDERED BOTH SIDES
12 oz COPPER SHEET

SECTION B

* ITEMS NOT NEEDED FOR WOOD FRAME COLLECTOR TO BE REPLACED WITH THESE:

1 EA.	96" x 36" x 3/8" TREATED A-B PLYWOOD
2 EA.	96 1/4" x 2 x 6 NO 2 PINE TREATED
2 EA.	40" x 2 x 6 NO. 2 PINE TREATED
2 EA.	96" x 2 x 2 NO.2 PINE TREATED
2 EA.	34" x 2 x 2 NO. 2 PINE TREATED

NOTE:
GLUE SHOULD BE USED AT ALL JOINTS. SCREWS SHOULD BE USED INSTEAD OF NAILS IF POSSIBLE. PILOT HOLES MUST BE DRILLED FOR ALUMINUM SCREWS.

Tools Required

PROPANE TORCH
HACKSAW
SAW
HAMMER
SCREWDRIVER
TAPE MEASURE
CLAMPS - 2
PAINT BRUSHES
ELECTRIC DRILL
CHISEL

2 x 2 (NOTCHES 2" WIDE; 3/4" DEEP)

2 1/2"
8 1/2"
14 1/2"
20 1/2"
26 1/2"
32 1/2"
37"

| Dwn. By JEH - RHR |
| Chkd. By JEH |
| Appr. By TCS |
| Date 10/10/75 |

Florida Cooperative Extension Service
Institute of Food and Agricultural Sciences
University of Florida and USDA Cooperating

SOLAR WATER HEATER
DESIGNED BY: AGRICULTURAL ENGINEERING DEPT.
I. F. A. S.   UNIVERSITY OF FLORIDA

Sheet 1 of 1   Job No. FL 1080-R

tion or by using a pump. The thermosyphon system requires no man-made energy to operate and it is based upon the fact that hot water rises. The rate of movement of hot water from the tank to the collector is controlled by the intensity of the sunlight.

Because this system is dependent upon hot water rising, the storage tank must be mounted so that the bottom is at least 2 feet above the top of the solar collector panel. This might require installing the tank in an attic or on a rooftop. Although a false chimney can help the appearance, problems of weight and construction might be encountered. Another possibility is mounting the collector on the ground and installing the tank in your house. This will aid in insulating your tank and eliminate the need for a weatherproof structure around the tank.

When using the thermosyphon system, it is essential that the connecting pipe or tubing have a continuous fall with no sections permitting the formation of air pockets. Circulation will stop if an air pocket is formed.

A pump adds flexibility to a solar water-heating system while using an insignificant amount of energy. Because the pump forces the hot water from the collector to the storage tank, the tank can be located in any convenient place. The pump must be controlled so that water circulates only through the collector when the sun is shining.

An inexpensive method for this control can be obtained by using a timer to control the pump. Of course, this has the disadvantage of operating during daytime hours even on days when there is little or no sunshine. Such conditions would actually cool the water and reduce the efficiency of the system.

A better, but more expensive control, is a *differential thermostat* with one sensing element on the storage tank and one on the collector. With this device, the pump operates only when the solar collector is hotter than the water in the storage tank. Another method is to use a *single-element thermostat* with the sensing element in the collector box and set at about 130 degrees Fahrenheit. The pump and controls add to the cost of a solar water-heating system, but this is often offset by the lower cost of installing the heavy storage tank at ground level.

Whatever circulation system you choose, it is necessary to consider some form of freeze protection, regardless of locale.

☐ Provide a means of manually draining the sys-

tem during hard freezes by placing an air-vent valve above the collector. This allows air to enter the system and produces complete drainage.

☐ Provide a source of heat to exposed plumbing and collector. You could circulate warm water through the collector or attaching electrical heating elements to the plumbing near the collector.

☐ Use a separate heat loop for the exposed collector and plumbing. Antifreeze can be added to this loop because it is not connected to the fresh-water supply. This system is considerably more expensive because a heat exchanger (usually consisting of tubes connected to the outside of the storage tank) is required to transfer heat from the heat loop to the storage tank. This system is also less efficient in its collection of solar energy. In spite of these disadvantages, it is probably the best freeze-protection system for cold climates. It deserves consideration for those in areas of the country with long winters. A basic system is shown in Fig. 2-39.

A TWO-TANK CONCEPT
FOR SOLAR-HEATED WATER

A two-tank concept for maximizing available solar energy is shown in Fig. 2-40. Solar systems operate more efficiently at low temperatures—(80-105°). The two-tank arrangement offers the best opportunity for the system to operate in a partial (low temperature) mode.

Most solar-heated water systems have a pump that circulates water through the collector on command of a differential thermostat (controller) whenever the temperature of the water in the collector (T2) is hotter than the temperature of the water in the solar storage tank (T1). Suppose on a cloudy day the temperature at (T2) averages about 105° F. If the supply water temperature (T0) in the tank enters at 70° F, that means that the pump will continue to circulate the water until all the water in the tank (T1) equals or approaches the temperature of the collector (T2). In this case it would be 105° F. If a family required water at 140° F (T4), the solar system will have supplied approximately 50 percent of that day's hot water requirement. If only one tank was used with the thermostat set at 140° F, the temperature (T2) would never have been high enough on that particular day to give any solar contribution. On a warm, sunny day, the temperature at the collector (T2) might exceed 150° F. This would supply 100 percent of the hot water requirement if the duration is long enough.

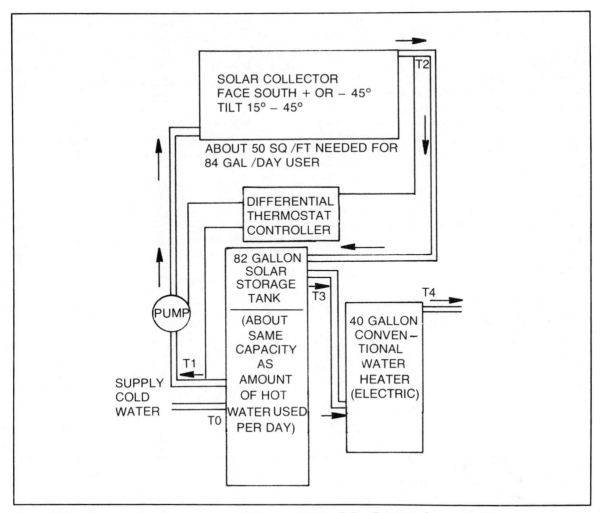

Fig. 2-40. Two-Tank concept for solar hot water (courtesy of Henry Fuller, Escambia County Agent).

Water Usage Patterns

The success of a solar water heating system in energy conservation and hot water delivery depends on usage patterns. It is advisable to determine how much hot water is needed at different times of the day so the family can plan its usage accordingly. You might find that dishes can be washed less frequently and that most of the laundry can be washed in cold water.

Laundry, dishwashing, and bathing should be done early enough in the day so that there are sufficient hours of sunshine to heat more water. For some families, this routine might not be possible. If this is true, a larger storage tank will improve the operation of your system.

General Instructions

Before you begin construction, check local building and plumbing codes and obtain the necessary permits. The plan, as outlined in Fig. 2-40, should provide the average person with the necessary information to construct a solar water heating system. Some construction operations, such as those for the collector box, are shown.

It is recommended that only copper sheet and tubing be used for constructing the absorber plate. Steel or some other material for the absorber could be used and provide satisfactory results. Nevertheless, the thickness of the sheet metal would have to be increased or more tubing would have to be used.

37

Because of this, the cost of construction using steel is equal to or greater than that for copper. Also, copper can be expected to last much longer than steel or other materials.

To make the soldering job easier, note that the plan (Fig. 2-40) indicates using three strips of copper sheet rather than a full 3'-×-8' sheet. If difficulty is encountered, use six strips of copper with one tube placed approximately in the center of each sheet. This procedure will prevent the solder on adjacent tubes from melting. This will not reduce the efficiency of the collector.

If you are building a system yourself, you might want to make other changes or substitutions so that you may have the option of using materials you already have on hand. Avoid the use of styrofoam adjacent to the metal absorber; Styrofoam will melt at these high temperatures. Styrofoam can be used as the second layer of insulation.

A large amount of total heat loss in a home during the winter occurs through exterior walls. This is particularly true for around windows and doors in those walls. Reconfiguring the Standard Practice House into a one-story rectangle does several things:

☐ The total exterior wall area is reduced.

☐ The interior rooms have less exposure to the outside, and the window area is also reduced somewhat.

☐ Roof area is increased. In conventional construction, it is possible to include more insulation in the roof than in the walls. This further reduces heat loss. This is not to suggest that all one-story homes are more energy efficient than two-story homes. Trading wall area for roof area, however, can save heating energy.

Chapter 3

Insulation

PROPERLY INSULATING A NEW home or making sure that an existing structure has sufficient insulation will save energy and provide additional comfort. There are many ways to save energy in your house such as dialing down thermostats in winter and setting them higher in the summer, turning off lights, shutting drapes, closing off unused rooms, and periodic maintenance of your heating and cooling equipment. But there are other effective ways to save energy and money on your monthly fuel bills. By investing in the energy conservation improvements outlined in this chapter, you can permanently reduce the amount of energy used to heat and cool your house.

Insulation can be added to most houses even if some is already in place. Insulating a ceiling is generally where the greatest savings can be accomplished. In the heating season alone, adequate insulation in the ceiling generally will save up to 20 percent on fuel bills. In an air-conditioned home, summer savings will add to the total. Insulation works in *all* seasons.

Other improvements include the installation of insulation in the walls, under floors, and around ducts in unheated areas. The percentage of savings will depend upon how much insulation you had before you added more, the attic area of your house in relation to

wall area, the number and size of windows and doors, and whether you can have storm windows and doors and good weather stripping.

The National Bureau of Standards and the Office of the Special Assistant to the President for Consumer Affairs have jointly said that, if you live in a region of relatively mild winters and have no ceiling insulation, an investment in 6 inches of ceiling insulation will be returned by fuel savings within one year!

The exact amount of money you will save is affected, of course, by the rates you pay for fuel and electricity in your locale and on your living habits as a family. No matter what those rates are, if you make energy-conserving improvements to your home now, you can expect even greater future dollar savings as energy costs rise with inflation.

In the following sections, each area of a house that requires insulation is treated separately. Details include how much material to buy, where to insulate, and how to do it.

TYPES OF INSULATION

Batts: glass fiber or rock wool. See Fig. 3-1. They are used to insulate unfinished attics and the underside of floors.

Fig. 3-1. Fiberglass Insulation Batts (courtesy of Owens-Corning Fiberglas Company).

Best suited for standard joist or rafter spacing of 16″ or 24″ and space between joists relatively free of obstructions.

Cut in sections 15″ or 23″ wide, 2″ to 12″ thick, 4′ or 8′ long.

With or without a vapor barrier backing.

Easy to handle because of relatively small size.

Use will result in more waste from trimming sections than use of blankets.

Fire resistant and moisture resistant.

Blankets: glass fiber or rock wool. See Fig. 3-2. The are used to insulate unfinished attics, attic rafters if attic floors are finished, and the underside of floors.

Best suited for standard joist or rafter spacing of 16″ or 24″ and space between joists relatively free of obstructions.

Cut in sections 15″ or 23″ wide, 1″ to 12″ thick in rolls to be cut to length by the installer.

With or without a vapor barrier backing.

A little more difficult to handle than batts because of size.

Fire resistant and moisture resistant.

Loose Fill (poured-in): glass fiber, rock wool, cellulose, vermiculite, or perlite. See Fig. 3-3. It is used to insulate unfinished attic floors.

Vapor barrier bought and applied separately.

Best suited for nonstandard or irregular joist spacing or when space between joists has many obstructions.

Glass fiber and rock wool are fire resistant and moisture resistant.

Cellulose is chemically treated to be fire resistant and moisture resistant. Treatment not yet proven to be heat resistant; it might break down in a hot attic. Check to be sure that bags indicate material meets federal specifications. If they do, they'll be clearly labeled.

Vermiculite and perlite have about the same insulating value.

All are easy to install.

Loose fill (blown-in): glass fiber, rock wool, or cellulose. It's used to insulate unfinished attics and finished frame walls.

A contractor is needed.

Vapor barrier is bought separately.

Same physical properties as poured-in loose fill.

Because it consists of smaller tufts, cellulose gets into small nooks and corners more consistently than rock wool or glass fiber when blown into closed spaces such as walls or joist spaces.

Rigid Board: extruded polystyrene, bead board (expanded polystyrene), urethane board, glass fiber. It's used to insulate basement walls, exterior walls and foundations and interior walls. When used on the interior of the home, polystyrene and urethane rigid board insulation must be covered with ½″ fire-rated (Type X) gypsum wallboard to assure fire safety.

Extruded polystyrene and urethane are their own vapor barriers; bead board and glass fiber are not.

Fig. 3-2. Fiberglass Insulation Blankets (courtesy of Owens-Corning Fiberglas Company).

High insulating value for relatively small thickness, particularly urethane.

Comes in 24-inch or 8-inch widths.

Variety of thicknesses from ½" to 4".

Foamed in Place. It's used to insulate finished frame walls.

A contractor is needed. The quality of application is sometimes inconsistent. Choose a qualified contractor who will guarantee his work.

More expensive than blown-in materials. See Fig. 3-4.

BUYING INSULATION

Your money's worth in insulation is measured in R-value. *R-value* is a measurement that tells you how much resistance the insulation presents to heat flow-

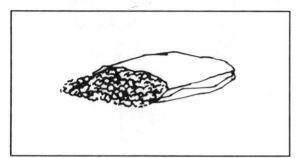

Fig. 3-3. Loose-fill insulation.

Fig. 3-4. Foamed-in-place insulation.

41

Table 3-1. Types of Insulation and R-Values.

Thickness Of Existing Insulation	How Much To Add	How Much To Add If You Have Electric Heat or If You Have Oil Heat and Live in A Cold Climate*	How Much to Add If You Have Electric Heat and Live in Cold Climate**
0″	R-38	R-38	R-38
0″-2″	R-22	R-30	R-38
2″-4″	R-11	R-11	R-30
4″-6″	R-11	R-11	R-19
6″-8″	None	None	R-11

* Add this much if you're doing it yourself and your heating and cooling factors add up to more than 0.4 or you're hiring a contractor and your heating and cooling factors add up to more than 0.6.

**Add this much if you're doing it yourself and your heating and cooling factors add up to more than 0.7 or you're hiring a contractor and your heating and cooling factors add up to more than 1.0.

ing through it. The larger the R-value the better the insulation. Study all of the types of insulation listed, the ways in which to use them, and then make your decision. See Table 3-1 for how many inches of each type of insulation it takes to achieve the R-value you need.

If you have a choice of insulating materials, and all the choices are available in your area, price the same R-values for each and get the better buy. Pay more only for more R-value.

Attic insulation is one of the most important energy-saving home improvements you can make. If your home has one of the three kinds shown in Fig. 3-5

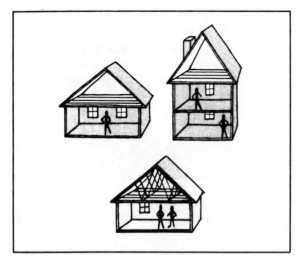

Fig. 3-5. Unfinished attics (no floor).

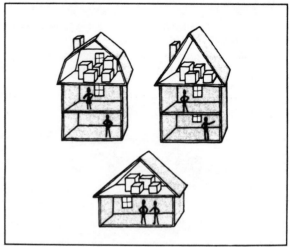

Fig. 3-6. Unfinished attics (with floor).

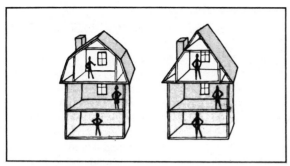

Fig. 3-7. Finished attics.

and Fig. 3-6 go straight to the section in this chapter that applies.

If your home has a combination of two kinds of attics (part of your attic might be finished and heated or part might be unused except for storage as in Figs. 3-7 and 3-8), treat each of the attic areas separately. If your home has a flat roof or a mansard roof, it will be harder and more expensive to insulate than the others. Talk to a contractor. See Fig. 3-9.

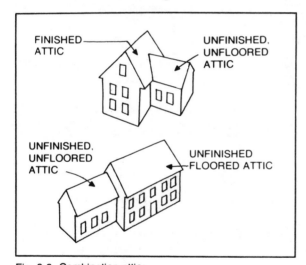

Fig. 3-8. Combination attics.

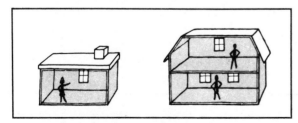

Fig. 3-9. Flat and mansard roofs.

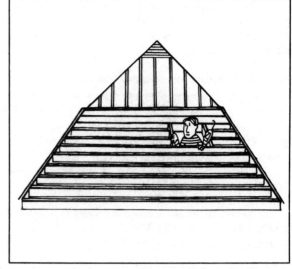

Fig. 3-10. Insulate your unfinished attic.

INSULATE AN UNFINISHED ATTIC

The kind of attic shown in Fig. 3-10 has, at most, some loose boards on which to walk. Should you insulate it? It depends on how much insulation is already there. To find out, go up into your attic and measure the depth of the insulation (Fig. 3-11).

If you already have 8 inches or more, you might have enough. If you have less than 8 inches, you might

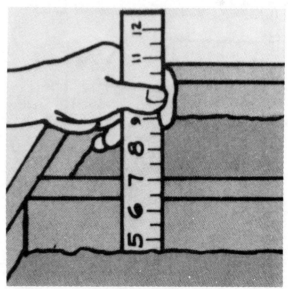

Fig. 3-11. Measure your existing insulation.

43

need more. Start by writing down the approximate thickness you have. Go through the steps marked 1, 2, and 3 in Fig. 3-12. Fill in the data in lower right-hand corner of Fig. 3-12.

How Much Insulation Should You Add?

For electrically heated homes or for homes in extremely cold climates, see Table 3-1. If Table 3-1 indicates a need for a greater thickness for your home, you can still use the figures in Table 3-2 to estimate insulation costs, but not fuel savings.

Read across and down the Table 3-2 from the boxes you've checked to find which square in the chart applies to you. Table 3-3 is an example.

You can do the work yourself if there is a way for you to get up into the attic. To measure your attic area, you don't even have to go up into the attic. Find out the area of the first floor of your home—not counting the garage, porch, and other unheated areas—and it will be the same as the area of your attic.

If it's a rectangle, measure its length and width in feet to the nearest foot and multiply. If it's a combination, break it down into rectangles, find the area of each one, then add the areas to get the total. See Fig. 3-12.

The attic shown in Fig. 3-13 is unfinished and unheated, but it has a floor. Should you insulate such an attic? It depends on how much insulation is already there. If there is any, it will be in either of two places:

☐ Between the rafters. The first place to look is up between the rafters and in the walls at the ends of the attic.

☐ Under the floor. If it's not between the rafters, it might be down under the floorboards. If so, it won't be

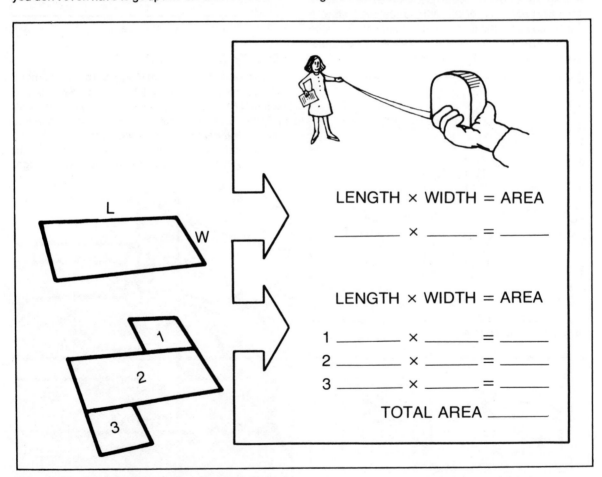

Fig. 3-12. Your computed figures after taking measurements.

Table 3-2. Check the Number of Square Feet Closest to Your Total Attic Area.

IF YOU HAVE THIS MUCH INSULATION		YOU NEED THIS MUCH MORE INSULATION *		600 Sq. Ft.	900 Sq. Ft.	1200 Sq. Ft.	1600 Sq. Ft.	2000 Sq. Ft.
NONE AT ALL	Do-it-yourself	R-38(10"-18")	Cost	$282	$423	$564	$752	$940
			Savings Factor	246	369	492	656	820
	Hire a contractor	R-38(10"-18")	Cost	$350	$525	$699	$932	$1166
			Savings Factor	246	369	492	656	820
UNDER 2 INCHES	Do-it-yourself	R-22(6"-10")	Cost	$168	$252	$336	$448	$560
			Savings Factor	56	86	115	154	206
	Hire a contractor	R-22(6"-10")	Cost	$198	$297	$396	$529	$661
			Savings Factor	56	86	115	154	206
2 TO 4 INCHES	Do-it-yourself	R-11(3"-5")	Cost	$78	$117	$156	$208	$260
			Savings Factor	22	33	44	59	74
	Hire a contractor	R-11(3"-5")	Cost	$86	$129	$172	$229	$286
			Savings Factor	22	33	44	59	74
4 TO 6 INCHES	Do-it-yourself	R-11(3"-5")	Cost	$78	$117	$156	$208	$260
			Savings Factor	12	18	24	32	40
	Hire a contractor	R-11(3"-5")	Cost	$86	$129	$172	$229	$286
			Savings Factor	12	18	24	32	40

Table 3-3. An Example of Insulating Costs and Savings.

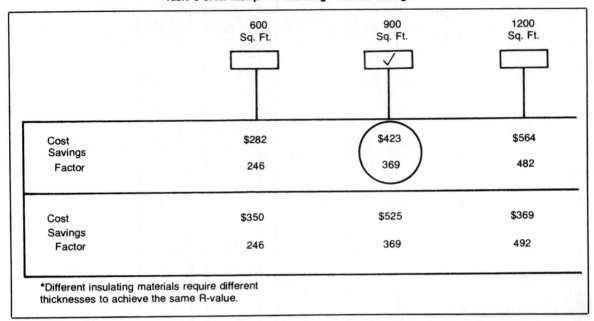

	600 Sq. Ft.	900 Sq. Ft. ✓	1200 Sq. Ft.
Cost	$282	$423	$564
Savings Factor	246	369	482
Cost	$350	$525	$369
Savings Factor	246	369	492

*Different insulating materials require different thicknesses to achieve the same R-value.

easy to see. You'll have to look around the edges of the attic or through any large cracks in the floor. A flashlight will come in handy, use a ruler to poke through the cracks. If there's any soft, fluffy material in there, that's insulation.

Wherever the insulation estimate it's thickness. If it's thicker than 4 inches, it's not economical to add more. If it's 4 inches thick or less, you might need more.

Costs and Savings

To get a quick estimate of your costs and savings, follow steps 1 and 2 below.

Step 1. There are two basic ways to insulate this type of attic. Insulate the rafters, end walls, and collar beams. This is the best way if you're doing it yourself, or if you think you might ever finish the attic. The other way is to blow loose insulation in under the attic floor. This is a job for a contractor. Don't have this done if you think you might ever finish the attic. But if you're going to call a contractor, this is the least expensive and most effective way.

For the method you've chosen, check one of the three boxes in Table 3-4. Check the top box if there's

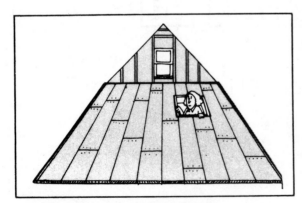

Fig. 3-13. An unfinished and unheated attic.

Fig. 3-14. A finished attic needing insulation.

Table 3-4. Insulation Costs and Savings.

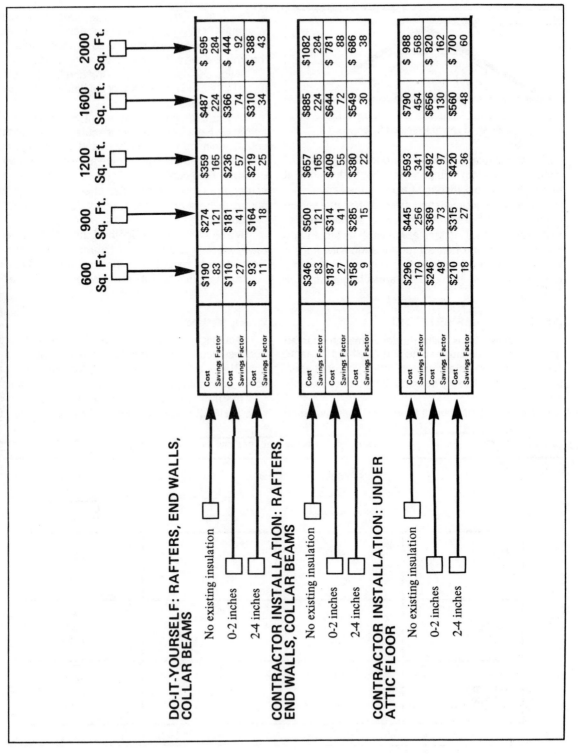

DO-IT-YOURSELF: RAFTERS, END WALLS, COLLAR BEAMS

		600 Sq. Ft.	900 Sq. Ft.	1200 Sq. Ft.	1600 Sq. Ft.	2000 Sq. Ft.
No existing insulation	Cost	$190	$274	$359	$487	$ 595
	Savings Factor	83	121	165	224	284
0-2 inches	Cost	$110	$181	$236	$366	$ 444
	Savings Factor	27	41	57	74	92
2-4 inches	Cost	$ 93	$164	$219	$310	$ 388
	Savings Factor	11	18	25	34	43

CONTRACTOR INSTALLATION: RAFTERS, END WALLS, COLLAR BEAMS

		600 Sq. Ft.	900 Sq. Ft.	1200 Sq. Ft.	1600 Sq. Ft.	2000 Sq. Ft.
No existing insulation	Cost	$346	$500	$657	$885	$1082
	Savings Factor	83	121	165	224	284
0-2 inches	Cost	$187	$314	$409	$644	$ 781
	Savings Factor	27	41	55	72	88
2-4 inches	Cost	$158	$285	$380	$549	$ 686
	Savings Factor	9	15	22	30	38

CONTRACTOR INSTALLATION: UNDER ATTIC FLOOR

		600 Sq. Ft.	900 Sq. Ft.	1200 Sq. Ft.	1600 Sq. Ft.	2000 Sq. Ft.
No existing insulation	Cost	$296	$445	$593	$790	$ 988
	Savings Factor	170	256	341	454	568
0-2 inches	Cost	$246	$369	$492	$656	$ 820
	Savings Factor	49	73	97	130	162
2-4 inches	Cost	$210	$315	$420	$560	$ 700
	Savings Factor	18	27	36	48	60

47

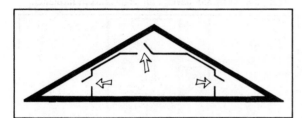

Fig. 3-15. Unfinished space indicated by arrows.

no existing insulation, the middle one if there's up to 2 inches of existing insulation, or the bottom one if there's from 2 to 4 inches of existing insulation.

Step 2. Your unfinished, floored attic area will be either shaped like a rectangle or a combination of rectangles. If it's a rectangle: Measure its length and width in feet to the nearest foot and multiply. If it's a combination, break it down into rectangles, find the area of each one, then add the areas to get the total. See Fig. 3-12.

INSULATE A FINISHED ATTIC

A finished attic is a little harder to insulate than an unfinished attic because some parts are hard to reach. A contractor can do a complete job. If you do it yourself, there will probably be parts that you can't reach. See Fig. 3-4.

You need to find out if there's enough insulation

there already. Depending on what your house is like, you might or might not be able to measure your insulation by getting into the unfinished spaces in your attic through a door or hatchway. See Fig. 3-15.

If you can get in, measure the depth of insulation. If you have 9 inches or more of insulation everywhere, you have enough.

If you can't get into the unfinished parts of your attic at all, have a contractor measure the insulation for you. Ask him how much is there and use the figures in Table 3-4 to complete and arrive at the total insulation. Be sure to record these figures. Read down and across from the boxes you've checked to find which square in the chart applies to you. See Table 3-5 for an example.

Make notes of the depth of insulation that's already there. You'll want this information in a minute. Remember to record all of the "amounts" you calculate from reading the Tables as you progress. See Fig. 3-16.

Which Method?

You might find that you can't do the work yourself because you can't get into the unfinished part of your attic. If you can get to all parts of the attic, there are some good things you can do yourself to insulate it.

Insulate the Attic Ceiling. You can insulate your attic ceiling if there's a door to the space above the

Table 3-5. An Example of Costs and Savings.

	600 Sq. Ft. ☐	900 Sq. Ft. ✓	1200 Sq. Ft. ☐
Cost	$190	$274	$359
Savings Factor	83	121	165
Cost	$110	$181	$236
Savings Factor	27	41	57
Cost	$93	$104	$219
Savings Factor	11	18	25

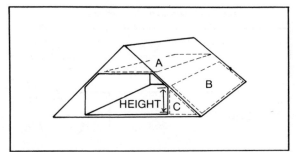

Fig. 3-16. The basics of measuring for attic insulation.

finished area. You should consider insulating it if there's less than 9 inches of insulation already there.

Insulate Outer Attic Rafters. Outer attic rafters are the parts of the roof shown in Fig. 3-17. You should consider insulating them if there's no insulation between the rafters or if there's room for more insulation in the outer attic floor and in the "knee walls" that separate the finished and unfinished parts of the attic.

Insulate Outer Attic Gables. Outer attic gables are the little triangular walls shown in Fig. 3-18. You should insulate them if you insulate the outer attic rafters.

If you want to find costs and savings for a do-it-yourself insulation job, use Tables 3-6 through 3-9.

Contractor Installation

Finished attics differ a lot in how much they cost for a contractor to insulate them. Therefore, Fig. 3-11 gives you only a rough estimate of how much it would cost you. If you want a better figure, get a contractor to give you a firm estimate.

Cost and Savings

To get a quick estimate of your cost and savings,

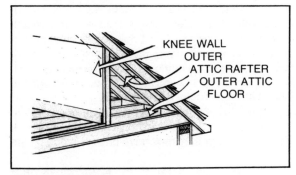

Fig. 3-17. Attic rafters.

Table 3-6. Costs and Savings for Do-It-Yourself Insulation.

1. How large are the areas you want to insulate? Multiply the length times the width (in feet) of each area that you can insulate.
   a. ATTIC CEILING: Length × width = area

   b. OUTER ATTIC RAFTERS (there might be several areas you'll need to add together here)

Length	× width	= area
_____	_____	= ___
_____	_____	= ___
_____	_____	= ___
		+

   Total _____

   c. OUTER ATTIC GABLES (the area of these triangles is only half the length times the height).
   length × height ÷2 = area
   _____ _____ ÷2 = ___
   Multiply by the number of gable ends to get the total area.

2. Your Savings Factor
   For each part of your attic that you've measured, check below about how much insulation is already there. For each row you've checked, multiply your area times the number written to the right:
   ATTIC CEILING

   _____ none _____ × .38 = _____
   _____ 0-2 inches _____ × .09 = _____
   _____ 2-4 inches _____ × .04 = _____
           area
   OUTER ATTIC RAFTERS (Existing insulation will be in the floor and knee walls)
   _____ none _____ × .23 = _____
   _____ 0-2 inches _____ × .09 = _____
   _____ 2-4 inches _____ × .05 = _____
           area
   OUTER ATTIC GABLES (Existing insulation will be in the floor and knee walls)
   _____ none _____ × .16 = _____
   _____ 0-2 inches _____ × .06 = _____
   _____ 2-4 inches _____ × .03 = _____
           area   +

   TOTAL _____

   Add the results from each row you've filled out to get your savings factor.

3. Your Cost
   ATTIC CEILING:
   If there's no existing insulation
   _____ × $0.37 = _____
     area
   If there's up to 2 inches of existing insulation
   _____ × $0.24 = _____
     area
   If there's 2 to 4 inches of existing insulation
   _____ × $0.13 = _____
     area
   OUTER ATTIC RAFTERS:
   If there's up to 2 inches of existing insulation
   _____ × $0.24 = _____
     area
   If there's from 2 to 4 inches of existing insulation
   _____ × $0.13 = _____
     area
   OUTER ATTIC GABLES:
   _____ × $0.13 = _____
     area

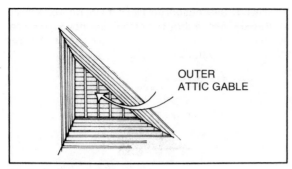

Fig. 3-18. Outer gables.

measure the depth of existing insulation. Measure the length and width of the finished part of your attic. Round them off to the nearest foot and multiply length times width to equal area. See Fig. 3-19.

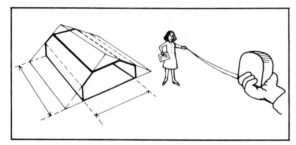

Fig. 3-19. How big is your attic?

Check the number of square feet (Table 3-7) that's closest to your finished attic area. Read down and across from the boxes you've checked to find which square in the Table applies to you. Table 3-8 is an example.

Measure the depth of existing insulation. Check the box that's closest to the depth you find. Usually, it will be the same thickness in all parts of the attic. If there are different thicknesses, figure the average

Table 3-7. Costs and Savings Example.

	300	550	800	1100	1400
None	$321 208	$469 316	$587 429	$641 572	$745 721
Under 2"	$233 68	$343 97	$418 126	$469 167	$555 205
2"-4"	$130 31	$214 44	$285 56	$322 74	$410 90

Table 3-8. Costs and Savings Example.

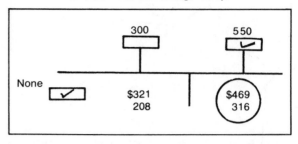

depth and check it in Table 3-7. Measure the length and width of the finished part of your attic. Round them off to the nearest foot and multiply. See Fig. 3-19. Check the number of square feet that's closest to your finished attic area.

Table 3-9. Costs and Savings Factors.

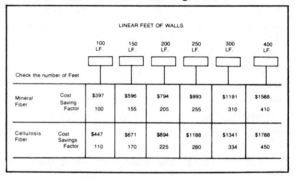

		LINEAR FEET OF WALLS					
		100 LF.	150 LF.	200 LF.	250 LF.	300 LF.	400 LF.
Check the number of Feet							
Mineral Fiber	Cost Saving Factor	$397 100	$596 155	$794 205	$993 255	$1191 310	$1588 410
Cellulosis Fiber	Cost Savings Factor	$447 110	$671 170	$894 225	$1188 280	$1341 334	$1788 450

INSULATE YOUR WALLS

Should you insulate walls? It depends on the size of your energy bills and what your walls are like. See Fig. 3-20. To find out if you should insulate walls, answer the following questions.

How Big are Your Energy Bills? If you have heating, but no whole-house air conditioning, look up the factor for your city in Table 1-6. The heating factor is a number that reflects the climate in your area and how much you pay for fuel. Look at the heating factor for the type of heating you have (gas, oil, electricity, or coal). It's one of the numbers in the first four columns. Then look up your cooling factor. It's the number in the fifth column of Table 1-6.

What are Your Walls Like? Most houses have frame walls. They have a wood structure (usually 2 by 4s) even though they may have brick or stone on the outside.

Some houses have brick or block masonry walls that form the structure. If there is no insula-

50

Fig. 3-20. Insulate your walls (contractor's job).

tion at all in them already, a contractor can fill them with insulation and cut energy waste by about two-thirds.

You might already know whether or not your walls have insulation in them. If you don't know, here's how to find out.

Turn off the current at the fuse box. Take the cover off a light switch on an outside wall. Shine a flashlight into the space between the switchbox and the wall material. Look for insulation. If there's some insulation there now, you might need more.

If you have masonry walls, it might be worthwhile to insulate them if they're uninsulated now. It's more complicated than insulating frame walls; call a contractor to find out what's involved.

Costs and Savings

Some kinds of wall insulation cost more than others, and some kinds work better than others. The least expensive is mineral fiber insulation. There are two kinds: rock wool and glass fiber. Either kind can be blown into the wall by means of a special machine.

A slightly more expensive, but more effective insulation is cellulosic fiber. This is another loose insulation that's blown in like mineral fiber.

How Big is Your House? Measure the perimeter—the total distance around the outside—of each story of your house that has frame walls. Measure around the heated parts only. Measure in feet to the nearest 10 feet. Then fill in the footage as indicated in Fig. 3-22.

Table 3-9 shows costs and savings factors for different types of insulation applied to different sizes of houses. To use Table 3-9, look at the column under the box you've checked. See Table 3-10 for an example.

Look at the top numbers in that column (Table 3-9) for the estimated costs for installing each type of material. See which you can afford. Remember that if the cost is higher, your savings will also be higher.

Crawl Spaces, Floors, and Basements

If you live in a climate where your heating bill is big enough to be a worry, it's a good idea to insulate the

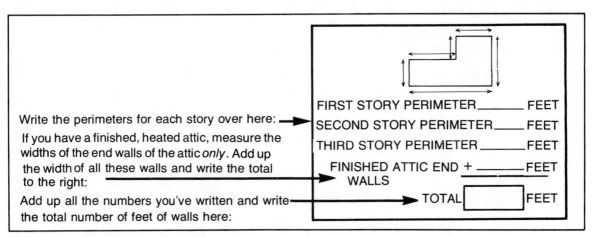

Write the perimeters for each story over here: ➡️

If you have a finished, heated attic, measure the widths of the end walls of the attic *only*. Add up the width of all these walls and write the total to the right:

Add up all the numbers you've written and write the total number of feet of walls here:

FIRST STORY PERIMETER_____ FEET
SECOND STORY PERIMETER_____ FEET
THIRD STORY PERIMETER _____ FEET
FINISHED ATTIC END + _____FEET
WALLS
➡️ TOTAL [   ] FEET

Fig. 3-21. How to measure your house for insulation.

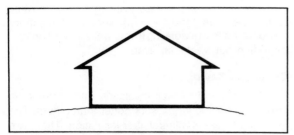

Fig. 3-22. A house without a crawl space.

underside of your house. It won't save much on air conditioning, but it will save on heating.

A Flat Concrete Slab Sitting on the Ground. There's not much that you can easily do to insulate this type of foundation. It's hard to tell how much insulation is already there. It's also hard to tell what your savings would be.

A Crawl Space with Walls Around It. If you have a crawl space that you can seal tightly in winter, you can insulate its walls and the ground around its outer edges.

A Floor Over a Garage, a Porch or an Open Crawl Space. If there's an open space under your floor that you can't seal off tightly from the outside air, the place to insulate is in the floor—between the joists.

Protruding Walls of a Heated Basement. If you have a basement that is heated and is used as a living area, it might be worth your while to insulate the basement walls down to a depth of 2 feet below the ground.

A Combination of the Above Factors. Your house might have a heated basement and crawl space, or some other combination. To estimate your costs and savings, treat each of the parts separately. See Figs. 3-22 and 3-23.

If your house (or part of it) sits on top of a crawl space that can be tightly sealed off from the outside air

in the winter, the least expensive and best place to insulate it is around the outside walls and on the adjacent ground inside the space. See Fig. 3-23.

Is there no insulation at all around the crawl space walls or under the floor? Is your crawl space high enough to get in there to do the work? If the answer to either of these questions is "no" don't insulate here. If your answer is "yes," measure the distance around the outside of the heated part of your crawl space (don't include areas underneath porches, and other unheated areas). Make a note of this computation for easy reference. See Fig. 3-25.

It makes a difference whether you want to do the work yourself or call a contractor. Doing it yourself is

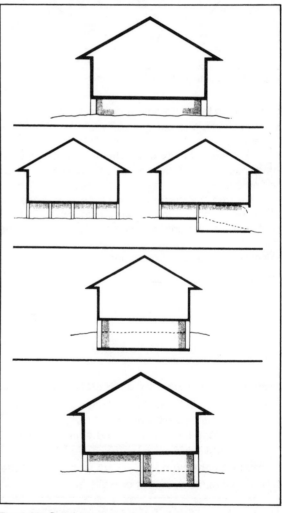

Fig. 3-23. Crawl spaces.

Table 3-10. Costs and Savings Example.

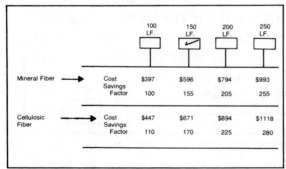

		100 LF.	150 LF.	200 LF.	250 LF.
Mineral Fiber →	Cost	$397	$596	$794	$993
	Savings Factor	100	155	205	255
Cellulosic Fiber →	Cost	$447	$671	$894	$1118
	Savings Factor	110	170	225	280

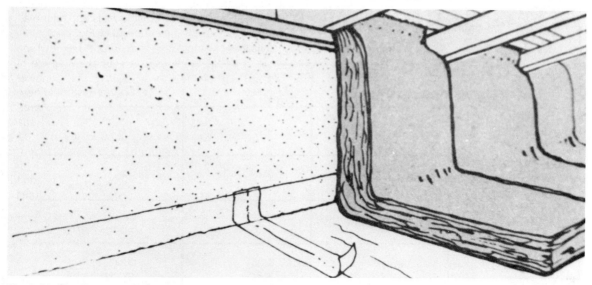

Fig. 3-24. Crawl-space walls insulated.

hard work, but you'll save a lot of money once you are through.

To estimate the cost if you're doing the work yourself, multiply the total distance around your crawl space times $0.80 (the approximate cost per running foot).

To estimate the cost if a contractor will do the work, multiply the distance around your crawl space, that you wrote in at the bottom of the last column (Fig. 3-25), by $1.10 (the approximate cost per running foot).

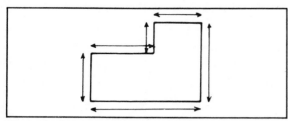

Fig. 3-25. How to measure a crawl space.

How much will you save?

To estimate your savings factor, multiply the distance around your crawl space times 0.54.

INSULATE YOUR FLOORS

There are two cases where it's good to insulate your floors.

One example is if you have a crawl space that you can't seal off in the winter. Perhaps your house stands on piers (Fig. 3-23). Another example is if you have a garage, porch, or other cold unheated space with heated rooms above it (Fig. 3-23).

If your answer to any of these examples is "no," don't insulate the floor. If your answer to both questions is "yes," decide whether you want to do the work yourself or call a contractor.

How Big is Your Floor?

Measure the area of the floor that you plan to insulate. If it's a rectangle, measure the length and width of the floor in feet and multiply. If it's a combination of rectangles, break it down into rectangles. For each rectangle, measure its length and its width and multiply. Add these numbers to get the total area.

Should You Insulate It?

Is your floor uninsulated? Is the floor accessible? If it's above a crawl space, is the crawl space high enough for a person to work in it? If your answer to any of these questions is "no," don't insulate the floor. If your answer to both questions is "yes," refer to Tables 3-11 and 3-12.

Choose either the "do-it-yourself" or "contractor" column in Table 3-11. Read down the column until you

53

Table 3-11. Costs and Savings Example.

Square Feet	Do-it-Yourself	Contractor	Cost/ Savings Factor
200_____	$ 24 58	$ 56 58	Cost Savings Factor
400_____	$ 48 116	$112 116	Cost Savings Factor
600_____	$ 76 173	$167 173	Cost Savings Factor
900_____	$106 260	$250 260	Cost Savings Factor
1200_____	$152 347	$334 347	Cost Savings Factor
1600_____	$189 462	$445 462	Cost Savings Factor

come to the row next to the number of square feet you've checked. Circle that box.

Check the number of square feet that's closest to the floor area to be insulated that you found in Table 3-11. Choose either the "do-it-yourself" or "contractor" column in the table. Read down that column until you come to the row next to the number of square feet you've checked. Circle that box.

INSULATE YOUR BASEMENT WALLS

If you have a basement that you use as a living space or work space, and that has air outlets, radiators, or baseboard units to heat it, you might find that it will pay to add a layer of insulation to the inside of the wall. The cost figures in Table 3-12 do not allow for the cost of refinishing as well as insulating.

Table 3-12. Costs and Savings Example.

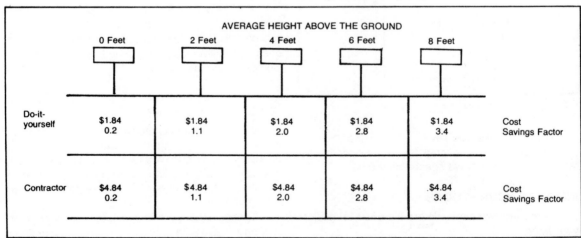

	0 Feet	2 Feet	4 Feet	6 Feet	8 Feet	
Do-it-yourself	$1.84 0.2	$1.84 1.1	$1.84 2.0	$1.84 2.8	$1.84 3.4	Cost Savings Factor
Contractor	$4.84 0.2	$4.84 1.1	$4.84 2.0	$4.84 2.8	.$4.84 3.4	Cost Savings Factor

AVERAGE HEIGHT ABOVE THE GROUND

Fig. 3-26. Insulate your floors.

Multiply the top number in the square you circled times the total length of the walls (from the measurements you will take as explained in the following).

If your basement walls aren't insulated and if your basement's average height above ground is 2 feet or more, then it pays to insulate them in almost any climate if you do the work yourself. If your basement's average height above ground is less than 2 feet, then it pays to insulate these walls if your heating factor is more than 0.7.

If you want to have a contractor do it, your heating factor should be 0.5 or more if your basement's average height above ground is 2 feet or more. If the height is less than 2 feet, you should not have the work done.

Measurements. Measure the length of each wall that sticks 2 or more feet above ground and add the

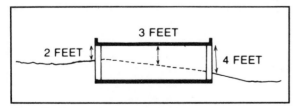

Fig. 3-27. Height above the ground.

lengths. Estimate, to the nearest foot, how far on the average these walls stick up above ground. For example, suppose your house is on a slope. The average height for this house is 3 feet. Record your average height above ground. See Fig. 3-27.

At the top of Table 3-12, check the height of the basement walls above ground that's closest to the amount you recorded. At the side of the chart, check either "do-it-yourself" or "contractor." Read across the row you checked until you come to the column you checked. Circle the square where the row and the column meet.

When you have recorded the number, multiply the bottom number in the square that you circled times the total length of the walls to get your savings factor. The result is your estimated cost.

HOW-TO INSULATION PROCEDURES

Insulating Your Unfinished Attic. This is an easy do-it-yourself project. Install batts or blankets between the joists or trusses in your attic, pour in loose fill between the joists or trusses, lay in batts, or pour in loose fill over existing insulation if you've decided you don't have enough already. Don't add a vapor barrier if you're installing additional insulation. *Note:* If your attic has trusses in it, this section still applies. The insulation goes in the same place, but the job is more difficult. See Figs. 3-28 through 3-31.

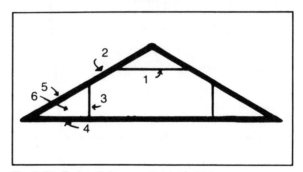

Fig. 3-28. End-wall diagram (finished attic).

Tools

Temporary lighting.
Temporary flooring.
Duct or masking tape (2″ wide).
Heavy-duty staple gun and staples, or a hammer and tacks.
Heavy-duty shears or a utility knife to cut batts or blankets and plastic for the vapor barrier. See Fig. 3-32.

55

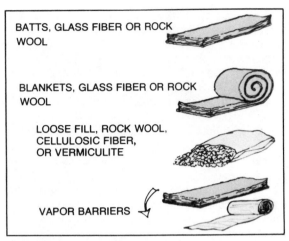

BATTS, GLASS FIBER OR ROCK WOOL

BLANKETS, GLASS FIBER OR ROCK WOOL

LOOSE FILL, ROCK WOOL, CELLULOSIC FIBER, OR VERMICULITE

VAPOR BARRIERS

Fig. 3-29. Various insulating materials.

Safety

Provide good lighting.

Lay boards or plywood sheets over the tops of the joists or trusses to form a walkway (the ceiling below won't support your weight).

Be careful of roofing nails protruding through roof sheathing.

If you use glass fiber or mineral wool, wear gloves and a breathing mask. Keep the materials wrapped until you're ready to put them in place.

Materials

Batts: glass fiber or rock wool.
Blankets: glass fiber or rock wool.

Loose fill: rock wool, cellulosic fiber, or vermiculite.

Vapor barriers. See Fig. 3-29.

Accurately determine your attic area. If necessary, divide it into rectangles and sum the areas.

Insulation area equals .9 times total area.

Vapor barrier area (if it is needed).

Batts or blankets with vapor barrier backing. Polyethylene (for use with loose fill, or if backed batts or blankets are not available). Plan on waste because the polyethylene will be installed in strips between the joists or trusses and you may not be able to cut an even number of strips out of a roll.

Insulation thickness. See Table 3-13. If it calls for R-30 or more, you will be adding two layers of insulation. Lay the first layer between the joists or trusses and the second layer across them. Only the first layer should have a vapor barrier underneath it. The second layer should be an unfaced batt or blanket, loose fill, or a faced batt or blanket with the vapor barrier slashed freely.

Preparation

Put in temporary lighting and flooring. Check for leaks and check need for ventilation and vapor barrier. Seal all places where pipes or wires penetrate the attic floor. *Note:* Some manufacturers recommend using polyethylene in a continuous sheet across the joists or trusses. If you aren't adding insulation that covers the tops of these framing members with at least 3½" of insulation, laying a continuous sheet might cause condensation along them; lay strips instead.

Table 3-13. Types of Insulation.

| | BATTS OR BLANKETS | | LOOSE FILL (POURED-IN) | | |
	Glass fiber	Rock wool	Glass fiber	Rock wool	Cellulosic fiber
R-11	3½"-4"	3"	5"	4"	3"
R-19	6"-6½"	5¼"	8"-9"	6"-7"	5"
R-22	6½"	6"	10"	7"-8"	6"
R-30	9½" - 10' ¼"*	9"*	13"-14"	10"-11"	8"
R-38	12"-13"*	10½"*	17"-18"	13"-14"	10"-11"

* Two batts or blankets required

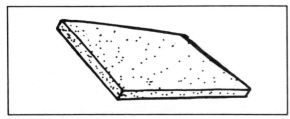

Fig. 3-30. Rigid-board insulation.

Fig. 3-31. Unfinished attic.

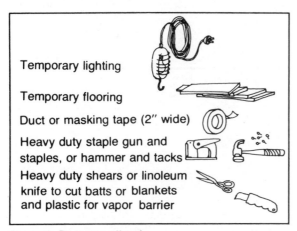

Temporary lighting

Temporary flooring

Duct or masking tape (2" wide)

Heavy duty staple gun and
staples, or hammer and tacks

Heavy duty shears or linoleum
knife to cut batts or blankets
and plastic for vapor barrier

Fig. 3-32. Do-it-yourself tools.

Keep insulation in wrappers until you are ready to install. It comes wrapped in a compressed state and expands when the wrappers are removed. See Fig. 3-33.

Check for roof leaks; look for water stains or marks. If you find leakage, make repairs before you insulate. Wet insulation is ineffective and can damage the structure of your home. See Fig. 3-34.

Fig. 3-33. Temporary flooring and lighting.

Install a separate vapor barrier if needed. Lay in polyethylene strips between joists or trusses. Staple or tack in place. Seal seams and holes with tape. Instead of taping, seams may be overlapped 6". See Fig. 3-35.

If you're using loose fill, install baffles at the inside of the eaves vents so that the insulation won't block the flow of air from the vents into the attic. Be sure the insulation extends out far enough to cover the top plate. See Fig. 3-36.

Fig. 3-34. Checking for roof leaks.

57

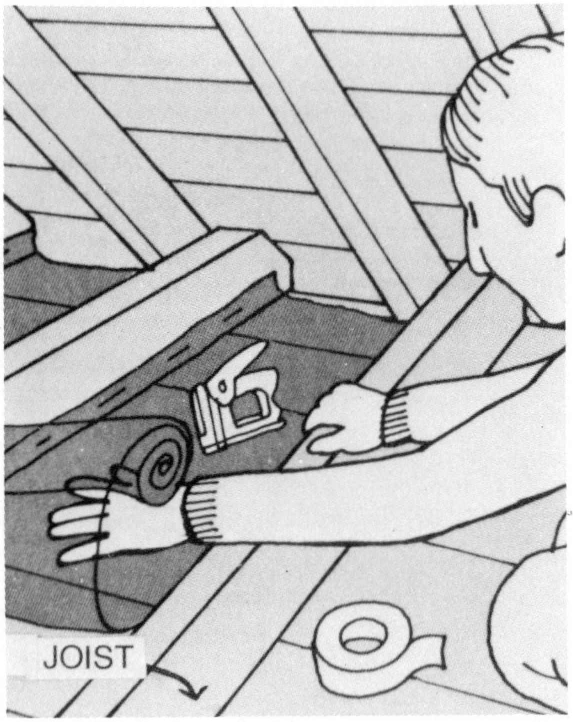

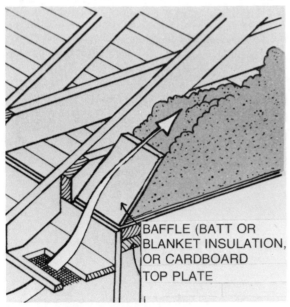

Fig. 3-35. Vapor barrier.

Installing Insulation

Lay in batts or blankets between the joists or pour in loose fill. If you're using batts or blankets with a vapor barrier, place the barrier on the side toward the living area.

Lay in blankets or batts between joists or trusses. (Note: batts and blankets are slightly wider than joist spacing so they'll fit snugly.) If blankets are used, cut long runs first to conserve material; use leftovers for shorter spaces. Slide insulation under wiring wherever possible. See Fig. 3-37.

Fig. 3-37. Laying blankets on batts.

Pour in loose fill insulation to the depth required. If you are covering the top of the joists, a good way to get uniform depth is to stretch two or three strings the length of the attic at the desired height, and level the insulation to the strings. Use a board or garden rake. Fill all the nooks and crannies, but don't cover recessed light fixtures or exhaust fans. See Fig. 3-38.

The space between the chimney and the wood framing should be filled with noncombustible material, preferably unfaced batts or blankets. Also, the Na-

BAFFLE (BATT OR BLANKET INSULATION, OR CARDBOARD TOP PLATE

Fig. 3-36. Baffle installation.

Fig. 3-38. Loose fill to the preferred depth.

Fig. 3-39. Fill the space between the chimney and the framing.

tional Electric Code requires that insulation be kept 3″ away from light fixtures. See Fig. 3-39.

Cut ends of batts or blankets to fit snugly around cross bracing. Butt the next batt in a similar way to allow the ends to butt tightly together. If Table 3-1 calls for an R-value that requires a second layer, place it at right angles to the joists. See Fig. 3-40.

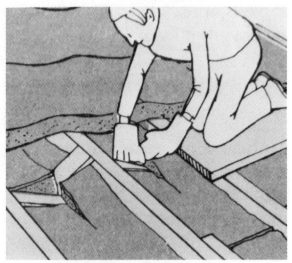

Fig. 3-40. Cut the ends of the blankets or batts.

Insulate Your Unfinished Floor Attic

Contractor Installed. The types of materials contractors use are blown-in insulation: glass fiber, rock wool, cellulosic fiber. See Fig. 3-41. Do you need ventilation in your attic? Check for roof leaks; look for water stains or marks. If you find any leaks, make repairs before you insulate. Wet insulation is useless and can damage the structure of your home.

What Your Contractor Will Do. The insulation is installed by blowing the insulating material under air pressure through a big flexible hose into the spaces between the attic floor and the ceiling of the rooms below. Bags of insulating material are fed into a blowing machine that mixes the insulation with air and forces it through the hose and into place. Before starting the machine, the contractor will locate the cross bracing between the joists in the attic. He'll then remove the floor boards above the cross bracing and install the insulation by blowing it in on each side of the cross bracing to make sure there are no spaces left unfilled. Because there's no effective way to partially fill a space, all of the spaces should be completely

59

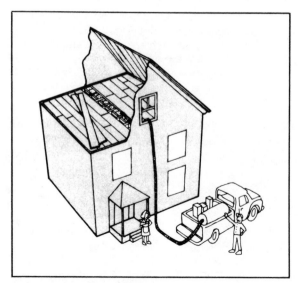

Fig. 3-41. Contractor installed.

After the job is finished, it's a good idea to drill ¼″ diameter holes in the floor about a foot apart. This will help prevent condensation from collecting under the floor in winter.

Do-It-Yourself Instructions. Install batts or blankets in your attic between the rafters and collar beams, and the studs on the end walls. See Fig. 3-42.

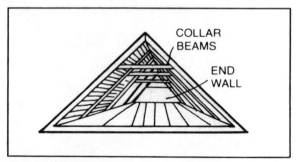

Fig. 3-42. Collar beam and end-wood studs.

filled to ensure proper coverage. Normally the job will take no longer than a day. See Fig. 3-41.

What You Should Check. First be very careful about choosing a contractor. Before you sign an agreement with your contractor, decide how much and what kind of insulation you're buying and make sure it's included in the contract. Insulation material properly installed will achieve a single insulating value (R-value) for the depth of your joist space. You should agree with the contractor on what that insulating value is before the job begins.

Check a bag of the type of insulation he intends to use. On it, there will be a table that will indicate how many square feet of attic floor that bag of material is meant to cover while achieving the desired insulating value. The information might be in one of several different forms (number of square feet per bag or number of bags per 1000 square feet), so you might have to do some simple division to use the number properly. Knowing this and the area of your attic, you should be able to figure out how many bags must be installed to give you the desired R-value. This number should be agreed upon between you and the contractor before the job is begun.

While the job is in progress, be sure the right amount is being installed. There's nothing wrong with having the contractor save the empty bags so that you can count them (5 bags more or less than the amount agreed on is an acceptable difference from the estimate).

This will involve installing 2 × 4 beams that span between each roof rafter at ceiling height if your attic doesn't already have them. This gives you a ventilation space above the insulation. *Note:* The materials, methods, and thicknesses of insulation are the same for both do-it-yourself and contractor jobs.

Safety

Provide good lighting.

Be careful of roofing nails protruding through the roof sheathing.

If you use glass fiber or mineral wool, wear gloves and a breathing mask. Keep the material wrapped until you're about to use it.

Tools

Temporary lighting.

Heavy-duty staple gun and staples.

A utility knife or heavy-duty shears to cut the insulation.

Duct tape or masking tape (2″ wide).

A hammer and nails (only if you're putting in collar beams).

A power saw or a hand saw (only if you're putting in collar beams). See Fig. 3-43.

Materials

Buy either batts or blankets made out of glass fiber or rock wool. *Exception:* For the area between the collar beam, if you're laying the new insulation on top

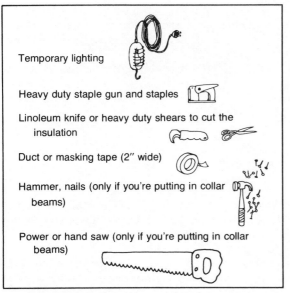

Temporary lighting

Heavy duty staple gun and staples

Linoleum knife or heavy duty shears to cut the
insulation

Duct or masking tape (2" wide)

Hammer, nails (only if you're putting in collar
beams)

Power or hand saw (only if you're putting in collar
beams)

Fig. 3-43. Tools needed.

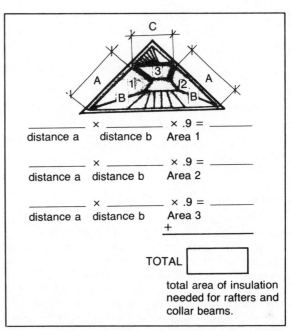

_____ × _____ × .9 = _____
distance a   distance b   Area 1

_____ × _____ × .9 = _____
distance a   distance b   Area 2

_____ × _____ × .9 = _____
distance a   distance b   Area 3
                      + _____

TOTAL [ ]

total area of insulation
needed for rafters and
collar beams.

Fig. 3-44. How to measure attic and compute insulation
needs.

of old insulation, buy insulation without a vapor barrier
if possible. Or slash the vapor barrier on the new
insulation.

For the area between the collar beams, follow the
guidelines in "unfinished attic" section.

Existing insulation means either insulation between the collar beams or in the attic floor.

For the rafters and end walls, buy insulation that's
thick enough to fill up the rafter and stud spaces. If
there's some existing insulation in there, the combined
thickness of the new and old insulation together
should fill up the spaces.

Figure out the area you want the insulation to
cover between your rafters and collar beams. In general, figure each area to be covered, and total the
areas. If your attic is like the one shown in Fig. 3-44
distances, a, b, and c, enter them in Fig. 3-44 in the
area marked Area 1, Area 2, and Area 3. Do the
figuring indicated. The .9 allows for the space taken up
by rafters or collar beams. Record your total findings in
"Total" in Fig. 3-44.

Calculate the length of 2-×-4 stock you'll need for
collar beams. Measure the length of span you need
between rafters (c) and count the number of collar
beams you need to install. Multiply to get the length of
stock you need. You can have the lumber yard cut it to
length at a small charge. If you cut it yourself, allow for
waste. If you plan to finish your attic, check with your
lumber yard to make sure 2 × 4's are strong enough to

support the ceiling you plan to eventually install.
Figure out the area of each end wall you want to
insulate. Measure (d) and (e) and multiply to determine the area. Multiply by (.09) to correct for the space
taken up by the studs, then multiply by the number of
end walls. See Fig. 3-45.

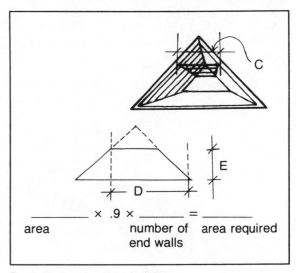

_____ × .9 × _____ = _____
area   number of   area required
                    end walls

Fig. 3-45. Area in attic calculation.

61

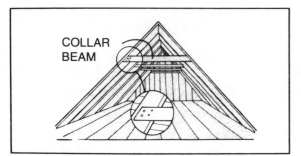

Fig. 3-46. Collar beam in attic.

Preparation and Installation

Check for roof leaks; look for water stains or marks. If you find any leaks, make repairs before you insulate. Wet insulation is useless and can damage the structure of your house. Determine your need for more ventilation. Put up temporary lights.

Install 2-×-4 collar beams spanning from rafter to rafter at the ceiling height you want (Fig. 3-46). Every pair of rafters should have a collar beam spanning between them.

If you're installing new insulation over existing insulation, *between the rafters and between the end wall studs*, cut the old insulation loose where it has been stapled, push it to the back of the new cavities, and slash the old vapor barrier (if any) before you lay the new insulation over it. *Between the Collar Beams,* lay the new insulation above the old. Lay it over the tops of the collar beams in an unbroken layer at right angles to the beams. Use insulation that does not have a vapor barrier for this part of the job. If you can't get insulation without a vapor barrier, slash the vapor barrier before laying it down so that moisture won't get trapped in the insulation.

Install batts or blanket sections in place between the rafters and collar beams. Install with the vapor barrier on the inside (the side toward you). Don't try to

Fig. 3-47. Trim with care.

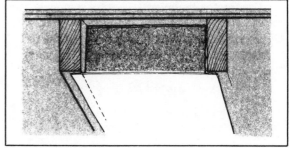

Fig. 3-48. Staple properly and carefully.

use a continuous length of insulation where the collar beams meet the rafters. It will only result in gaps that are very hard to fill. Install batts in the end walls the same way. Be sure to trim carefully to fit the angles on the end walls. See Fig. 3-47.

Install batts or blanket sections by stapling the facing flange to the edge of the rafter or collar beam. Don't staple to the outside of the rafters. The vapor barrier will have a break at every rafter and you might compress the insulation against the sheathing, reducing its insulation value. See Fig. 3-48.

Fig. 3-49. Finished attic.

Insulate Your Finished Attic

The options available, if there is under 4 inches of insulation already in your finished attic, are to do the work yourself or to hire a contractor. Insulation should be installed in the attic ceiling, rafters, knee walls, outer attic floors or outer attic rafters, and end walls. See Fig. 3-50.

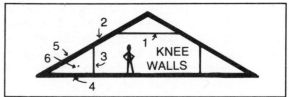

Fig. 3-50. Where to install insulation.

Contractor Installed. Types of materials contractors use are blown-in insulation or batts or blankets (glass fiber or rock wool).

How thick should the insulation be? See Table 3-1. Check your need for ventilation and a vapor barrier. Check for roof leaks; look for water stains or marks. If you can find any leaks, make repairs *before* you insulate. Wet insulation is useless and can damage the structure of your house.

Your contractor will blow insulation into the open joist spaces above your attic ceiling, between the rafters, and into the floor of the outer attic space, and then install batts in the knee walls. If you want to keep the outer attic spaces heated for storage or any other purpose, you should have the contractor install batts between the outer attic rafters instead of insulating the outer floors and knee walls. This process is much the same for open joists with no floor over them. See Figs. 3-41 and 3-51.

Fig. 3-51. Contractor installation.

Do-It-Yourself Procedures. You can insulate wherever you can get into the unfinished spaces. Installing insulation in your attic ceiling is the same as insulating it in an unfinished attic (as shown in Figs. 3-3 and 3-8).

If you want to insulate your outer attic spaces yourself, install batts between the rafters and the studs

in the small triangular end walls. See Figs. 3-46 through 3-48.

Insulate Your Wood Frame Walls

Insulating material is blown or pumped into the spaces in a wood frame wall through holes drilled from the outside or from the inside. See Fig. 3-20.

Be very careful about selecting a contractor. Before you sign an agreement with your contractor, define what you're buying and make sure it's spelled out in the contract. Insulation material properly installed will add an R-value of 8 for rock wool or 10 for cellulosic fiber in a standard wood frame wall. You should agree on what that R-value is with the contractor before the job begins.

Check a bag of the type of insulation the contractor intends to use (mineral fiber or cellulosic fiber). On it, there will be a table that will indicate how many square feet of wall space that bag is meant to fill and the R-value of the insulation. The information could be in different forms (number of square feet per bag or number of bags per 1000 square feet). You will have to do some simple division to use the number properly. You should be able to figure out about how many bags should be installed to give you the preferred R-value.

This number should be agreed upon between you and the contractor before the job is started. While the job is in progress, be sure the proper amount is being installed. There's nothing wrong with having the contractor save the empty bags so you can count them. About four or five bags more or less than the amount you agreed on is an acceptable difference from the estimate.

Insulate Your Crawl Space Walls

If you insulate crawl space walls yourself install batt or blanket insulation around the walls and perimeter of your crawl space. Lay a plastic vapor barrier down in the crawl space earth.

If your crawl space presents access- or working-space problems, you might want to consider having a contractor do the work for you. The contractor will probably follow a method similar to the do-it-yourself method described. If he suggests something different, have him price both methods and explain which is better. *Note:* This method of insulation should not be used by residents of Alaska, Minnesota, and Northern Maine. The extreme frost penetration in areas such as these can cause heaving of the foundation if the insulation method shown in Fig. 3-24 is used.

Tools

Staple gun and staples.
Heavy-duty shears or a utility knife.
Temporary lighting.
Portable fan or blower to provide ventilation
Tape measure.
Duct tape or masking tape (2″ wide) see Fig. 3-52.

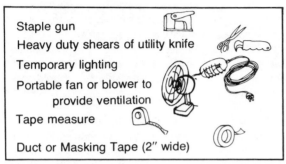

Staple gun

Heavy duty shears of utility knife

Temporary lighting

Portable fan or blower to
    provide ventilation

Tape measure

Duct or Masking Tape (2″ wide)

Fig. 3-52. Tools needed for use in crawl-space walls.

Safety

Provide adequate temporary lighting.
Wear gloves and a breathing mask when working with glass fiber or rock wool.
Provide adequate ventilation.
Keep lights, fan, and all wires well off wet ground.

Materials

R-11 (3-3½″ thick) blankets or rock wool or glass fiber; without a vapor barrier.
Six-mil polyethylene plastic to lay on each for vapor barrier (mils are measure of thickness). See Fig. 3-53.
Determine the area to be insulated. Measure the length and average height of the wall to be insulated. Add 3′ to the height (for perimeter insulation) and multiply the two to find total insulation area.
Determine the area to be covered by the vapor barrier by finding the area of your crawl space. Length times width equals area. You might have to divide your crawl space into several rectangles in order to measure them.

Installation

Where the joists run at right angles to the wall, press short pieces of insulation against the header. They should fit snugly. Install the wall and perimeter insulation by stapling the top of each strip to the sill. Make sure the batts fit snugly against each other and

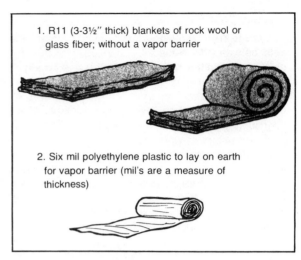

1. R11 (3-3½″ thick) blankets of rock wool or glass fiber; without a vapor barrier

2. Six mil polyethylene plastic to lay on earth for vapor barrier (mil's are a measure of thickness)

Fig. 3-53. Materials needed.

that you cut them long enough to cover 2 feet of floor (as shown in Fig. 3-54).

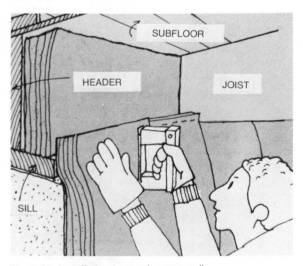

Fig. 3-54. Installation in crawl space walls.

Where the joists run parallel to the wall, you don't need the short pieces of insulation. Install the wall and perimeter insulation by stapling the top of each strip to the band joist. See Fig. 3-55.
When all batts have been installed, lay down the polyethylene vapor barrier. Tuck it under the batts all the way to the foundation wall. Turn it up at least 6″ at the wall. Tape the joints of the vapor barrier or lap them at least 6″. Plan your work to minimize stepping or crawling on the vapor barrier.

Insulate Your Floor

Do-It-Yourself Procedures. Install batts or blankets between floor joists by stapling wire mesh or chicken wire to the bottom of the joists and sliding the batts or blankets in on top of the wire. Place the vapor barrier up.

The job is quite easy to do in most cases. If you are insulating over a crawl space, there might be some problems with access or working room. Careful planning can make things go much more smoothly and easily.

Check your floor joist spacing. This method will work best with standard 16" or 24" joist spacing. If you have nonstandard or irregular spacing, there will be more cutting and fitting and some waste of materials.

Tools

Heavy-duty shears or a utility knife.

Temporary lighting with waterproof wiring and connectors.

Portable fan or blower to provide ventilation.

Tape measure.

Heavy-duty staple gun and staples. See Fig. 3-52.

Safety

Provide adequate, temporary lighting.

Wear gloves and a breathing mask when you are working with glass fiber or rock wool.

Provide adequate ventilation.

Keep lights and all wires off wet ground.

Materials

R-11 (3"-3½") batts or blankets or rock wool or glass fiber, preferably with foil facing.

Wire mesh or chicken wire of convenient width for handling in tight space. See Fig. 3-56.

Determine the area to be insulated by measuring the length and width, and multiplying to get the area. You might find it necessary to divide the floor into smaller areas and add them: (.9) (total area) = area of insulation. Total area equals the area of wire mesh or chicken wire.

Installation

Start at a wall at one end of the joists and work out. Staple the wire to the bottom of the joists, and at right angles to them. Slide batts in on top of the wire. Work with short sections of wire and batts so that it won't be

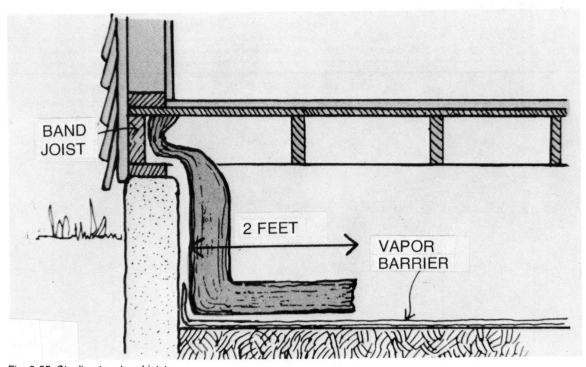

BAND JOIST

2 FEET

VAPOR BARRIER

Fig. 3-55. Stapling to a band joist.

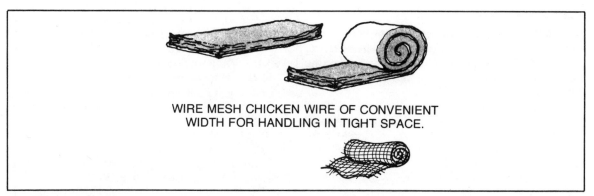

WIRE MESH CHICKEN WIRE OF CONVENIENT
WIDTH FOR HANDLING IN TIGHT SPACE.

Fig. 3-56. Materials needed.

too difficult to get the insulation in place. Plan sections to begin and end at obstructions such as cross bracing. See Fig. 3-26.

Buy insulation with a vapor barrier. Install the vapor barrier facing up (next to the warm side) leaving an air space between the vapor barrier and the floor. Get foil-faced insulation if you can; it will make the air space insulate better. Be sure that ends of batts fit snugly up against the bottom of the floor to prevent loss of heat up end. Don't block combustion air-openings for furnaces. See Fig. 3-57.

Insulate Your Basement Walls

Insulating basement walls is a moderately easy do-it-yourself project. Install 2-×-4 studs (needed for thickness of insulation) along the walls to be insulated. Add glass fiber insulation between the studs. If you prefer, finish with wallboard or paneling. The thickness

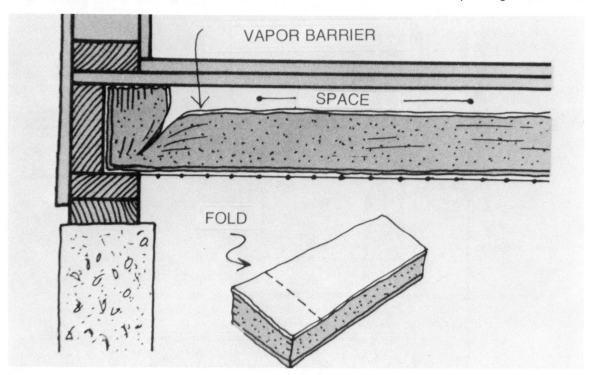

Fig. 3-57. Vapor barrier.

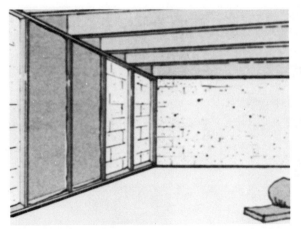

Fig. 3-58. Basement walls.

of the finished wall material will determine the spacing for the studs. See Fig. 3-58.

Tools

Saw.
Hammer and nails.
Heavy-duty staple gun and staples (or hammer and tacks).
Tape measure.
Utility knife or heavy-duty shears.
Level.
Small sledge hammer and masonry nails. See Fig. 3-59.

Safety

Provide adequate, temporary lighting.

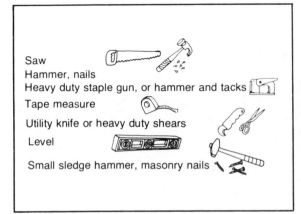

Fig. 3-59. Tools needed for wall insulation.

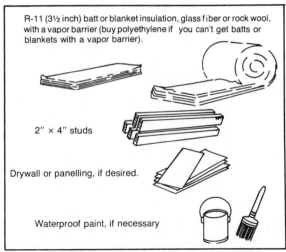

Fig. 3-60. Materials for basement walls.

If you use glass fiber or rock wool, wear gloves and a breathing mask and keep the material wrapped until you are ready to use it.

Materials

R-11 (3½ inch) batt or blanket insulation, glass fiber or rock wool, with a vapor barrier (buy polyethylene if you can't get batts or blankets with a vapor barrier).
2'-×-4' studs.
Drywall or paneling (if preferred).
Waterproof paint (if necessary). See Fig. 3-60.
Measure the height and length of the walls you intend to insulate. Multiply these two figures to determine how many square feet of insulation is needed.

Find the linear feet of studs you'll need by multiplying the length of the walls you intend to insulate by 6. (6) × (length) = (linear feet).

The area of wall covering equals the basement wall height times the length of wall you intend to finish. (height) × (length) = area.

Installation

Nail the bottom plate to the floor ¾" out from the base of the wall with a hammer and masonry nails. Install studs 16 or 24 inches apart after the top plate is nailed to the joists above. Where the wall runs parallel to the joists, you might not be able to fasten the top plate in this way. You might have to fasten a ¾" thick horizontal furring strip to the wall near the top, and fasten the studs to it. Block between studs at ceiling

67

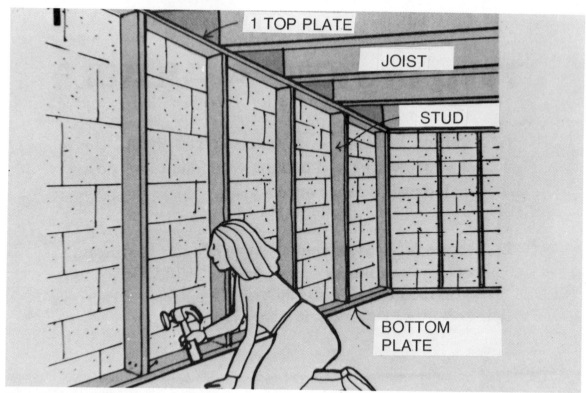

Fig. 3-61. Bottom plate.

Fig. 3-62. Cut and staple blankets.

68

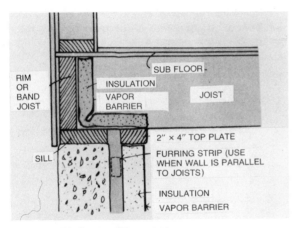

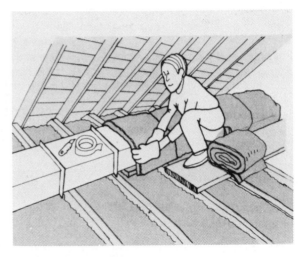

Fig. 3-63. Work around new studs.

Fig. 3-65. Duct insulation.

after studs are in place if you need backing for finish wall material. See Fig. 3-61.

Cut blankets into sections the height of the wall. Staple them into place with the vapor barrier toward the living space. Fig. 3-62.

Install another small piece of insulation above the new studs and against the sill to insulate the sill and band joist. See Fig. 3-63.

For a more finished look, install finish wall board or paneling over the insulation and studs. See Fig. 3-64.

Duct Insulation

If the ducts for your heating or air-conditioning system run exposed through your attic or garage (or any other space that is not heated or cooled), they should be insulated. Duct insulation comes (generally) in blankets 1″ or 2″ thick. Use the thicker variety, and particularly if you've got rectangular ducts. If you're doing this job at all, it's worth it to do it right. For air-conditioning ducts, make sure you get the kind of insulation that has a vapor barrier (the vapor barrier goes on the outside). Seal the joints of the insulation tightly with tape to avoid condensation. Check for leaks in the duct and tape them tightly before insulating. See Fig. 3-65.

Mobile Home Insulation

Insulate overhead where the greatest heat loss occurs. Foam insulating materials can be applied to the existing roof.

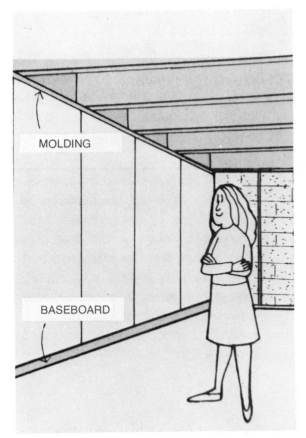

Fig. 3-64. Use wall board or paneling for a finished look after insulating basement walls.

69

Top coat the roof with a protective liquid glass sealer to prevent discoloration and deterioration. Cooling comfort can also be increased through the use of a reflective roof coating. This thick fibrous substance contains aluminum particles that migrate to the surface as the coating dries. A thick coating should be applied.

Install fiberglass batts beneath the floor. Buy batts with a vapor barrier and place the vapor barrier toward the inside of the home. Keep the batts in place by attaching chicken wire to the joists. Use an insulation with an R-9 to R-11 value over unheated spaces.

Chapter 4

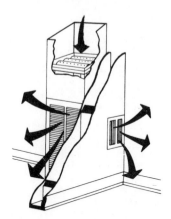

Heating and Cooling

AIR CONDITIONING IS UNDOUBTEDLY one of the largest financial and energy consumptive costs in residences. Using an air conditioner during hot weather will consume more electricity than all of your other appliances combined.

In addition to cooling your home, most air conditioning equipment can dehumidify, filter, and circulate air. Some units also can provide ventilation. Although many homes now have central air conditioning (and heating) units, there are still those who use window units. Size, efficiency, and economy must be taken into consideration when choosing any unit.

Air conditioners vary considerably in efficiency and in the amount of energy used. Select equipment on the basis of the energy efficiency ratio (commonly referred to as EER). The EER is a means for comparing the unit's capacity to provide cooling. The ratio is calculated by dividing the cooling capacity of the unit expressed as Btuh (British thermal unit hours) by the power it uses in watts.

For example, a 12,000-Btu air conditioner that uses 2000 watts has an EER of 6. An EER of 8 will use 25 percent less energy than a unit with an EER of 6. A

general rule of thumb is that an EER of 10 or more is excellent, 8 or 9 is good, and 6 or 7 is adequate. Equipment with an EER below 6 should not be used. If the EER is not provided, it can be calculated from the Btu rating and watts requirements. See Fig. 4-1.

The EER should be given close attention when you are checking the different brands of equipment. Read the manufacturers' information bulletin with each particular unit to determine the efficiency rating. This is given in terms of EER or coefficients of performance (COP).

Central systems heat or cool a whole house or apartment. They are more expensive to buy and install than a window unit, but they provide a more uniform temperature. *Zoned heating* should be considered. Zoned heating and cooling simply means that each room, or a group of rooms, has an individual element, but each specific area in which you place the system is either put in as a separate thermostatically controlled unit placed on the baseboards, for instance, or in the ceiling (baseboard selection is preferred in order to accommodate maintenance work). This permits the heating or cooling of specific rooms or areas in the home frequently occupied.

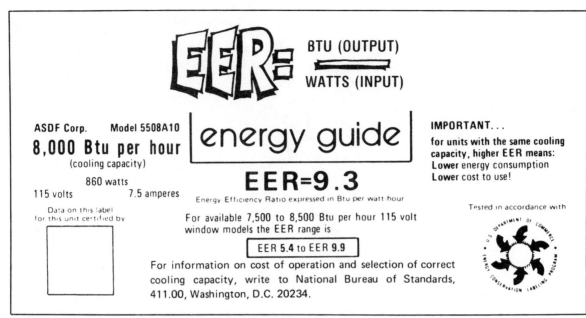

EER= BTU (OUTPUT) / WATTS (INPUT)

ASDF Corp.   Model 5508A10

8,000 Btu per hour
(cooling capacity)

860 watts
115 volts   7.5 amperes

Data on this label
for this unit certified by

energy guide

EER=9.3
Energy Efficiency Ratio expressed in Btu per watt-hour

For available 7,500 to 8,500 Btu per hour 115 volt window models the EER range is

EER 5.4 to EER 9.9

For information on cost of operation and selection of correct cooling capacity, write to National Bureau of Standards, 411.00, Washington, D.C. 20234.

IMPORTANT. . .
for units with the same cooling capacity, higher EER means:
Lower energy consumption
Lower cost to use!

Tested in accordance with

U.S DEPARTMENT OF COMMERCE
ENERGY CONSERVATION LABELING PROGRAM

Fig. 4-1. An EER rating and a sample of plate information.

CHOOSING AN AIR CONDITIONER

An appropriately-sized air conditioner reduces humidity and cools the air. If the cooling capacity is too small, the unit will not adequately cool and dehumidify your home. Conversely, if the unit is too large it will be more expensive and will not dehumidify properly.

Room air conditioners are noiser than central systems and they will not cool more than one room effectively. If more than two or three rooms require cooling, a central system should be considered.

Window units come in various sizes; they can be mounted in walls, with a sash, or in casement windows. Window air-conditioning units can be used for ventilating, cooling, and dehumidifying. Direct sunlight falling on a window unit increases the work load. When a choice is possible, locate a window unit on the north or shady side of the house.

During the summer, controls should be positioned at a setting that will be more comfortable to the homeowner. The American Society of Heating and Refrigeration and Air Conditioning (ASHRAC) suggests that 78 degrees is a comfortable temperature for most during the hot summer months. Each degree higher setting on an air conditioning unit results in energy savings. See Fig. 4-2. Take into consideration that there will be times when an increase of daytime temperatures will require that the thermostat

be set several degrees above or below the desired level. This will usually *not* enable a system to cool faster. The system will most likely overshoot and waste energy.

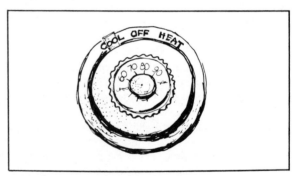

Fig. 4-2. Degrees for heat/cooling settings.

REDUCING ENERGY
USAGE OF WINDOW UNITS

Window units are designed to cool small areas. Nevertheless central air-conditioning units usually cost approximately 20 percent less to operate than a window unit that has an equivalent cooling capacity. In order to receive the ultimate efficiency from a window unit, you should:

☐ Place units on the shady side of the house.

☐ Shade them from the sun.

☐ Cover and close floor and wall registers so that cool air does not escape into the duct work of your heating system.

☐ Turn temperature controls up or shut them off when out of the cooling area.

☐ Use a bathroom exhaust fan or open the bathroom window (with the door closed) with bathing or showering to remove the heat and moisture so that your air conditioner isn't overworked. You can use exhaust fans to carry away any excess heat and moisture as well as cooking odors. Don't leave the exhaust fan on for more than 15 minutes after cooling. If you do you will be taking out your air conditioning.

☐ Use an automatic timer on room air conditioners. Set the timer to turn the unit on an hour or so before you expect to arrive so that the house will be comfortable when you get home.

There are innumerable ways to have sensible comfortable control systems. An outside air duct can flush out unwanted odors. A dehumidification cycle, working on a timer, reduces moisture build-up from such activities as cooking and bathing.

Light colors on the outside of the house will reflect sunlight. This can reduce the temperature inside. A home with a light-colored roof will cost less to cool than the same home with a dark roof.

Minimize the use of heat-generating appliances while your air conditioner is working. Similarly, less artificial illumination cuts down on the cooling load.

Schedule such tasks as ironing, cooking, and baking for the coolest part of the day.

Pilot lights required by flame-type heating units, ranges, dryers or water heaters add to the cooling requirements.

In many instances, such as the early morning and late evenings, a fan can be used effectively in place of the window unit and it will not require nearly as much energy. A window fan requires only about 150 watts while a typical window air conditioner uses 10 times more energy.

Use a fan in your attic to save on air conditioning. Without an attic fan, your attic temperature can be as much as 35 degrees higher than the outside temperature during hot days. Your air conditioner does not have to work as hard or use as much energy if it is not fighting this extra heat.

A thermostatically controlled power vent could be one of your best energy conserving investments.

Ventilated awnings or other shading devices for windows exposed to direct sunlight reduces the amount of the solar heat penetrating the room.

MOBILE HOME COOLING

If your mobile home is equipped with a central cooling system, set the thermostat no lower than 78 to 80 degrees. If you use a room air-conditioning unit, be sure to choose one that is sized for the space to be cooled. A properly sized air conditioner cools, dehumidifies and provides comfort with great efficiency.

When purchasing a room air conditioner for a mobile home, be sure to check the energy efficiency ratio (EER). The higher the EER number, the more efficient the air conditioner and the less it costs to operate compared to units of similar cooling capacity. Room air conditioning units range from 4 to 12 EER. An air conditioner with an EER of 10 will provide the same amount of cooling with half the electricity as one with an EER of 5.

CHECKLIST FOR COOLING SYSTEMS

☐ Set thermostats between 68 and 78° F.

☐ Raise the thermostat by several degrees or turn off air conditioner if you are away from the home for several hours. For extended periods, a timer should be installed to operate the unit periodically to help prevent mildew.

☐ Ceiling or window fans should be used in lieu of central air conditioning units.

☐ If outside awnings or window covers are used that are insufficient or undesirable, sun control film on interior of windows is available. Transparent polyester and aluminum film is inexpensive and causes a mirror effect.

☐ If your house has large overhanging eaves, the windows will probably not be suitable for many types of houseplants. Nevertheless, the cost of installation and savings in fuel consumption is significant.

HEATING SYSTEMS

Much can be done to reduce heating requirements in the home. This reduces heating costs, increases personal comfort, and saves energy. If you have a fireplace, the chimney is a part of the heating plant. Proper construction and maintenance are important. Chimneys should extend a minimum of 2 feet above the roof ridge.

Area Heating

Area heating units include stoves, circular heaters, and "pipeless" furnaces. They are installed in the room or area to be heated. In central systems, the heating unit is located in the basement or other out-of-the-way place, and heat is distributed through ducts.

Central Heating

Central heating systems are the most efficient and economical method of heating. Forced-warm-air heating systems are the most efficient. They cost less to install than gravity-warm-air heating systems. Forced-warm-air systems consist of a furnace, ducts, and registers. See Fig. 4-3. A blower in the furnace circulates the warm air to the various rooms through supply ducts and registers. Turn grilles and ducts carry the cooled room air back to the furnace where it is reheated and recirculated.

Forced-warm-air systems heat uniformly and respond rapidly to changes in outdoor temperatures. They can be used in homes with or without base-

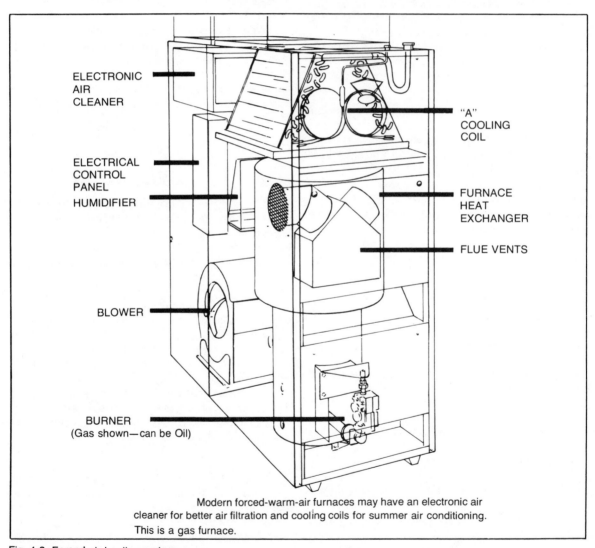

ELECTRONIC AIR CLEANER

ELECTRICAL CONTROL PANEL

HUMIDIFIER

BLOWER

BURNER
(Gas shown—can be Oil)

"A" COOLING COIL

FURNACE HEAT EXCHANGER

FLUE VENTS

Modern forced-warm-air furnaces may have an electronic air cleaner for better air filtration and cooling coils for summer air conditioning. This is a gas furnace.

Fig. 4-3. Forced-air heating system.

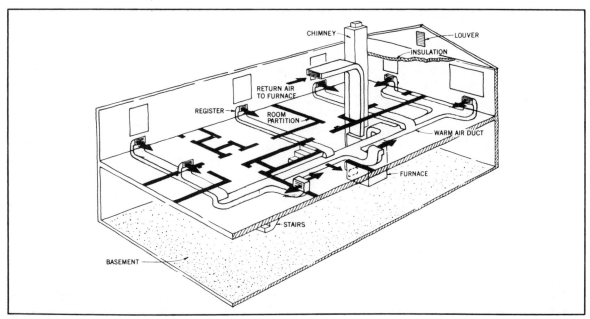

Fig. 4-4. An efficient forced-air system.

ments. The furnace does not have to be below the rooms to heat them and the unit does not need to be centrally located. Some systems can be adapted for summer cooling by the addition of cooling coils. Combination heating and cooling systems, as shown in Fig. 4-3, use the same ducts for both heating and cooling. These central units are not only more energy efficient, but they help remove pollen, fine dust, and other irritants that pass through ordinary filters.

As shown in Fig. 4-4, forced-warm-air systems are the most popular type of heating systems. Most installations have a cold air return in each room (except the bathroom and kitchen). If the basement is heated, additional ducts should deliver hot air near the basement floor along the outside walls. In cold climates, a separate perimeter-loop heating system, as shown in Fig. 4-6, might be the best way to heat the basement.

Locate warm-air supply outlets along outside walls. They should be low in the wall, in the baseboard, or in the floor where air cannot blow directly on room occupants. Floor registers tend to collect dust and trash, but you might have to install this type of system in an old house.

If your house does not have a basement, perhaps you could install horizontal furnaces (that burn gas or oil) in the crawl space or hang them from ceiling joists

in a utility room or adjoining garage. Gas furnaces can also be installed in attics. Allow adequate space for servicing the furnaces. Heavily insulate attic furnaces and ducts to prevent excessive heat loss.

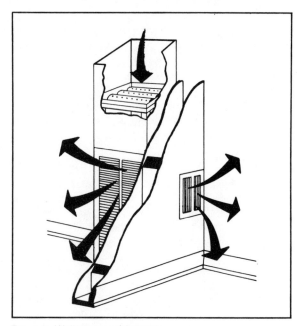

Fig. 4-5. Wall recessed furnace.

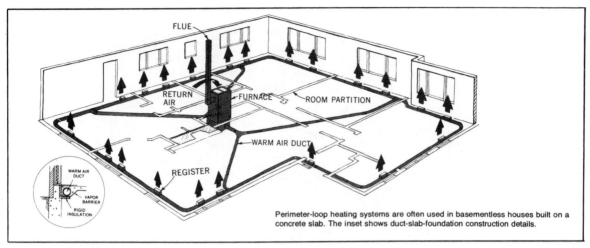

Perimeter-loop heating systems are often used in basementless houses built on a concrete slab. The inset shows duct-slab-foundation construction details.

Fig. 4-6. Loop heating system.

Vertical gas or oil furnaces designed for installation in a closet or wall recess or against a wall are popular for small houses. The counterflow type furnace discharges the hot air at the bottom to warm the floor. Figure 4-5 shows a gas-fired unit that has discharge grilles for several rooms.

Up-flow vertical furnaces can discharge the warm air through attic ducts and ceiling diffusers. Without return air ducts, these furnaces are less expensive, but they also heat less uniformly.

If your house is built on a concrete slab, it might be heated by a perimeter-loop heater system (Fig. 4-6). Warm air is circulated by a counterflow-type furnace through ducts cast in the outer edge of the concrete slab. The warm ducts heat the floor, and the warm air is discharged through floor registers to heat the room. To prevent excessive heat loss, insulate the slab from the foundation walls and separate it from the ground by a vapor barrier.

FORCED-HOT-WATER HEATING SYSTEMS

Forced-hot-water heating systems are more efficient than gravity-hot-water heating systems. In a forced-hot-water system, a small booster—or circulating pump—forces or circulates the hot water through the pipes to the room radiators or convectors. See Fig. 4-7.

There are two types of systems: a one-pipe system and a two-pipe system. With a one-pipe system, one (main) pipe serves for both supply and return. It makes a complete circuit from the boiler and back again. Two risers extend from the main to each room heating unit. A two-pipe system has two (main) pipes. One carries the heated water to the room heating units. The other pipe returns the cooled water to the boiler.

A one-pipe system takes less pipe than a two-pipe system. In the one-pipe system, cooled water from each radiator mixes with the hot water flowing through the main, and each succeeding radiator receives cooler water. Be sure to allow for this in sizing the radiators because larger ones might be required further along in the system.

ELECTRIC HEATING

The following electric heating systems are available:

Ceiling units.
Baseboard heaters.
Heat pumps.
Central furnaces (most commonly used in new construction).
Floor furnaces.
Wall units.

All but the heat pump are *resistance heaters*. Resistance-type heaters produce heat the same way as the familiar electric radiant heater. Heat pumps are usually supplemented with resistance heaters.

Ceiling heat can be provided with electric heating cable laid back and forth on the ceiling surface (Fig. 4-8) and covered with plaster or a second layer of gypsum board. Other types of ceiling heaters include infrared lamps and resistance heaters with reflectors or fans.

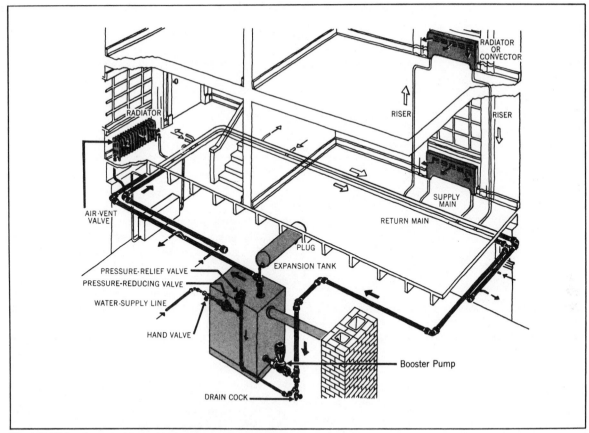

Fig. 4-7. Piping layout of forced hot-water heating system.

Baseboard heaters resemble the water baseboard heaters except that they simply have electrical coils in them. These are ideal for individual room zoning. Baseboard radiator units are designed to replace the conventional wood baseboard. In the hollow types, water or steam flows directly behind the baseboard face. Heat from that surface is transmitted to the room. In the finned-tube type, the water or steam flows through the tubes and heats the tube and the fins. Air passing over the tube and fins is heated and delivered to the room through the slots. See Fig. 4-9.

Wall units (Fig. 4-10) that are radiant or convection or both are designed for recessed or surface wall mounting. They come equipped with various types of resistance heating elements. The warm air can be circulated either by gravity or by an electric fan. The better types of electric wall heaters discharge the warm air from the bottom and circulate it by means of a fan.

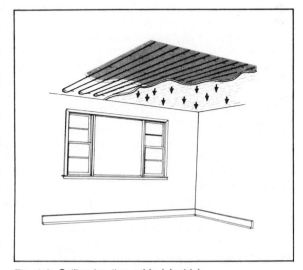

Fig. 4-8. Ceiling heating cable (electric).

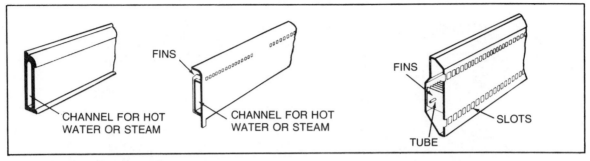

Fig. 4-9. Baseboard heating units.

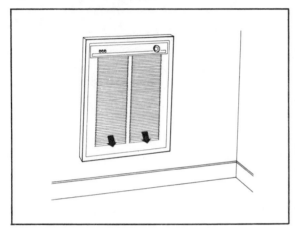

Fig. 4-10. Electric wall heater.

MOBILE HOME HEATING

Mobile home gas and oil heating systems should be equipped with automatic cut-off devices. For all types of heating systems, set your thermostat no higher than 65 to 68 degrees. Do *not* block the furnace's fresh air intake, outside draft opening, or inside outlets.

HEAT PUMPS

Heat pumps are heat transferral systems. Even in the coldest weather, heat is present in the outside air. There are three types of heat pumps. The most common is the air-to-air or air-source heat pump. It transfers heat from outdoor air to indoors during the heating cycle. The water-to-air or water-source heat pump transfers heat from a water source to the indoor air system. If you can supply a source of water (if you live beside a lake for instance), this system has the greatest potential for efficient and economical operation. Ground-to-air heat pumps have also been tried,

but they are difficult to maintain efficiently.

Heat pumps come as package units that fit into the wall and as connected split systems. Split units are more expensive, but more versatile than the smaller units because the inside unit can be located anywhere in the house. Heat pumps provide heat or cooling on demand. They are more expensive than other systems, but where the climate is not severe operating costs can be one-third to one-half that of conventional electric heating.

The heat pump uses electricity efficiently because it can deliver as much as two units of heat for every one heat unit of electricity used during the heating season. See Fig. 4-11. Switch over between heating and cooling can be made completely automatic—if you want it—from season to season, within the same day, or even hourly. See Fig. 4-12.

How Does a Heat Pump Work?

A heat pump works similar to a refrigerator in that heat is removed from inside a refrigerator. A heat pump is like a two-way refrigerator. In summer, it cools

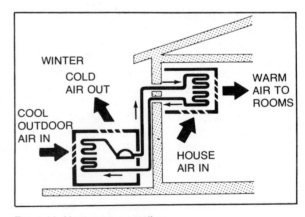

Fig. 4-11. Heat pump operation.

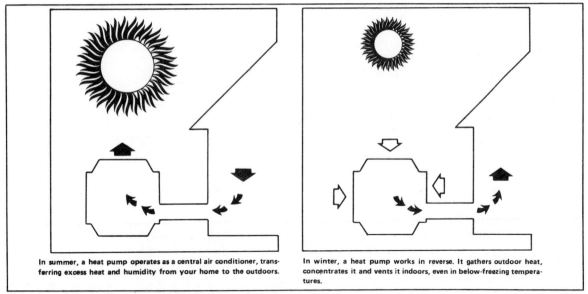

In summer, a heat pump operates as a central air conditioner, transferring excess heat and humidity from your home to the outdoors.

In winter, a heat pump works in reverse. It gathers outdoor heat, concentrates it and vents it indoors, even in below-freezing temperatures.

Fig. 4-12. Summer and winter operations.

the house by absorbing heat from the inside air and transferring it outside. In winter, it heats the house by absorbing heat from the outside air and transferring it inside. Winter heating is made possible because very cold air contains *some* heat. The heat pump is able to extract this heat from outside air to heat the inside space.

Most of the time that's all that is needed. But there is a supplemental heat source that will operate automatically, if needed, on extremely cold days.

Is the Heat Pump Reliable?

Heat pumps of the type now on the market have been in use for many years. Experience proves the heat pump is a practical, dependable heating and cooling unit.

Are Heat Pumps Expensive?

Prices for heat pumps vary with different manufacturers and different unit sizes, but generally the initial cost of a heat pump is about 20 percent more than the cost of an electric furnace, plus electric air conditioning of comparable performance.

During periods when supplemental electric heat is required, operating costs will be higher. Nevertheless, the heat pump's efficiency during periods when the outdoor temperature is above 35 to 45 degrees F can produce significant savings. Actual savings depend on such factors as climate and the cost and availability of natural gas, oil, and electricity.

Where Do You Install a Heat Pump?

Because a heat pump does not have to be vented and requires no outside air to support combustion, design flexibility is allowed in its installation. A heat pump looks like a conventional central heating and air conditioning unit and it can be fitted into almost any space of sufficient size you might choose. Any home that can be air conditioned can use a heat pump for heating and cooling.

Efficiency

When the outside temperature is above 35 to 40 degrees F, all the heat necessary is supplied by the heat pump's outdoor unit. Below that temperature, supplemental electric resistance heat strips automatically turn on to supply additional heating needs of your home.

Points to Consider

Capacity (Size). Determine the amount of cooling required. Electric resistance heaters are added to supplement the heat pump at low outside temperatures. This way the system will produce the right amount of heating and cooling. A heat pump is most economical if it is used year-around for both heating and cooling.

Duct System. It is important that the duct system is adequately designed, sized, and insulated. The efficient performance of the heat pump depends on an adequate duct system.

Home Insulation. Proper insulation is a must for efficient economical operation of your heating and cooling system. Insulation, caulking and weather stripping not only ensures comfort and economy, but add value to your home and help conserve energy.

Efficiency Ratings. The COP (Coefficient of Performance) for heating and the EER (Energy Efficiency Ratio) for cooling are indicators of the heat pump's efficiency. The higher the COP and EER, the greater the heating and cooling efficiency of the unit. A COP of 2.5 to 3 and an EER of 8 to 10 are considered energy efficient for the heat pump. Heating and cooling loads should be estimated by an experienced heat pump dealer who can advise you on selection, installation, and operation.

Should you buy a heat pump? The choice depends on the following:

Climate.
Initial cost and estimated life.
Operational costs.
Maintenance service costs.
Size and design of your house.
Personal preference.
Adaptability to summer cooling.
Convenience.

HOT-WATER SYSTEMS

Hot water circulating pumps should be lubricated if they are not sealed. Check the manufacturer's recommendations for amount and frequency. They usually require 2 or 3 *drops* of oil once or twice a year.

Clean radiators and hot-water baseboards by vacuuming. Bleed air from radiators and hold a container under it until water comes out. See Fig. 4-13. The water need not be drained (only the air). Paint the radiators with special radiator paints. A sheet of aluminum or other shiny metal placed behind radiators near cold walls will help reflect more heat into the room.

CHIMNEY INSPECTION AND CLEANING

A chimney might have one or more flues. The flue that serves heating systems fueled by oil or coal will

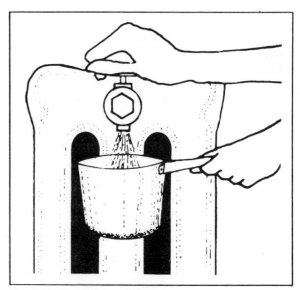

Fig. 4-13. Bleeding a radiator.

require an occasional—once a year usually—cleaning.

The chimney, brickwork, and flashings should be inspected each fall. Loose bricks, mortar, cracked linings, and leaks should be repaired. See Fig. 4-14.

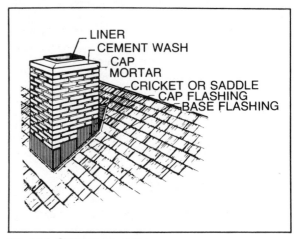

Fig. 4-14. Chimney inspection.

FUELS AND BURNERS

Wood. The use of wood requires more labor and more storage space than do other fuels. Nevertheless, wood fires are easy to start, burn with little smoke, and leave little ash.

Most well-seasoned hardwoods have about half as much heat value per pound as does good coal. A cord of hickory, oak, beech, sugarmaple, or rock elm weighs about 2 tons and has about the same heat value of 1 ton of good coal.

Coal. Two kinds of coal are used for heating homes: anthracite (hard) and bituminous (soft). Bituminous is used more often.

Anthracite coal sizes are standardized; bituminous coal sizes are not. Heat value of the different sizes of coal varies little, but certain sizes are better suited for burning in firepots of given sizes and depths.

Both anthracite and bituminous coal are used in stoker firing. Stokers are installed at the front, side, or rear of a furnace or boiler. Leave space for servicing the stoker and for cleaning the furnace. Furnaces and boilers with horizontal heating surfaces require frequent cleaning because *fly ash* (powdery fine ash) collects on these surfaces.

Oil. Oil is the most popular heating fuel, and especially in cold regions. It requires little space for storage, no handling by the homeowner, and it leaves no ash.

There are two grades of fuel commonly used for home heating. No. 1 is higher and slightly more expensive and No. 2 has higher heat value per gallon. The plate on the burner tells you which oil should be used in your particular facility. Usually No. 1 is used in pot-type burners and No. 2 is used in gun-and-rotary-type burners.

There are two kinds of oil burners: *vaporizing* and *atomizing*. Vaporizing burners premix the air and oil vapor. The pot-type burner (Fig. 4-15) is a vaporizing

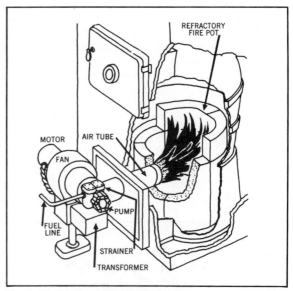
Fig. 4-16. Gun or pressure oil burner.

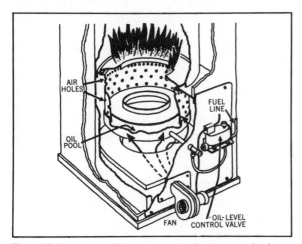
Fig. 4-15. Vaporizing oil burners are the least expensive type.

burner and it consists of a pot containing a pool of oil. An automatic or handset valve regulates the amount of oil in the pot. Heat from the flame vaporizes the oil. In some heaters, a pilot flame or electric arc ignites the oil pot when heat is required. In others, the oil is ignited manually and burns continuously at any set fuel rate between high and low fire—until shut off. There are few moving parts and operation is quiet. Some pot-type burners can be operated without electric power.

There are two general types of atomizing burners: *gun* (or pressure) and *rotary*. The gun burner (Fig. 4-16) is by far the more popular type for home heating. It has a pump that forces the oil through a special atomizing nozzle. A fan blows air into the oil fog. An electric spark ignites the mixture which burns in a refractory-lined firepot.

Gas. Gas is supplied at low pressure to a burner head (Fig. 4-17) where it is mixed with the right amount of air for combustion. Designs vary but they all operate on much the same principle. The controls shown are essential for safe operation.

A room thermostat controls the gas valve. A pilot light is lit at the beginning of the heating season and, in some cases, can be turned off when heat is no longer required. If it is kept burning during nonheating seasons, condensation and rapid corrosion of the system will be prevented. The pilot light takes little energy in comparison to having to replace a system. Make sure the pilot light is equipped with a safety thermostat to

81

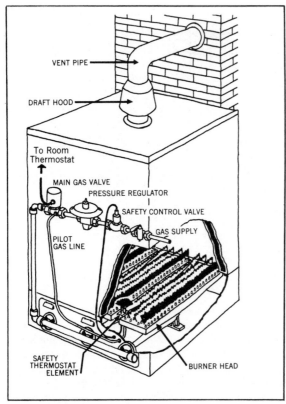

VENT PIPE

DRAFT HOOD

To Room Thermostat

MAIN GAS VALVE

PRESSURE REGULATOR

SAFETY CONTROL VALVE

GAS SUPPLY

PILOT GAS LINE

SAFETY THERMOSTAT ELEMENT

BURNER HEAD

Fig. 4-17. Gas burner.

keep the gas valve from opening if the pilot goes out. Then no gas will then escape into the room.

There are three kinds of gas: natural, manufactured, and bottled. Bottled gas (usually propane) is sometimes called LPG (liquified petroleum gas). This is particularly popular with mobile-home dwellers, and people who live in rural areas. If you heat with gas, you should know that:

☐ Different gasses have different heat values when burned.

☐ A burner adjusted for one gas must be readjusted when another gas is used.

☐ You must vent gas-burning equipment to the outside.

☐ You must chimneys and smoke pipes free from leaks.

☐ Connect all electrical controls for gas-burning equipment on a separate switch so that the circuit can be broken in case of trouble.

☐ Gas-burning equipment should be cleaned, inspected, and properly adjusted yearly.

☐ Bottled gas is heavier than air. If it leaks into the basement, it will accumulate at the lowest point and create an explosive hazard. When bottled gas is used, make sure that the safety control valve is placed so that it shuts off the gas to the pilot as well as to the burner when the pilot goes out.

Electricity. Electric heating offers convenience, cleanliness, evenness of heat, safety, and freedom from odors and fumes. With proper insulation, weather stripping, double- or triple-glazing windows, and good vapor sealing of the home, electricity is still the most popular home-heating method, and especially so for new homes. The heating equipment should be only large enough to handle the heat load. Oversized equipment costs more and requires heavier wiring than does properly sized equipment.

AUTOMATIC CONTROLS

All heating plant systems require special control features. But even the simplest control system should include *high-limit controls* to prevent overheating. Limit controls are usually recommended by the equipment manufacturer.

The high-limit control, which is usually a furnace or boiler thermostat, shuts down the fire before the furnace or boiler becomes dangerously or wastefully hot. In steam systems, it responds to pressure. In other systems, it responds to temperature.

The high-limit control is often combined with fan or pump controls. In a forced-warm-air or forced-hot-water system, controls are usually set to start the fan or the pump circulating when the furnace or boiler warms up, and to stop it when the heating plant cools down. Usually, they are set just high enough to insure heating without overshooting the preferred temperature and they can be adjusted to suit climatic conditions.

Other controls insure that all operations take place in the right order. Room thermostats control the burner or stoker on forced systems. They are sometimes equipped with timing devices that can be set to automatically change the preferred temperatures at night and in the daytime.

Oil Burner Controls

The oil burner controls allow electricity to pass through the motor and ignition transformer and shut them off in the right order. They also stop the motor if the oil does not ignite or if the flame goes out. This is

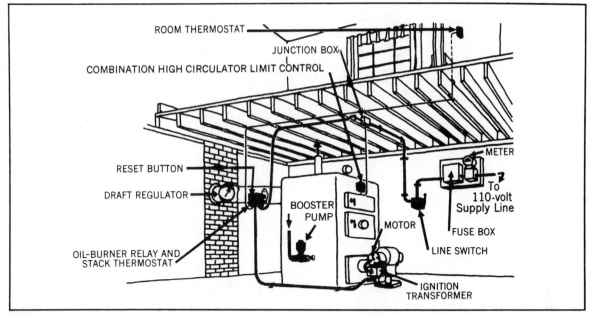

Fig. 4-18. Forced hot-water system controls.

done by means of a stack thermostat built into the relay. The sensing element of the stack control is inserted into the smoke pipe near the furnace or boiler. Some heating units are equipped with "electric eye" (cadmium sulfide) flame detectors, that are used in place of a stack control.

The stack thermostat or electric eye are safety devices. Without such a device, a gun or rotary-type burner could flood the basement with oil if it failed to ignite. With such protection, the relay allows the motor to run only a short time if the oil fails to ignite. Then it opens the motor circuit and keeps it open until it is reset by hand.

Figure 4-18 shows controls for an oil burner with a forced-hot-water system. The boiler thermostat acts as high-limit control if the water in the boiler gets too hot.

Stoker-Fired, Coal-Burner Controls

These systems are popular in colder regions of the country and the control systems are much like that used for an oil burner. An automatic timer is included to operate the stoker for a few minutes every hour or half hour to keep the fire alive during cool weather when little heat is required.

A stack thermostat is not always used, but in communities where electric power failures might be

long enough to let the fire go out, a stack thermostat or other control device is needed to keep the stoker from filling the cold fire pot with coal when the electricity comes on again. A light-sensitive electronic device such as an electric eye can be used. In the stoker-control setup for a forced-warm-air system, the furnace thermostat acts as high-limit and fan control. See Fig. 4-19.

ROOM VENTILATION

Proper ventilation of your house reduces or eliminates the need for summer air conditioning in many areas. Use screened windows, doors and other natural ventilation or use electric fans. Natural ventilation might not be as cooling, but it might be sufficient and it certainly will cost less than air conditioning.

Ventilate your living space in the evening and at night. Do not ventilate when the house is cooler inside than out. Keep the cool air trapped. Open vents or windows near the ceiling, If you can, to remove trapped hot air. Ventilation fans are particularly useful where evening breezes are not strong enough to move air through the house.

Your attic is a heat trap. While it serves as a buffer for the sun's heat, heat from the attic flows into the living area and increases the air-conditioning load. Attics reach temperatures above the outside air early

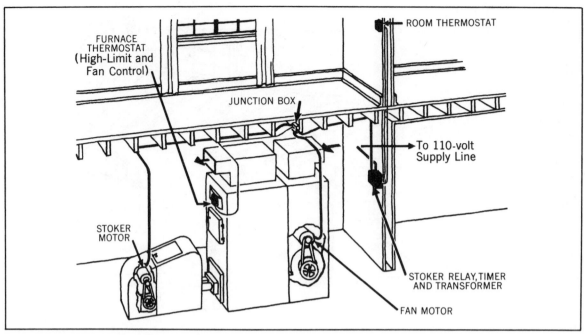

FURNACE
THERMOSTAT
(High-Limit and
Fan Control)

ROOM THERMOSTAT

JUNCTION BOX

To 110-volt
Supply Line

STOKER
MOTOR

STOKER RELAY, TIMER
AND TRANSFORMER

FAN MOTOR

Fig. 4-19. Controls for stoker-fired coal burner.

in the day. The attic should be ventilated by a fan as soon as its temperature rises above that of the outside in order to prevent a heat buildup.

Attics can be ventilated by natural air currents or by fans. Either way, lots of air must pass through to be effective. Roof vents or louvres should provide a lot of open air for natural ventilation. Most homes have minimal louvre openings (only enough to avoid winter moisture problems).

Frequently, a combination of soffit, gable, or ridge vents is used to ventilate attics without using a blower. Soffit and ridge vents are quite effective because the air flow is shorter. The ridge vent exhausts at a higher elevation than a gable opening. This creates a strong natural draft. Gable vent efficiency can be improved by locating a new house to permit prevailing winds to flow through the attic. For winter ventilation, the exhaust vent area (a similar area is needed for intake air) is 1 square foot for every 150 square feet of attic space. Effective summer ventilation requires much larger vent areas.

Ridge vents also increase natural ventilation by providing a short, direct airflow through the attic. The rotating cap of the cyclone acts as a low-capacity turbine. It can use wind power from any direction.

Powered fans operated from a thermostat reduce attic temperature levels automatically. The cost of operating the blower will be offset by savings in air conditioning loads. The more insulation in your attic, however, the less necessity for a powered fan. When ceiling R-values are high (above 30), it is still economical to install ventilation that operates on natural air currents.

FAN BELTS

A fan belt that's too tight causes excessive wear on the bearings. If it is too loose, it will slip. This increases belt wear and reduces blower efficiency. Allow a ¾-inch depression in the belt for each foot of distance between shaft and pulleys when the belt is pressed with a finger midway between the pulley. Check belt tension and alignment every 6 weeks when the air filters are inspected. If a new belt is needed, be sure to:

☐ Purchase the proper size.

☐ Purchase the proper length.

☐ When installing the new belt, release the take-up adjustment on the motor and do not roll the belt onto the pulley.

☐ Check the vanes on the fan and remove accumulated dirt.

☐ Be sure the power to the motor is shut off so it will not come on while you are working on the motor, belts, or fans.

THERMOSTATS AND HUMIDISTATS

Thermostats and humidistats are controls that cause the heating, cooling, and humidifying systems to operate automatically. They are used to turn the equipment on and off, when needed, so that temperature and humidity are kept at a constant level. This adds to the comfort of the occupants and reduces the system's operating cost.

How a Thermostat Works

The thermostat is a temperature-sensitive switch that turns the heating or cooling system on and off. The switch is equipped with a temperature-sending element that opens or closes the switch when the preferred temperature is reached or when additional heating or cooling is needed.

How a Humidistat Works

Humidistats have elements that are sensitive to moisture. Increases in moisture in the air cause a switch to open, and this turns off the humidifying equipment. The humidifying equipment is turned on when moisture levels decrease below the setting on the humidistat. See Fig. 4-20.

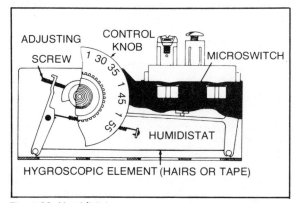

Fig. 4-20. Humidistat.

Thermostat Location

The thermostat should be located on an inside wall about 4 feet above the floor (Fig. 4-21). Do *not* put them near heat outlets, fireplaces, on walls above lamps or television sets, at the foot of an open stair-

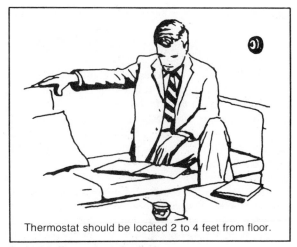

Thermostat should be located 2 to 4 feet from floor.

Fig. 4-21. Thermostat placement.

way, above a heat register, or any place where it will be affected by direct heat from sunlight.

Temperature Setting

The thermostat should be set at the point at which the occupants are most comfortable and *left at that setting* except for special circumstances. A setting above the desired temperature will not make the temperature rise any faster. A lower setting in the summer will not cause the house to cool any faster. The speed at which a house is cooled or heated depends on the heating or cooling system and *not* on the thermostat (Fig. 4-22). A thermostat setting higher than 60° will not make the room temperature reach 68° any faster.

Adjusting the Thermostat

The actual setting of your thermostat is not necessarily the "exact setting." They can be off 2 to 5

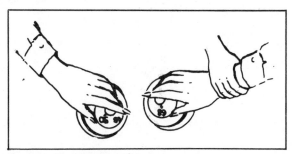

Fig. 4-22. Thermostat setting.

degrees. The only way this can be determined is by calibration of the thermostat in the home. Judicious control of the thermostat contributes to energy conservation. Frequent changes of thermostat settings is unwise because it increases the heating costs in the winter and cooling costs in the summer. During the winter, a maximum daytime temperature setting of 68 degrees is recommended. For each degree above, an additional 2 percent is added to your heating bill. In the Northeastern United States, 15-to-20 percent savings are possible with a reduction of 5 to 8 degrees in house temperature.

Setting the thermostat down at night to 55 or below makes sleeping more comfortable. For the forgetful, clock-controlled thermostats can insure that temperature settings are adjusted on schedule. Lowering the thermostat 5 to 10 degrees for a period of at least 8 hours or more will produce energy savings of 5 to 10 percent.

It also is useful to set the thermostat back during the daytime if the house will be unoccupied. Besides the thermostats that can automatically lower the temperature settings at night, some thermostats are available that allow two set-backs per day.

Inside Controls on Thermostats

Most thermostats used on central systems are equipped with small, built-in heaters that give the thermostat a false reading so that the switch opens just before the temperature setting is reached during the heating season (Fig. 4-23).

This controls allows the residual heat in the furnace or boiler to bring the room to the desired temperature without overheating the house. If there is not enough residual heat, the thermostat senses the deficiency and turns the system on again and repeats the process until the air in the house reaches the desired temperature. In this way, the heating is done in small increments so that energy is not wasted by the air being overheated.

Zone Control

In most cases, one thermostat is sufficient to control the temperature in the entire house. In some houses, it might be more desirable to divide the house into several areas or zones. Each zone would be controlled by a separate thermostat.

With systems such as electric cable or electric baseboard, zoning is easily achieved. With ducted or piped systems, special dampers or valves are needed. The ducts and pipes must be specifically designed for zoned control.

Zoning can be used to maintain slightly different temperatures in various areas of the house. It is most useful in maintaining even temperatures in rooms with varying sun and wind exposure (Fig. 4-24).

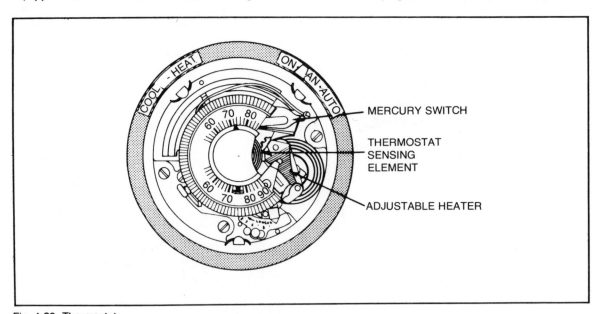

Fig. 4-23. Thermostat.

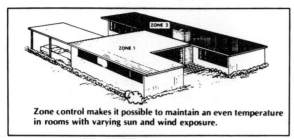

Zone control makes it possible to maintain an even temperature in rooms with varying sun and wind exposure.

Fig. 4-24. Zone control outline.

Thermostat Maintenance

Thermostats occasionally lose their calibration. For example, setting the thermostat on 68 might produce house temperatures of 70 to 72 degrees. This can be easily corrected by simply setting the thermostat at the number that produces the desired temperature. Checking to see if the thermostat you have has adjustable screws that are placed especially for calibration purposes.

Thermostats require some maintenance. Here are some helpful hints to make them more energy efficient:

☐ Check them regularly to make sure they are mounted level.

☐ Clean them at least once yearly to remove dust and grime.

☐ During the daytime, bedroom thermostats should be set with slightly lower temperatures than other living areas.

☐ Care should be taken *not* to block heating outlets with return air registers and obstacles such as furniture, draperies or doors.

☐ Circulated air will allow a more comfortable heat setting in the winter.

☐ Overhead doors of attached garages should be closed to block the cold winds from infiltrating connecting doors between the house and the garage.

☐ If you live in cold areas, exterior louvres in foundation walls should be closed during the coldest season.

☐ Portable electric heaters used to heat small areas should be put to limited use and should be thermostatically controlled.

☐ Furnaces are more efficient if they are slightly undersized. The smallest adequate system is the most economical.

Humidistat Maintenance

Maintenance and calibration of humidistats can be very difficult. Dust on the sensing element causes the humidistat to give incorrect readings or even stick on one setting. Each time the humidistat is cleaned, it will need calibration. Be *sure* to check the manufacturer's manual. If you do not have a manual, call a repairman. It will save you time, energy, and money in the long run.

AIR LEAKS

Air infiltration, or air leakage, is the largest single factor in your home's heating and air conditioning load. It can account for one-third to one-half of your winter heating and summer cooling bill. This loss is an unnecessary expense, and it is a waste of energy resources.

Infiltration. This is the uncontrolled leakage of outside air coming into your home. Air enters through cracks and bad joints in the exterior walls of the building such as around doors, windows, chimneys, or any other opening.

Ventilation. This is the controlled exchange of air necessary for providing fresh air, combustion air for furnace systems, and for removing odors from household activities, including cooking.

Causes of Air Leakage

Weather influences air leakages in two ways. Wind blowing directly on a wall forces air into the house through any available opening. On other walls, warm air is sucked out of the house. Because of temperature differences between the inside and outside, buoyant warm air rises to the top of the building, escapes, and is replaced by cold incoming air.

People cause air leakage by opening windows and doors, and by operating ventilating fans in kitchens, bathrooms, and laundry rooms. To run an energy-efficient home, every member of the family should recognize that these activities cause heat or cooling loss.

Air Leakage Affects Your Home

Air leakage is a burden on your furnace. Whenever warm air escapes, it is replaced by cold outside air that must be heated. In most houses, the entire volume of air in the house is exchanged every hour. This requires that the furnace run far more often than if the air leakage were reduced. Besides this, there are two other factors:

Humidity. When leaks are reduced, dry cold winter air is kept out, and you can maintain a comfortable relative humidity inside the house without using a humidifier.

Moisture. Bathing, washing, cooking, house plants, and normal respiration and perspiration produce moisture inside your house. After being tightened up, your house will have increased moisture levels. If this bothers you, simply running any exhaust fan or opening a window for a short time should clear up the problem.

A sealed home is a more comfortable one. Keeping the cold air out will result in few drafts and cold wall surfaces. And there will be higher indoor relative humidity. With a well-sealed house, you can lower your thermostat without decreasing comfort. If you are considering using solar energy, sealing air leaks is the necessary first step. It decreases fuel needs, and that lowers the size and cost of a solar-heating system.

Know Your House

Do a quick check of your house and make a list of the obvious leaks.

Fix broken windows. Don't forget basement windows.

Check the fireplace damper and make sure it is closed. Remember to open it before you use the fireplace. A pocket mirror held at an angle is an easy way of seeing the damper.

See that the basement and attic doors are kept tightly closed. Leaving the basement door open creates a large updraft throughout the house.

Pull drapes at night to cut down on drafts.

Keep the track of sliding glass doors clean. Dirt here can throw the doors out of alignment and cause air leakage.

Teach your children the need for keeping doors and windows closed when you are heating or air conditioning your home.

Make a thorough inspection of your house and look for the small leaks. Air can enter through any crack or space. To effectively keep the heat in, you will have to seal many small cracks. Keep a list of all cracks and leaks you find so you can caulk and repair these areas.

How to Locate Leaks

Make a simple leak detector by clipping a piece of tissue paper or light plastic to a coat hanger. Hold the coat hanger in front of a suspected crack and any movement of the paper will indicate air leakage. See Fig. 4-25.

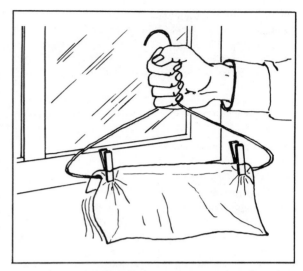

Fig. 4-25. Handmade draft gauge (courtesy of the Canadian Department of Energy Mines and Resources).

Choose a cold windy day to find many leaks with your hand.

COMMON AREAS FOR LEAKS

Windows and Doors. Check how tightly windows and doors seal when closed. Inspect the framing of the window. Frames often shift, and leave cracks between the frame and the wall.

Pipes and Wires. Check holes cut into the walls for pipes or electrical wiring. Pipes under sinks in kitchens and bathrooms are often poorly sealed into the floor or wall.

Electrical Outlets. Hold your draft gauge up to electrical wall outlets to test for leakage. Remember that these outlets are just holes cut into the walls and that they are seldom sealed properly or at all. If they aren't sealed do it!

Foundation Seal. A major leakage area is around the foundation seal. Wherever different materials come together, they can shrink and pull apart—causing leaks. These should be checked annually, and especially after seasons of hard freezing.

Mail Chutes. Don't overlook a mail chute in your front door. If the flap doesn't close tightly, a lot of cold air will enter the house. Oil the hinges periodically.

Fireplaces. Place a wood panel across the opening to reduce air leakage when the fireplace is not in use.

Exhaust Fans. Seal exhaust fans in the kitchen and bathroom in the wall or ceiling. Keep the filter in your kitchen fan clean so odors and smoke move out quickly. This will allow you to turn the fan off sooner.

Attics. It is especially important to check for attic leaks. Holes in the ceiling from pipes and electrical wires should be sealed. Place a board across the stringers when you are working in the attic so you won't fall through the ceiling.

Garage Doors. Check to see if the bottom edge is adequately weather stripped and that it seals tightly. Attached garages act as a buffer in keeping air from leaking into the house, but they can be quite leaky.

Siding Cracks. Replace damaged siding. Small cracks should be nailed closed.

Masonry Cracks. Mortar joints in masonry deteriorate with age. Although the weight of masonry itself is usually sufficient to seal small cracks, some gaps might require caulking.

Old Caulk and Weather Stripping. Periodically inspect all caulk and weather stripping. Even though most weather stripping materials last many years, it is important to keep them in good shape.

Checklist for House Leaks

Starting at the basement of your house and working your way up. Don't overlook the following areas:

- ☐ Basement windows.
- ☐ Basement ceiling holes cut for wires and plumbing.
- ☐ Basement door. Crawl space access door.
- ☐ Heating ducts in the crawl space.
- ☐ Exterior lights, electrical outlets, and water pipes.
- ☐ Windows: sashes, frames, and trim.
- ☐ Doors: mail slots and glass panels.
- ☐ Sliding glass doors.
- ☐ Fireplace dampers.
- ☐ Electrical wall outlets.
- ☐ Attic floor holes cut for wires and plumbing.

HEATING- AND COOLING-SYSTEM MAINTENANCE

To increase the energy efficiency of heating and cooling systems, and reduce the over-all energy consumption in your home, proper maintenance is necessary. The heating system should be checked in the fall and the cooling system should be checked in the spring. Routine maintenance can be done by the homeowner.

Checking compressors, pumps, motors, and adjusting pilot lights, thermostats and other devices must be done by a properly trained person. If you feel you do not know enough about these things, call a professional. It will save you time, energy, and money in the long run.

With a forced-air heating and cooling system, the blower and motor are protected from dirt and dust by filters located in the return-air side of the blower unit. Therefore, little is required in this type of system. See Fig. 4-26.

Check your heating systems prior to each season's use. Correct adjustments reduce fuel consumption.

Change the filters at least twice yearly in *all* cases. Depending upon the amount of use, check monthly, they might need changing as much as once monthly. Make it a point to check your filters on a monthly basis. The amount of time you have to change the filters depends on the amount of usage and the amount of dust in the air.

Clogged filters will not allow a sufficient amount of air to pass across the heat exchanger or the cooling coil. This will waste energy and result in inadequate heating or cooling.

Clean the furnace room, supply ducts and return ducts with a vacuum cleaner to reduce dust accumulation. See Fig. 4-27.

The blower bearings and blower motor should be oiled unless they are sealed. The manufacturer's recommendations should be checked for amount and frequency of oiling. Unless specified otherwise, bearings on electric motors should receive 2 or 3 *drops* of oil once or twice a year. Check fan belts and pulleys for wear and proper tension. See Fig. 4-28.

The air-conditioning condensing unit (usually located outside the house) also should be cleaned. The grille and coils—which collect insects, dirt, and trash—should be brushed and hosed as needed.

The evaporator coil (usually located within the house in the heating and cooling unit) functions as a dehumidifier as well as a cooling element. It condenses water that collects in a pan beneath the coil and is conducted to a drain. This drain line can easily become obstructed and will require periodic cleaning to remove dust and algae. Water overflowing during cooling is an indication that the drain line needs to be cleaned.

Humidifiers and dehumidifers should be cleaned and dried thoroughly, oiled as required, and checked for rusting. Spot paint all rusted areas. Check humidifiers for calcium deposits and dehumidifiers for

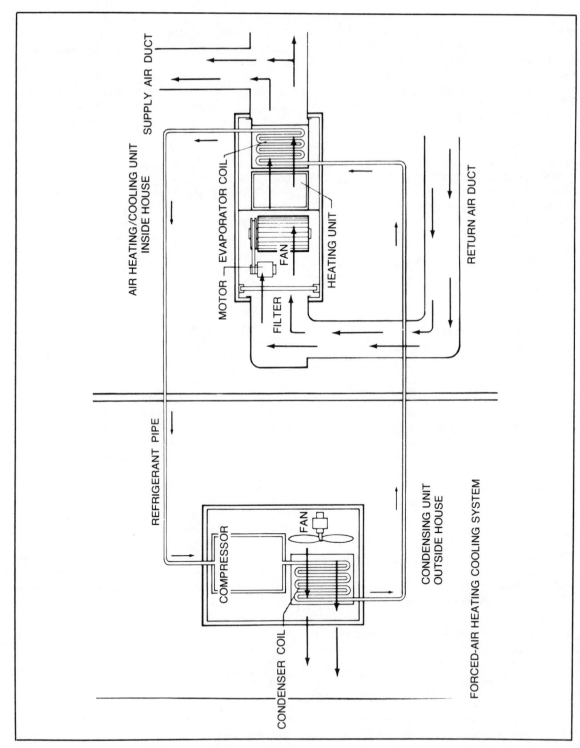

AIR HEATING/COOLING UNIT
INSIDE HOUSE

SUPPLY AIR DUCT

EVAPORATOR COIL

MOTOR

FAN

HEATING UNIT

FILTER

RETURN AIR DUCT

REFRIGERANT PIPE

COMPRESSOR

FAN

CONDENSING UNIT
OUTSIDE HOUSE

CONDENSER COIL

FORCED-AIR HEATING COOLING SYSTEM

Fig. 4-26. Forced-air System.

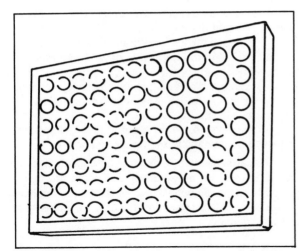
Fig. 4-27. Filter.

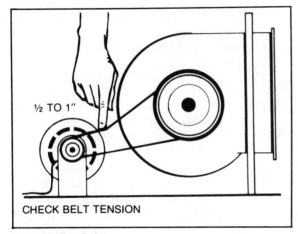
CHECK BELT TENSION

½ TO 1"

Fig. 4-28. Fan Belts.

algae growth. Algae can be removed with household chlorine bleach.

Inspect ductwork every year and use duct tape to seal holes that could leak air. Duct tape is a cloth tape (usually grey in color) that is available in hardware stores. Ductwork in attics or unheated crawl spaces should be fully covered by insulation (R-11 unfaced batts). Do not store flammable materials in the furnace or boiler room. See Fig. 4-29.

Keep condenser coils cleaned and finned, and free from lint and other foreign material.

If you have an oil fired system:

☐ Clean the oil lines and filters.

☐ Check all leads, connections, and valves for leaks.

Fig. 4-29. Inspecting duct work.

☐ Check the chimney or the exhaust stack for obstructions.

☐ Check the solenoid valve shut-offs when burning shuts off.

☐ Check the chimney exhaust stack for obstructions or exhaust gas flow.

☐ If a yellow flame appears at the burner or excess smoke from the chimney appears, the burner probably needs adjusting. This should be done by a professional serviceman.

If you have a gas-fired furnace you should:

☐ Make sure a clear blue flame consistently appears.

☐ Remove rust and soot, from the heat exchanger, as it appears.

☐ Light the pilot light and leave it lit all summer in order to reduce corrosion.

☐ Replace stacks that have leaks.

GENERAL GUIDELINES

Don't heat or cool space not being used. If you have excessive cooling or heating bills, it could be that you can operate your home more efficiently by changing your current heating and cooling routine as follows.

If you can get along without heat in some areas of your house, turn it off.

Some rooms or areas may need only a minimum amount of heat; others need heating or cooling only occasionally. Regulate the heating or cooling in this way and reduce your energy costs.

When practical, heat or cool the rooms in the center of the house and let the outside rooms serve as an insulating barrier.

Adjust the heating and cooling in rooms by opening and closing registers. If your registers aren't adjustable, replace them.

If you have a water system or steam radiator that can't be turned off, install bypass lines or shutoff valves as needed to control the system and protect it against freezing.

Thermostatically controlled valves in each room will provide the most effective system.

Single-room heating units in large homes will help reduce demand on a central system. The central unit can be operated at a low temperature setting throughout the house while the small units can boost the temperatures in rooms being used the most.

Storm windows that are color coated reduce demand on the central system.

Each time the door is opened, hot air comes in so keep them closed. Your air conditioner has to work harder to keep you cool.

An air-conditioning unit that runs continuously and does not adequately cool the area might be low on refrigerant. It might not be large enough to cool the area. It might be working overtime because the filter needs cleaning or changing.

On sunny days, light-colored draperies, blinds, and shades should be closed on the sunny side of the house to lighten cooling loads. Dark colors absorb heat. Make sure your draperies are insulated or lined.

Crawl space vents should be opened in the summer to reduce humidity or moisture load on the cooling unit.

Turn off lights, radios, and television sets not being used. They add heat.

Checklist for Cooling/Heating Systems

☐ Keep garage doors closed if the garage is attached to the house.

☐ Set the thermostat at 68 degrees or lower during the day. Set the thermostat at 55 degrees during the night or while you are away from the house for an extended period of time. This procedure will vary for individuals and areas.

☐ Shades, blinds, and drapes should be drawn during the night and on cloudy days. Open them on sunny days.

☐ Electric blankets are comfortable, efficient, and inexpensive to use. They can be substituted for regular blankets.

☐ Be sure to file, in a safe place, instructions supplied by manufacturers for *all* equipment.

Regardless of the heating or cooling system used, make sure all windows and doors are tightly closed and that air outlets are not blocked by furniture or draperies. Heat or air condition only the rooms most frequently used.

SEASONAL HOUSE CHECKS

The preceding measures are not a one-time project. Your house, like the weather, is constantly changing. Weather effects and small shifts in the house are always opening new cracks and leaks to "drag" out the heat or cooling air that you want to keep in the house.

Make a habit of going over your entire house twice a year. Inspect all the potentially leaky areas. In the fall, make sure everything is well sealed before the winter heating season. In the spring, it is important to look for damage done by winter weather.

In the Fall

☐ Inspect all windows and doors to make sure caulking and weather stripping are in good condition. If caulk has dried and cracked, it should be scraped clean and redone. Weather stripping should seal tightly against moving parts.

☐ Look for damaged or bent sections that need to be replaced.

☐ Check and see that the fireplace damper hinge is operable and that the damper will close tightly when the fireplace is not in use.

☐ Replace filter in furnace several times during the operating season to allow heating systems to operate more efficiently. This is important in realizing the benefits of a comfortably sealed home.

In the Spring

☐ Inspect windows and doors again for damaged caulk and weather stripping, and replace where necessary.

☐ Remember that it is important to keep an air-conditioned house well sealed against moisture-laden air during the summer months.

☐ Plant shrubs, hedges, or trees to act as a windbreak and shelter.

Seasonal temperatures and *degree-days* compromise heating and cooling seasons. They are better defined by local climatic conditions than seasons of the year. Important facts to consider are average monthly temperatures and the local demand for heating—expressed in degree-days.

Heating degree-days are calculated by subtracting the average daily temperature on a given day from an established base temperature. For heating this is usually set at 65° F. For instance, if the average daily temperature is 64° F it represents one degree day. If the average temperature is 63° F it represents two degree days. The sum of an entire month's degree-days represents the monthly heating load. Similarly, the sum of all monthly degree-days represents the yearly heating demand. A similar procedure is used for cooling degree-days, but a different base temperature is usually used (70 to 75° F).

Chapter 5

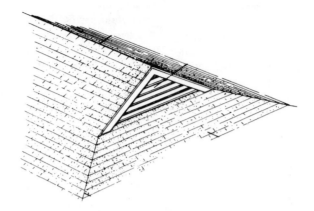

Condensation and Ventilation

INSTALLING INSULATION CAN ALTER the movement of moisture through walls, ceilings, and floors. The control of condensation through the use of vapor barriers and ventilation should be practiced regardless of the amount of insulation used.

Normally, winter condensation problems occur in those parts of the United States where the average January temperature is 35° F or lower. Figure 5-1 shows this condensation zone. The northern half of the condensation zone has a lower average winter temperature and, of course, more severe conditions than the southern portion. Areas outside this zone, such as the Southeast, the West Coast area and the Southern states, seldom have condensation problems.

Vapor barriers should be installed in new homes at the time of construction. Proper ventilation procedures should be followed to insure control over normal condensation problems.

During the heating season, warm indoor air holds more moisture than cold outdoor air. See Fig. 5-2. This creates vapor pressure inside which constantly forces water vapor out through walls and ceilings as it seeks lower moisture levels outside. When moisture levels within walls, attics, or crawl spaces become high, the

water vapor tends to condense on cold surfaces. In most structures, moisture can escape to the outside. But if moisture moves into the walls, ceiling, or crawl space faster than it can escape to outside air, the moisture will build up. There are three things you can do to control moisture buildup:

- ☐ Control humidity in the house
- ☐ Install vapor barriers in walls, floors, and ceilings
- ☐ Ventilate attics and crawl spaces

CONDENSATION

Condensation can be described as the change in moisture from a vapor to a liquid. Condensation will take place anytime the temperature drops below the dewpoint (100 percent saturation of the air with water vapor at a given temperature). Commonly under such conditions, some surface accessible to the moisture in the air is cooler than the dewpoint and the moisture condenses on that surface.

In homes not properly protected, condensation caused by high humidities often results in excessive maintenance costs and low energy efficiency. Water vapor within the house, when unrestricted, can move

94

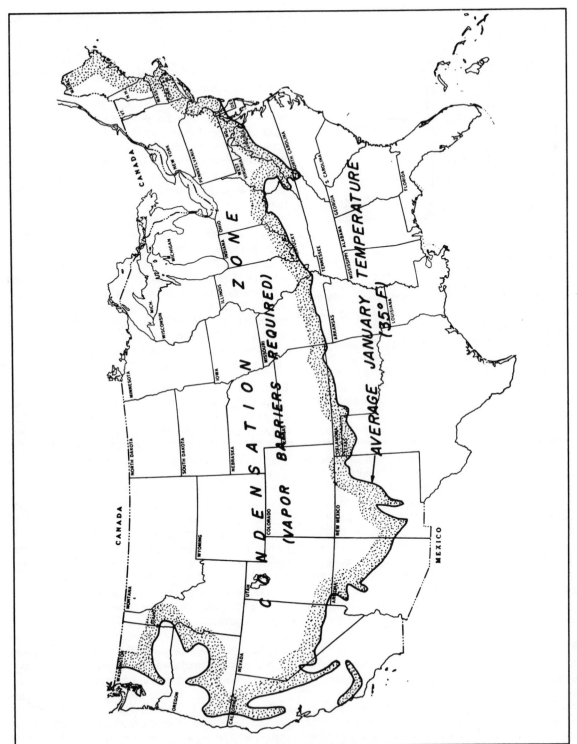

Fig. 5-1. Condensation zone map.

95

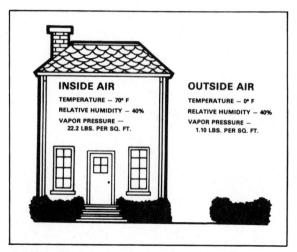

INSIDE AIR
TEMPERATURE — 70° F
RELATIVE HUMIDITY — 40%
VAPOR PRESSURE —
22.2 LBS. PER SQ. FT.

OUTSIDE AIR
TEMPERATURE — 0° F
RELATIVE HUMIDITY — 40%
VAPOR PRESSURE —
1.10 LBS. PER SQ. FT.

Fig. 5-2. Vapor pressure.

through the wall or ceiling during the heating season to solid cold surfaces where it condenses and collects, generally, in the form of ice or frost. During warm periods the frost melts.

When conditions are severe, the water from melting ice in unvented attics might drip to the ceiling below and cause damage to the interior finish. Moisture can also soak into the roof sheathing or rafters and set up conditions which could lead to decay. In walls, water from melting frost might run out between siding laps and cause staining, or soak into the siding and cause paint blistering and peeling.

Wood and wood-base materials used for sheathing and panel siding can swell from this added moisture and result in bowing, cupping, or buckling. Thermal insulation also becomes wet and provides less resistance to heat loss. Efflorescence can occur on brick or stone of an exterior wall because of such condensation.

The cost of heat losses, painting, redecorating, and excessive maintenance and repair caused by cold-weather condensation can be easily reduced or eliminated when proper construction techniques are used.

Factors in Condensation Problems

Changes in construction design, materials, and methods have resulted in houses that are easier to heat and more comfortable. But these changes have accentuated the potential for condensation problems. The latest types of weather stripping, storm sash, and sheet material for sheathing in new houses provide tight air-resistant construction that restricts the escape of moisture generated in the house. Today's homes are generally smaller and have lower ceilings. This results in less atmosphere to hold moisture.

It is estimated that a typical family of four converts 3 gallons of water into water vapor per day. Unless excess water vapor is properly removed in some way—such as ventilation—it will either increase the humidity or condense on cold surfaces such as window glass. More seriously, it can move in or through the entire construction. It will often condense within the wall, roof, or floor cavities. Heating systems equipped with winter air-conditioning systems also increase the humidity.

Most houses have from 2 to 3½ inches of insulation in the walls and 6 or more inches in the ceilings. Unfortunately, the more efficient the insulation is in retarding heat transfer, the colder the outer surfaces become. Moisture, therefore, must be restricted from entering the wall or ceiling to eliminate the greater potential for moisture condensation. Moisture migrates toward cold surfaces and will condense or form as frost or ice on these surfaces.

The proper use of vapor barriers and good ventilating practices will prevent condensation problems.

Concealed Condensation

During cold weather, visible condensation is usually first noticed on windows, but might also be discovered on cold surfaces of closet and unheated bedroom walls and ceilings. It might also be visible in attic spaces on rafters or roof boards near the cold cornice area. Darkened areas on roof boards and rafters in attic area indicate stain that stemmed from condensation. This usually can be prevented by having a vapor barrier in the ceiling and good attic ventilation (Fig. 5-3). It can also form as frost. This type of condensation or melting frost often results in excessive maintenance such as the need for refinishing of windows sash and trim, or worse, decay. Water from melting frost in the attic can also damage ceilings below.

A prime area for visible condensation is in crawl spaces under occupied rooms. This area usually differs from those on the interior of the house and in the attic because the source of the moisture is usually from the soil or from warm, moisture-laden air that enters through foundation ventilators.

Moisture vapor then condenses on the cooler surfaces in the crawl space. Surface condensation on floor joists in crawl space are shown in Fig. 5-4. A vapor barrier ground cover can prevent this because it

Fig. 5-3. Darkened areas on roof boards (courtesy of USDA).

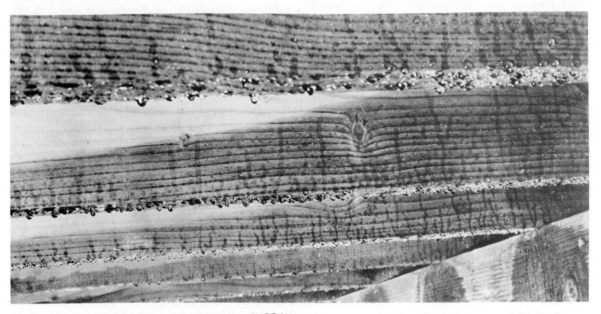

Fig. 5-4. Moisture condensation on joists (courtesy of USDA).

restricts water vapor movement from the soil and thus avoids high humidity of crawl space and subsequent surface condensation. Such conditions often occur during warm periods in late spring.

An increase in relative humidity of the inside atmosphere increases the potential for condensation on inside surfaces. When the inside temperature is 70° F, surface condensation will occur on a single glass window when the outside temperature falls to – 10° F, and inside relative humidity is 10 percent.

When inside relative humidity is 20 percent, condensation can occur on the single glass when outside temperature only falls to about 7° F. When a storm window is added or insulated glass is used, surface condensation will not occur until the relative humidity has reached 38 percent when the outdoor temperature is –10° F.

The above conditions apply only where storm windows are tight and there is good circulations of air on the inside surface of the window. Where drapes or shades restrict circulation of air, storm windows are not tight, or lower temperatures are maintained in such areas as bedrooms, condensation will occur at a higher outside temperature.

Visible Condensation

Condensation in concealed areas, such as wall spaces, often is initially noticed by stains on the siding or by peeling paint. Water vapor moving through permeable walls and ceilings is usually responsible for such damage. Water vapor also escapes from houses by constant out-leakage through cracks and crevices, around doors and windows, and by ventilation. This moisture-vapor loss is usually insufficient to eliminate condensation problems.

MOISTURE

Interior. Moisture produced in a home or that enters a home changes the relative humidity of the interior atmosphere. Some household functions that generate a good share of the total amount of water vapor include dishwashing, cooking, bathing, and laundering. Also included is human respiration and evaporation from house plants. Houses might also be equipped with central winter air conditioners or room humidifiers. Yet another source of moisture comes from unvented or poorly vented clothes dryers. Several sources and their effects in adding water vapor to the interior of the house are shown in Table 5-1.

Crawl Space. Water vapor from the soil or from

Table 5-1. Moisture Sources.

PINTS OF WATER	
Plants	-1.07 for each plant in 24 hours
Showers	-0.5 for each shower and
	-0.1 for each bath
Floor Mopping	-2.9 per 100 square feet, each washing
Kettles and Cooking	5.5 per day
Clothes (washing, steam ironing and drying)	-29.4 per week

crawl spaces in houses does not ordinarily affect the occupied areas. Nevertheless, without good construction practices or proper precautions it can be a factor in causing problems in exterior walls over the area as well as in the crawl space itself. It is another source of moisture that must be considered in providing protection.

Water from Construction. People moving into a newly constructed house in the fall or early winter sometimes experience temporary moisture problems. Surface condensation on windows, damp areas on cold closet walls where air movement is restricted, and even stained siding indicate an excessive amount of moisture. Such conditions can often be traced to water used in the construction of a house.

Basement floors, concrete walls, and plastered walls and ceilings require a tremendous amount of water during their construction. While much of this water has evaporated from the surface after a month or so, the addition of heat aids in driving off more moisture as these elements reach moisture equilibrium with the surrounding atmosphere. This moisture creates higher than normal humidities, and the increased amount of vapor drives vapor toward colder areas in attics or in the walls.

A concrete floor in the basement of a small home contains more than 240 gallons of water when it is poured. The concrete basement walls of a small (the same) home contain over 480 gallons of water. If the house is plastered, over 300 gallons of water are used. It is often a common occurrence to have some moisture problems when a house is just completed. These are normally corrected after the first heating season. There are several methods of reducing excessive moisture, but the simplest is to heat and ventilate a new house so that excessive moisture is dissipated outdoors before the occupants arrive.

There are other sources of moisture that are often unsuspected and that can be the cause of condensation problems. One such source can be a gas-fired furnace. It is desirable to maintain flue-gas temperatures, within the recommended limits, throughout the appliance, in the flue, the connecting vent, and other areas. Otherwise excessive condensation problems will result. If all sources of excessive moisture have been exhausted in determining the reasons for a condensation problem, have the heating unit examined by a competent heating engineer.

The relationship between indoor relative humidity and outdoor temperatures is distinct in all homes. The humidity is generally high indoors when outdoor temperatures are high and decreases as outdoor temperatures drop. To reduce relative humidity in an exceptionally tight modern house where moisture buildup can be a problem, outside air should be introduced into the cold air return ducts.

VAPOR BARRIERS

Materials such as plaster, drywall, wood paneling, and plywood permit water vapor to pass slowly through them during cold weather. Temperatures of the sheathing or siding on the outside of the wall are often sufficiently low to cause condensation of water vapor within the cavities of a framed wall.

When the relative humidity within the house at the surface of an unprotected wall is greater than that within the wall, water vapor will transfer through the plaster or other finish into the stud space where it will condense if it comes in contact with surfaces colder than its dewpoint temperature. Vapor barriers are used to resist this movement of water vapor or moisture in various areas of the house.

The amount of condensation that can develop within a wall depends on:

☐ The resistance of the intervening materials to vapor transfusion.
☐ Differences in vapor pressure.
☐ Time.

Plastered walls or ordinary drywalls have little resistance to vapor movement. When the surfaces are painted with oil-base paint, the resistance is increased. High indoor temperatures and relative humidities result in high indoor vapor pressures. Low outdoor vapor pressures always exist at low temperatures. Therefore, a combination of high inside temperatures will normally result in vapor movement into the wall if no vapor barrier is present. Long periods of severe weather will result in condensation problems. Though few homes are affected by condensation in mild winter weather, it appears that the minimum relative humidities in affected homes are 35 percent or higher.

Vapor barrier requirements can be satisfied by the use of materials used in construction. In addition to integral vapor barriers that are a part of many types of insulation materials such as plastic-faced hardboard can be used. The *permeability* of the surface to such vapor movement is expressed in *perms* which are grains of water vapor passing through a square foot of material per hour per inch of mercury difference in vapor pressure. A material with a low perm value (1.0 or less) is a barrier; one with a higher perm value (greater than 1.0) is a "breather."

The perm value of the cold side materials should be several times greater than those on the warm side. A ratio of 1 to 5 or greater from inside to outside is the basic rule of thumb when selecting material and finish. When this is not possible due to virtually impermeable outside construction—such as a built-up roof or resistant exterior wall membranes—there is a need to ventilate the space between the insulation and the outer covering.

There are three specific areas of the house where vapor barriers should be used to minimize condensation or moisture problems.

—Walls.
—Ceilings.
—Floors.

Vapor barriers used on the warm side of all exposed walls, ceilings, and floors greatly reduce movement of water vapor to colder surfaces where harmful condensation can occur. For such uses, select materials with perm values of 0.25 or less. Such vapor barriers can be a part of the insulation or a separate film. Some materials used are:

☐ Asphalt-coated or laminated papers.
☐ Kraft-backed aluminum foil.
☐ Plastic films such as polyethylene, and others.
☐ Foil-back gypsum board and various coatings.
☐ Coatings such as oil-base or aluminum paint or similar coatings are often used in older homes that did not have other vapor barriers installed during their initial construction.

Concrete Slabs

Vapor barriers under concrete slabs resist the movement of moisture through the concrete and into living areas. Such vapor barriers should normally have a maximum perm value of .0.50. But the material must also have adequate resistance to the hazards of pouring concrete. A satisfactory material must be heavy enough to withstand such damage and at the same time have an adequate perm value. Heavy asphalt laminated papers, papers with laminated films, roll roofing, heavy films such as polyethylene, and other materials are commonly used as vapor barriers under slabs.

Crawl Space Covers

Vapor barriers in crawl spaces prevent ground moisture from moving up and condensing on wood members (Fig. 5-4). A perm value of 1.0 or less is considered satisfactory for such use. Asphalt-laminated paper, polyethylene, and similar materials should be used. Strength and resistance of crawl space covering to mechanical damage can be lower than that for vapor barriers used under concrete slabs.

Exterior Materials

In structures without vapor barriers, a low permeance material or coating on the outside can retard the escape of moisture that has been forced into the wall from the inside. An alternative finish for such a situation is a penetrating stain that does not form a coating on the wood surface and, therefore, does not retard the movement of moisture. Penetrating stains are very durable and easily refinished because they do not fail by blistering or peeling.

Where an older home has a paint peeling problem due to condensation, paint the siding with white latex paint, which is very porous, and then spot-paint annually wherever peeling occurs. White paint should be used because it does not fade and it retains a good exterior appearance between yearly touchups.

In new construction where low permeance vapor barriers are properly installed, most commercially available sheathing and siding materials and coatings are used without creating condensation problems.

Thermal Insulation

Thermal insulation has a major influence on the need for vapor barriers. The inner face of the wall sheathing in an insulated wall, for instance, is colder than the sheathing face in an uninsulated wall and consequently has a greater attraction to moisture. Thus there is greater need for a vapor barrier in an insulated wall than in an uninsulated wall.

Ventilation

A recognized means of controlling condensation in buildings is the use of ventilation in proper amounts and locations. Inlet and outlet ventilators in attic spaces, ventilation of rafter spaces in flat roofs, and crawl space ventilation aid in preventing accumulation of condensation in those areas. By introducing fresh air into living quarters during the winter, some humid air is forced out of the house while the incoming air has a low water-vapor content. Well installed vapor barriers will increase the need for ventilation in living quarters because little of the moisture generated can get out and it will build up.

The use of inlet and outlet ventilators in attic spaces aids in keeping the air moving and preventing the accumulation of frost or condensation on roof boards in cold climates. "Dead" air pockets in the attic can normally be prevented by good distribution of inlet ventilators in the soffit areas. Nevertheless, there is still a need for vapor barriers in the ceiling. Ventilation alone, when insulation is used, does not prevent condensation problems. A good vapor barrier is especially needed under the insulation in a flat roof where ventilation can normally be provided only in the overhang.

Crawl space moisture, which results in high moisture content of the wood members, can be almost entirely eliminated by a vapor barrier over the soil. When such protection is used, the need for ventilation is usually reduced to only 10 percent of that required when a soil cover is not present.

During warm damp periods in early summer, moisture often condenses on basement walls or around the perimeter of the floor in concrete slab houses. Soil temperatures in the northern part of the United States remain quite low until summer, and surface temperatures of the floor or wall are often below the dewpoint. When concrete reaches normal temperature and the atmosphere changes, such problems are normally reduced or eliminated.

Location of Vapor Barriers

A good general rule to keep in mind when installing vapor barriers in your house is to place the vapor barrier as close as possible to the interior or warm surface of all exposed walls, ceilings, and floors. This normally means placing the vapor barrier—separated or as a part of the insulation—as follows:

☐ The inside edge of the studs just under the rock lath or drywall finish.

☐ On the under side of the ceiling joists of a one-story house or the second-floor ceiling joists of a two-story house.

☐ Between the subfloor and finished floor or just under the subfloor of a house with an unheated crawl space in addition to the one placed on the ground.

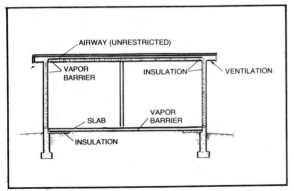

Fig. 5-5. Location of vapor barriers and insulation in concrete slab and flat deck roof.

The insulation, of course, is normally placed between studs or other frame members on the outside of the vapor barrier. The exception is the insulation used in concrete floor slabs where a barrier is used under the insulation to protect it from ground moisture.

Placement of vapor barriers and insulation in a one-story house is shown in Fig. 5-5 (flat roof and

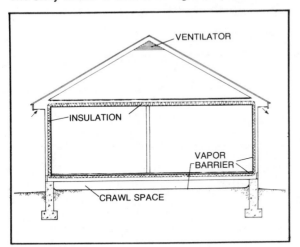

Fig. 5-6. Location of vapor barriers in the crawl space of a one-story house.

concrete floor slab) and Fig. 5-6 (pitched roof and crawl space). Figure 5-7 shows barriers and insulation in a 1½-story house with a full basement. Figure 5-8 shows a two-story house with a full basement. Other

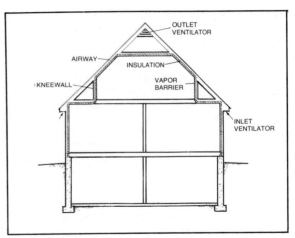

Fig. 5-7. Location of vapor barriers in 1½-story house with basement.

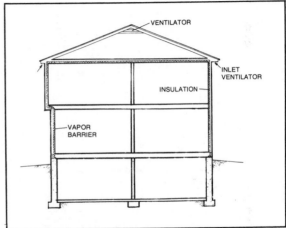

Fig. 5-8. Location of vapor barriers in a full two-story house with basement.

combinations of slabs, crawl spaces, and basements in houses with 1 story, 1½ stories, or 2 stories, should follow the same general recommendations.

CONCRETE SLABS

A house constructed over a concrete slab must be protected from soil moisture that could enter the slab. Protection can be provided by a vapor barrier that completely isolates the concrete and perimeter insulation from the soil. Thermal insulation of some type is required around the house perimeter in colder climates. This reduces heat loss and minimizes condensation on the colder concrete surfaces. Some type of rigid insulation impervious to moisture absorption, such as expanded plastic insulation (polystyrene), should be used.

Figure 5-9 shows one method of installing this insulation. Another method consists of placing it vertically along the inside of the foundation wall. Both methods require insulation at the slab notch of the wall. See Chapter 3 for details. If the insulation is placed vertically, it should extend a minimum of 12 inches below the outside finish grade. In colder climates, a minimum 24-inch width or depth should be used.

In late spring or early summer, periods of high humidity can cause surface condensation on exposed concrete slabs or on coverings such as resilient tile before the concrete has reached normal tempera-

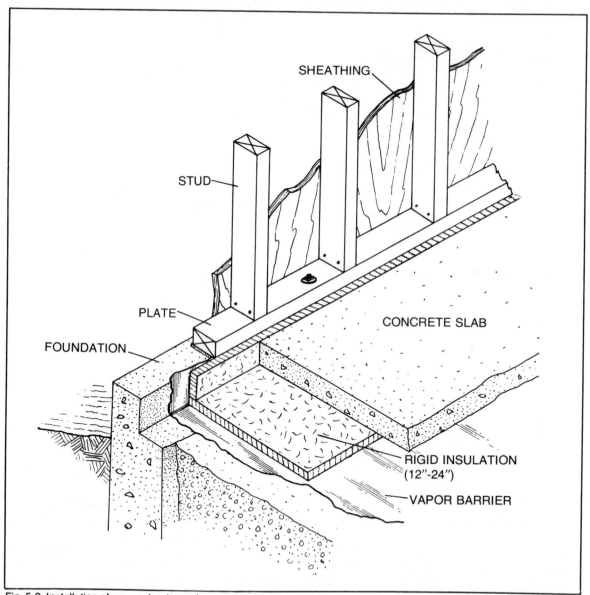

Fig. 5-9. Installation of a vapor barrier under a concrete slab.

tures. A fully insulated slab or a wood floor installed over wood furring strips minimizes, if not eliminates, such problems.

Because the vapor barriers slow the curing process of the concrete, final steel troweling of the surface is somewhat delayed. Do *not* punch holes through the barrier to hasten the curing process because this will destroy its effectiveness.

CRAWL SPACES

Enclosed crawl spaces require some protection to prevent problems caused by excessive soil moisture. In an unheated crawl space this usually consists of a vapor barrier over the soil, together with foundation ventilators. In heated crawl spaces, a vapor barrier and perimeter insulation is used but foundation ventilators are eliminated.

Unheated Crawl Space

To provide complete protection from condensation problems, the conventional unheated crawl space usually contains:

☐ Foundation ventilators.
☐ Ground cover (vapor barrier).
☐ Thermal insulation between the floor joists.

Foundation ventilators are normally located near the top of the masonry wall. In concrete block foundations, the ventilator is often made in a size to replace a full block. See Fig. 5-10.

The amount of ventilation required for a crawl space is based on the total area of the house in square feet and the presence of a vapor barrier. Table 5-2 lists the recommended minimum net ventilating areas for crawl space with or without vapor barriers.

The flow of air through a ventilator is restricted by the presence of screening and by the louvers. This reduction varies with the size of the screening or mesh and by the type of louvers used. Louvers are sloped about 45 degrees to shed rain when used in a vertical position. Table 5-3 outlines the amount by which the total calculated net area of the ventilators must be increased to compensate for screens and thickness of the louvers.

In placing the vapor barrier over the crawl-space soil, adjoining edges should be lapped slightly and ends should be turned up on the foundation wall. See Fig. 5-11. To prevent movement of the barrier, weight down laps and edges with bricks or other small masonry sections.

An unheated crawl space in cold climates offers insufficient protection to supply and disposal pipes during winter months. It is common practice to use a large vitrified or similar tile to enclose the water and sewer lines in the crawl space. Insulation is then placed within the tile to the floor level.

Insulating batts, with an attached vapor barrier, are normally located between the floor joists. They can be fastened by placing the tabs over the edge of the joists before the subfloor is installed when the cover (vapor barrier) is strong enough to support the insulation batt. See Fig. 5-11. There is often a hazard of the insulation becoming wet before the subfloor is installed and the house is enclosed. Therefore, it is advisable to use one of the following alternative methods.

☐ Friction-type batt insulation is made to fit tightly between joists and can be installed from the crawl space. See Fig. 5-12(A).

☐ Use small dabs of mastic adhesive to insure that it remains in place against the subfloor. When the vapor barrier is not a part of the insulation, a separate film should be placed between the subfloor and the finish floor.

When standard batt or blanket insulation containing an integral vapor barrier is not installed from above before the subfloor is applied, several alternative methods, as follows, can be used.

☐ If the vapor barrier and enclosing paper wrap is strong enough, it can be installed with a mastic adhesive in the same manner as the friction tape. See Fig. 5-12(A).

☐ Floor insulation can also be supported by a wire mesh held in place by wood strips. See Fig. 5-12(B).

☐ Small wood strips can be applied across the joist space. See Fig. 5-12(C). Cut the strips slightly longer than the width of the space and spring in place so that they bear against the bottom of the insulation.

When only a small amount of insulation is required between the joists because of moderate climates, several other insulating materials can be used.

One type of material is reflective insulation; it usually consists of a kraft paper with aluminum foil on each face. The reflective face must be placed at least ¾ of an inch away from the underside of the subfloor or other facing to be fully effective. See Fig. 5-13(A). Multiple or expanded reflective insulation might also be used. A thick blanket insulation can also be used

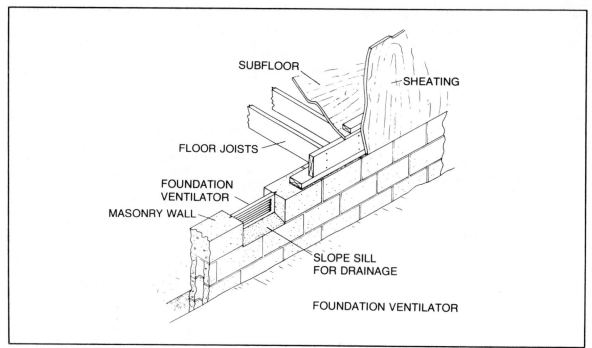

Fig. 5-10. Ventilation.

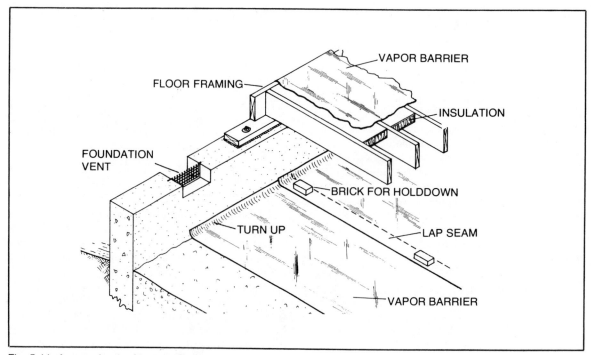

Fig. 5-11. A vapor barrier for a crawl space.

104

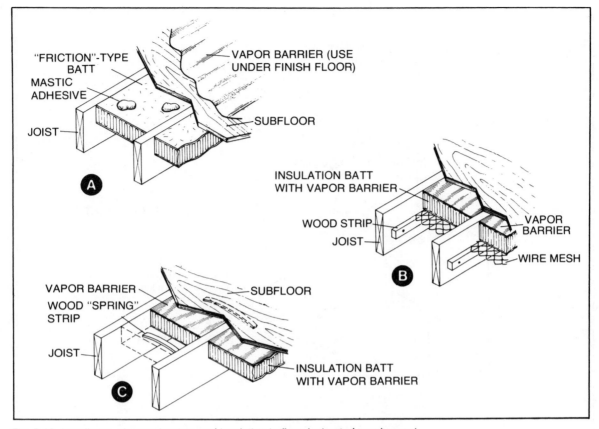

Fig. 5-12. Installation of vapor barriers and insulation in floor (unheated crawl space).

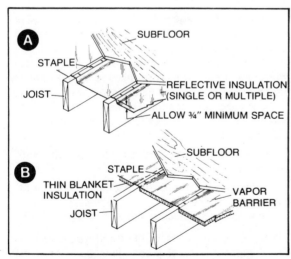

Fig. 5-13. Installation of vapor barriers and insulation over crawl space.

between the joists. See Fig. 5-13(B). This is installed in much the same manner as thicker insulations (as shown in Figs. 5-11 and 5-12). When vapor barriers are a part of the flexible insulation and properly installed, no additional vapor barrier is ordinarily required.

Heated Crawl Space

One method of heating crawl spaces uses the crawl space as a *plenum chamber*. Warm air is forced into the crawl space, which is somewhat shallower than those normally used without heat, and through the walls and into the rooms above.

When such a system is used, insulation is placed along the perimeter walls. See Fig. 5-14. Flexible insulation, with the vapor barrier facing the interior, is used between joists (at the top of the foundation wall). A rigid insulation, such as expanded polystyrene, is placed along the inside of the wall to extend below the

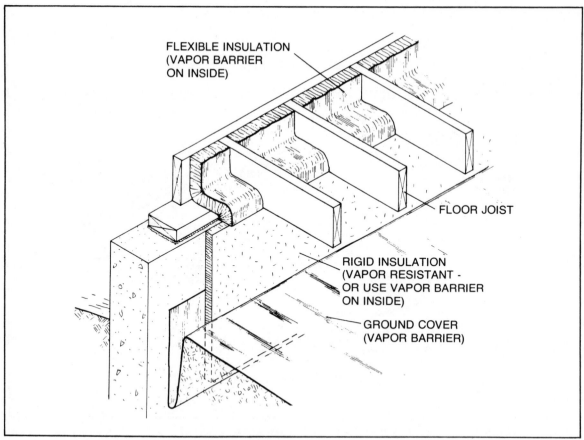

FLEXIBLE INSULATION
(VAPOR BARRIER
ON INSIDE)

FLOOR JOIST

RIGID INSULATION
(VAPOR RESISTANT -
OR USE VAPOR BARRIER
ON INSIDE)

GROUND COVER
(VAPOR BARRIER)

Fig. 5-14. Installation of vapor barrier in a heated crawl space.

groundline in order to reduce heat loss. Insulation can be held in place with an approved mastic adhesive. To protect the insulation from moisture and to prevent moisture entry into the crawl space from the soil, a vapor barrier is used over the insulation below the groundline. See Fig. 5-14. Seams of the ground cover should be lapped and held in place with bricks or other bits of masonry. The crawl space of such construction is seldom ventilated.

For houses with crawl spaces, as well as other types, the finish grade outside the house should be sloped to drain water away from the foundation wall.

FINISHED BASEMENT ROOMS

Finished basement areas with fully or partly exposed walls are treated much the same as a framed wall with regard to the use of vapor barriers and insulation. See Fig. 5-15. When a full masonry wall is involved, other factors to consider are as follows:

☐ When drainage in the area is poor and soil is wet, the drain tile should be installed on the outside of the footing for removing excess water.

☐ In addition to an exterior wall coating, a waterproof coating should also be applied to the interior surface of the masonry to insure a dry wall.

☐ A vapor barrier should be used under the concrete floor slab to protect untreated wood sleepers or other materials from becoming wet.

Furring strips (2-by-2-inch or 2-by-3-inch members) used on the walls will provide:

☐ space for the blanket insulation with the attached vapor barrier.

☐ a nailing surface for interior finish (Fig. 5-15).

One or 1½-inch thicknesses of friction-type insulation with a vapor barrier of plastic film, such as 4-mil polyethylene or other materials, could also be used for the walls.

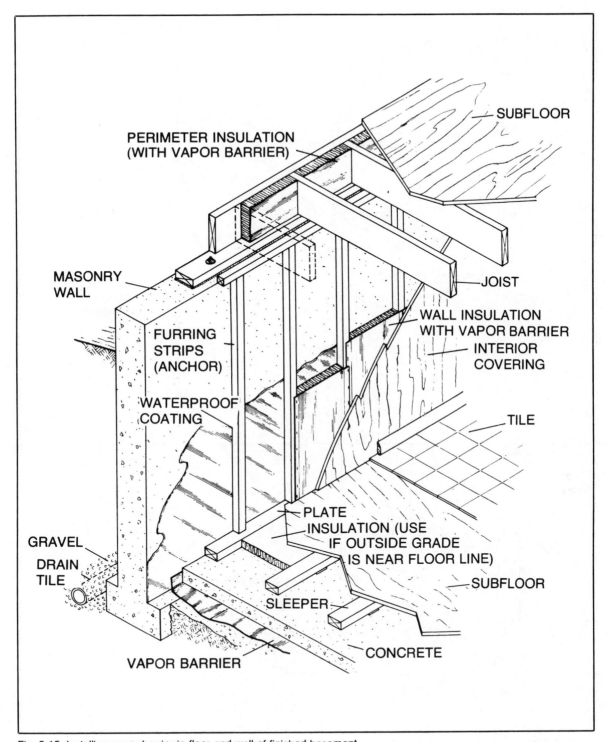

Fig. 5-15. Installing vapor barrier in floor and wall of finished basement.

107

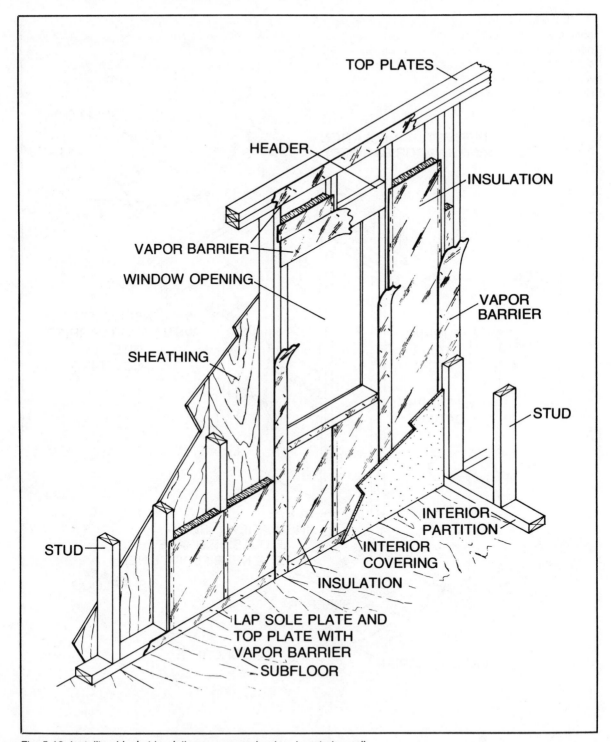

Fig. 5-16. Installing blanket insulation over vapor barriers in exterior wall.

If a vapor barrier has not been used under the concrete slab, place some type over the slab itself before applying the sleepers. Use treated 1-by-4's sleeps fastened to the slab with mastic followed by the vapor barrier and then by a second set of 1-by-4's sleepers placed over and nailed to the first set. Sub-floor and finish floor are then applied over the sleep-ers.

When the outside grade is near the level of the basement floor, use perimeter insulation around the exposed edges. See Fig. 5-15.

To prevent heat loss and minimize escape of water vapor, use blanket or batt insulation with at-tached vapor barriers around the perimeter of the floor framing above the foundation wall. See Fig. 5-15. Place the insulation between the joists or along stringer joists with the vapor barrier facing the base-ment side. The vapor barrier should fit tightly against the joists and subfloor.

WALLS

Blanket Insulation. To minimize vapor loss and possible condensation problems when flexible insula-tion in blanket or batt form is used in an entire wall, you can staple the tabs over the edge of the studs. See Fig. 5-16. If the tabs are fastened only to the inner faces of the studs, it usually results in some openings along the edge of the vapor barrier and, of course, a chance for vapor to escape and cause problems. Another technique is to staple a polyethylene vapor barrier to the studs.

Another factor in the use of flexible insulation having an integral vapor barrier is the protection re-quired around window and door openings. When the vapor barrier on the insulation does not cover doubled studs and header areas, use additional vapor barrier materials for protection. See Fig. 5-15.

At junctions of interior partitions with exterior walls, care should be taken to cover this intersection with some type of vapor barrier. For best protection, insulating the space between the doubled exterior wall studs and the application of a vapor barrier should be done before the corner post is assembled. See Fig. 5-16. The vapor barrier should at least cover the stud intersections at each side of the partition wall.

Friction Insulation. The development of this new process of installing insulation and vapor barriers has practically eliminated condensation problems in the walls. *Enveloping* is a process of installing a vapor barrier over the entire wall. This type vapor barrier

ordinarily consists of 4-mil or thicker polyethylene or similar material used in 8-foot wide rolls. After insula-tion has been placed, rough wiring or duct work finished, and window frames installed, the vapor bar-rier is placed over the entire wall. Staples are used where necessary to hold it in place. See Fig. 5-17.

Fig. 5-17. Installing vapor barrier over wall (courtesy of Owens-Corning Fiberglas Company).

Window and door headers, top and bottom plates, and other framing are completely covered. See Fig. 5-18. After rock lath plaster base or drywall finish is installed, the vapor barrier can be trimmed around window openings.

Reflective Insulations. Reflective insulations ordinarily consist of either a Kraft sheet faced on two sides with aluminum foil (A of Fig. 5-19) or the multiple-reflective "accordian" type (B of Fig. 5-19). Both are made to use between studs or joists. It is important in using such insulation that there is at least

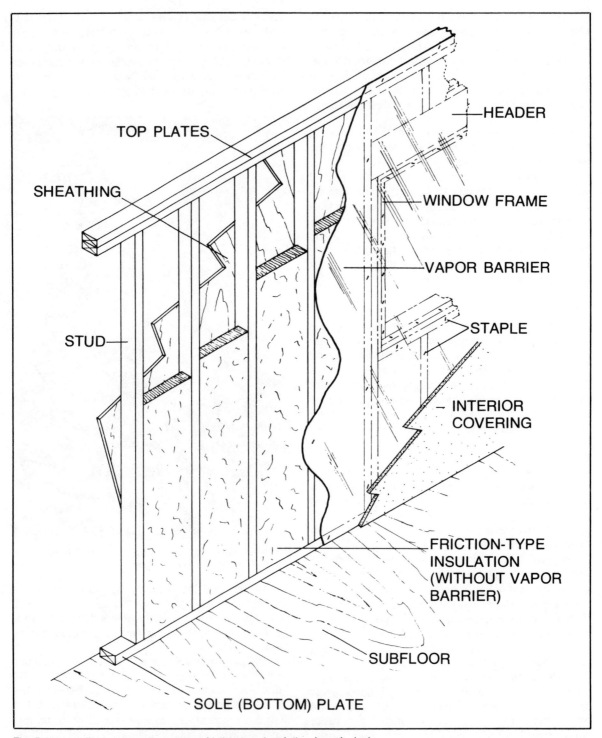

TOP PLATES

SHEATHING

STUD

HEADER

WINDOW FRAME

VAPOR BARRIER

STAPLE

INTERIOR COVERING

FRICTION-TYPE INSULATION (WITHOUT VAPOR BARRIER)

SUBFLOOR

SOLE (BOTTOM) PLATE

Fig. 5-18. Installing a vapor barrier over friction-type insulation (enveloping).

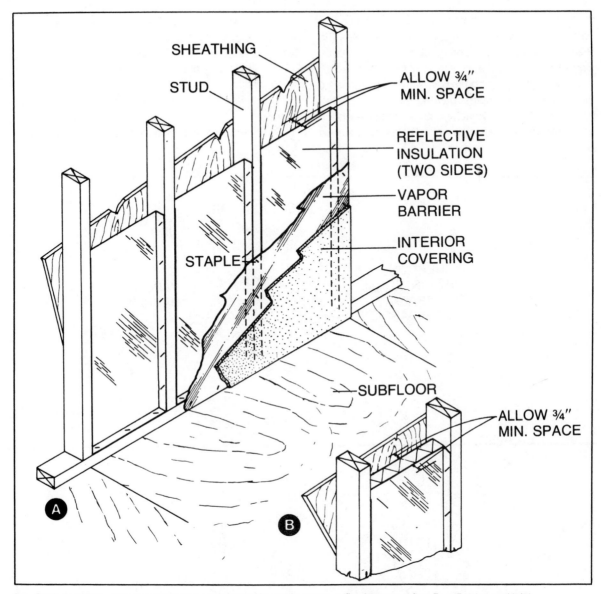

Fig. 5-19. Installing reflective insulation as barrier (A: single sheet, reflective two sides; B: reflective multiple).

a ¾-inch space between the reflective surface and wall, floor, or ceiling surface. When a reflective insulation is used, it is good practice to use a vapor barrier over the studs or joists. Place the barrier over the frame members just under the drywall or plaster base (A of Fig. 5-19). Gypsum board commonly used as a drywall finish can be obtained with an aluminum foil on the inside face which serves as a vapor barrier. When such material is used, the need for a separate vapor barrier is eliminated.

VAPOR BARRIER IN A TWO-STORY HOUSE

One area often overlooked in a two-story house, where a vapor barrier and additional insulation are often overlooked, is at the perimeter area of the second floor joists. Protect the space between the joists at the header and along the stringer joists by sections of batt insulation that contain a vapor barrier. See Fig. 5-20. Fit the sections together tightly so that both the vapor barriers and the insulation fill the joist spaces.

If your two-story house is designed so that part of the second floor projects beyond the first, usually a projection of about 12 inches, the projections should be insulated and vapor barriers should be installed. See Fig. 5-21.

Install insulation and vapor barriers in exposed second floor walls (Fig. 5-20) in the same manner as for walls of single-story houses. This would include:

☐ Standard blanket insulation with its integral vapor barrier.

☐ Friction-type insulation with separate vapor barrier.

☐ Reflective insulation with the protective vapor barrier.

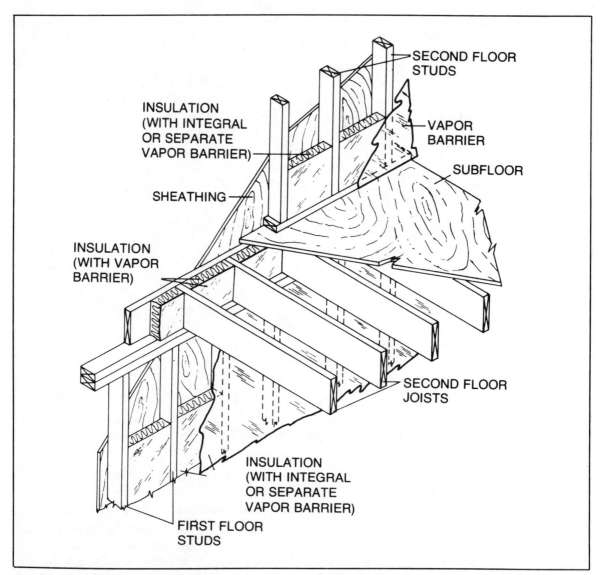

Fig. 5-20. Vapor barriers in walls and joist space of a two-story house.

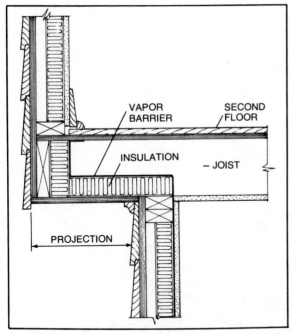

Fig. 5-21. Insulation and vapor barrier at a second-floor projection.

KNEE WALLS

In a 1½-story house, containing bedrooms and other occupied room son the second floor, *knee walls*—partial walls that extend from the floor to the rafts as shown in Fig. 5-22—usually have a height varying between 4 and 6 feet. Such areas must normally contain vapor barriers and insulation in the following area:

—In the first floor ceiling area.
—At the knee wall.
—Between the rafters.

Place insulation batts with the vapor barrier facing down between joists from the outside wall plate to the knee wall. Fill the entire joist space under the knee wall with insulation (Fig. 5-22). Take care to allow an airway for sttic ventilation at the junction of the rafter and exterior wall when placing the insulation.

Insulation in the knee wall can consist of blanket or batt-type instulation with integral vapor barrier or with separately applied vapor barriers.

Batt or blanket insulation is commonly used between the rafters at the sloping portion of a heated room (Fig. 5-22). Be sure that the vapor

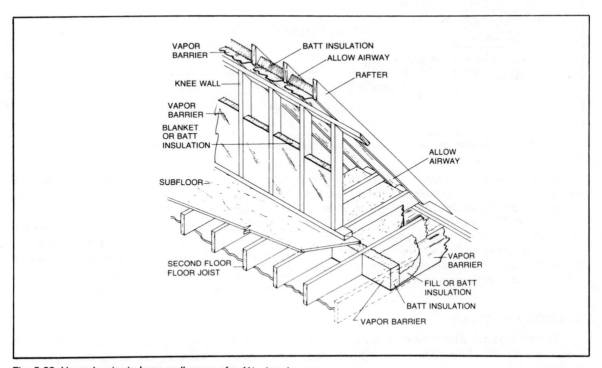

Fig. 5-22. Vapor barrier in knee wall areas of a 1½-story house.

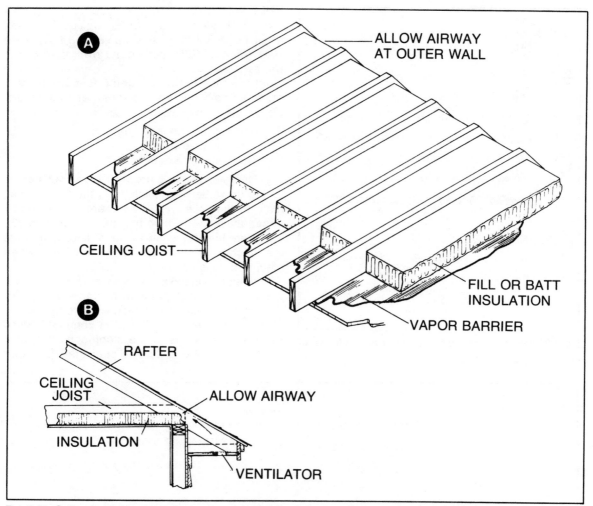

Fig. 5-23. Ceiling insulation and vapor barrier. (A: vapor barrier and insulation; B: airway for ventilation).

barrier faces the inner or warm side of the roof or wall. An airway should be allowed between the top of the insulation and the roof sheathing at each rafter space. This should be at least 1 inch clear space without obstructions such as might occur when solid blocking. This allows movement of air in the area behind the knee wall to the attic area above the second floor rooms (Fig. 5-7).

CEILINGS AND ATTICS

To provide for good condensation control, a vapor barrier should always be provided in ceilings and attics (Fig. 5-23). When an insulation batt is supplied with a vapor barrier on one face, no additional protection is required. Place the batts with barrier side down so that they fit tightly between ceiling joists. Batts with the vapor barrier attached can also be stapled to the bottom edge of the joists before the ceiling finish is applied. At the junction of the outside walls and rafters, leave a space below the roof boards to provide a ventilating airway. See Fig. 5-23.

VENTILATION

Ventilation of attic spaces and roof areas is important to minimize water vapor building. While good ventilation is important, there is still a need for vapor

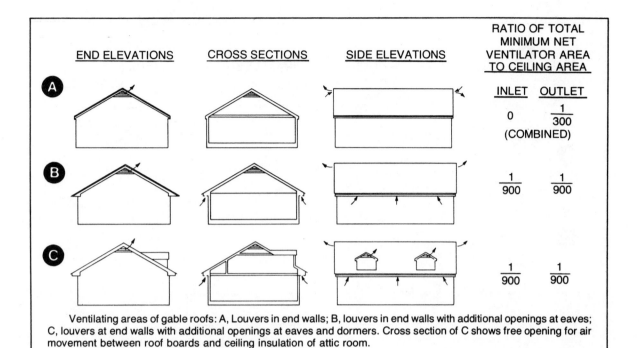

			RATIO OF TOTAL MINIMUM NET VENTILATOR AREA TO CEILING AREA	
END ELEVATIONS	CROSS SECTIONS	SIDE ELEVATIONS	INLET	OUTLET
A			0	$\frac{1}{300}$ (COMBINED)
B			$\frac{1}{900}$	$\frac{1}{900}$
C			$\frac{1}{900}$	$\frac{1}{900}$

Ventilating areas of gable roofs: A, Louvers in end walls; B, louvers in end walls with additional openings at eaves; C, louvers at end walls with additional openings at eaves and dormers. Cross section of C shows free opening for air movement between roof boards and ceiling insulation of attic room.

Fig. 5-24. Ventilating areas of gable roofs.

barriers in ceiling areas. This is especially true of the flat or low-slope roof where only a 1 to 3 inch space above the insulation might be available for ventilation.

In houses with attic spaces, the use of both inlet and outlet ventilation is recommended. Placing inlet ventilators in soffit or frieze-board areas of the cornice and outlet ventilators, as near the ridgeline as possible, will assure air movement through a "stack" effect.

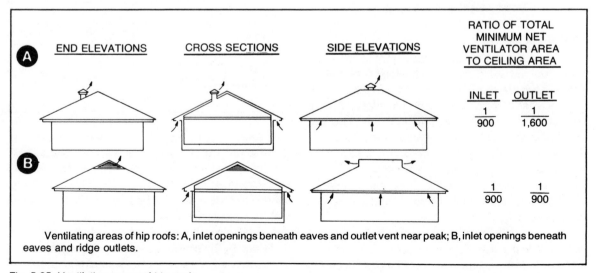

			RATIO OF TOTAL MINIMUM NET VENTILATOR AREA TO CEILING AREA	
END ELEVATIONS	CROSS SECTIONS	SIDE ELEVATIONS	INLET	OUTLET
A			$\frac{1}{900}$	$\frac{1}{1,600}$
B			$\frac{1}{900}$	$\frac{1}{900}$

Ventilating areas of hip roofs: A, inlet openings beneath eaves and outlet vent near peak; B, inlet openings beneath eaves and ridge outlets.

Fig. 5-25. Ventilating areas of hip roofs.

115

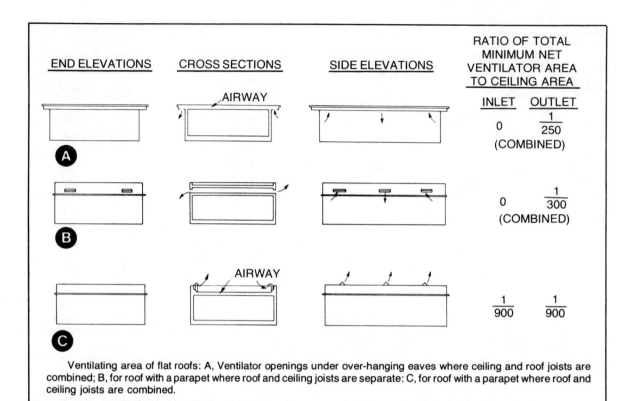

END ELEVATIONS	CROSS SECTIONS	SIDE ELEVATIONS	RATIO OF TOTAL MINIMUM NET VENTILATOR AREA TO CEILING AREA	
			INLET	OUTLET
A	AIRWAY		0	$\frac{1}{250}$ (COMBINED)
B			0	$\frac{1}{300}$ (COMBINED)
C	AIRWAY		$\frac{1}{900}$	$\frac{1}{900}$

Ventilating area of flat roofs: A, Ventilator openings under over-hanging eaves where ceiling and roof joists are combined; B, for roof with a parapet where roof and ceiling joists are separate: C, for roof with a parapet where roof and ceiling joists are combined.

Fig. 5-26. Ventilating area of flat roof.

This is due to the difference in height between inlet and outlet ventilators and it normally assures air movement even on windless days or nights.

Ventilating Areas

The minimum amount of attic or roof space ventilation required is determined by the total ceiling area. These ratios are shown in Figs. 5-24 through 5-26 for various types of roofs. The use of both inlet and outlet ventilators is recommended whenever possible. The total net area of ventilators is found by application of the ratios shown in Fig. 5-24 through 5-26. To find the total area of the ventilators, use the data provided in Table 5-2. Divide this total area by the number of ventilators used to find the recommended square-foot area of each.

For example, a gable roof similar to Fig. 5-24(B) with inlet and outlet ventilators has a minimum required total inlet and outlet ratio of 1/900 of the ceiling area. If the ceiling area of the house is 1350 square

Table 5-2. Crawl-Space Ventilation.

Crawl Space	Ratio of Total Net Ventilating Area To Floor Area[1]	Minimum Number of Ventilators[2]
Without vapor barrier	1/150	4
With vapor barrier	1/1500	2

1. The actual area of the ventilators depends on the type of louvers and the size of screen used (See Table 5-3)
2. Foundation ventilators should be distributed around foundation to provide best air movement. When two are used, place one toward the side of prevailing wind and the other on opposite side.

feet, each net inlet and outlet ventilating area should be 1350 divided by 900 or 1 1/3 square feet.

If ventilators are protected with No. 16-mesh insect screen and plain metal louvers (Table 5-2) the minimum gross area must be 2 times 1½ or 3 square feet. When one outlet ventilator is used at each gable end, each should have a gross area of 1½ square feet (3 divided by 2). When distributing the soffit inlet ventilators to three on each side, for a small house (total of 6), each ventilator should have a gross area of 0.5

116

Table 5-3. Ventilation Area Increase Required if Louvers and Screening are used in Crawl Spaces and Attics.

	To determine total area of ventilators[2], multiply required net area in square feet by
¼-inch-mesh hardware cloth	1¼
⅛-inch-mesh screen No. 16-mesh screen (with or without plain metal louvers)	2
Wood louvers and ¼-inch mesh hardware cloth[3]	2
Wood louvers and ⅛-inch-mesh screen[3]	2¼
Wood louvers and No. 16-mesh insect screen[3]	3

1. In crawl-space ventilators, screen openings should not be larger than ¼ inch; in attic spaces no larger than ⅛ inch.
2. Net area for attics determined by ratios in Figs. 5-24, 5-25 and 5-26.
3. If metal louvers have dripedges that reduce the opening, use same ratio as shown for wood louvers.

square feet. For long houses, use 6 or more on each side.

Inlet Ventilators

Inlet ventilators in the soffit can consist of several designs. Distribute them as much as possible to prevent "dead" air pockets in the attic where moisture might collect. A continuous screened slot (A of Fig. 5-27) takes care of this. Small screened openings such as in B of Fig. 5-27 can be used.

For flat-roof houses where roof members serve as both rafters and ceiling joists, use continuous slots or individual ventilators between roof members. Lo-

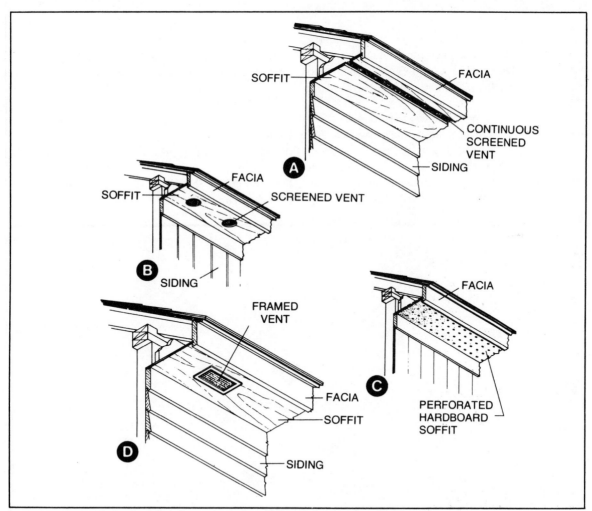

Fig. 5-27. Inlet ventilators in soffits (A: continuous vent; B: round vents; C: perforated; D: single).

117

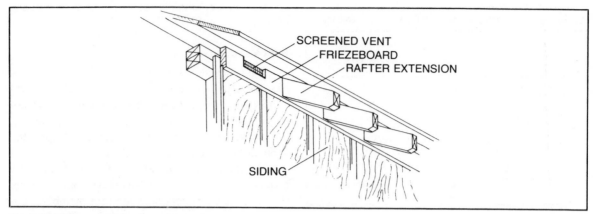

Fig. 5-28. Frieze ventilator for open cornice.

cate the openings away from the wall line to minimize the possible entry of wind-driven snow. A soffit consisting of perforated hardboard (C of Fig. 5-27) can also be used to advantage, but holes should be no larger than ⅛ inch in diameter.

Small metal frames with screened openings are also available and can be used in soffit areas (D of Fig. 5-27). For open cornice design, the use of a frieze board with screen ventilating slots would be satisfactory (Fig. 5-28). Perforated hardboard might also be used for this purpose. The minimum inlet ventilating ratios shown in Figs. 5-24 through 5-26 should be followed in determining total net ventilating areas for both inlet and outlet ventilators.

Outlet Ventilators

To be most effective, outlet ventilators should be located as close to the highest portion of the ridge as possible. They can be placed in the upper wall section of a gable-roofed house in various forms as shown in Fig. 5-29 (A and B). In wide gable-end overhangs with ladder framing, a number of screened openings can

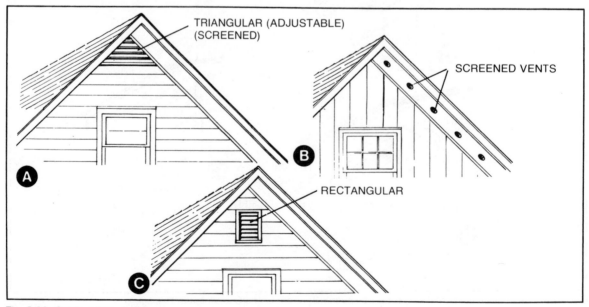

Fig. 5-29. Gable outlet ventilators.

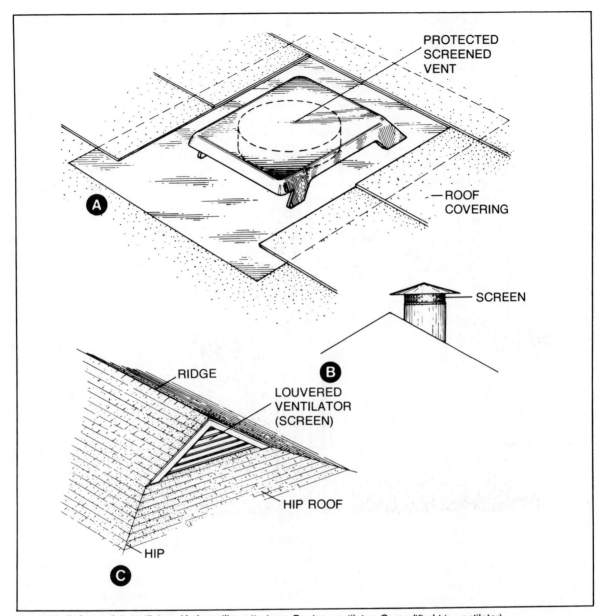

Fig. 5-30. Ridge outlet ventilators (A: low silhouette type; B: pipe ventilator; C: modified hip ventilator).

be located in the soffit area of the lookouts (C of Fig. 5-29).

Ventilating openings to the attic space should not be blocked. Outlet ventilators on gable or hip roofs can also consist of some type of roof ventilator. See Fig. 30 (A and B). Hip roofs can use a ventilating gable (modified hip). See Fig. 5-30(C).

Protection from blowing snow must be considered. This often restricts the use of a continuous ridge vent. Locate the single roof ventilators (Fig. 5-30 A and B) along the ridge toward the rear of the house so that they are not visible from the front. Outlet ventilators can also be located in a chimney as a false flue. A screened opening to the attic would be used.

SNOW BELT PROTECTION

Water leakage into walls and interiors of houses in the snow belt area of the country is sometimes caused by ice dams and is often mistaken for condensation. Such problems occur after heavy snowfalls when there is sufficient heat loss from the living quarters to melt the snow along the roof surface. The water moves down the roof surface to the colder overhang of the roof where it freezes. This causes a ledge of ice and backs up water that can enter the wall or drip down onto the ceiling finish (A of Fig. 5-31).

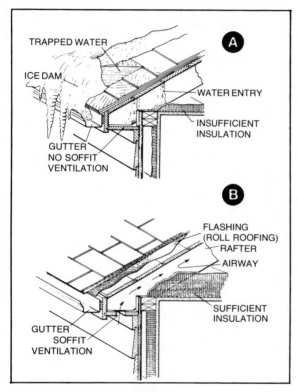

Fig. 5-31. Ice dams. A: Insufficient insulation and ventilation can cause ice dams and water drainage. B: Good ventilation inside and roof flashing minimizes moisture.

Ice dams can be minimized by reducing attic temperatures, by adequate insulation, and by ventilation. Good insulation, 6 inches or more in the Northern sections of the country, greatly reduces heat loss from the house. Adequate ventilation, in turn, tends to keep attics dry with temperatures only slightly above outdoor temperatures. This combination of good ventilation and insulation is the answer to reducing ice dam problems.

An additional protective measure is provided by the use of a flashing material. A 36-inch width of 45-pound roll roofing along the eave line will provide such added protection. See Fig. 5-31A.

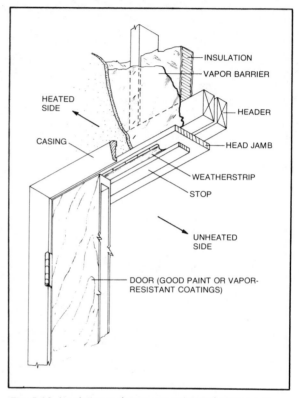

Fig. 5-32. Insulating a door to an unheated attic space.

PROTECTION AT UNHEATED AREAS

Walls and doors to unheated areas such as attic spaces should be treated to resist water vapor movement as well as to minimize heat loss. This includes the use of insulation and vapor barriers on all wall areas adjacent the cold attic (Fig. 5-32). Vapor barriers should face the warm side of the room.

In addition, some means should be used to prevent heat and vapor loss around the perimeter of the door. One method is through some type of weather strip (Fig. 5-32). The door should be given several finish coats of paint or varnish. This will resist the movement of water vapor.

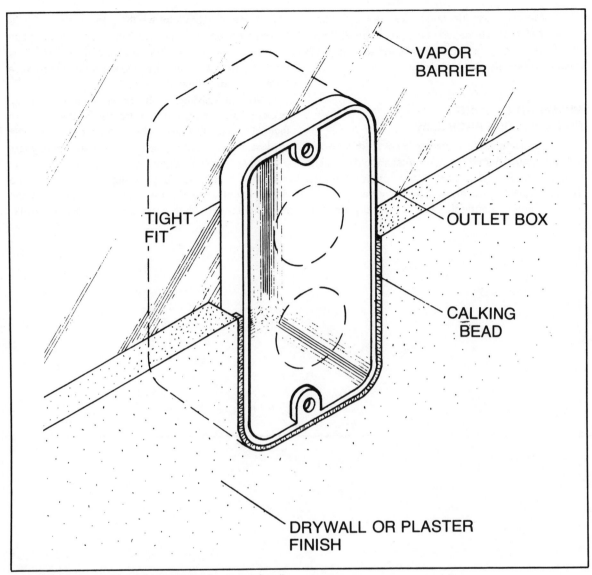

Fig. 5-33. Protection around outer boxes in exposed walls.

If further resistance to heat loss is needed, a covering of ½ inch (or thicker) rigid insulation, such as insulation board or foamed plastic, can be attached to the back of the door.

PROTECTION AT OUTLET BOXES

Outlet (switch) boxes or other openings in exposed (cold) walls often are difficult to treat to prevent water vapor escape. Initially, whether the vapor barrier is a separate sheet or part of the insulation, as tight a fit as possible should be made when trimming the barrier around the box. See Fig. 5-33.

This is less difficult when the barrier is separate. As an additional precaution, apply a bead of caulking compound around the box after the dry wall or the plastic base has been installed (Fig. 5-33). The same caulking can be used around the cold-air return ducts or other openings in exterior walls.

Some switch and junction boxes are more difficult to seal than others because of their makeup. A simple polyethylene bag or other enclosure around such boxes will provide some protection.

MINIMIZING EXISTING CONDENSATION PROBLEMS

Control household humidity. In cold climates, controls for relative humidity in the winter should be set no higher than 35 to 40 percent. When outdoor temperatures are 20° F or lower, reduce the humidity to less than 35 percent. Although a higher humidity might be healthier and might improve the performance of your heating system, it could cause serious condensation problems in your home. When condensation develops on insulated glass windows, you know that the relative humidity is definitely too high.

Normal activities in the home such as bathing, cooking, and doing the laundry add to the moisture level. Exhaust fans in baths and kitchens will help eliminate this moisture before it spreads throughout the house. Clothes dryers should be vented to the outdoors. If high humidity persists, consider using a dehumidifier and set the controls higher than the humidity that is recommended for your climate zone.

Chapter 6

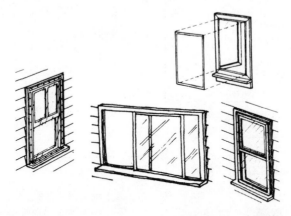

Windows and Doors

DOORS AND WINDOWS REPRESENT 15 to 20 percent of the wall space of an average house. Poorly insulated windows and doors will account for an important percentage of the total heat loss no matter how well or poorly insulated the house is otherwise.

Good windows should have sashes that fit tightly in their frames, but still allow smooth operation. The channels or grooves that hold the sash should have weather stripping installed to keep wind from blowing through the window. Wood windows provide natural insulation. See Figs. 6-1 through 6-3.

There are many ways to use doors and windows that will provide energy efficiency and home beauty. Today's windows are picked more for the view and the light they let in than for the amount of ventilation they give. Even door designs are stressing views (such as the wide-sliding patio doors).

Ventilation has taken a back seat due to the more sophisticated heating and cooling systems of today's homes. But with the concerns for energy conservation, ventilation might come back as a substitute for air conditioning.

How do you choose which window and which type of door to use? How do you go about doing all of the necessary items such as caulking, weatherizing, and installing? With windows, you can narrow down the field by asking yourself four questions:

- ☐ What kind of view will you have?
- ☐ How easy is it to clean?
- ☐ Will it be easy to open and close where it is located?
- ☐ Will it provide good ventilation (if needed)?

There are three basic types of windows to consider:
- —Fixed.
- —Sliding.
- —Swinging.

There are many variations in design and style under these categories. Choosing the type of window you feel is best for your needs is only one part of window selection. You must also pay attention to materials used in the makeup of that window. What's the glass made of? How about the frame around it? And what about the quality of the hardware? Cost too is a major factor in making any purchasing decision. Compare total costs by:

- ☐ Finding the cost of the window unit.

Fig. 6-1. Double-hung window with weather stripping.

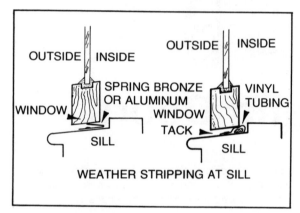

Fig. 6-2. Sill display.

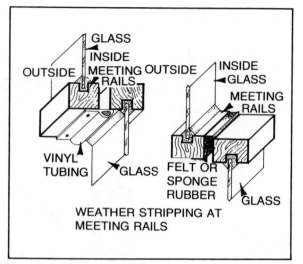

Fig. 6-3. Meeting rails.

□ Adding to the basic costs the extras such as hardware and screens, plus installation and finishing costs. If you are doing it yourself, the installation costs can be deleted.

In general it is wise to purchase the best quality windows and doors you can afford. The guide for window shoppers, Table 6-1, and the guide for window materials, Table 6-2, provide breakdowns for types of windows and their relevant information.

If you're looking at wood doors, the solid door is the highest quality and the highest priced. The hollow-core doors might have high-quality veneer faces, but the lower-priced ones are covered with less durable wood-composition board. The solid door has a wood-filled core between two slabs of high-quality wood veneer such as birch, oak, or mahogony.

Modern insulated steel doors are gaining favor for exterior use. They can be used in cold areas and in hot areas because they are extremely beneficial for energy efficiency. They keep the hot air out and the cool (air conditioning) air in. They do not warp, shrink, or swell with weather changes. And they need painting less often.

Like wood doors, steel doors come in designed styles and they can be fitted with glass openings for viewing. Those with magnetic gaskets that grip like a refrigerator door give the tightest seal against the weather. They are usually prehung so the frame and hinges are included when you purchase. The cost for steel doors is quite comparable with commonly used wood doors.

Whether you buy wood, steel or glass, give the width of the doorway careful consideration. To move major pieces of furniture in and out, at least one door in the house needs to be a minimum of 36 inches wide. This generally is the front door. But width can be a factor in interior doorways as well.

Interior doors are usually either wood or metal. And some plastic is used. For wood doors used inside, hollow-core construction is most commonly used. Solid wood is also available. Thickness of an interior door is less than that of doors made for exterior use because this thinner construction is not meant to stand outside use. See Table 6-3.

Most wood doors are sold unfinished, but factory-finished doors are available. Metal doors are usually factory-primed. Most metal doors are made of steel.

Before you choose windows and doors, make yourself a checklist as follows. Must your windows:

Table 6-1. Guide for Window Shoppers.

Window Type	How Does It Operate?	Is it Easy to clean?	How is it for Viewing?	How is it for Ventilating?
FIXED	Does not open, requires no screens or hardware	Outside job for exterior of window	No obstruction to views or light	No ventilation Minimum air leakage
SLIDING Double-Hung	Sash pushed up and down. Easy to operate except over sink or counter	Inside job if sash is removable	Horizontal can cut view	Only half can be open
Horizontal Sliding	Sash pushes sideways in metal or plastic tracks	Inside job if sash is removable	Vertical divisions cut view less than horizontal divisions	Only half can be open
SWINGING Casement (Side-Hinged)	Swings out with push-bar or crank. Latch locks sash tightly	Inside job if there is arm space on hinged side	Vertical divisions cut view less than horizontal	Opens fully. Can scoop air into house
Awining (Top Hinged)	Usually swings out with push-bar or crank. May swing inward when used high in wall.	Usually an inside job unless hinges prevent access to outside of glass	Single units offer clear view. Stacked units have horizontal divisions that cut view	Open fully. Upward airflow if open outward; downward flow when open inward
(Bottom Hinged)	Swings inward, operated by a lock handle at top of sash	Easily cleaned from inside	Not a viewing window, usually set low in wall	Airflow is directed upward
Jalousie	A series of horizontal glass slates open outward with crank	Inside job, but many small sections to clean	Multiple glass divisions cutting horizontally across view	Airflow can be adjusted in amount and direction

Capture a view outside.
Let plenty of daylight stream in.
Ventilate the house adequately.
Make your home weathertight.
Open and close easily.
Clean easily from the inside.
Enhance the appearance of your house.
Must you have doors that:
Won't interfere with each other.
Insulate well against cold.
Won't interfere with house traffic.
Require the least upkeep.
Are wide enough to meet needs.

By installing the proper doors and windows, you might be able to cut your heating bill in half. Even if you do have storm windows and doors, they might not be giving you the best protection. The key to success in weatherizing windows and doors is providing a "dead" air space between panes of glass or plastic (an air gap between ¼ of an inch and 2 inches is satisfactory, but a ¾ inch gap is best). Any of the following methods will be useful in providing this air space.

INSULATED GLASS

An excellent permanent solution is to use insulated glass windows (sheets of glass with an air space between) in place of single panes. There are several good insulated windows on the market. They are the most practical for new construction. Cleaning insulated glass windows is easier than cleaning storm windows. Insulated glass, however, is more expensive to replace when broken.

Table 6-2. Guide for Window Materials.

GLASS AREA

Single-strength glass	Suitable for small panes. Longest dimensions are about 40 inches
Double-strength glass	Thicker, stronger glass suitable for larger panes. Longest dimensions are about 60 inches
Plate glass	Thicker and stronger for still larger panes
Insulating glass	Two layers of glass separated by a dead-air space and sealed at edges. Desirable for all windows in cold climates to reduce heating costs. Noise transmission is also reduced
Safety glass	Acrylic or plexiglass panels eliminate the hazard of accidental breakage. Panels scratch more easily than glass. Laminated glass as used in automobiles also reduces breakage hazard

FRAME

Wood	Preferable in cold climates as there is less problem with moisture condensation. Should be treated to resist decay and moisture absorption. Painting needed on outside unless frame is covered with factory-applied vinyl shield or other good coating
Aluminum	Painting not needed unless color change is desired. Condensation a problem in cold climates unless frame is specially constructed to reduce heat transfer. Often less tight than wood frames.
Steel	Painting necessary to prevent rusting unless it is stainless steel. Condensation a problem in cold climates.
Plastic	Lightweight and corrosion-free. Painting not needed except to change color
HARDWARE	Best handles, hinges, latches, locks, etc., usually are steel or brass. Aluminum satisfactory for some items but not often less durable. Some plastics and pot metal are often disappointing.

If metal (aluminum) windows are used, they should be the type with *thermal break*. This is also known as dead air space (Fig. 6-4). Windows should have locks that provide security and also hold the window tight in its frame. Tight-fitting windows help prevent wind from blowing into the house. Good doors also should fit their frames and they should be weather stripped. A solid threshold of wood or aluminum with a vinyl insert should be fitted tightly against the bottom of the door. See Figs. 6-5 through 6-7.

STORM WINDOWS

Either prefabricated metal windows or wooden storm windows will do the job. Metal storm windows usually come completely assembled and ready for installation. You will probably have to make adjustments when you install the windows. These units usually are displayed where they are sold so you can examine them closely before you buy. If you install your own units, carefully follow instructions from the dealer.

Wooden storm windows are just as useful, but they require periodic painting and space for summer storage. Single-pane, wood-frame storm windows are usually removed in the summer and replaced with screens. The windows usually must be painted every two or three years to preserve the wood frames. Putty holding the glass in place also must be checked and replaced regularly. See Fig. 6-8.

Table 6-3. Guide for Interior Doors.

TYPE OF DOOR	
Hinged	The most common type for openings 18 to 36 inches wide. Use wherever there is no objection to a swinging door.
Bi-fold	A special type of hinged door. Panels fold against each other to reduce swing-out space. Gives access to full width of closets. Use in openings 3-8' wide.
Glide-by	Two or more door panels slide by each other. Main use is on closets where door projection is not permissible. Gives access to only half the opening at once.
Pocket	Door which slides into wall. Use where a hinged door would interfere with traffic or other doors.
Folding	A special type of sliding door with accordion-fold sections. It can substitute for the other types, but door width is reduced unless a stacking pocket is provided

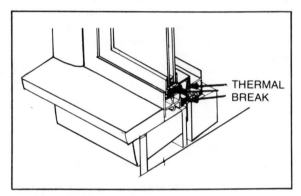

Fig. 6-4. Metal window with a thermal break.

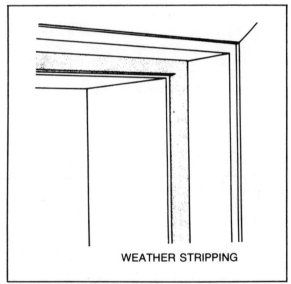

Fig. 6-6. Weather stripping a door.

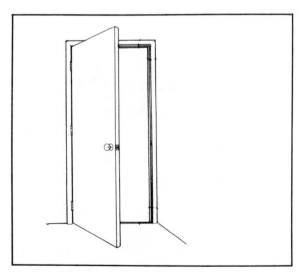

Fig. 6-5. Wood door with weather stripping.

Combination storm and screen units store the storm windows and screen in place and make converting for winter to summer an easy project. The units are usually made of aluminum with either a natural finish or a baked-enamel finish. Well-made aluminum storm windows have hardware that is easy to manipulate, strong corner joints, weather stripping and ventilation holes where the storm window rests on the window sill. The vents drain away condensation that can accumulate on the storm window during the winter and rainwater that can collect behind the frame when the screen is in place. See Fig. 6-9.

Fig. 6-7. Aluminum threshold and weather stripping.

Most storm windows have frames for windows with either two or three tracks for the up-and-down movement of glass and screen inserts. Regardless of the number of tracks, you should be able to remove all the inserts from the inside of the house.

The triple-track frame allows you to move all the inserts separately to up or down positions. You can also remove them separately from the frame. Although triple-track frames are more expensive, there free movement of inserts does permit you to clean and ventilate easier at either the top or bottom of the window. You can also get frames with inserts that you can tilt in.

For the double-track frame, the screen insert is under the outside top glass inserts and supports it. You can raise or lower the bottom glass insert for ventilation. You must remove the screen from the outside track before you can remove the upper glass insert from the frame.

Factory-built storm windows or panels for casement, sliding, awning, and picture windows require special designs, depending upon the style of the original window. You can insulate most windows of this type by removing the screen panels and replacing them with glass or plastic panels on the inside of the existing window.

Storm windows also are available for basement casement windows; they open either to the inside or outside of the basement.

Fig. 6-8. Wooden storm window with a single pane.

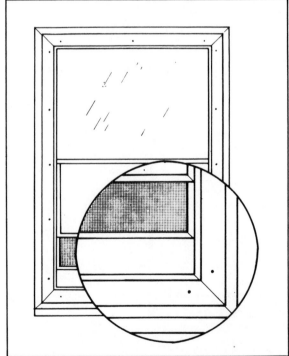

Fig. 6-9. Combination storm window and screen window.

PLASTIC COVERS
FOR DOORS AND WINDOWS

Plastic can give you the same effective insulation as permanent storm units. People living on fixed incomes should consider this type of energy-efficient window covering in lieu of remodeling. You can either use the plastic to cover your present doors, windows, or screens, or you can mount the plastic covering on its own separate fitted frame.

Plastic comes in rolled sheets or already cut and packed in kits that include tacking strips, tacks, and instructions for installation. The plastic film varies in thickness, clearness, and resistance to deterioration by sunlight. Polyethylene, for example, is cloudy, flexible, and it lasts from 2 to 3 years in direct sunlight. Polyester film is clear and rigid, but might rattle when the wind is high. It is usually finished in 7-mil thickness and stays clear from 6 to 7 years or longer. Plastic sheets of the same thickness as glass are available and they can be effectively used in place of glass. It is not, however, nearly as scratch resistant as glass. During warm months, plastic will have to be removed for ventilation. See Fig. 6-10.

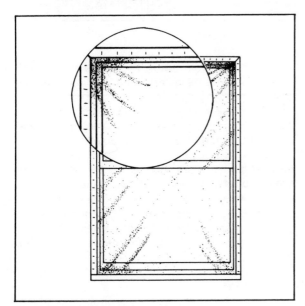

Fig. 6-10. Plastic sheeting.

STORM DOORS

Storm doors can be wood frames with screens to replace the glass during the summer or combination storm and screen doors that allow you to switch for summer to winter without having to remove the glass or screen. Safety glass or plastic should be used in storm doors to prevent injuries that can occur if glass is broken. See Fig. 6-11.

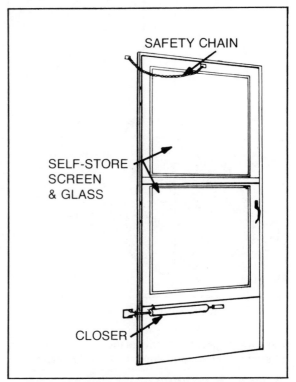

Fig. 6-11. Combination storm and screen door.

There are several types of metal storm doors. Pick one that suits the style of your house. Look especially for strength and rigidity of framing. Combination screen and storm doors are popular. Self-storing glass panels that slide out of the way for ventilation are convenient, but they will probably cost more.

Buy storm doors with tempered safety glass or nonbreakable rigid plastic to reduce breakage hazards. A grille or bar across the door at the point where your body is most likely to press against the door will also help reduce breakage. See Figs. 6-12 and 6-13.

Kick plates at the bottom prevent damage from continued use. Automatic closing devices and strong safety springs are important. This is particularly true in windy locations. Wooden storm doors are equally as effective as metal storm doors, if not slightly more so, but they require painting. Table 6-4 compares some of

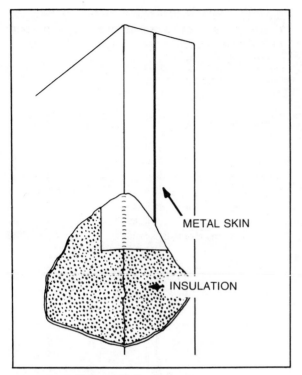

Fig. 6-12. Cutaway view of a metal door.

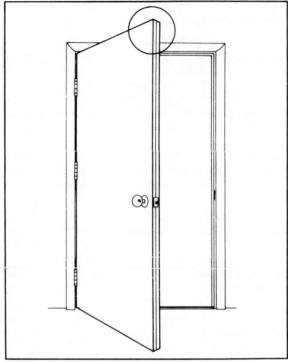

Fig. 6-13. A metal door.

the advantages and disadvantages of the three types of storm windows and doors that are available.

MAKING SELECTIONS

When selecting storm doors and windows, consider the following points.

The strength of the main frames and frames for the glass or screen inserts is important. Also look for good design to assure easy and efficient handling.

Look for weathertightness to prevent the entrance of water, cold air, dust, and insects. An opening or weep system is standard at the base of all storm windows to release excessive moisture.

You should be able to remove the glass and

screen inserts from the inside of the house. This makes house cleaning easier and requires no outside climbing.

Think ahead to possible repair problems. Does the dealer offer repair service or can you get replacement parts and do the repairs yourself?

When you buy new units, check to see that you have all the hardware such as hinges, closers, wind chains, locking latches, vinyl base weatherstripping, and screws. Check the quality and sturdiness.

Are materials, workmanship, finish, and assembly under warranty for an adequate period?

Select the appropriate finish to match your exterior finish.

Table 6-4. Storm Windows and Doors.

	Initial Cost	Durability	Maintenance	Operational Ease	Installation
Plastic	Low	Poor	High	Difficult	Easy
Single Pane	Medium to high	Good	Medium	Difficult	Easy
Combination	High	Excellent	Low	Easy	Difficult

Table 6-5. Recommended Humidity Levels.

Outside Air Temperature	Recommended Relative Humidity
−20 degrees F or below	Not more than 15%
−20 degrees F to −10 degrees F.	Not more than 20%
−10 degrees F to 0 degrees F	Not more than 25%
0 degrees F to 10 degrees F	Not more than 30%
10 degrees F to 20 degrees F	Not more than 35%

When metal framed storm panels are placed on metal storm windows, use a gasket to prevent metal-to-metal contact.

AVOIDING MOISTURE PROBLEMS

You'll have less condensation on the inside surfaces of glass panes when you install storm doors and windows. There might be some condensation if you draw drapes or shades at night or if the inside air is especially moist. Remember that while plastic storm covers should be snug, they need not be completely airtight. Weep vents in aluminum storm windows also allow a small circulation of air to prevent condensation.

Weatherstripping on sashes of the house windows can prevent moisture condensation inside the storm windows. Table 6-5 indicates the recommended

Table 6-6. Window Problems and Solutions.

Problems	Solutions
Cracks between plaster and frames of windows or doors Cracks in nonoperating parts of windows or doors	Caulking
Cracks in and around operating parts of windows	Weather stripping
Single glazing in relatively draft-free windows and doors	Storm Windows and Doors
Gusts of cold wind entering when door is opened	Storm Doors
Deteriorated doors or windows	New Doors, New Windows with insulating glass and/or storm window. Made-to-fit windows and doors make replacement quick, easy and economical.
Condensation on windows	Storm windows or multiple layers of glass and control humidity.

humidity levels for your home in relationship to outside temperatures. These recommended humidity levels will reduce the possibilities of condensation problems. The relative humidities assume 70 degrees indoor air temperature. Lower humidities would be required for higher indoor temperatures.

If condensation problems are evident on your inside windows, in the form of fog or frost, even at recommended humidity levels, the following are additional steps you can take to reduce condensation on your windows. (Also see Table 6-6.) They are especially appropriate if you don't have storm windows:

☐ Add storm windows or double glazing.
☐ Shut off the furnace.
☐ Make sure attic louvers are open.
☐ Run ventilating fans longer and more often.
☐ Ventilate the entire house briefly and more often.
☐ Get the most condensation-free window you can.

CAULK AND WEATHERSTRIPPING

Caulking and weatherstripping are good inexpensive ways to save energy. It's worth your while to check to see if you need caulking, putty, or weatherstripping on your windows and doors.

Look at a typical window and a typical door. Look at the parts shown in Fig. 6-14. Check the box next to the description that best fits what you see for your individual problem.

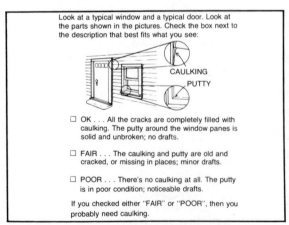

Look at a typical window and a typical door. Look at the parts shown in the pictures. Check the box next to the description that best fits what you see:

CAULKING
PUTTY

☐ OK . . . All the cracks are completely filled with caulking. The putty around the window panes is solid and unbroken; no drafts.

☐ FAIR . . . The caulking and putty are old and cracked, or missing in places; minor drafts.

☐ POOR . . . There's no caulking at all. The putty is in poor condition; noticeable drafts.

If you checked either "FAIR" or "POOR", then you probably need caulking.

Fig. 6-14. A typical window-check system.

Windows. Look at the parts shown in Fig. 6-15. This is a typical window. Check the box next to the description that best suits your individual needs.

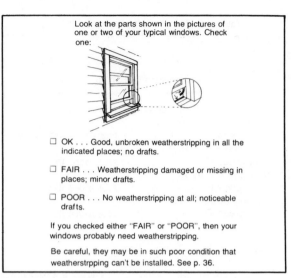

Look at the parts shown in the pictures of one or two of your typical windows. Check one:

☐ OK . . . Good, unbroken weatherstripping in all the indicated places; no drafts.

☐ FAIR . . . Weatherstripping damaged or missing in places; minor drafts.

☐ POOR . . . No weatherstripping at all; noticeable drafts.

If you checked either "FAIR" or "POOR", then your windows probably need weatherstripping.

Be careful, they may be in such poor condition that weatherstrpping can't be installed. See p. 36.

Fig. 6-15. Do your windows need weatherstripping?

Doors. Look at the parts of doors shown in Fig. 6-16. Check one. If you checked "OK" for all items, then you don't need caulking, putty, or weatherstripping. If you checked "Fair" or "Poor" for any item, use Table 6-7 to find your cost. Use the spaces in Fig. 6-17 for ease in finding your cost.

This cost is your estimated do-it-yourself cost. If you get a contractor to do it, your costs will be greater (at least two to four times as much). Prices vary from area to area and from job to job, so check with local contractors for an estimate if you don't do it yourself.

Look at the parts of your doors shown in the picture. Check one:

☐ OK . . . Good, unbroken weatherstripping in all the indicated places; no drafts.

☐ FAIR . . . Weatherstripping damaged or missing in places; minor drafts.

☐ POOR . . . No weatherstripping at all; noticeable drafts.

If you checked either "FAIR" or "POOR", then your doors probably need weatherstripping.

Fig. 6-16. Check your door.

Table 6-7. Find Your Cost.

1. Multiply the number of windows that need caulking and putty times the cost per window_____ × \$0.90 = _____
   No. of windows

2. Multiply the number of windows that need weather stripping times the cost per window_____ × \$4.00 = _____
   No. of windows

3. Multiply the number of doors that need caulking times the cost per door_____ × \$0.85 = _____
   No. of doors

4. Multiply the number of doors that need weather stripping times the cost per door _____ × \$6.75 = _____
   No. of doors

5. Add these numbers to get the total cost
   TOTAL COST \$_____

Tools

Besides weatherstripping materials and caulking compounds, you will need these simple tools:

—Hammer and nails.
—Scissors or tin snips.
—Screwdriver.
—A steel measuring tape.
—A caulking gun.
—A putty knife (Fig. 6-18).

Weatherstripping Windows

Weatherstripping windows can be accomplished by even the most inexperienced handyman. A minimum of tools and skills is required. Before starting, make sure that both the moving parts of your windows (the sash) and the channels that the sash slide in aren't so rotted that they won't hold the small nails used for weatherstripping. If they are badly rotted,

Find Your Savings Factor
Fill out only the lines that apply to your house:

A YOUR WINDOWS

Multiply these two numbers

caulking and putty:

in FAIR condition: _____ X 0.3 = [   ]
number of windows

in POOR condition: _____ X 1.0 = [   ]
number of windows

weather stripping:

in FAIR condition: _____ X 1.0 = [   ]
number of windows

in POOR condition: _____ X 8.4 = [   ]
number of windows

B YOUR DOORS

Multiply these two numbers

caulking:

in FAIR condition: _____ X 0.3 = [   ]
number of doors

in POOR condition: _____ X 0.9 = [   ]
number of doors

weather stripping:

in FAIR condition: _____ X 2.0 = [   ]
number of doors

in POOR condition: _____ X 16.8 = [   ] **+**
number of doors

C Add up all the numbers you've written in the boxes to the right and write the total here: This number is your savings factor. _____ SAVINGS FACTOR [   ]

Fig. 6-17. Savings chart.

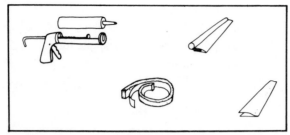

Fig. 6-18. Tools needed.

don't weatherstrip. Consider replacing the entire window unit first. Call your lumberyard or window dealer for an evaluation or cost estimate. See Fig. 6-19.

Tools

Hammer and nails.
Screwdriver.
Tin snips.
Tape measure (Fig. 6-20).

Safety

Upper-story windows can be a problem. You should be able to do all work from the inside, but avoid awkward leaning out of windows when tacking weather stripping in place. If you find that you need to use a ladder, observe the following precautions.

☐ Level and block the ladder in place. Have a helper hold it if possible.

☐ Don't try to reach that extra little bit; get down and move the ladder.

☐ Carry your caulking gun with a sling so that you can use both hands climbing the ladder. Carry other tools the same way.

Fig. 6-19. Weather stripping your windows.

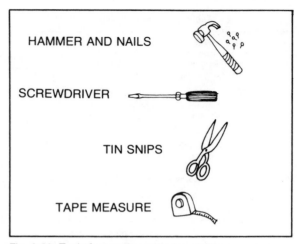

Fig. 6-20. Tools for weather stripping windows.

Materials

Thin Spring Metal. Installed in the channel of the window so it is virtually invisible. Somewhat difficult to install. Very durable.

Rolled Vinyl. With or without metal backing. Visible when installed. Easy to install. Durable.

Foam Rubber Adhesive Backing. Easy to install. Breaks down and wears rather quickly. Not as effective a sealer as metal springs or rolled vinyl. Never use where friction occurs. See Fig. 6-21.

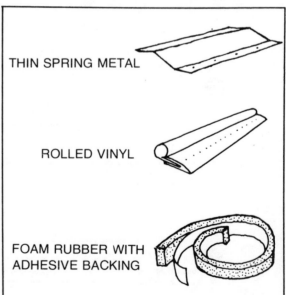

Fig. 6-21. Materials needed.

Weather stripping is purchased either by the running foot or in kit form for each window. In either case, you'll have to make a list of your windows, and measure them to find the total length of weather stripping you'll need. Measure the total distance around the edges of the moving parts of each window type you have. Be sure to allow for waste. If you buy the kit form, be sure the kit is intended for your window type and size. See Fig. 6-22.

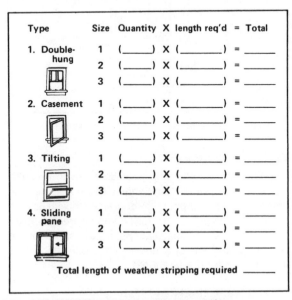

Type	Size	Quantity	X	length req'd	=	Total
1. Double-hung	1	(_____)	X	(_____)	=	_____
	2	(_____)	X	(_____)	=	_____
	3	(_____)	X	(_____)	=	_____
2. Casement	1	(_____)	X	(_____)	=	_____
	2	(_____)	X	(_____)	=	_____
	3	(_____)	X	(_____)	=	_____
3. Tilting	1	(_____)	X	(_____)	=	_____
	2	(_____)	X	(_____)	=	_____
	3	(_____)	X	(_____)	=	_____
4. Sliding pane	1	(_____)	X	(_____)	=	_____
	2	(_____)	X	(_____)	=	_____
	3	(_____)	X	(_____)	=	_____
Total length of weather stripping required						_____

Fig. 6-22. Complete for your particular window.

Installation

Install by moving sash to the open position and sliding strip in between the sash and the channel. Tack in place into the casing. Do not cover the pulleys in the upper channels. See Fig. 6-23.

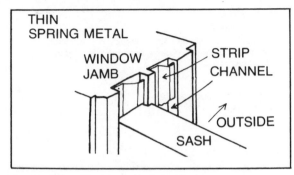

Fig. 6-23. Installation of weather stripping.

Install strips the full width of the sash on the bottom of the lower sash bottom rail and the top of the upper sash top rail. See Fig. 6-24.

Then attach a strip the full width of the window to the upper sash bottom rail. Countersink the nails slightly so they won't catch on the lower sash top rail. Fig. 6-25.

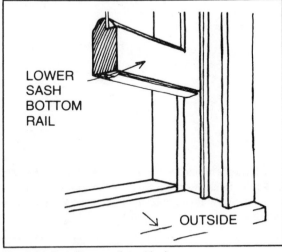

Fig. 6-24. Installing weather stripping.

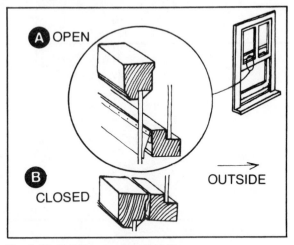

Fig. 6-25. Installing weather stripping.

For Rolled Vinyl

Nail on vinyl strips on double-hung windows as shown in Fig. 6-26. A sliding window is much the same and can be treated as a double-hung window turned on its side.

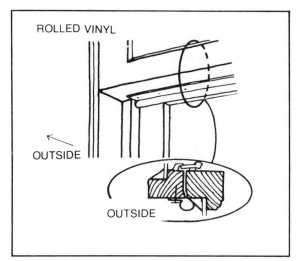

Fig. 6-26. Installing rolled vinyl.

Casement and tilting windows should be weatherstripped with the vinyl nailed to the window casing so that, as the window shuts, it compresses the roll. See Fig. 6-27.

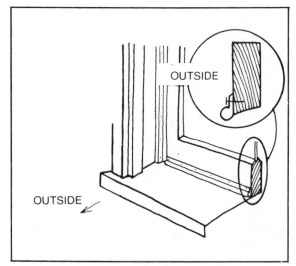

Fig. 6-27. Rolled vinyl installation.

Adhesive-backed Foam Strip

Install adhesive backed foam, on all types of windows, only where there is no friction. On double-hung windows, this is only the bottom (as shown) and top rails. Other types of windows can use foam strips in many more places. See Fig. 6-28.

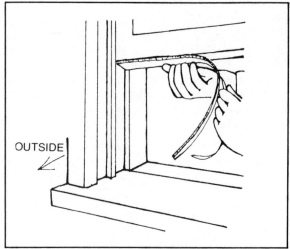

Fig. 6-28. Installing adhesive-backed foam strip.

Weatherstrip Doors

You can weatherstrip your doors even if you're not an experienced handyman. There are several types of weatherstripping for doors, each with its own level of effectiveness, durability, and degree of installation difficulty. The installations are the same for the two sides and top of a door, with a different, more durable one for the threshold.

Alternative Methods and Materials

Adhesive Backed Foam. Tools: Knife or shears; tape measure. Evaluation: Extremely easy to install, invisible when installed, not very durable, more effective on doors than windows. Installation: Stick foam to inside of jamb (Fig. 6-29).

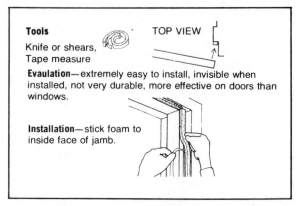

Fig. 6-29. Alternative methods and materials.

Rolled Vinyl with Aluminum Channel Backing.
Tools: Hammer, nails, tin snips, tape measure. Evaluation: Easy to install, visible when installed, durable. Installation: Nail strip snugly against door on the casing. See Fig. 6-30.

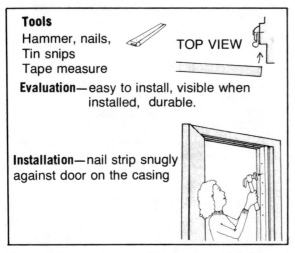

Tools
Hammer, nails,
Tin snips
Tape measure

TOP VIEW

Evaluation—easy to install, visible when installed, durable.

Installation—nail strip snugly against door on the casing

Fig. 6-30. Rolled vinyl with aluminum channel backing.

Foam Rubber with Wood Backing. Tools: Hammer, nails, handsaw, tape measure. Evaluation: Easy to install, visible when installed, not very durable. Installation: Nail strip snugly against the closed door. Space nails 8 to 12 inches apart. See Fig. 6-31.

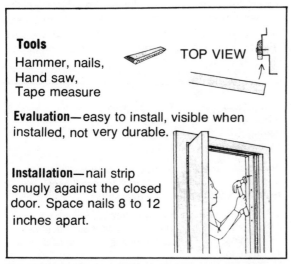

Tools
Hammer, nails,
Hand saw,
Tape measure

TOP VIEW

Evaluation—easy to install, visible when installed, not very durable.

Installation—nail strip snugly against the closed door. Space nails 8 to 12 inches apart.

Fig. 6-31. Installation of foam rubber with wood backing.

Spring Metal. Tools: Tin snips, hammer, nails, tape measure. Evaluation: Easy to install, invisible when installed, extremely durable. Installation: Cut to length and tack in place. Lift outer edge of strip with screwdriver after tacking for better seal. See Fig. 6-32.

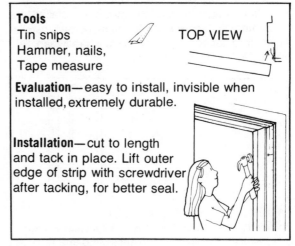

Tools
Tin snips
Hammer, nails,
Tape measure

TOP VIEW

Evaluation—easy to install, invisible when installed, extremely durable.

Installation—cut to length and tack in place. Lift outer edge of strip with screwdriver after tacking, for better seal.

Fig. 6-32. Installing spring metal.

Interlocking Metal Channels. Note: The following methods are more difficult than the first four methods. Tools: Hacksaw, hammer, nails, tape measure. Evaluation: Difficult to install (alignment is crucial), visible when installed, durable but subject to damage, because they're exposed, excellent seal. Installation: Cut and fit strips to head of door first. Male

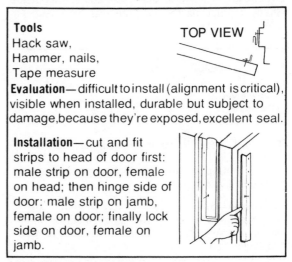

Tools
Hack saw,
Hammer, nails,
Tape measure

TOP VIEW

Evaluation—difficult to install (alignment is critical), visible when installed, durable but subject to damage, because they're exposed, excellent seal.

Installation—cut and fit strips to head of door first: male strip on door, female on head; then hinge side of door: male strip on jamb, female on door; finally lock side on door, female on jamb.

Fig. 6-33. Interlocking metal channels.

strips on door and female on head. Then hinge side of door. Male strip on jamb and female on door. Lock side on door with female on jamb. See Fig. 6-33.

Fitted Interlocking Metal Channels (J-Strips). Evaluation: Very difficult to install, exceptionally good weatherseal, invisible when installed, not exposed to possible damage. Installation: Should be installed by a carpenter. Not appropriate for do-it-yourself installation unless done by an accomplished handyman. See Fig. 6-34.

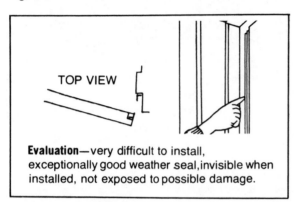

Fig. 6-34. Filled interlocking channels.

Sweeps. Tools: Screwdriver, hacksaw, tape measure. Evaluation: Useful for flat thresholds; might drag on carpet or rug. Models that flip up when the door is opened are available. Installation: Cut sweep to fit 1/16 inch in from the edges of the door. Some sweeps are installed on the inside and some outside. Check instructions for our particular type. See Fig. 6-35.

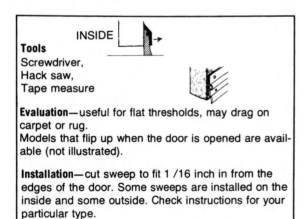

Fig. 6-35. Sweeps.

Door Shoes. Tools: Screwdriver, hacksaw, plane, tape measure. Evaluation: Useful with wooden threshold that is not worn, very durable, difficult to install (must remove door). Installation: Remove door and trip required amount of bottom. Cut to door width. Install by sliding vinyl out and fasten with screws. See Fig. 6-36.

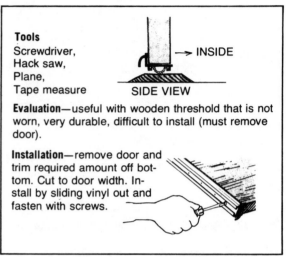

Fig. 6-36. Door shoes.

Vinyl Bulb Threshold. Tools: Screwdriver, hacksaw, plane, tape measure. Evaluation: Useful where there is no threshold or where the wooden one is worn out. Difficult to install. Vinyl will wear but replacements are available. Installation: Remove the door and the trim off the bottom. The bottom should have about a ⅛" bevel to seal against vinyl. Be sure bevel is cut in the right direction for the opening. See Fig. 6-37.

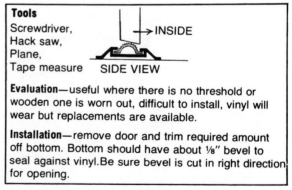

Fig. 6-37. Vinyl built threshold.

138

Interlocking Threshold. Evaluation: Very difficult to install. Exceptionally good weather seal. Installation: Should be installed by a skilled carpenter. See Fig. 6-38.

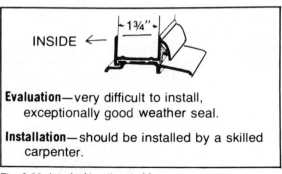

Evaluation—very difficult to install, exceptionally good weather seal.

Installation—should be installed by a skilled carpenter.

Fig. 6-38. Interlocking threshold.

WINDOW INSTALLATION

There are several kinds of storm windows:

☐ Plastic (polyethylene sheet). These come in rolls. You may have to put up replacements each year.

☐ Single-panel glass or rigid plastic. You put them up and take them down each year.

☐ Triple-track glass (combination). These have screens and you can open and close them. They are for double-hung or sliding doors.

All of these are about equally effective. The more expensive ones are more durable, attractive, and convenient. See Fig. 6-39.

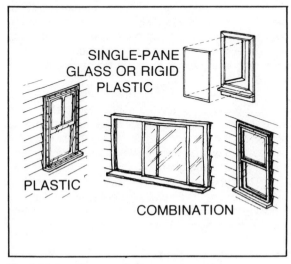

SINGLE-PANE GLASS OR RIGID PLASTIC

PLASTIC

COMBINATION

Fig. 6-39. Install storm windows.

Plastic Storm Windows

Tack the plastic sheets over the outside of your windows or tape sheets over the inside instead of installing permanent storm windows. See Fig. 6-40.

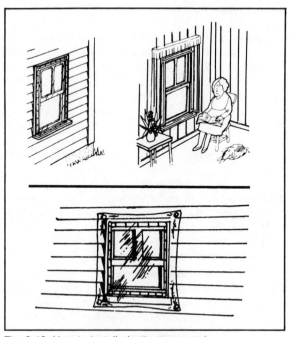

Fig. 6-40. How to install plastic storm windows.

Tools and Materials

Six-mil thick polyethylene plastic in rolls or kits.
Shears to cut and trim plastic.
Two-inch wide masking tape or a hammer and tacks.
Wood slats (¼″ × 1¼″) See Fig. 6-41.

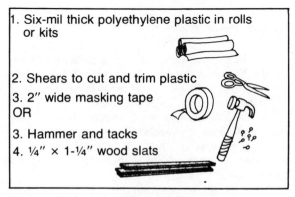

1. Six-mil thick polyethylene plastic in rolls or kits

2. Shears to cut and trim plastic

3. 2″ wide masking tape
OR

3. Hammer and tacks

4. ¼″ × 1-¼″ wood slats

Fig. 6-41. Tools and materials needed.

Installation

Measure the width of your largest window to determine the width of the plastic rolls to buy. Measure the length of your windows to see how many linear feet and therefore how many rolls or the kit size you need to buy.

Attach to the inside or outside of the frame so that the plastic will block airflow that leaks around the moveable parts of the window. If you attach the plastic to the outside, use the slats and tacks. If you attach it to the inside, masking tape will work.

Inside installation is easier and will provide greater protection to the plastic. Outside installation is more difficult. This is especially true on a 2-story house, and the plastic is more likely to be damaged by the elements.

Be sure to install the material tightly and securely. Remove all excess material. Besides looking better, this will make the plastic less susceptible to deterioration during the course of the winter.

Jalousie Windows

Jalousie windows are particularly difficult to insulate against the cold. A homemade plastic covering can be slipped over the screen of a jalousie window to prevent the movement of air. See Fig. 6-42.

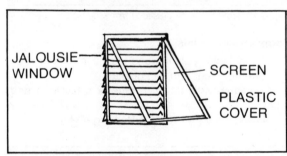

Fig. 6-42. Jalousie storm windows.

Use lighter-weight plastic such as 2-mil to 4-mil plastic. The width of the plastic covering is determined by the width of the screen on the jalousie window.

Measure the length of the screen.

Double the measurement in order to determine the length of plastic needed.

Fold the plastic in half.

Sew up the sides on your machine using the longest stitch.

Pull the plastic covering over the screen like a large plastic pillow case. The plastic covering can be put on and removed easily. It does an effective job of insulating against cold.

Single-Pane Storm Windows

Rigid Plastic. These are available in do-it-yourself kits.

Glass. Storm window suppliers will build single-pane glass storm windows to your measurements that you then install yourself. Another method is to make your own with do-it-yourself materials available at some hardware stores. See Fig. 6-43.

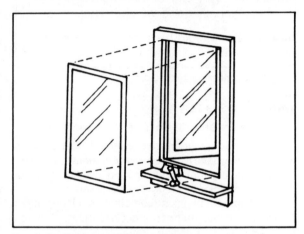

Fig. 6-43. Single pane storm windows.

Rigid plastic windows are always installed on the inside. Follow the instructions on the do-it-yourself kit.

Glass windows can be installed either inside—if the way the window is built will permit it—or on the outside. If you install them on the outside, then they only cover the moving part of the window and you'll save less energy, but they will be permanently installed.

Determine how you want the windows to sit in the frame. Your measurements will be the outside measurements of the storm window. Be as accurate as possible, and then allow ⅛″ along each edge for clearance. You'll be responsible for any errors in measurement; so do a good job.

When your windows are delivered, check the actual measurements carefully against your order. Install the windows and fix in place with moveable clips so you can take them down for cleaning.

Advantages and Disadvantages

Single-pane storm windows aren't as expensive

as the double-track or triple-track windows. The major disadvantage of the single-pane windows is that you can't open them easily after they're installed.

Frame Finish (glass windows). A mill finish (plain aluminum) will oxidize quickly and degrade in appearance. Windows with an anodized or baked enamel finish look better.

Weather Stripping. The side of the storm window frame that touches the existing window frame should have a permanently installed weather strip or gasket to make the joint as airtight as possible.

Install Combination Storm Windows. Triple-track combination (window and screen) storm windows are designed for installation over double-hung and sliding windows. They are permanently installed and they can be opened at any time for ventilation.

Double-track combination units are also available and they cost less. Both kinds are sold almost everywhere, and can be bought with or without the cost of installation. Perfect for the do-it-yourselfer. Fig. 6-44.

Fig. 6-44. Combination storm windows.

Installation. You can save a few dollars (10 percent to 15 percent of the purchase price) by installing the windows. But you'll need some tools:

—Caulking gun.
—Drill.
—Screwdriver.

In most cases, it will be easier to have the supplier install your windows for you (but it will cost more).

The supplier will first measure all the windows where you want storm windows installed. It will take anywhere from several days to a few weeks to make up your order before the supplier returns to install them.

Installation should take less than one day; much depends on how many windows are involved. Two very important items should be checked to make sure that the installation is properly done. Make sure that both the window sashes and screen sash move smoothly and seal tightly when closed after installation. Poor installation can cause misalignment. Be sure there is a tightly caulked seal around the edge of the storm windows. Leaks can hurt the performance of storm windows a lot.

Most combination units will come with two or three ¼-inch-diameter holes (or other types of vents) drilled through the frame where it meets the window sill. This is to keep winter condensation from collecting on the sill and causing rot. Keep these holes clear, and drill them yourself if your combination units don't already have them.

Judging Quality

Frame Finish. A mill finish (plain aluminum) will oxidize. This reduces ease of operation and degrades appearance. An anodized or baked-enamel finish is better.

Corner Joints. Quality of construction affects the strength and performance of storm windows. Corners are a good place to check construction. They should be strong and airtight. Normally, overlapped corner joints are better than mitered joints. If you can see through the joints, they will leak air.

Sash Tracks and Weather Stripping. Storm windows are supposed to reduce air leakage around windows. The depth of the metal grooves (ash tracks) at the sides of the window and the weather stripping quality makes a big difference in how well storm windows can do this. Compare several types before deciding.

Hardware Quality. The quality of locks and catches has a direct affect on durability and is a good indicator of overall construction quality.

STORM DOORS

Storm doors of wood or steel can be purchased within the same price range. The choice between doors of similar quality but different material is primarily up to your own taste. Installing storm doors is one step homeowners can easily take to cut down rising bills for heating/cooling.

Engineered in every detail to maximize insulating value, ready-to-install storm door packages offer up to six times more energy economy than conventional wood entrances. These doors come complete with a prehung door in a frame and a threshold (ready to fit into the rough opening). Fully weather sealed, the unit can be quickly installed in new homes or as replacements.

Basically, an insulated door is a foam-filled insulating core sandwiched between two deep-embossed sheets of steel. Thick density of polyurethane is foamed-in-place and bonds to the door to form an insulation blanket of tiny trapped cells.

Extra-strength magnetic weather strips on head and strike jambs "reach out" for positive sealing like a refrigerator door. Double compression vinyl weather strip on the hinge jamb adds to weather stripping action.

Sealing out air and water leakage between threshold and door bottom is a flexible door sweep that can be adjusted for a snug fit. Resilient pads at both lower corners complete the weather blocking design.

Some specific features of these doors are the insulated glass designs that provide an added energy-saving feature. Energy-saving systems block out weather nine ways.

Energy Saving Jamb. Extra-wide (6½″) matches the wider "energy construction" method in home building. Other options for inswing and outswing doors in standard widths.

Double Weather Strip. Double compression vinyl weather strip forms weather seal at hinge jamb.

Engineered Edges. Doors are all-steel design. There are no stiles or rails of wood at hinge jamb.

Insulating Sandwich. Thick density (2.8-pounds per cubic foot) of foamed-in-place polyurethane bonds to steel faces. Gives natural insulation of tiny trapped cells.

Adjustable for Snug Fit. Door bottom sweep with flexible fingers can be adjusted for tight fit against threshold to stop air and water leakage.

Frost-Break Heat Barrier. Rigid polymer connector blocks heat transfer in sturdy aluminum thresholds.

Choice of Thresholds. Wider aluminum threshold for "energy construction" homes, or standard inswing or outswing thresholds of similar energy-saving design.

Flexible Corner Pads. Resilient pads at both lower corners stop wind and water.

Extra-Strong Magnetic Weather Strip. Positive, refrigerator-like action with magnetic weather strips on head and strike jambs. See Fig. 6-45.

Energy Savings with Insulated Doors

The amount of energy a homeowner can save depends on the efficiency of the materials used for insulating to block heat flow—in or out. To help in selecting for energy savings, various rating systems are used to compare these materials.

Consumers are sometimes confused because this is a numbers game that's also played with letters. Here's a simplified explanation of the most common letters that represent the values being compared.

R-value stands for resistance (how well a material resists the flow of heat). Higher R ratings reflect stronger resistance to thermal movement. This is the most commonly used yardstick, and it gives a total picture of the efficiency of the material or component.

With Benchmark energy-efficient doors, the R value—with its dense core of polyurethane foam—is 14.58. For comparison, a solid wood door is rated at 2.75.

Now there is a new and easier way to compare the insulating efficiency of various door systems. This is the *door insulating systems index* (DISI) developed by the Insulated Steel Door Systems Institute.

The DISI rating gives a single number that includes heat flow through the door/frame system and from the inflow/outflow of air. Heat loss (or gain) is calculated, in Btu per day, and divided by 1000 to give the rating number.

A homeowner can multiply the DISI ratings of various doors by 1000 to arrive at the total heat (or cooling) loss per day. With a DISI rating of 1.5, a typical Benchmark door would lose only 1500 Btu daily. Maximum allowable loss set by the Institute for the doors is 8600 Btu loss per day under the DISI standards.

U-value stands for a unit factor used to calculate how much heat is transmitted through a material in a given amount of time (generally per hour). The lower U-ratings mean less heat moving in or out of a space.

A typical solid-wood door has a U-factor of .46. That is roughly six times less efficient than an insulated door, such as the Benchmark door, with a measurement of 36″ × 68″ having a U-value of .069.

A fourth rating value, sometimes called the K-factor, is a measure of the heat flow through a material of 1″ thickness.

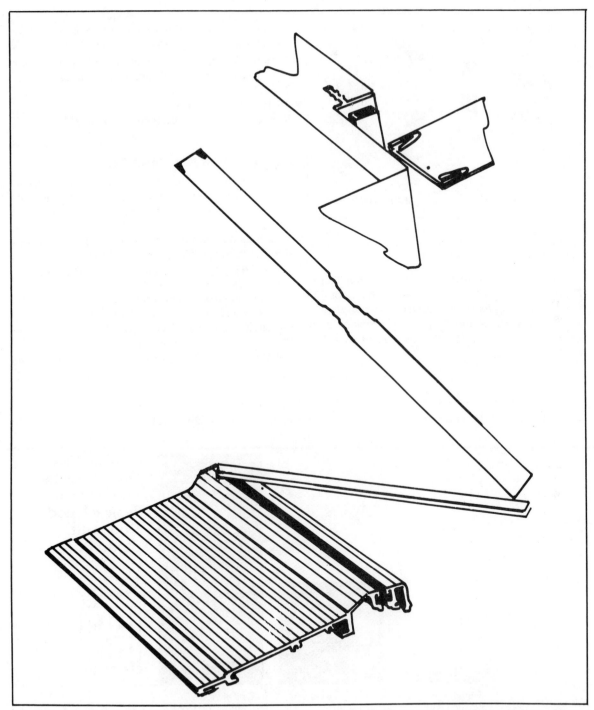

Fig. 6-45. Cutaway of an insulated door (courtesy of Benchmark Doors, Mr. R. Morton Miller and Mr. Hunter Morin, General Products Company).

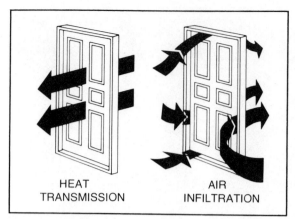

HEAT
TRANSMISSION

AIR
INFILTRATION

Fig. 6-46. How the door insulating system works (courtesy of Benchmark Doors, Mr. R. Morton Miller and Mr. Hunter Morin, General Products Company).

Under the new door insulating system index (DISI) that combines energy loss through a door and from air leaking around the edges, a standard insulated door, such as the Benchmark entrance door system, provides a high efficiency rating of 1.5 to homeowners.

The Btu loss in entranceways is calculated by adding the two essential sources of heat loss: heat transmission and air infiltration. See Fig. 6-46. Some comparisons of Btu loss per day for entrance systems are shown in Fig. 6-47. Ratings are for actual Btu lost, converted to an index. For example, 19.1 means 19,100 Btu lost per day. Doors such as the Benchmark insulated steel entrance system is rated at 1.5 or 1500 Btu per day.

Threshold With Frost-Break Design

Engineered to block heat flow across an entrance sill, an energy-efficient aluminum threshold cuts energy loss. This frost-break feature has a rigid polyurethane polymer connector built into the extruded aluminum threshold. It is designed to form a thermal barrier while preserving the strength of the metal. An energy-saving threshold group features a 6″ width one-piece aluminum threshold for the 2″-×-6″ stud wall energy construction method. See Fig. 6-48.

Homeowner benefits from this aluminum threshold, in addition to energy savings, include exceptional durability, ease of cleaning, no maintenance, and absence of rotting or splitting problems.

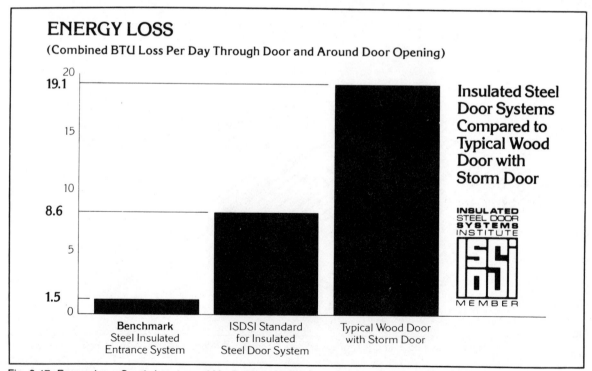

Fig. 6-47. Energy Loss Graph (courtesy of Mr. R. Morton Miller and Mr. Hunter Morin, General Products Company).

Fig. 6-48. Threshold (courtesy of Mr. R. Morton Miller and Mr. Hunter Morin, General Products Company).

Tools You Will Need

Carpenters' level.
Shim materials.
Hammer.
16d galvanized finish nails.
Screwdriver.
Caulking gun, exterior caulk.
Drill and ½" bit.
Saw, trim stripping tool.

Measuring for Replacement Unit

Temporarily remove interior trim casings.

Width is the distance between rough opening studs (not jambs).

Height is measured from bottom of rough header to top of finished floor.

Determine distance from top of finish floor to bottom of header. Allow space for extra-thick carpet. See Fig. 6-49.

Handing is always taken from the outside. See Fig. 6-49.

Shimming and Plumbing Your Door

Shim your door with beveled shims. Insert the first shim with the thin end toward you. Drive the other shim in until the door is plumb and secure. Cedar shims make good shims. Plumb your door carefully. The most important part of your installation is making sure your door is plumb in both directions (from left to right and from inside to outside). See Fig. 6-50.

Single and double door units require the same basic installation steps as follows. Also see Figs. 6-51 and 6-52.

☐ Remove the old door. Carefully remove the interior casings. See Fig. 6-53.

☐ Strip off outside casing. See Fig. 6-54.

☐ Take out the old sill, and fill void up to level of finish floor. See Fig. 6-55.

☐ Saw through side jambs for easier removal of the old frame. Fig. 6-56.

Installation Steps

Preparation. Check rough opening dimensions and be sure the sill is level. See Fig. 6-57. Raise the sill to the *finished floor* level if necessary and make sure to leave the extra space for carpeting. Apply continuous beads of construction adhesive to the bottom of

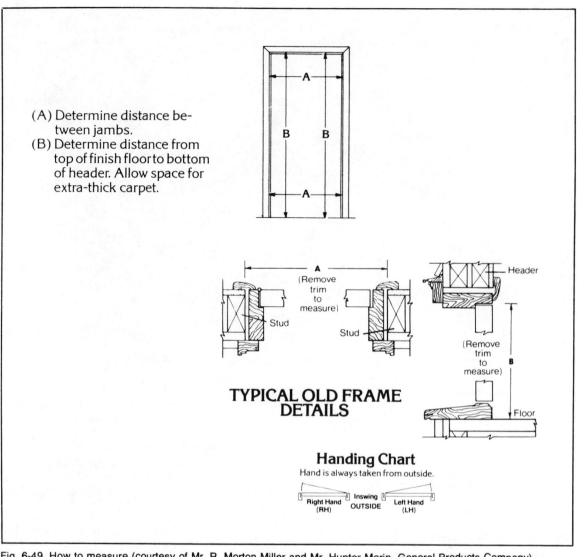

(A) Determine distance be-
    tween jambs.
(B) Determine distance from
    top of finish floor to bottom
    of header. Allow space for
    extra-thick carpet.

TYPICAL OLD FRAME DETAILS

Handing Chart

Hand is always taken from outside.

Right Hand (RH)   Inswing OUTSIDE   Left Hand (LH)

Fig. 6-49. How to measure (courtesy of Mr. R. Morton Miller and Mr. Hunter Morin, General Products Company).

aluminum threshold on all contact surfaces. Do *not* remove braces. The door *must not* be opened until the unit is in place, plumbed and shimmed. For a double door, the active jamb must be securely nailed.

Center the Unit in the Rough Opening. Allow at least ¾″ between jambs and rough studs on each side to accommodate shims. From outside, plumb both sides of door unit. Nail through brickmold for tempo- rary support at two points on each side. Do not drive nails completely until the unit is thoroughly plumbed and shimmed. See Fig. 6-58.

Go Inside (through another entry). On the hinge side of the unit, insert shims between the jamb and the stud. Shim behind each hinge. Constantly check to be sure it is *level*. Note: For double doors, insert shims between the jamb and the stud on both active and inactive side of the unit. Shim behind each hinge on both sides of the doors.

Shim Behind the Strike Jamb. Shim at top, bot- tom, and at the strike location. Again, check constantly to be sure jamb is *plumb* in both directions. Note: For

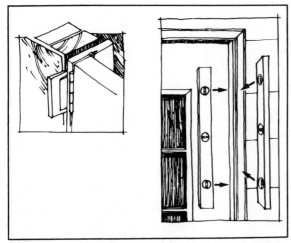

Fig. 6-50. Shimming and plumbing a door (courtesy of Mr. R. Mortin Miller, and Mr. Hunter Morin, General Products Company).

Fig. 6-51. A single-door unit (courtesy of Mr. R. Morton Miller and Mr. Hunter Morin, General Products Company).

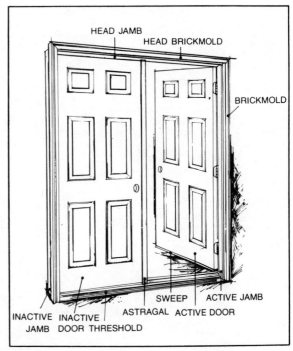

Fig. 6-52. Double door unit (courtesy of Mr. R. Morton Miller and Mr. Hunter Morin, General Products Company).

double doors, go outside and nail only the active hinge jamb securely at the three hinge locations. Use 16d finish nails to nail through jamb into stud.

Then go back inside and remove the remainder of bracing. The active door can now be opened. With the top astragal bolt locked, check to be sure active door contacts the weather strip of the astragal evenly from top to bottom. Adjust an inactive jamb if necessary to make good contact. Do *not* use a level, but adjust for even contact. Open, close, and lock the bolt to test the operation. Make adjustments to the door unit, if necessary, to insure easy operation.

Hinge Jamb. Go outside and nail the hinge jamb securely at each hinge location. Use 16d finish nails to nail through the jamb into the stud. Then go back inside and carefully remove bracing. At this point, your unit should be plumb, level, and held securely with the shims, hinge jamb nailing and temporary nailing outside.

Open the door, remove spacers struck to the jambs and spacer on strike end of sweep. Step outside and carefully close the door. Check to be sure the door makes even contact, top to bottom, with the magnetic weather seal on the strike jamb and header. If contact

147

Fig. 6-53. Remove an old door (courtesy of Mr. R. Morton Miller and Mr. Hunter Morin, General Products Company).

Fig. 6-54. Strip off outside casing (courtesy of Mr. R. Morton Miller and Mr. Hunter Morin, General Products Company).

149

Fig. 6-55. Taking out an old sill (courtesy of Mr. R. Morton Miller and Mr. Hunter Morin, General Products Company).

Fig. 6-56. Sawing through a door jamb (courtesy of Mr. R. Morton Miller and Mr. Hunter Morin, General Products Company).

Fig. 6-57. Make sure the door sill is shimmed to floor level (courtesy of Mr. R. Morton Miller and Mr. Hunter Morin, General Products Company).

Fig. 6-58. Remodeling the unit into an opening and nail the frame to existing wood frame (courtesy of Mr. R. Morton Miller and Mr. Hunter Morin, General Products Company).

Fig. 6-59. For maximum strength and security, the hinge jamb is screwed into the stud behind the wood frame (courtesy of Mr. R. Morton Miller and Mr. Hunter Morin, General Products Company).

is not complete, adjust the strike jamb in or out at the top or bottom until even contact is achieved.

Do *not* use a level but adjust for good contact. For double doors (final nailing), use 16d finish nails to nail through the inactive jamb and into studs at all shim locations. Nail the head jamb at shim locations. Complete nailing of brickmold on both jambs and header.

Final Nailing. Use 16d finish nails to nail through the strike jamb and into studs at all shim locations except the shim behind strike plate. This area should be nailed securely only after lockset is installed (to allow for final adjustment). Frequently check the weather seal contact by carefully opening and closing door while nailing. Nail the head jamb at shim locations.

Complete nailing brickmold on both sides and header. Caulk nail holes. Note: for double doors, put a small dab of caulk on threshold at location of home that needs to be drilled to accept bottom bolt. Move bottom bolt to locked position to mark caulk for *exact* location of hole. Drill ½" hole at that position.

Hinge Support. For extra hing support Benchmark provides 4 long (2") screws. Install two in the top hinge and one each in the center and bottom hinges. These screws will pass completely through the jamb and into the studs for added support of door. Note: for double door, there are eight 2" screws. See Fig. 6-59.

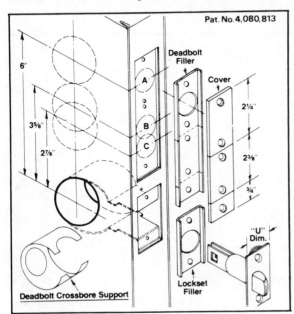

Fig. 6-60. Latch preparation (courtesy of Mr. R. Morton Miller and Mr. Hunter Morin, General Products Company).

Locket and Strike Plate. Install as shown in Fig. 6-50. Note that the illustration includes a provision for installing deadbolt. Remember to nail the jamb at the strike location after the lockset is installed and any final shim adjustments made. Note: For double doors, the strike plate attaches to the astragal.

Adjusting Sweep. Loosen screws on bottom sweep just enough to adjust sweep up or down. Adjust the sweep so that "fingers" compress by 1/16" on threshold. Tighten screws.

For additional weather stripping, pack insulating material between side jambs, header, and studs. Use a caulking gun to caulk around brickmold, along the front edge and at ends of the threshold.

How to Install Patio Doors

Elegance combines with security and energy efficiency in the Vista insulated steel patio doors system by Benchmark, a product of the General Products Company, Fredericksburg, Virginia. The ready-to-install units are designed to replace sliding glass doors and other patio entrances.

Energy-saving efficiency is engineered into these Vista patio door systems. Doors have the standard insulating "sandwich" of foamed-in-place, high-density polyurethane, and they are factory-glazed with insulated safety glass. They are prehung in a preassembled frame complete with refrigerator-like weather sealing and a frost-break threshold.

Begin by removing the old doors to install new Vista doors by removing metal sliding doors from tracks and metal frame from inside jamb. This frame is usually screwed to jamb. See Fig. 6-61.

Remove any remaining sill or threshold and fill void to level of finished floor. See Fig. 6-62.

Strip off old brickmold from outside and trim from inside. Remove inside trim carefully and you can reuse it to trim your new door. See Fig. 6-63.

Take out old jamb to expose rough opening. Saw through side jambs for easier removal. See Fig. 6-64.

Start by removing old sliding glass doors and screen (Fig. 6-65).

Remove old metal channel frame from opening (Fig. 6-66).

Remove old sill. If necessary, fill into finished floor level (Fig. 6-67).

Carefully remove inside trim casing (Fig. 6-68).

Pry off the outside casing to expose jamb and header (Fig. 6-69).

Saw through jambs for easier removal of jambs and header (Fig. 6-70).

Fig. 6-61. Removing old doors to install Vista Patio Doors (courtesy of Mr. R. Morton Miller and Mr. Hunter Morin, General Products Company).

Fig. 6-62. Removing old doors to install Vista Patio Doors. Remove any remaining sill or threshold and fill to level off the finished floor (courtesy of Mr. R. Morton Miller and Mr. Hunter Morin, General Products Company).

Fig. 6-63. Removing old doors to install Vista Patio Doors. Strip off old brickmold from outside and trim from inside. Remove inside trim carefully and you can reuse it to trim your new door (courtesy of Mr. R. Morton Miller and Mr. Hunter Morin, General Products Company).

Fig. 6-64. Removing old doors to install Vista Patio Doors. Take out the old jamb to expose the rough opening. Saw through side jambs for easier removal.

Fig. 6-65. Start by removing old sliding glass doors and screens (courtesy of Mr. R. Morton Miller and Mr. Hunter Morin, General Products Company).

Place new Vista unit into rough opening. Plumb the unit with level and shim as necessary (Fig. 6-71).

Nail Vista jambs to studs (4 points each jamb) or use long screws (Fig. 6-72).

Replace interior trim casings, and caulk around exterior brick mold. See Fig. 6-73.

Finished interior scene. See Fig. 6-74.

Paint and apply other finishing touches. Optional sliding screen may be added at this point. See Fig. 6-75.

A COLORFUL IDEA

You can create an elegant look with energy economy by installing decorative insulated sidelights. See Fig. 6-76. Sidelights offer choices in leaded-, stained- and clear-glass styled designs to complement traditional or contemporary architecture decor.

The sidelights shown in Fig. 6-76 have energy savings built into them with an inner core of dense polystyrene tightly bonded to steel outer faces. A thermal break between inner and outer faces blocks heat flow both ways. Another thermal barrier is across the aluminum threshold.

Weather that could rob heating or cooling energy is sealed out with caulking inside and outside. Plus there is a rubber sill gasket between the sash and

Fig. 6-66. Remove old metal channel frame from the open (courtesy of Mr. R. Morton Miller and Mr. Hunter Morin, General Products Company).

Fig. 6-67. Remove the old sill. If necessary, fill in to finished floor level (courtesy of Mr. R. Morton Miller and Mr. Hunter Morin, General Products Company).

Fig. 6-68. Carefully remove inside casing (courtesy of Mr. R. Morton Miller and Mr. Hunter Morin, General Products Company).

Fig. 6-69. Pry off the outside casing to expose jambs and header (courtesy of Mr. R. Morton Miller and Mr. Hunter Morin, General Products Company).

162

Fig. 6-70. Saw through jambs for easier removal of jambs and header (courtesy of Mr. R. Morton Miller and Mr. Hunter Morin, General Products Company).

threshold. All lights are insulated safety glass, factory-glazed and sealed to prevent energy loss.

These energy-saving sidelights can be combined with the doors shown into an insulated entrance system that's quickly installed for new homes or remodeling plans.

INSTALLING DECORATIVE PANELS

Caulk all inner flanges of cutout with acrylic latex caulk or equivalent as shown in Fig. 6-77.

Spread the Uni-Panel adhesive on the back of both decorative panels. Keel 1″ from edges.

Center the Masonite filler on the back of one panel. Determine which will be the exterior side of door, and place this panel/filler unit into that side of cutout. Press unit firmly against caulking.

Lay the door, exterior side down, on a smooth flat surface with panel rigidly supported from underneath. Interior side cutout opening will now be exposed to receive second panel. After placing the panel, start screws from this interior side. Use screws in a pattern, as shown in Fig. 6-77, to secure panels and filler

Fig. 6-71. Place the new Vista unit into rough opening. Plumb the unit with level and shim as necessary (courtesy of Mr. R. Morton Miller and Mr. Hunter Morin, General Products Company).

together. Prepare the screw locations with a slight countersink to allow screw heads to sink below the panel surface; Fill with putty or spackle. Caulk the seams between panel edges and door.

Paint the decorative panels with a low to medium glass oil base.

To install the type of panels shown in Fig. 6-77, (1, 2, and 4), you will need:

☐ 6 #6 × 1″ type A, flat-head screw.
☐ 1 masonite filler panel (6½ -× 17¼ ∶× ¼″).
☐ 2 decorative panels (each ¾″ thick).
☐ 1 tube of Uni-Panel adhesive.

HOW TO INSTALL SLIDING SCREENS

1. Center the top track right to left on the header brickmold. The horizontal leg of the track should be

164

back against the frame. This spaces the vertical leg of the track out ⅝″ from the frame. Secure the track with self-tapping screws. See Fig. 6-78.

2. Center the bottom track right to left on the threshold. The horizontal leg of the track should be back against the frame. This spaces the vertical leg of the track out ⅝″ from the frame. Secure the track with self-tapping screws. See Fig. 6-79.

3. Remove the bag from the door handle to find instructions for adjusting rollers in step 5. See Fig. 6-80. Most screen doors direct from the factory have this.

Fig. 6-72. Nail Vista jambs to studs—four points each jamb—or use long screws (courtesy of Mr. R. Morton Miller and Mr. Hunter Morin, General Products Company).

Fig. 6-73. Replace interior trim casings and caulk around exterior brick mold (courtesy of Mr. R. Morton Miller and Hunter Morin, General Products Company).

Fit upper rollers onto the flange of the top track. Pushing up on the door, place the bottom rollers over their track. See Fig. 6-81.

Use a Phillips screwdriver to adjust both top and bottom roller assemblies (total of four) for correct tension to insure smooth action. See Fig. 6-82.

Close the screen and mark the correct position for the latch on the jamb brickmold. Then secure the latch with screws. See Fig. 6-83.

PATIO DOORS

The Benchmark Vista Patio Door, produced by

166

General Products Company, is just one of the many ways in which you can turn an ordinary back porch into a beautiful sunroom. Before a patio door system was installed in house shown Fig. 6-84, it had a plain back porch rarely used for anything, but flower pots and old doormats.

But with this type of economical doors, this commonplace back porch became a fully insulated, useful sunroom. The exterior appearance of the house was enhanced and the value was increased.

This beautiful patio can be used for bright morning breakfasts, casual lunch gatherings, late-evening parties, or as a playroom for children.

With a center-hinged active door that swings in against an inactive panel, this patio door provides free space adjacent walls for placing furniture.

Fig. 6-74. Finished interior scene shows Vista advantages (courtesy of Mr. R. Morton Miller and Hunter Morin, General Products Company).

Fig. 6-75. Paint and apply other finishing touches. Optional sliding screen can be added at this point (courtesy of R. Morton Miller and Hunter Morin, General Products Company).

Figure 6-85 shows a Vista prehung patio door system that transformed a screened porch into a fully insulated sunroom (with a minimum of carpentry). These doors come with a choice of 15-light or single-light styles. Almost any opening can be quickly filled with ready-to-install two door or three-door units in preassembled packages. Sturdy center jambs with center swing doors do away with the sticking, track-jumping, and leaking problems of sliding doors.

Table 6-8. provides a breakdown of sealing materials. Caulking compounds are available in disposable cartridges made to be used with a caulking gun. Compounds are also sold in 1-gallon and 5-gallon cans. Some compounds come in rope form—that you can unwind and force into cracks with your fingers—or in sqeeze tubes that work like toothpaste tubes. Because each of the many varieties is designed for a specific use, be careful to choose the right one for the

Fig. 6-76. Decorative sidelights (courtesy of R. Morton Miller and Hunter Morin, General Products Company).

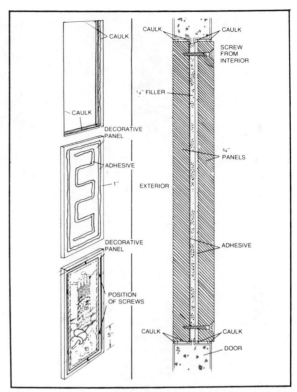

Fig. 6-77. How to install decorative panels (courtesy of R. Morton Miller, and Hunter Morin, General Products Company).

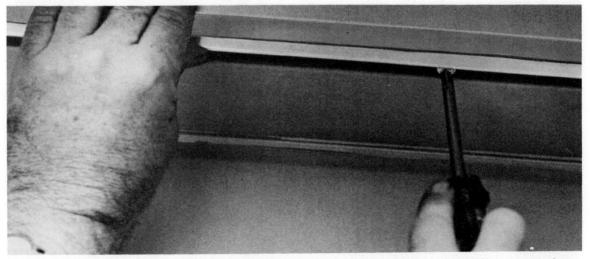

Fig. 6-78. Center the top track right to left on the header brickmold. The horizontal leg of the track should be against the frame. This spaces the vertical leg of the track out ⅝″ from the secure. Secure the track with self-tapping screws (courtesy of R. Morton Miller and Hunter Morin, General Products Company).

169

Fig. 6-79. Center the bottom track right to left on the threshold. The horizontal leg of the track should be back against the frame. This spaces the vertical leg of the track ⅝" from the frame. Secure the track with self-tapping screws (courtesy of R. Morton Miller and Hunter Morin, General Products Company).

170

Fig. 6-80. Remove the bag from the door handle to find instructions for adjusting rollers (courtesy of R. Morton Miller and Hunter Morin, General Products Company).

Fig. 6-81. Fit upper rollers onto the flange of the top track. Pushing up on the door, place the bottom rollers over their track (courtesy of R. Morton Miller and Hunter Morin, General Products Company).

Fig. 6-82. Use a Phillips screwdriver to adjust both top and bottom roller assemblies (total of four) for correct tension to insure smooth action (courtesy of R. Morton Miller and Hunter Morin, General Products Company).

Fig. 6-83. Close the screen and mark the correct position for the latch on the jamb brickmold. Then secure the latch with screws (courtesy of R. Morton Miller and Hunter Morin, General Products Company).

Fig. 6-84. Before remodeling, this screened porch was rarely used (courtesy of R. Morton Miller and Hunter Morin, General Products Company).

Fig. 6-85. Vista prehung patio doors transformed this screened porch into a fully insulated, handsome sunroom. Decorating options are available with a choice of styles. Almost any opening can be quickly filled with ready-to-install 2-door or 3-door units. Sturdy center jambs with center swing doors do away with the sticking, track-jumping, and leaking problems of sliding doors (courtesy of R. Morton Miller and Hunter Morin, General Products Company).

Table 6-8. Uses and Properties of Common Sealing Materials.

MATERIAL	RECOMMENDED USES	CLEAN-UP SOLVENT	SHRINKAGE	ADHESION	REMARKS
Silicone	Seals joints between bath and kitchen fixtures and tile; adhesive for tiles and metal fixtures; seals metal joints as in plumbing and gutters. Seals most dissimilar building materials (i.e., wood and stone; metal flashing and brick).	Dry cloth will remove if area is cleaned up immediately. Use mineral spirits, naphtha or paint thinner.	Little or none	Good to excellent	Readily available. Remains flexible for life. Permits joints to stretch or compress. Silicones will stick to painted surfaces, but paint will not adhere to cured silicone. Cost: High
Butyl Rubber	Seals most dissimilar materials glass, metal, plastic, wood, concrete; Seals around windows and flashing, or bonds loose shingles.	Use mineral spirits, naphtha or paint thinner.	Minimal	Good to excellent	Less resilient than silicone. Allows for joint movement but does not become brittle with age. Can be painted after a skin forms. Apply when temperature is above 40° F. Cost: High
Latex	Seals joints around tub and shower; fills cracks in tile, plaster, glass, and plastic; fills nail-holes.	Use water.	Minimal	Good to excellent, except to metal	Easy to use. Seams can be trimmed or smoothed with moist finger or tool. Good water resistance when dry. Can be sanded and painted. Less elastic than above materials. Easy to clean up. Cost: Moderate
Oil-Base Caulks	Seals exterior seams and joints on building materials	Use mineral spirits, naphtha or paint thinner.	Shrinks when dry.	Good	Readily available. Least expensive of the four types. Rope and tube form. Oils dry out and cause material to harden and fall out. Cost: Low

job. Be sure you have the right color for the job. Caulking comes in white, gray, black and other colors. The most popular types are packed in individual containers to be used with a caulking gun.

Caulking compounds should be selected on the basis of their capability to adhere to other materials such as wood, glass, metal, plaster, or masonry because these materials expand and contract. Resistance to weathering, cracking, shrinkage, water, and mildew are also important.

The time to caulk is during the spring or fall. Below 40° F (4C), caulking will not cure properly. And condensation of moisture can prevent a solid bond.

Chapter 7

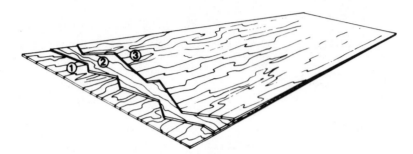

Plywood

PLYWOOD IS THE STRONGEST construction material available for its weight.It's strong because of the way it's put together: cross-laminated. *Cross-lamination* distributes along-the-grain strength in both directions.

Plywood is durable. The waterproof glue in *exterior*-type plywood won't come apart even when exposed to extreme moisture conditions or to agricultural acids from silage, manure, or fertilizer. Plywood can withstand dry temperatures to nearly 150° F for a year or more without any important loss of strength. When temperatures fall below normal, plywood actually becomes stronger.

Plywood is stable. Because it comes from the mill as a very dry material, and because of the way it's made, plywood swells, shrinks, and warps very little (even with repeated wetting and drying).

Plywood is a natural insulator. This is very important for an energy efficient home. In winter, it cuts condensation (sweating) and makes for warm walls and ceilings. Just as heat loss through the walls is reduced in winter, heat gain is reduced in summer to help keep rooms cool. Plywood construction is tight. There are fewer joints (openings or cracks between pieces) than with boards. And the panel is nonporous.

Plywood is economical. In most cases, plywood is less expensive to start with than other materials and it is frequently more readily available. Plywood goes on fast and that cuts time spent completing a job.

Plywood is easy to work with. It's a real labor-saver. That's why it's one of America's best building materials for do-it-yourselfers.

PLYWOOD CHARACTERISTICS

Plywood is made of wood and glue. Plywood is a flat panel built up of sheets of veneer called *Plies*. Veneers are produced by "peeling" a log. The log is placed in a giant lathe and the log is turned against a long knife. The veneer comes from the knife in a long, continuous ribbon that is cut into convenient widths for kiln drying and assembly into plywood. Peeling veneers and putting them together as plywood provides a means for making a structural material much larger than could be produced as solid wood.

In manufacturing plywood, the dried veneers are assembled with grain direction of each layer at right angles to the one next to it, starting with the grain running the long way of the panel. This is called cross-laminating. Wood is much stronger in the direction of the grain than it is across the grain. The cross-lamination in plywood distributes wood's along-the-grain strength in both directions. A panel is made that is very strong for its weight and that is split- and puncture-resistant.

Plywood always has an odd number of layers. A layer can consist of a single ply or 2 or more plies laminated with the grain direction parallel. The layers are joined under high pressure and temperature to produce a structural bond between layers and that is as strong as, or stronger than, the wood itself. Figure 7-1 shows some typical plywood constructions.

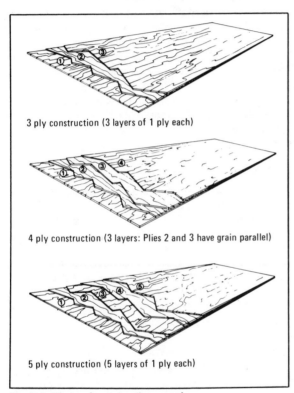

3 ply construction (3 layers of 1 ply each)

4 ply construction (3 layers: Plies 2 and 3 have grain parallel)

5 ply construction (5 layers of 1 ply each)

Fig. 7-1. Plywood construction panels.

The standard size for plywood panels is 4 feet wide and 8 feet long. Longer panels can be manufactured. Thickness ranges from ¼ inch to 1¼ inches.

Types of Plywood

Plywood produced under PS1 (Product Standard for Construction and Industrial Plywood) is a national standard developed by the plywood industry and the U.S. Department of Commerce. The standard is a detailed specification of how plywood must be man-ufactured. There are two types of plywood: Interior and Exterior.

Exterior Plywood

This plywood is made with very high-quality veneers and is bonded with a waterproof glue. Exterior plywood has the best durability. The glue does not weaken even with age or after long exposure to weather. It's so durable that boiling water won't hurt it.

Interior Plywood

This plywood has either highly moisture-resistant or else waterproof glue. That's up to the manufacturer. Veneers used in Interior plywood can be lower quality than those in Exterior plywood. Interior plywood is durable if it gets wet during construction, but it should not be exposed permanently to the weather.

Interior Bonded With Plywood Interior Glue

Plywood of this type is moisture resistant. It is for all indoor uses. It should not be damaged if it is exposed to the elements for short periods during construction.

Interior Bonded Plywood With Exterior Glue

The only difference between this type of plywood and true Exterior plywood is the quality of the veneers used for the inner plies and back of the panel. The glue is the same and is completely waterproof. Interior plywood bonded with exterior glue can be used where it will eventually be protected from exposure to weather. It is not a substitute for Exterior plywood, and it should not be used for permanent outdoor exposure. Most Interior plywood is now made with Exterior glue.

Although the plywood is manufactured under the Product Standard (usually called PS1), plywood companies who are members of the American Plywood Association also must qualify their products against additional quality requirements. Association quality supervisors go to member mills unannounced to make random sampling of the plywood production. These are tested in any of eight laboratories located in major production areas throughout the country. Products that can pass this rigid testing and inspection program may have the APA grade-trademark applied to it.

The APA Grade-Trademark

This trademark is like a table of contents. It tells about plywood type, wood species, veneer grade,

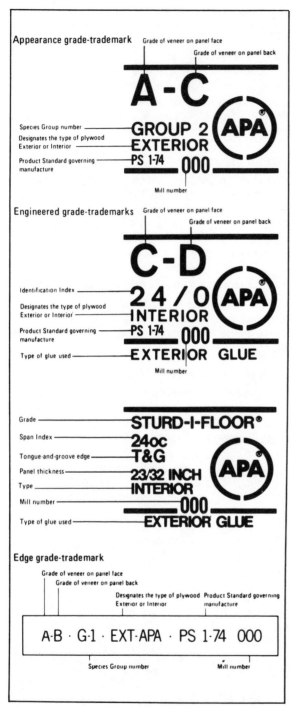

Appearance grade-trademark

Grade of veneer on panel face
Grade of veneer on panel back

A-C

Species Group number
Designates the type of plywood
Exterior or Interior
Product Standard governing
manufacture

GROUP 2
EXTERIOR
PS 1-74   000

Mill number

Engineered grade-trademarks

Grade of veneer on panel face
Grade of veneer on panel back

C-D

Identification Index
Designates the type of plywood
Exterior or Interior
Product Standard governing
manufacture
Type of glue used

24/0
INTERIOR
PS 1-74   000
EXTERIOR GLUE

Mill number

Grade
Span Index
Tongue-and-groove edge
Panel thickness
Type
Mill number
Type of glue used

STURD-I-FLOOR®
24oc
T&G
23/32 INCH
INTERIOR
000
EXTERIOR GLUE

Edge grade-trademark

Grade of veneer on panel face
Grade of veneer on panel back
Designates the type of plywood   Product Standard governing
Exterior or Interior   manufacture

A-B · G-1 · EXT·APA · PS 1-74 000

Species Group number   Mill number

Fig. 7-2. Grade trademarks (courtesy of the American Plywood Association).

glue, and manufacture. The grade-trademarks of "appearance" grades are a little different from those of "engineered" grades, but each tells the story of the panel it marks. Grade-trademarks may be stamped on the panel edge instead of the back if appearance grade veneers are used on both sides, or if both surfaces have a special overlay. Figure 7-2 explains each part of the grade-trademark.

SPECIES GROUPS

There are some 70 species used in manufacturing plywood. Strength and stiffness of the wood varies somewhat among species. So that you don't have to worry about 70 different strength levels, the species have been classified into five groups. The species in each group meet the same set of standards. The groups are numbered from 1 through 5; the woods in species Group 1 are the strongest and stiffest. For example, Douglas fir is stiffer and stronger than Alaska cedar. Table 7-1 shows a breakdown of the various woods in each group.

PLYWOOD GRADES

Just as wood species are classified according to a set of stiffness and strength standards, the veneer made from the wood is separated into grades based on wood characteristics such as knots, splits, and the like. Letters are assigned to veneer grades: N, A, B, C, C-Plugged, and D. N is the most nearly perfect (and is a special-order item), and D is the lowest allowable grade. Any panel that has a D veneer in it is considered and graded as Interior plywood. Table 7-2 summarizes grading characteristics.

Appearance of Grades

Appearance grades of plywood are those used where looks are the most important factor. Figure 7-3 is a breakdown of Interior and Exterior plywoods and their best uses. Plywood sidings, registered as the 303[r] line, come in many different surface patterns that are imparted to the plywood face by sawing, scratch sanding, or grooving. The sidings are used indoors for paneling as well as outdoors. Medium-density overlay (MDO) and high-density overlay (HDO) have resin-treated fiber overlays bonded to one or both sides of a plywood panel. These overlays make the surfaces very smooth and durable. MDO is an ideal base for paint. HDO needs no finishing at all, and it is used primarily for concrete forms and signs.

Table 7-1. Species Group Classification.

Group 1	Group 2	Group 3	Group 4	Group 5
Aputigb a,b.	Cedar, Port Orford	Alder, Red	Aspen	Basewood
Beech, American	Cypress	Birch, Paper	Bigtooth	Fir, Balsam
Birch	Douglas Fir 2c	Cedar, Alaska	Quaking	Poplar, Balsam
Sweet	Fir	Fir. Subalpine	Calivo	
Yellow	California Red	Hemlock, Eastern	Cedar	
Douglas Fir 1c	Grand	Maple, Bigleaf	Incense	
Kapur a	Mobile	Pine	Western Red	
Keruing a,b	Pacific Silver	Jack	Cottonwood	
Larch, Western	White	Lodgepole	Eastern	
Maple Sugar	Hemlock, Western	Ponderosa	Black (Western	
Pine	Lauan	Spruce	Poplar)	
Caribbean	Almon	Redwood	Pine	
Ocote	Bagikan	Spruce	Eastern White	
Pine, Southern	Mayapis	Black	Sugar	
Loblolly	Red Lauan	Englemann		
Shortleaf	Tangle	White		
Slash	White Lauan			
Tanoak	Maple, Black			
	Mengkulang a.			
	Meranti, Red, a.d.			
	Mersawa a.			
	Pine			
	Pond			
	Red			
	Virginia			
	Western Pine			
	Spruce			
	Red			
	Sitka			
	Sweetgum			
	Tamarack			
	Yellow Poplar			

a - represents trade group of closely related species; b - species of same genus collectively; Apitong if originating in Phillipines; c - Douglas fir 1 grown in WA, OR, CA, ID, MT, WY, and Alberta and British Columbia, Canada, Douglas fir 2. grown in NY, UT, CO, AZ and NM, d - limited to species having specific gravity of 0.41 or more based on green volume and oven dry weight.

Table 7-2. Veneer Grade Summary.

N = Smooth surface "natural finish" veneer. Select, all heartwood or all sapwood. Free of open defects. Allows not more than 6 repairs, wood only, per 4-×-8 panel, made parallel to grain and well matched for grain to color.

A = Smooth, paintable. Not more than 18 neatly made repairs, boat, sled, or router type, and parallel to grain, permitted. May be used for natural finish in less demanding applications.

B = Solid surface. Shims, circular repair plugs and tight knots to 1 inch across grain permitted. Some minor splits permitted.

C = Improved C veneer with splits limited to ⅛ inch across grain and some to 1½ inch if total width of knots and knotholes is within specified limits. Synthetic or wood repairs. Discoloration and sanding effects that do not impair strength permitted. Limited splits allowed.

D = Knots and knotholes to 2½ inch width across grain and 1/3 inch larger within specified limits. Limited splits are permitted. Limited to Interior grades of plywood.

Most veneer can be repaired to raise its quality to the next higher grade. Repairs are made in the veneer as soon as it comes from the dryer. A machine cuts out a knot or other defect and at the same time fills the hole with a wood patch of the same thickness. The patches may be any of several shapes (oval, round, or long and narrow).

Use the grade guide in Fig. 7-3 to help you choose the right plywood for a particular job. First, find the job listed in the "use" column. Read across to find the type and grade you need to specify, what a typical grade-trademark looks like, and what thicknesses are available. For example, a soffit is exposed to the weather so you will want an Exterior type panel. Look in the section called "Exterior type." Find soffits in the use column. A-C is the recommended grade, and it is available in the following inch thicknesses: ¼, ⅜, ½, ⅝, and ¾.

Engineered Grades

Engineered grades are the workhorse grades of plywood. They are specially built for strength rather than appearance. They are the panels that enclose a house or give you a solid comfortable floor to walk on. The engineered grades are not sanded, except for Plyform[r] (a concrete form panel), underlayment (a panel for application over subflooring), and Sturdi-I-Floor[r] (a combined, subfloor-underlayment panel). Plyform is fully sanded. Underlayment and Sturdi-I-

	Common uses and descriptions	Use these terms when you specify plywood	Typical grade-trademarks	Grade inner ply	1/4	5/16	3/8	1/2	5/8	3/4
Interior Type	Natural finish cabinets • Furniture (Special order item)	N-N, N-A, N-B INT-APA	N·N·G·1·INT·APA·PS 1·74 / N·A·G·2·INT·APA·PS 1·74	C						•
	Paneling • Cabinets (Special order item)	N-D INT-APA	N-D GROUP 3 INTERIOR PS 1.74 000 (APA)	D	•					
	Built-ins • Cabinets • Furniture • Partitions (Paintable, 2 smooth solid faces)	A-A INT-APA	A·A·G·4·INT·APA·PS 1·74	D	•		•	•	•	•
	Same as A-A except appearance of 1 side less important. (Paintable, 1 smooth face.)	A-B INT-APA	A·B·G·4·INT·APA·PS 1·74	D	•		•	•	•	•
	Paneling • Shelving • 1-good-side partitions (Paintable, 1 smooth solid face)	A-D INT-APA	A-D GROUP 2 INTERIOR PS 1.74 000 (APA)	D	•		•	•	•	•
	Shelving • Walls • Workshop furniture (Utility panel, 2 solid sides)	B-B INT-APA	B·B·G·3·INT·APA·PS 1·74	D	•		•	•	•	•
	Sides of built-ins • Shelving • Bins (Utility panel, 1 solid side)	B-D INT-APA	B-D GROUP 3 INTERIOR PS 1.74 000 (APA)	D	•		•	•	•	•
	Paneling • Interior accent walls Built-ins • Counter facing (Usually textured)	DECORATIVE PANELS-APA	DECORATIVE B·D·G·1 INT·APA PS 1·74	D			•	•	•	
Exterior Type	Fences • Outdoor built-ins • Signs • Boats (Paintable, 2 smooth solid faces)	A-A EXT-APA	A·A·G·3·EXT·APA·PS 1·74	C	•		•	•	•	•
	Same as A-A except appearance of 1 side less important. (Paintable, 1 smooth face.)	A-B EXT-APA	A·B·G·1·EXT·APA·PS 1·74	C	•		•	•	•	•
	Siding • Soffits • Fences • Tanks (Paintable, 1 smooth solid face)	A-C EXT-APA	A-C GROUP 2 EXTERIOR PS 1.74 000 (APA)	C	•		•	•	•	•
	Service buildings • Shelving outdoors, e.g., in carports, garages (Utility panel, 2 solid sides)	B-B EXT-APA	B·B·G·1·EXT·APA·PS 1·74	C	•		•	•	•	•
	Farm buildings • Bins • Ag equipment Tile backing (Utility panel, 1 solid side)	B-C EXT-APA	B-C GROUP 2 EXTERIOR PS 1.74 000 (APA)	C	•		•	•	•	•
	Cabinets • Counter tops • Tanks Concrete forms (Hard, smooth resin-fiber overlay 2 sides)	HDO EXT-APA	HDO·A·A·G·1·EXT·APA·PS 1·74	C or C-Plugged			•	•	•	•
	Siding • Built-ins • Furniture (Smooth, paintable, resin-fiber overlay 1 or 2 sides)	MDO EXT-APA	MDO·B·B·G·4·EXT·APA·PS 1·74	C			•	•	•	•
	Siding • Paneling • Accent walls Counter facing • Fences • Ceilings Storage buildings • Open soffits (Usually textured)	303 SIDING EXT-APA T 1-11 EXT-APA	303 SIDING 6-S/W T 1-11 GROUP 2 24 oc SPAN EXTERIOR PS 1.74 000 (APA); 303 SIDING 6-S GROUP 1 24 oc SPAN EXTERIOR PS 1.74 000 (APA)	C			•	•	•	•
	Boat hulls (A or B face and back. Available also HDO and MDO.)	MARINE EXT-APA	MARINE A·A EXT·APA PS 1·74	B	•		•	•	•	•

Fig. 7-3. Appearance grades (courtesy of the American Plywood Association).

Floor panels are usually "touch sanded." They are sanded only enough to bring them to the proper thickness. Structural and sheathing (unsanded) grades have a set of numbers called the *Identification Index* in the grade-trademark. Sturdi-I-Floor panels carry a *span index* in their grade-trademarks. See Fig. 7-2.

Structural I and II Grades

This family of plywood grades was designed especially for use where extra structural strength is needed, such as gusset plates in trusses, or wall and roof sheathing in high wind and earthquake areas. All engineered graded can be obtained in Structural I or Structural II.

Structural I grades are made only with group 1 woods. Structural II grades may also have Group 2 or 3 woods in their makeup. All structural grades are made only with exterior glue. Structural II grades are generally limited-production items and might not be available everywhere. It's wise to check before specifying Structural II grades.

C-D Interior Sheathing

This grade is one of the most commonly used on the market. It is the panel that's most often called for as the structural covering for wall and roof framing, for subflooring, crates, shelves, and pallets. Most C-D-grade plywood is manufactured with exterior glue. C-D with exterior glue, CDX, should be used if the plywood will be exposed to moisture during construction. D-D with interior glue will withstand limited exposure to moisture during construction. A specification calling for the grade should allow for use of CDX to insure availability.

PLYFORM

Plyform is an American Plywood Association trade name for a special Exterior concrete-forming panel with a B veneer face and back. It can be used many times and it is manufactured in Classes I and II. Class I, due to the wood species used in its manufacture, is somewhat stronger and stiffer than class II and it is more readily available. The engineered grades, their uses, and their available thicknesses are shown in Fig. 7-3.

SELECTING AN ENGINEERED PANEL

Use both the Engineered Grades Guide, Fig. 7-4, and the Identification Index, Table 7-3. Example: Sim-

ple roof decking on supports of 24 inches on center. Because the roof deck (sheathing) will be covered by the finish roof material (shingles, built-up roofing, etc.), you could use an Interior panel. In Fig. 7-3, you see roof sheathing listed in the uses for C-D Interior, which is available in thicknesses from 5/16 to ¾ inch. In Table 7-3, find the indexes with the left hand number 24. The Table shows Interior Group 1, or ½-inch C-D Interior Group 2, 3, or 4.

SPECIFYING AND BUYING PLYWOOD

Whether you order one panel of plywood or enough to build a house, give your dealer the information he needs to properly fill your order. To estimate how much plywood you need:

☐ Multiply length by width of each wall, floor or roof. (Half of the roof at a time if it's a pitched roof.)

☐ For each kind of plywood you need (subflooring, siding, etc.), subtract length times width of each opening such as stairwells and ducts in floors, fireplaces, windows, doors and chimneys.

☐ Divide the number of square feet in each answer by 32 (there are 32 square feet in a plywood panel).

☐ Round off your answer to the next highest whole number.

☐ That will be the number of pieces of plywood you need.

Remember to allow for a little waste even though there isn't much waste with plywood.

Appearance Grades

Designate the thickness, grade, group number, APA grade-trademark, dimensions, and number of pieces. For example: ¼" A-A Group 1, Interior, APA grade-trademarked, 48" × 96", 100 pieces.

Engineered Grades

Designate the thickness, grade, identification index (or span index or group number), type APA grade-trademark, dimensions, number of pieces. For example: 4/8" C-D 24/0, Interior, APA grade-trademarked, 48" × 96", 100 pieces (Note "exterior glue" if preferred).

How Plywood is Made

At the mill, logs are separated and stacked by wood species. They may also be sorted by length and

	Common Uses	Use these terms when you specify plywood	Typical grade-trademarks	Grade inner ply	Common thicknesses (inch)					
					1/4	5/16	3/8	1/2	5/8	3/4
Interior Type	Wall sheathing ● Roof sheathing ● Subflooring	C-D INT-APA WITH EXTERIOR GLUE	C-D 32/16 (APA) INTERIOR PS 1-74 000 EXTERIOR GLUE	D		●	●	●	●	●
	Roof decks ● Structural diaphragms Box beams ● Gusset plates Stressed skin panels ● Pallet bins	STRUCTURAL I C-D INT-APA STRUCTURAL II C-D INT-APA	STRUCTURAL I C-D 24/0 (APA) INTERIOR 000 EXTERIOR GLUE	Improved D		●	●	●	●	●
	Subfloor-underlayment	STURD-I-FLOOR INT-APA	STURD-I-FLOOR 48oc 24 1 1 1 INCH INTERIOR (APA) 000 EXTERIOR GLUE	C & D	(1)19/32, 5/8, 23/32, 3/4, 1-1/8 (2·4·1)					
	Underlayment	UNDERLAYMENT INT-APA	UNDERLAYMENT GROUP 1 (APA) INTERIOR 1 000	C & D	●		●	●	●	●
	Cabinet and built-in backs Wall and ceiling tile backing (Not a substitute for UNDERLAYMENT)	C-D PLUGGED INT-APA	C-D PLUGGED GROUP 2 (APA) INTERIOR PS 1-74 000	D			●	●	●	●
Exterior Type	Subflooring ● Roof decking Siding on service and farm buildings Pallet bins	C-C EXT-APA	C-C 32/16 (APA) EXTERIOR PS 1-74 000	C		●	●	●	●	●
	All engineered uses that demand full Exterior type plywood, as outdoor exposure of uses listed in Interior STRUCTURAL grades	STRUCTURAL I C-C EXT-APA STRUCTURAL II C-C EXT-APA	STRUCTURAL I C-C 48/24 (APA) EXTERIOR PS 1-74 000	C		●	●	●	●	●
	Subfloor-underlayment in moist conditions, as balcony decks	STURD-I-FLOOR EXT-APA	STURD-I-FLOOR 24oc 24 1 (APA) EXTERIOR 000	C	(1)19/32, 5/8, 23/32, 3/4, 1-1/8 (2·4·1)					
	Underlayment ● Shower tile backing Fruit pallet bins ● Tanks	UNDERLAYMENT C-C PLUGGED EXT-APA	UNDERLAYMENT C-C PLUGGED GROUP 2 (APA) EXTERIOR PS 1-74 000	C	●		●	●	●	●
	Same as UNDERLAYMENT C-C Plugged EXT-APA	C-C PLUGGED EXT-APA	C-C PLUGGED GROUP 3 (APA) EXTERIOR PS 1-74 000	C	●		●	●	●	●
	Concrete forms	B-B PLYFORM CLASS I OR II EXT-APA	B-B PLYFORM CLASS I (APA) EXTERIOR PS 1-74 000	C					●	●

(1)Or other solid wood-base material.

Fig. 7-4. Guide to engineered grades of plywood (courtesy of the American Plywood Association).

grade quality before they are cut into peeler blocks. See Fig. 7-5.

Bark, removed from the log, is used as garden mulch or fuel at the plant to provide power. Bark can be removed by a high pressure water jet, chipped off by knurled wheels, or peeled off with knives. See Fig. 7-6.

The last premanufacturing step in plywood production is to cut the peeler blocks. These are the sections of log that will fit the veneer-cutting lathes. Peeler blocks are 8 feet 4 inches long. Blocks are usually soaked in a hot water vat or steamed before peeling. See Fig. 7-7.

Peelable block next travels to a lathe spotter and charger. The spotter elevates and levels the block to the charger. The charger then moves the block forward to lathe chucks that will hold the block against the lathe knife.

Lathe chucks revolve the block against a long knife that peels a continuous thin ribbon of veneer at up to 600 lineal feet per minute. Softwood veneer is usually peeled in thickness ranging from 1/10 inch to 1/4 inch. Fig. 7-8.

Clippers cut the veneer ribbon into usable widths (up to 54 inches) and cut out sections with nonrepair-

Table 7-3. Identification Index of Engineered Grades.

| Thickness Inch | C-D Int - APA C-d Ext - APA | | |
	Group 1 and Structural 1	Group 2[2] or 3 & Structural II[2]	Group 4 (3)
5/16	20/0	16/0	12/0
3/8	24/0	20/0	16/0
1/2	32/16	24/0	24/0
5/8	44/20	32/16	30/12
3/4	48/24	42/20	36/16
7/8		48/4	42/20

Notes: (1) Sheathing/subflooring is ordinarily ordered by Identification Index. Check local availability if a specific combination of thicknesses and Identification Index is desired. Some panels, for example Structural II of all thicknesses, and panels with Identification Indexes of 30/02 and 36/16, may be difficult to obtain (2) Panels with Group 2 outer plies and special thickness and construction requirements, or STRUCTURAL II panels with Group 1 faces, may carry the Identification Index numbers shown for Group 1 Panels. (3) Panels made with Group 3 panels when they conform to special thickness and construction requirements detailed in PS1

Fig. 7-5. Logs ready for separating and grading at the mill (courtesy of the American Plywood Association).

Fig. 7-6. Bark being removed from a log (courtesy of the American Plywood Association).

Fig. 7-7 The final step in manufacturing plywood (courtesy of the American Plywood Association).

184

Fig. 7-8. Peeling veneer on plywood (courtesy of the American Plywood Association).

Fig. 7-9. Clipping plywood into usable lengths (courtesy of the American Plywood Association).

Fig. 7-10. Removing knotholes by diecutting (courtesy of the American Plywood Association).

Fig. 7-11. Glueing and sandwiching plywood sheets (courtesy of the American Plywood Association).

Fig. 7-12. Veneered/sandwiched plywood traveling through a hot press (courtesy of the American Plywood Association).

Fig. 7-13. Completed and graded plywood ready to ship (courtesy of the American Plywood Association).

able defects. Veneers are dried in ovens as much as 100 feet long to a moisture content of about 5 percent. Then they are sorted by grade. See Fig. 7-9.

Small defects, such as knotholes, are removed by diecutting. The holes are filled with patches that will be oval or boat shaped. Grain of wood patches runs the same direction as that of the veneer. Synthetic patches are also used in repairing panels. See Fig. 7-10.

After drying and patching, veneer sheets are glued and sandwiched together in one continuous operation. See Fig. 7-11.

The veneer sandwiches travel to the hot press where they are loaded into racks for bonding under heat and pressure. Generally, the heat range is 230° F to 315° F. The pressure ranges are 175 to 200 pounds per square inch. See Fig. 7-12.

Rough plywood panels are then trimmed to size, sanded (if required), graded, and stamped. Finished panels will move by railroad car or truck to building supply wholesalers and distributors. See Fig. 7-13.

Look around. You'll probably see something made of plywood. It could be a building or chairs, desks, cabinets, shelves, wall paneling, doors or the floor. And if you don't see any plywood, that's because it's probably covered by another material. See Figs. 7-14 and 7-15.

PLYWOOD FLOOR CONSTRUCTION

These days it's almost impossible to get along without using plywood in floor construction. Plywood makes a smooth, solid base for any kind of floor, and usually does it for less money than other materials. In frame construction, basic floor framing—installation of floor joists—is the same whether the building is a house or a livestock building. What changes is the spacing, or span between framing members, and the plywood grade and thickness. The changes are necessary because of different kinds of floor loads.

In residential construction, there are two basic floor systems. There are subfloor with underlayment over it and Sturdi-I-Floor (combined subfloor-underlayment).

Plywood Subfloors

Plywood subflooring is used where it will be covered with an underlayment layer or where a "structural" material such as wood strips or blocks will be the finished surface. The plywood forms a smooth level base for the finished floor. One man can usually put in the entire subfloor of a house in a single day.

Choose the Plywood Subflooring

Use the method given in the Identification Index section. C-D Interior is a good panel to use for subfloorings. Just be sure to specify C-D Interior with exterior glue if the plywood might be exposed for a long time during construction.

In a typical house, the floor joists are 16 inches on center. You can use a C-D INT-APA panel that has a right-hand Identification Index Number of 16 (e.g., 32/16). If your house plans show joists 24 inches on center, use a 48/23C-D INT-APA panel. See Table 7-4.

Fig. 7-14. Plywood has many uses (courtesy of the American Plywood Association).

Fig. 7-15. Plywood on the outside of a home (courtesy of the American Plywood Association).

Table 7-4. Plywood Subflooring.

Panel Identification Index	Plywood Thickness (inches)	Maximum Span (inches)	Nail Size & Type	Nail Spacing=inches Panel Ends	Intermediate Supports
30/12	5/8	12*	8d common	6	10
32/16	1/2 5/8	16**	6d common 8d common	6 6	10 10
36/16	3/4	16**	8d common	6	10
42/20	5/8, 3/4, 7/8	20**	8d common	6	10
48/24	3/4, 7/8	24	8d common	6	10
1 1/8" Groups 1 and 2	1 1/8	48	10d common	6	6
1 1/4" Groups 3 and 4	1 1/4	48	10d common	5	5

*May 16" if 25/32" wood strip flooring is installed at right angles to joists.
**May be 24" if 25/32" wood strip flooring is installed at right angles to joists.
Note: Nominal 20-inch support spacing is actually constructed to be 19.2 inches.

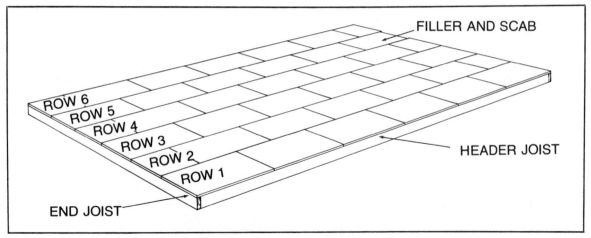

Fig. 7-16. Plywood subfloor (courtesy of the American Plywood Association).

When laying out a plywood subfloor, it is not necessary to stagger end joints of panels, but it is a better practice. End joints must fall over framing. See Fig. 7-16.

How to Lay the Subfloor

Start at one corner of the house. To help you put the panels down in a straight line, snap a chalk line the length of the house (across the floor joists) exactly 4 feet in from the outside edge of the header joists. This will be row 1 of panels. Start row 1. Use a full 4-foot-by-8-foot plywood panel. Lay it flush with the edges of the end and header joists.

Nail the first row 1 panel to floor joists. A good rule of thumb for choosing nail size is 6d for ½-inch and thinner panels and 8d for ⅝-inch and thicker panels. Common nails are called for as all APA testing and recommendations are based on their use. Some, however, find box nails work satisfactory for floor installation even though they tend to bend more easily than common nails and their strength is not as great. See Fig. 7-16.

Place nails ⅜ of an inch from the edge of the plywood and space them 6 inches apart along the outside of the house and along panel ends. Drive nails at a slight angle to make sure they go solidly into the floor joists. Also nail the panel to the joists underneath it. Space nails 10 inches apart along these intermediate joists and 17 inches along each 8-foot supported panel edge. Drive nails accurately so as not to miss the joist. Nails that miss or angle out the side of a joist allow the floor to move and can cause it to squeak.

A subfloor nailing pattern is shown in Fig. 7-17.

Install the rest of the panels in row 1. Always leave a little space between panels to make room for the slight natural expansion of the floor when it is wet. This is *important*. Leave a 1/6-inch space between panel ends (a penny is about that thick) and a ⅛-inch between panel edges. If conditions are very wet or very humid, double the spacing. Trim the end of the last panel flush with the end joist. You likely will have a very narrow scrap or a bit more than a half panel. If you should need an odd-sized panel section to fill in the end of the row, be sure the plywood goes across at least two spans. Also be sure the section is placed with the face grain across the supports like the rest of the panels. If the last panel in the row comes out 1 inch or more short of the inside edge of the end joist (because of an odd building dimension, for instance), nail a 2 × 4 "scab" or block to the end joist to support the panel end. Then use a filler strip of scrap. As an alternate, you can increase the space between the panel ends slightly to gain a little length in a row. See Fig. 7-18.

Install row 2. Use a half panel to start row 2 (Fig. 7-16). Make certain the face grain goes across the floor joists. Remember to leave a ⅛-inch space between the first and second rows. If you need to, trim a panel end slightly as you go down the row to keep end joists roughly centered over the joists.

Install the Remaining Subfloor

Start row 3 using a full-size panel.
Row 4 has a half panel.
Continue the pattern.

191

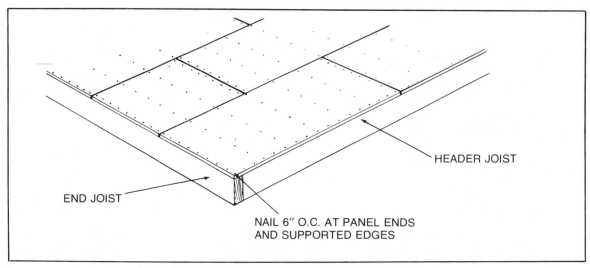

Fig. 7-17. Nailing plywood subfloor (courtesy of the American Plywood Association).

Finish the floor one row at a time. When you come to the centering girder of the house, you might find that the floor joists are overlapped. See Fig. 7-19. If the lap is enough so that panels do not end over the joist for solid nailing, simply trim off the first panel in the row 1½ inches to allow for the lap. Another way to take care of the problem is to scab a 2 × 4 on the side of a joist every 8 feet to support the panel end. See Fig. 7-20. A recommended minimum stapling schedule is shown in Table 7-5.

PLYWOOD UNDERLAYMENT

A "nonstructural" finish flooring material—carpet, vinyl tile, or linoleum—needs a very smooth, solid base under it. The smoothness is needed because rough or high places can cause the material to wear out quickly in those spots. A solid surface is needed to avoid punch through. An example would be a shoe heel poking a hole through a carpet or thin linoleum into a weak spot beneath it. Plywood underlayment is specially designed to go down flat and stay flat, to be solid, and to be smooth. It bridges unevenness the subfloor might have. Plywood underlayment can go over either plywood or lumber subflooring.

When purchasing your plywood underlayment, be sure to specify one of the APA (American Plywood Association) underlayment grades. They have the special inner ply construction that resists punch

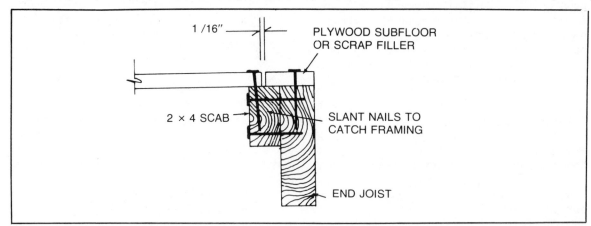

Fig. 7-18. Filler support for plywood subflooring (courtesy of the American Plywood Association).

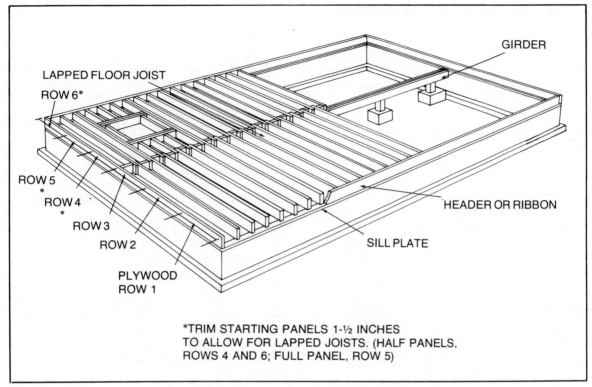

GIRDER

LAPPED FLOOR JOIST

ROW 6*

ROW 5
*

ROW 4
*

ROW 3

ROW 2

PLYWOOD
ROW 1

HEADER OR RIBBON

SILL PLATE

*TRIM STARTING PANELS 1-½ INCHES
TO ALLOW FOR LAPPED JOISTS. (HALF PANELS,
ROWS 4 AND 6; FULL PANEL, ROW 5)

Fig. 7-19. Installing the remaining subfloor (courtesy of the American Plywood Association).

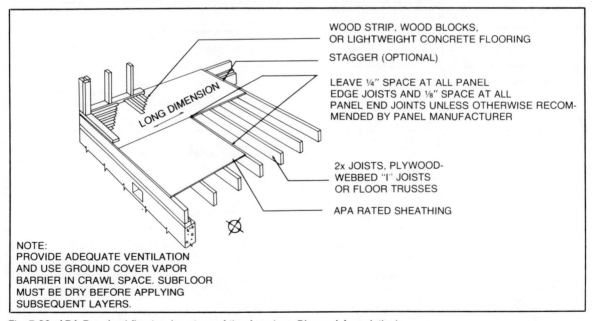

WOOD STRIP, WOOD BLOCKS,
OR LIGHTWEIGHT CONCRETE FLOORING

STAGGER (OPTIONAL)

LEAVE ¼" SPACE AT ALL PANEL
EDGE JOISTS AND ⅛" SPACE AT ALL
PANEL END JOINTS UNLESS OTHERWISE RECOM-
MENDED BY PANEL MANUFACTURER

LONG DIMENSION

2x JOISTS, PLYWOOD-
WEBBED "I" JOISTS
OR FLOOR TRUSSES

APA RATED SHEATHING

NOTE:
PROVIDE ADEQUATE VENTILATION
AND USE GROUND COVER VAPOR
BARRIER IN CRAWL SPACE. SUBFLOOR
MUST BE DRY BEFORE APPLYING
SUBSEQUENT LAYERS.

Fig. 7-20. APA Panel subflooring (courtesy of the American Plywood Association).

Table 7-5. Recommended Minimum Stapling Schedule.

Plywood Thickness	Staple Length (inches)	Spacing Around Entire Perimeter of Sheet (inches)	Spacing at Intermediate Members (inches)
½	1⅝	4	7
⅝	1⅝	2½	4

(A) Values are for 16-ga. galvanized wire staples with a minimum crown width of ⅜ inch.

through, dents from dropping sharp things, and concentrated loads in small areas from such things as a water-heater or furniture legs.

Table 7-6 shows the grades and thickness recommended for underlayment installed over plywood or boards. It also lists the fasteners to be used. Use UNDERLAYMENT IN-APA with exterior glue for kitchens and bathrooms, and UNDERLAYMENT CC Pluggex EXT-APA in extremely damp places where humidity is extremely high. Remember that C-D Plugged Interior is not a good substitute for underlayment because it lacks the special inner ply construction needed for the job.

FINISHING PLYWOOD FOR EXTERIOR EXPOSURE

Energy efficiency relates itself to dollar and cents savings. That is one of the primary reasons we need to learn how to have more energy efficient homes. A good product deserves a quality finish. Whether you are finishing a new house or refinishing an older home, a quality stain or paint can keep the plywood looking good. Care in applying the finish can be the difference in the length of its life.

A finish's primary functions are to protect siding from weathering processes and to help maintain its appearance. Weathering erodes unfinished wood. Different finishes give varying degrees of protection. The type of finish, its quality, quantity and the application method, must be considered in selecting and planning the finish or refinish job. The finish is the final touch on any building. It's important to do it right the first time.

Water-repellent preservatives help reduce the effects of weathering, if reapplied often enough, but they offer only minimum protection. Semitransparent stains are next in effectiveness. They are followed by solid color stains and by a two-coat paint system consisting of primer and top coat. The paint system gives the greatest protection against weathering and erosion of surface.

Table 7-6. Grades and Thickness for Underlayment.

Plywood Group Number and Grades	Subfloor Type	Plywood Thickness (inch	Approximate Fastener Size and Type	Fastener Spacing-inches Panel Edges	Panel Interior
All Groups:	Plywood	¼	3d ring-shank nails	3	6 each way
			18-gauge staples	3	6 each way
Groups 1,2,3, 4,5 UNDERLAYMENT INT-APA (with interior or exterior glue) or UNDERLAYMENT C-C Plugged EXT-APS	Lumber or other uneven surface	⅜ or ½	3d ring-shank nail	6	8 each way
			16-gauge staples	3	6 each way
		⅝ or ¾	4 d ring-shank nail	6	8 each way
			16-gauge staples	3	6 each way
Group 1 only: Grades as above	Lumber to 4" wide	¼	3d ring-shank nails	3	6 each way
			16 gauge staples	3	6 each way

Care and Protection

Plywood should be stored and handled with care to avoid damaging exposure before it is finished. Storage in a cool, dry place out of the sunlight and weather is best. If left outdoors, any straps on the plywood bundles should be loosened or cut and the stacks covered. The covering should allow for good air circulation between the plywood and the cover itself to prevent condensation and mold growth.

At least the first finishing coat should be applied as soon as possible because there is a definite relationship between the finish's performance and the exposure time of the raw wood. This is especially true for exposure to sunlight, wetting, and drying. Do not apply finishes to a hot surface.

Edge Sealing

End grain picks up and loses moisture much faster than side grain so all panels should be edge sealed to help minimize possible damage. Horizontal edges, especially lower drop edges, should be treated with special care because of the greater exposure to wetting from rain and water. Sealing both blind and exposed edges increases the life of the siding and the final finish. Edges cut during construction should be sealed too.

A liberal application of a good water repellent preservative compatible with the final finish should be used for edge sealing if a stain is to be used on the siding's face. If the siding will be painted, use the same exterior house paint primer that will be used on the face. Edge sealing is easiest when the panels are in a stack. A brush should be used to apply the primer. See Fig. 7-21.

Stain Finished

High-quality stains best meet the architectural style of textured plywood sidings. They add color and penetrate the surface for a durable, breathing finish. Stains add to the beauty of plywood siding and show off its rustic rough texture.

Semitransparent Stains

Available in a variety of hues, semitransparent stains give maximum grain show through. Only oil base semitransparent stains are recommended. Other types do not provide adequate protection for the siding.

Semitransparent stains are normally used to emphasize the wood's natural characteristics. This type of stain will show color differences in the wood itself or between the wood and any repairs.

One or two coats of stain should be applied in accordance with the manufacturer's directions. Greater depth of color and a longer life for the finish results from two coats.

Fig. 7-21. Edge sealing of plywood increases its life (courtesy of the American Plywood Association).

Fig. 7-22. Solid color stains (courtesy of the American Plywood Association).

Semitransparent stains are recommended for plywoods that are clear with no patches. Semitransparent stains may be used on other grades if it is desirable to show color contrasts. The stain should be tested on a sample containing color differences between the wood and any patches or within the wood itself to demonstrate the finished appearance.

Brushed plywood surfaces should be finished according to the plywood manufacturer's recommendations; otherwise use an oil base semitransparent stain.

Semitransparent stains are not recommended for an overlaid panel such as MDO.

Solid Color Stains

These highly pigmented, opaque stains cover the wood's natural color, but allow its texture to show. Either oil base or latex emulsion solid color stains may be used.

These stains give a solid, uniform color and work well to mask the wood's own color differences. They also tend to obscure panel characteristics such as

knots and repairs. Correctly applied, quality opaque stains provide a good bond to the panel. See Fig. 7-22. If a solid color stain in light hue is to be used on wood where extractive staining is anticipated, use an oil base. Do not use a latex (water-thinned) stain.

Application Methods

The application method is as important as the finish material itself. It is poor economy to buy a quality stain or paint and then cause it to fail prematurely because of improper application methods.

Apply finishes only to clean and reasonably dry surfaces under good weather conditions. If siding is very dry, application and performance of a latex finish is improved if the surface is dampened first.

☐ Remove construction dirt and loose wood fiber with a stiff brush.

☐ Final brushing should be along the grain to erase any marks.

☐ Do not paint or stain in the rain or when temperatures are low or in direct sunlight when the panel is hot.

☐ Minimum temperatures are 50° F for latex and 40° F for oil systems.

☐ A clean surface is the first step in achieving satisfactory performance from the finish.

STAINING

For best performance, stains should be brushed on. The brush works the stain into the woods' surface and gives a more uniform appearance. See Fig. 7-23.

Application with a long-napped roller is next in order of preference. It tends to work the stain into the surface, although not as well as brushing. When using latex, solid-color stains in hot weather, the siding may be dampened first to prevent too rapid drying and improve performance.

Spraying is the least desirable method and usually results in the poorest performance. If used, the spray must be applied liberally and then back-brushed. Back-brushing, or similar methods, work the stain into the surface and under loose particles, particularly on rough sawn surfaces. The back-brushing also helps to even out spray patterns. This gives a more uniform appearance.

If spray is fogged onto the siding, too little is applied and it adheres only to the extreme surface of loose dust and fibers. These easily erode in the natural weathering process.

Surface Preparation

Thorough surface preparation is essential for good performance of the new finish. Stain or paint applied over dirt, dust or a severely weathered surface that has not been cleaned of debris will not last long.

The amount of surface preparation required will depend upon the siding's condition as well as the type and condition of the original finish.

Clean siding before refinishing.

A brush removes loose dirt and fibers.

Solid color stains will need a more vigorous cleaning. This is especially true if a film shows evidence of flaking. A high pressure water blaster, available from many rental agencies, can be used to remove the loose stain. For previously painted plywood, remove all loose paint, dirt, and chalk before refinishing.

A stiff brush will usually work on textured plywood.

Use a water blaster on more stubborn areas.

Fig. 7-23. Brush application (courtesy of the American Plywood Association).

303 Series Plywood Siding Grades		Stains		Paints Minimum 1 Primer Plus 1 Top Coat (acrylic latex)
		Semi-Transparent (oil)	Solid Color (oil or latex)	
303	-0C	✔	✔	✔
	-0L	Not Recommended	**	✔
	-NR	✔	✔	✔
	-SR	*	✔	✔
303	-6-W	✔	✔	✔
	-6-S	*	✔	✔
	-6-S/W	*	✔	✔
303	-18-W	*	✔	✔
	-18-S	*	✔	✔
	-18-S/W	*	✔	✔
303	-30-W	*	✔	✔
	-30-S	*	✔	✔
	-30-S/W	*	✔	✔

Legend: C-clear; L-overlaid; NR-natural rustic (wood and synthetic patches not permitted); SR-synthetic rustic (permits only natural-defect shaped synthetic repairs); W-wood patch; S-synthetic patch; S/W-both wood and synthetic patches. Number indicates maximum number of patches allowed.

✔ Recommended with provisions given in text.
* Finish may be semi-transparent oil stain if color contrast between repairs and surrounding wood is acceptable. (See text.)
** Some panel manufacturers recommend a single coat of solid color acrylic latex stain. Consult the manufacturer's recommendations.

Continuing government restrictions of ingredients used in formulating stains and paints have resulted in uncertainties about performance. Testing of the new formulations continues and recommendations are being revised as new information becomes available. Be sure to use the latest APA recommendations. This brochure revised December, 1978.

Fig. 7-24. Finishes (courtesy of the American Plywood Association).

The suitability of a cleaned surface for repainting is easily checked with an adhesive bandage. Apply tape with finger pressure to a small area of cleaned and repainted surface. If tape is free of paint when it is removed by a quick pull, the surface is satisfactory for repainting.

Severe checks in sanded plywood should be filled to provide a more even surface and give better appearance and performance to the new finish. Paint usually will not fill cracks and seldom remains intact if used for this.

To fill checks, remove the loose paint, feather the edges of the remaining paint, and clean the surface. Then work a pliable patching compound, such as Tuff Kote (available in most paint stores), into open checks with a broad knife. Work across checked areas. Allow the compound to cure thoroughly, sand smooth, and wipe clean.

Removing Mildew

Mildew can develop on either a stained or painted surface, and especially in warm, humid conditions or in areas with poor air circulation. It usually begins as dark spots that look like surface dirt. It disappears when household bleach is applied. In severe cases, it can cause a uniform gray or black discoloration on large areas. Mildew must be killed and removed before refinishing or it will continue to grow through the newly applied finish.

Mild cases of mildew can be removed by scrubbing the surface with a solution of 1 part household bleach mixed in 3 parts by volume of warm water. Then wash with a detergent and rinse well with water.

More severe cases might require repeated applications. Dirt and chalk from the finish will not bleach and should be removed by scrubbing with a detergent solution. After cleaning, rinse with plenty of water and allow to dry. When using bleach, wear rubber gloves and use goggles to prevent eye damage. This is especially important when you are working overhead.

FOR A LASTING FINISH

☐ Protect the siding on the jobsite.

☐ Seal the edges of all panels. This is especially important for lower drip edges.

☐ Select a high-quality stain or paint system suitable for the siding grade.

☐ Always follow manufacturer's instructions.

☐ Apply finishes to clean surfaces in good weather. Surfaces must be dry for oil finishes but may be dampened for latex.

☐ Recommended finishes are shown in Fig. 7-24.

Chapter 8

Lumber

LUMBER IS CATEGORIZED BY SIZE into boards, dimension, and timbers. See Figs. 8-1 and 8-2. The nominal and minimum-dressed sizes and corresponding surfaces sizes are referred to as 1 × 2s, 2 × 4s, 4 × 10s, etc., and are outlined more fully in Table 8-1. Nominal and minimum-dressed dry sizes of siding at 19 percent maximum-moisture content are given in Table 8-2.

GRADING

Grading of lumber is stated as structural light framing, studs, light framing, structural joists and planks. See Table 8-3. The Western Wood Products Association uses what has become, more or less, a standard grading process that will apply to most of the lumber you purchase. Their grade stamp contains five elements identifying the manufacturer, grade, species, moisture content and certification.

Certification. Each piece of lumber has a symbol that indicates a piece bearing such a symbol has been graded under supervision.

Manufacturer. The originating mill is identified by an assigned number.

Grade. The grade is shown by the grade name or abbreviation such as *Const.* (Construction), *Stand.* (Standard), *Sel. Str.* (Select Structural).

Species Mark. Species or species grouping is indicated by an appropriate symbol.

Moisture Content. Moisture content at time of surfacing is shown by appropriate abbreviations such as *S-Gan* (Surfaces Green), standard size unseasoned lumber with moisture content of 20 percent or more.

FAMILIARITY

The quickest, easiest, and best way to learn about and become familiar with the many woods is gained by a visit to your local lumber dealer. The following are a few descriptions of species and their particular uses. With these points in mind, you will be more easily able to recognize what to look for in the lumber you are about to purchase.

Structural Light Framing (Hem-Fir). Knots must be of same type as in Select Structural grade up to 1½″. Unsound or loose knots or holes are limited to 1″, one per 3 lineal feet. In Fig. 8-3, piece #8 appears to be above grade, but the centerline knot of more than ⅞″ makes it No. 1.

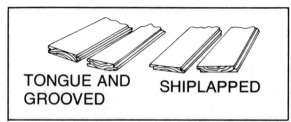

Fig. 8-1. Tongue and groove and shiplapped.

Light Framing (Douglas Fir-Larch). Construction: sound, firm, encased and pith knots, are tight and limited to no larger than 1½″. Unsound or loose knots and holes are limited to 1″, one per 3 lineal feet. Some pieces would be No. 1 or better under Structural Light Framing grading. See Fig. 8-4.

Light Framing (Hem Fir) Steel-knots are not restricted as to quality, but must be well-spaced and of sizes up to what is allowed in Utility grade. This separate grade, suitable for all stud uses, including load-bearing walls, places limitations on crook, wane and edge knots. Lengths are limited to a maximum of 10 feet. See Fig. 8-5.

Structural Joists and Planks (DF-L) Select Structural. Knots are limited to sound, firm, encased and pith knots, if tight and well-spaced, with one unsound or loose knot or hole per 4 lineal feet. Center-line knots range from maximum of 1½″ on 5″ widths to 3¼″ on 14″ widths. Edge knots range from maximums of 1 ″ on 5″ widths to 2⅜″ on 15″ widths. Unsound or loose knots or holes range from maximums of ⅞″ on 5″ widths to 1¼″ on 14″ widths, one per 4 linear feet. See Figs. 8-6 and 8-7.

Select Structural Douglas Fir-Larch No. 2 has well-spaced knots of any quality allowable, with one hole from any cause per 2 lineal feet. See Fig. 8-8.

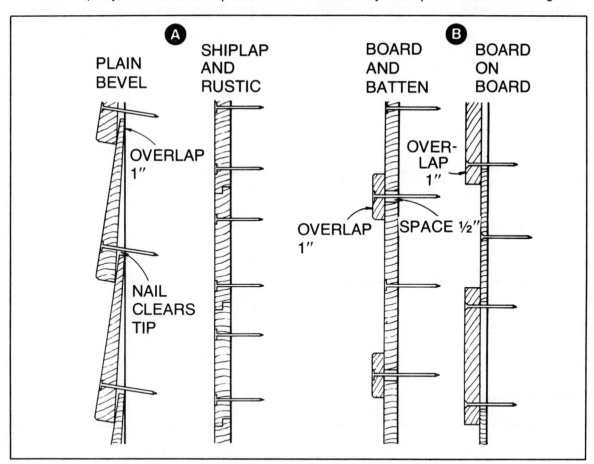

Fig. 8-2. Patterns of wood siding and recommended nailing practices (A: Horizontal; B: Vertical).

Table 8-1. Nominal and Minimum-Dressed Sizes of Finish Boards, Dimension, and Timbers. (The Thicknesses Apply to All Widths and All Widths to all Thicknesses).

ITEM	THICKNESSES				FACE WIDTHS			
	NOMINAL	MINIMUM DRESSED			NOMINAL	MINIMUM DRESSED		
		Inches				Inches		
Select or Finish (19 per cent moisture content)	3/8 1/2 5/8 3/4 1 1-1/4 1-1/2 1-3/4 2 2-1/2 3 3-1/2 4	5/16 7/16 9/16 5/8 3/4 1 1-1/4 1-3/8 1-1/2 2 2-1/2 3 3-1/2			2 3 4 5 6 7 8 9 10 11 12 14 16	1-1/2 2-1/2 3-1/2 4-1/2 5-1/2 6-1/2 7-1/4 8-1/4 9-1/4 10-1/4 11-1/4 13-1/4 15-1/4		
		Dry Inches	Green Inches			Dry Inches	Green Inches	
Boards	1 1-1/4 1-1/2	3/4 1 1-1/4	25/32 1-1/32 1-9/32		2 3 4 5 6 7 8 9 10 11 12 14 16	1-1/2 2-1/2 3-1/2 4-1/2 5-1/2 6-1/2 7-1/4 8-1/4 9-1/4 10-1/4 11-1/4 13-1/4 15-1/4	1-9/16 2-9/16 3-9/16 4-5/8 5-5/8 6-5/8 7-1/2 8-1/2 9-1/2 10-1/2 11-1/2 13-1/2 15-1/2	
Dimension	2 2-1/2 3 3-1/2	1-1/2 2 2-1/2 3	1-9/16 2-1/16 2-9/16 3-1/16		2 3 4 5 6 8 10 12 14 16	1-1/2 2-1/2 3-1/2 4-1/2 5-1/2 7-1/4 9-1/4 11-1/4 13-1/4 15-1/4	1-9/16 2-9/16 3-9/16 4-5/8 5-5/8 7-1/2 9-1/2 11-1/2 13-1/2 15-1/2	
Dimension	4 4-1/2	3-1/2 4	3-9/16 4-1/16		2 3 4 5 6 8 10 12 14 16	1-1/2 2-1/2 3-1/2 4-1/2 5-1/2 7-1/4 9-1/4 11-1/4	1-9/16 2-9/16 3-9/16 4-5/8 5-5/8 7-1/2 9-1/2 11-1/2 13-1/2 15-1/2	
Timbers	5 & Thicker		1/2 Off		5 & Wider		1/2 Off	

Source, PS 20-70 American Softwood Lumber Standard

Select Structural Douglas Fir-Larch No. 3. Well-spaced knots of any quality are allowable, with one hole from any cause per lineal foot. See Fig. 8-9.

Structural Joists and Planks (Hem-Fir). Knots are limited to sound, firm, encased and pitch knots if tight and well-spaced, with one unsound or loose knot or hole per 4 lineal feet. Centerline knots range from maximum of 1½″ on 5″ widths to ¾″ on 14″ widths. Edge knots range from maximums of 1″ on 5″ widths to 3 ⅜″ on 14″ widths. Unsound or loose knots are holes range from maximums of 7/7″ on 5″ widths to 1¼″ on 14″ widths, one per 4 lineal feet. See Fig. 8-10.

Structural Joists and Planks (Hem-Fir) No. 1. Knots must be of the same type as in Select Structural grade, but can be slightly larger, with one unsound or loose knot or hole permitted per 3 lineal feet. See Fig. 8-11.

Structural Joists-Planks (Hem-Fir) No. 2. Well-

Table 8-2. Nominal and Minimum-Dressed Dry Sizes of Siding at 19 Percent Maximum-Moisture Content. (The Thicknesses Apply to all Widths and all Widths to all Thicknesses).

ITEM	THICKNESSES		FACE WIDTHS	
	NOMINAL [1]	MINIMUM DRESSED	NOMINAL	MINIMUM DRESSED
		Inches		Inches
Bevel Siding	½ 9/16 ⅝ ¾ 1	7/16 butt, 3/16 tip 15/32 butt, 3/16 tip 9/16 butt, 3/16 tip 11/16 butt, 3/16 tip ¾ butt, 3/16 tip	4 5 6 8 10 12	3½ 4½ 5½ 7¼ 9¼ 11¼
Bungalow Siding	¾	11/16 butt, 3/16 tip	8 10 12	7¼ 9¼ 11¼
Rustic and Drop Siding (shiplapped, ⅜-in. lap)	⅝ 1	9/16 23/32	4 5 6	3 4 5
Rustic and Drop Siding (shiplapped, ½-in. lap)	⅝ 1	9/16 23/32	4 5 6 8 10 12	2⅞ 3⅞ 4⅞ 6⅝ 8⅝ 10⅝
Rustic and Drop Siding (dressed and matched)	⅝ 1	9/16 23/32	4 5 6 8 10	3⅛ 4⅛ 5⅛ 6⅞ 8⅞

[1] For nominal thicknesses under 1 inch, the board measure count is based on the nominal surface dimensions (width by length). With the exception of nominal thicknesses under 1 inch, the nominal thicknesses and widths in this table are the same as the board measure or count sizes.

Table 8-3. Dimension Lumber Grades (National Grading Rule).

GRADE	
2″-4″ Thick, 2″-4″ Wide	
Structural Light Framing	Sel Str (Select Structural) No. 1 No. 2 No. 3
Studs Light Framing	Stud Const (Construction) Std (Standard) Util (Utility)
2″-4″ Thick, 6: Wide	
Structural Joists and Planks	Sel Str (Select Structural) No. 1 No. 2 No. 3
2″-4″ Thick, 2″ and Wider	
Appearance Framing	A (appearance)

spacea knots of any quality are allowable, with one hole from any cause per 2 lineal feet. See Fig. 8-12.

Structural Joists-Planks (Hem-Fir) No. 3. Well-spaced knots of any quality are allowable, with one hole from any cause per lineal foot. See Fig. 8-13.

Structural Joists and Planks (PP-Ponderosa Pine). Knots are limited to sound, firm, encased and pith knots, if tight and well-spaced, with one unsound or loose knot or hole per 4 lineal feet. Centerline knots range from maximums of 1½″ on 5″ widths to 3¼″ on 14″ widths. Edge knots range from maximums of 1″ on 5″ widths to 2 ⅜″ on 14″ widths. Unsound or loose knots or holes range from maximums of ⅞″ on 5″ widths to 1¼″ on 14″ widths, one per 5 lineal feet. In Fig. 8-14, piece No. 2 shows pitch streaks and piece No. 4 shows stain. Both are allowable.

Structural Joists-Planks Ponderosa Pine No. 1. Knots must be of the same type as in Select Structural grade, but can be slightly larger, with one unsound or loose knot or hole permitted per 3 lineal feet. See Fig. 8-15.

INSTALLING WOOD SIDING

Because wood siding is precision-manufactured to standard sizes, it is easily cut, fitted, and fixed in place with ordinary tools.

Rows of horizontal siding (courses) should be spaced so that a single board runs continuously above and below windows and above doors without notching. Bevel siding, 6 inches wide, should have at least 1 inch of overlap between courses. Siding 8 inches or wider will overlap 1-1½″, depending on spacing required between window heights. See Fig. 8-16.

Butt siding snugly against door and window casings, corner boards, and adjoining boards. Corner boards should lie flat against the sheathing.

If metal corner covers are used, siding board should be carefully cut to avoid leaving a hollow place under the corner cover where water could collect. Mitered corners should be precisely fitted for the same reason. See Fig. 8-17.

Fasten siding in place with either zinc-coating aluminum or any other nonporous nails. Do not use

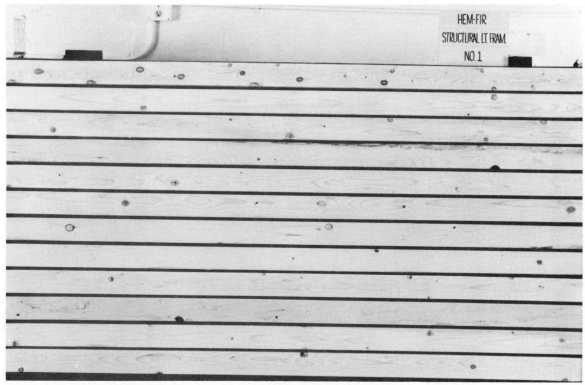

Fig. 8-3. Hem-Fir structural light framing #1 (courtesy of Western Wood Products).

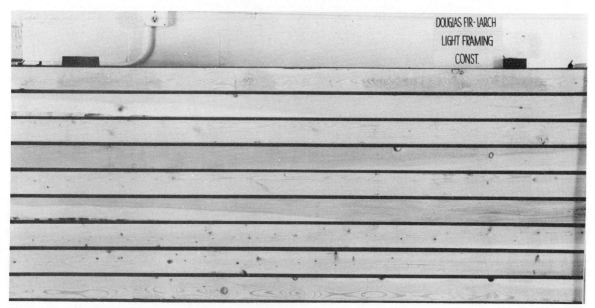

Fig. 8-4. Douglas Fir-Larch light framing (courtesy of Western Wood Products).

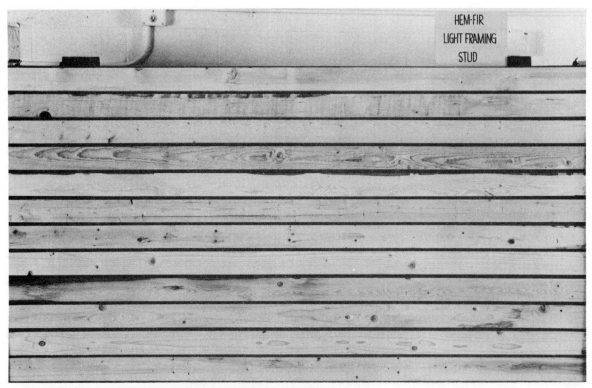

Fig. 8-5. Hem-Fir light framing stud (courtesy of Western Wood Products).

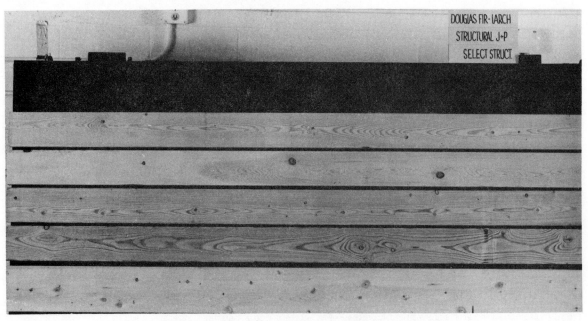

Fig. 8-6. Douglas Fir-Larch, structural joists, and planks (courtesy of Western Wood Products).

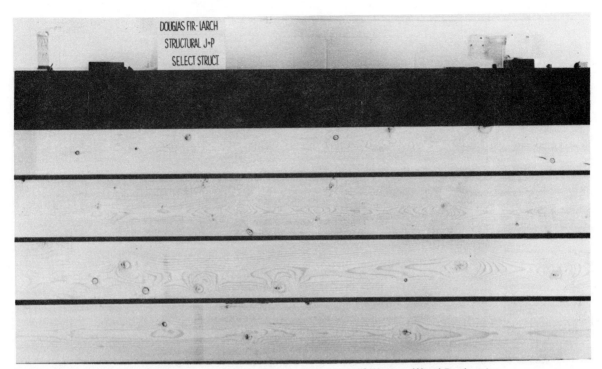

Fig. 8-7. Douglas Fir-Larch structural joists and planks select (courtesy of Western Wood Products).

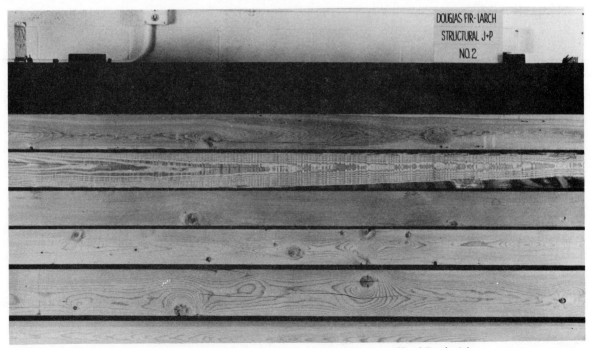

Fig. 8-8. Douglas Fir-Larch structural joists and planks #2 (courtesy of Western Wood Products).

207

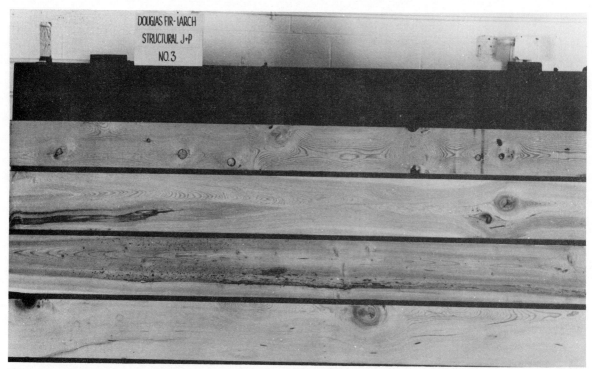

Fig. 8-9. Douglas Fir-Larch joists and planks, #3 (courtesy of Western Wood Products).

Fig. 8-10. Hem-Fir structural joists and planks, select (courtesy of Western Wood Products).

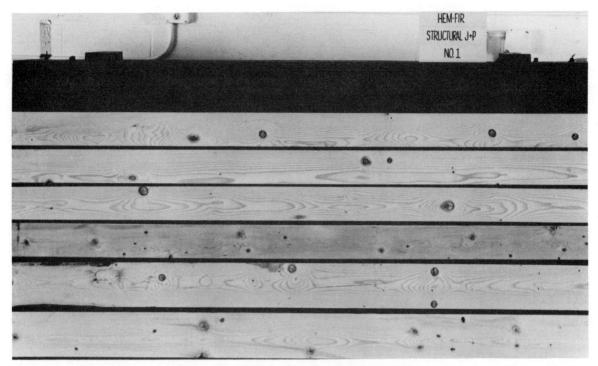

Fig. 8-11. Hem-Fir structural joists and planks #1 (courtesy of Western Wood Products).

Fig. 8-12. Hem-Fir structural joists and planks #2 (courtesy of Western Wood Products).

Fig. 8-13. Hem-Fir structural joists and planks #3 (courtesy of Western Wood Products).

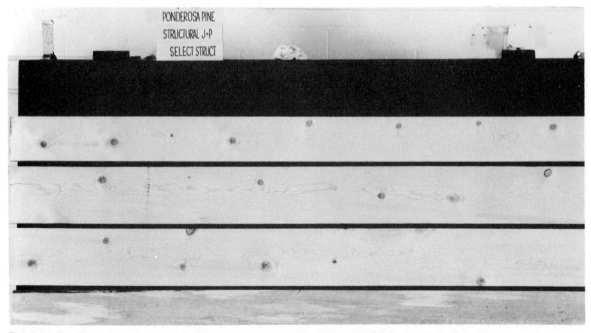

Fig. 8-14. Ponderosa pine structural joists and planks, select (courtesy of Western Wood Products).

210

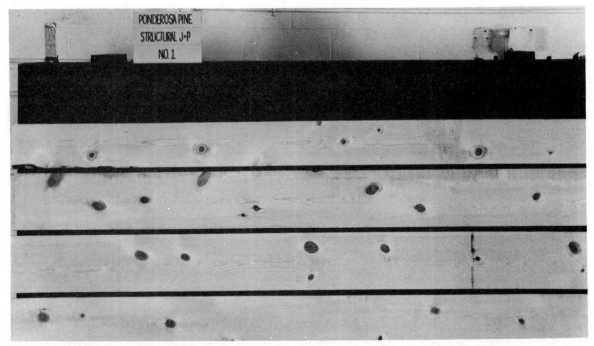

Fig. 8-15. Ponderosa pine structural joists and planks #1 (courtesy of Western Wood Products).

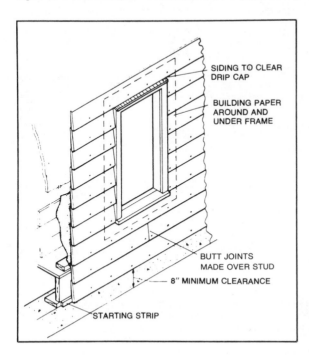

SIDING TO CLEAR DRIP CAP

BUILDING PAPER AROUND AND UNDER FRAME

BUTT JOINTS MADE OVER STUD

8″ MINIMUM CLEARANCE

STARTING STRIP

Fig. 8-16. Installing beveled siding.

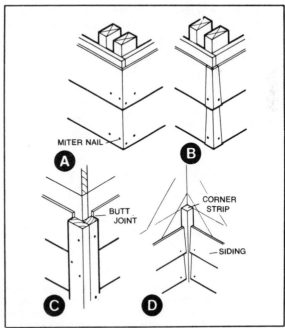

MITER NAIL

BUTT JOINT

CORNER STRIP

SIDING

Fig. 8-17. Recommended procedures for corners of siding: A, miter; B, metal; C, corner boards, D; Interior Corners.

plain steel-wire nails (especially the large headed type). The large headed type are designed for flush driving because they make unsightly rough spots on most paints. Even small-headed plain steel nails, countersunk and puttied, are likely to spot the finish with rust. Natural finished siding is installed best with aluminum nails.

THE HOUSE AND MOISTURE

Wood siding is a part of the house; therefore, its performance is vitally affected by the rest of the structure. The whole house must be properly built to insure long-lasting service.

Insulation, weather stripping, and generally tight construction reduce fuel bills and make for comfort. But their misuse can create some paint problems.

Water vapor formed within a house moves through the inner surfaces for the outer walls because of differences in temperature between the inside and outside. This water vapor condenses and collects as water or frost in the siding during the winter. With the return of warm weather during spring this moisture can, and often does, cause the exterior paint to blister. Other factors, such as air conditioning and humidifying enhance the problem. See Fig. 8-18.

A number of measures can be taken to help keep moisture out of walls which, in turn, keeps the lumber in excellent shape for many years. One of the most effective measures is to put a good vapor barrier under the plaster, drywall, or paneling. Asphalt-coated paper, aluminum foil, and polyethylene film are good vapor barriers. See Chaper 3 and Chapter 5 for details.

Rain and snow water also must be kept out. Some ways to do this are:

☐ Slope roof gutters.

☐ Have sufficient downspouts so that the roof gutters won't overflow during rainstorms and let water seep through the siding.

☐ Attic flooring should be well insulated and attic spaces ventilated so that heat losses do not melt snow on roofs to produce ice dams and clog gutters. See Fig. 8-19.

☐ Wide roof overhangs help in keeping moisture out. So does metal flashing in roof valleys, along dormers, and around chimneys.

☐ Window and door frames must also be adequately capped with flashing.

TREATMENT FOR SIDING

Siding can be dipped in a water-repellent preservative before it is installed or the water-repellent preservative can be brushed on after the siding is installed and before it is painted. These preservatives contain fungicides, resins, and waxes that are water repellent. Water runs off instead of penetrating into the wood at end and lap joints.

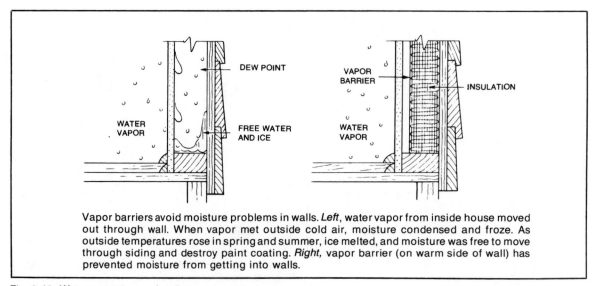

Vapor barriers avoid moisture problems in walls. *Left,* water vapor from inside house moved out through wall. When vapor met outside cold air, moisture condensed and froze. As outside temperatures rose in spring and summer, ice melted, and moisture was free to move through siding and destroy paint coating. *Right,* vapor barrier (on warm side of wall) has prevented moisture from getting into walls.

Fig. 8-18. Water vapor in wood walls.

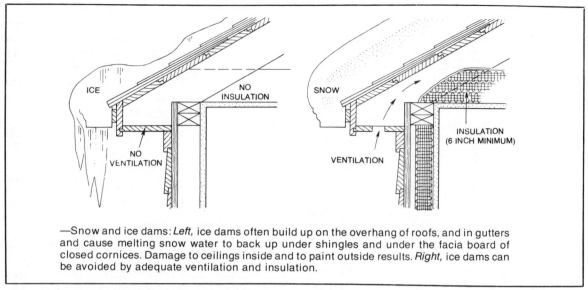

—Snow and ice dams: *Left,* ice dams often build up on the overhang of roofs, and in gutters and cause melting snow water to back up under shingles and under the facia board of closed cornices. Damage to ceilings inside and to paint outside results. *Right,* ice dams can be avoided by adequate ventilation and insulation.

Fig. 8-19. Measure to help keep moisture control.

Wood Finishes

The initial finish on lumber siding is the most important because it is the foundation for all subsequent finishes and will probably remain there for the life of the house. Selection of the finish must be made from two broad classes:

—Natural finishes.
—Paints.

Natural finishes are stains or preservatives. The choice will depend to a great degree on your preference. Consideration should be given to advantages and disadvantages of each class of finish. See Fig. 8-20. Paint is best for smooth surfaces; stains and preservatives are best for rough surfaces.

Natural Finishes

Natural finishes either form a surface coat or penetrate the wood. Natural finishes that form a surface coating provide a lustrous, even glossy coating. These are chiefly *spar varnishes*. A completely durable natural finish of this type has not yet been developed.

Fig. 8-20. Wood finishes.

Penetrating natural finishes leave little or no continuous coating on the surface. Because there is no coating, there is no failure by blistering or peeling. These finishes are, therefore, ideally suited for rough and flat-grained surfaces that are difficult to paint effectively.

Penetrating natural finishes include oil-base penetrating pigmented stains and water-repellent preservative finishes. Water-repellent preservatives penetrate wood readily and protect it from end staining, excessive cupping or twisting, and mildew.

Wood finished in this manner will weather to a clean buckskin color or a light tan color. Preservative finishes usually need refurbishing every two years. Adding pigment to the water repellent preservatives will enhance durability. Penetrating pigmented stains can be applied at any time over the water-repellent preservative treatment.

Good penetrating pigment stains are inexpensive and much more durable than water-repellent preservative finishes. Stains penetrate and color wood. This partially obscures the grain, but leaves little or no surface film. Rough-sawn weathered wood and absorptive surfaces are especially suitable for stains. Good stains should last at least 5 years, and many last as long as 10 years. Even or planned surfaces allow them to last at least as long as many paints before needing renewal.

Paints last longer on edge-grained soft woods of low density that are load swelling than on dense flat grained woods. Such flat-grained boards are better left rough sawn and finished with a stain. In painting flat grained surfaces with broad bands of summerwood, special care should be taken in selecting high-quality nonporous primers and topcoats that will protect the wood surface from excessive moisture.

Any wood surfaces, such as plywood and fiberboards that are overlaid with resin-treated paper, are excellent for painting. The overlay will serve as a stabilizer against swelling from moisture.

Because stains form little or no coating on the surface of the wood, they do not blister, crack, curl, flake, or scale. They are easily maintained and are ideal for finishing surfaces such as plywood and flat-grained surfaces that are difficult to paint.

HOUSE PAINTS

House paint consists of the solid parts (*pigments*) and a liquid part (the *vehicle*). The pigments include hiding (opaque) and transparent (extending) pigments.

The vehicle of an oil-based paint generally consists of a drying oil (usually linseed oil), an oil modified with an alkyd resin, a solvent (mineral spirits or turpentine), and a small amount of paint dryer to harden the paint promptly after application. The vehicle of latex paint consists of a suspension of resin particles, usually acrylic or vinyl, in water.

The performance characteristics of a paint depend to a great extent on the nature of the pigment, the proportion of pigment to vehicle, and the kind of vehicle. House paint is the most widely used finish for wood (lumber) siding. White is the most popular color. A good house paint should last from 3 to 5 years before it must be renewed.

Oil-base and Alkyd House Paints

White house paints can be classified simply according to the kind of white pigments used in them. The white pigments used have included white lead oxide, zinc oxide, and titanium dioxide. Each type has some characteristics generally considered as good in house paint. These include durability sufficient to last up to six years before needing renewal, a normal form of wearing that insures a good paint surface with a minimum of preparatory work, and a normally fast rate of wear from the surface. The wear requirement prevents the accumulation of an excessively thick film of paint when a reasonable maintenance schedule is followed (a single coat every four or five years or two coats every six years).

All paints have some desirable features and some are not so desirable. To select the type of paint likely to give the most satisfactory service, you should be familiar with the conditions in your area to which house paints are subjected. Paint should also have a clean, highly reflective color and ability to remain free from excessive dirt collection in service. It should be nonsensitive to moisture. It should not be stained by metal corrosion and wood extractives. Nor should it be discolored by hydrogen sulfide or organic sulfides. No one type of house paint on the market has all of these characteristics.

The homeowner must also determine the types of paint that will stand up best under the above conditions, which of the various paint properties are important to him under the circumstances, and which are relatively unimportant.

In terms of years of service, white lead paint has been used the longest. It has been used on houses since Colonial times, and it is still preferred by some painters and homeowners to any other type of house paints. Nevertheless, it accounts for only a very small fraction of the total house paint now used in the United States.

White lead paint is a durable paint that normally fails by chalking and crumbling. Probably the most important of its properties, however, is its nonsensitiveness to water. Even when exposed to water for a long period of time, it swells only about as much as wood does when wet. Consequently, it has little tendency to blister, and can be used where moisture blistering is an obvious paint problem.

One of the objections to white lead paint is its retention of dirt. Another objection is that it discolors on contact with hydrogen sulfide gases that cause the formation of black lead sulfide.

Paints pigmented with a combination of white lead and titanium are sold as "titanized white lead." Paints of the titanium lead type are nonsensitive to moisture. Therefore, they are very blister resistant. Because of this property, titanium and lead pigments were used universally for many years in house paint primers.

Paint with zinc oxide pigment usually has a brilliant and highly reflective color, remains uniformly clean in service, and it is mildew resistant. It is highly desirable for areas where humidity is high and mildew is excessive. It is generally hard and it wears away slowly.

Paints of this type normally fail by cracking, curling, and flaking. With paints that fail in this manner, the coating on the wood must not be permitted to become too thick, and the cracking failure must not be permitted to advance too far before repainting. Because zinc-containing paints swell when wet, they blister more readily on contact with water than do the other types of paint.

Paints containing zinc are more likely to become stained by nail rust and by the corrosion products of iron and copper screens reacting with zinc. House paints made with zinc oxide and titanium dioxide, often called "fume-proof" paint, do not discolor on exposure to hydrogen sulfide or organic sulfide gases.

Paints with titanium pigment combined with alkyd-oil resin vehicles are widely used. Alkyd paints are sold as "flat-alkyd, low-luster, breather-type, blister-resistant, and self-priming" paints. They will have little or no glass and will also be very porous. The performance of alkyd paints relates to quality; the better the quality the better the performance.

Titanium-alkyd paints normally fail by cracking and peeling and will chalk excessively if formulated

with an excessively low-vehicle content. The porous nature of the flat-alkyd type paints makes them quite susceptible to extractive staining over redwood and cedar. These paints should, therefore, be applied over a nonporous, zinc oxide-free primer that will protect the wood surface from excessive moisture in the form of rain and dew. They resist sulfide discoloration.

Dark-color paints, sometimes called *trim paints* or *trim-and trellis* paints consist chiefly of dark-color pigments with little, if any, white pigment or extending pigment. In most trim paints, the major part of the vehicle is varnish (usually an alkyd-resin varnish). Iron oxide-paints—the familiar red barn paints—can also be classified as dark-color paints. Sometimes used on houses, they are very durable if of good quality. In general good paints of dark colors are more durable than white or light-color paints.

Latex House Paints

Exterior latex white paints are usually based on suspensions of either acrylic or vinyl resins and titanium dioxide pigment. Latexes of this type can also be modified with alkyd-oil resins. These paints can have an excellent adhesion to wood surfaces, blister resistance, tint retention, and durability. Their ease of application and cleanup with water makes them very popular. Like the flat-alkyd paints, however, they are porous, and should be applied over a nonporous, oil-base primer on both new wood, which contains colored extractives, and old chalky oil-base paint.

Paint Primers

Some paints can be used as self-primers; whereas others require a special primer for the first coat on new wood. The proper choice of primer can do much to insure long-lasting, trouble-free paint performance. In particular, a primer should be nonporous, flexible, and blister resistant. It should, therefore, not contain zinc oxide pigment. Most paint manufacturers provide special, zinc-free, house-paint primers or undercoaters for use with paints containing zinc. As a rule, it is wise to use primer and finish paint of the same brand.

The *breather paints* and titanium flat-alkyd resin paints are usually used as self-primers. But they can be too porous to provide complete protection against moisture.

Very refractory wood surfaces, such as those of dense pine or fir, flat grain, wood with knots, and exterior plywood, will need the protection from moisture in many situations that only aluminum primers can provide. Aluminum paint for wood is the most impervious of the primers.

Some general points to consider prior to selecting house paints are:

☐ Where moisture troubles are widespread, a zinc-free paint of a high-quality latex should be used.

☐ The construction of the house must also be considered. Does it have a wide roof overhang to shield the walls?

☐ Does it have adequate gutters and downspouts? Are they properly installed?

☐ Is there a good vapor barrier, plus insulation?

☐ Are the attic spaces well insulated and vented?

If the answer to the above questions is "yes", the probabilities for minimal and successful paint performance are very good.

Finishing Wood Siding and Trim

When to paint, when to begin, and how many coats should you use are a few of the factors to consider when you are thinking about painting your home. Remember that painting and maintaining the outside, as well as the inside of your home, provides home energy efficiency and economy.

Finish paint can be applied with a brush, a spray, or a roller. Most professionals and do-it-yourselfers will use a brush. There are three basic steps for painting exterior woods:

☐ Apply water-repellent preservative by brush, roller, or squit can to all joints—wherever two pieces of wood come together—and ends of boards. Allow to dry for two days before priming. Water repellent preservatives should be applied to all joints before painting. See Fig. 8-21.

☐ Apply nonporous, zinc-free, oil-base primer thick enough to cover the wood grain.

☐ Within two days to two weeks after applying primer, apply latex or oil-base topcoats. Two topcoats should be applied in areas fully exposed to the weather.

Finish is best applied during warm weather when several weeks of sunshine can be expected. If a new house is built during fall or winter, it could create a problem because many builders let the house stand with a prime coat until spring before finishing the job. The best practice in this instance is to brush water-repellent preservatives on the siding, after which it can go without finish until spring.

How Many Coats?

While it depends largely on the type of paint used, as a rule three coats are recommended for new wood. The third coat can be applied only to areas exposed to severe weathering. A first paint job of oil-base paint should be 4½ to 5 mils (thousandths of an inch) thick; that is approximately the thickness of a dollar bill.

Exceptionally heavy coats, where oil-base paint is applied at a rate of 450 to 500 square feet a gallon, are likely to result in wrinkling, loss of gloss, and slow drying during cold weather. The optimum thickness of a three-coat latex system is 3 to 3.5 mils. See Fig. 8-22.

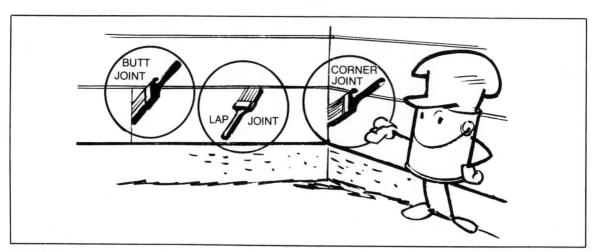

Fig. 8-21. Application of water-repellent preservatives.

Fig. 8-22. Three coats of paint will last twice as long as two coats.

With paint, an old craftsman's rule is follow the sun around the house. The north side should be painted early in the morning, the east side late in the morning, the south side well after noon, and the west side during late afternoon.

Morning dew or the water of a brief shower should be wiped off, and, after waiting about half an hour painting can begin. After many hours of hard rain, painting should be held up for up to two days to make sure the surface is completely dry.

If you are a beginner to house painting, you can learn to gauge spreading rates by applying a pint of paint evenly over a measured area. For example:

☐ At a spreading rate of 450 square feet to the gallon, a pint covers 55 square feet (or an area of 5 by 11 feet).

☐ At 550 square feet a gallon, a pint covers approximately 70 square feet (or an area of 5 by 14 feet).

For modern oil paints of average composition, a total thickness of between 4½ and 5 mils results when one coat of housepaint primer is applied at 450 square feet a gallon and two coats of finish paint at 550 square feet a gallon each.

In warm, dry weather, allow each coat of oil-base paint to dry for two days prior to applying the next coat. In cold, damp weather, allow paint to dry for three to four days, but not as long as two weeks. Coats of latex paint can be applied within a few hours of each other.

STAINING

Penetrating stains are very easy to apply. For smooth surfaces that are not too absorptive, two coats of stain should be avoided because the second coat will not penetrate. This results in holdout of the stain in certain areas to produce unsightly glossy spots.

On smoothly planed wood surfaces, a one-coat application will last approximately three years. Rough-sawn and weathered-wood surfaces are much more absorptive than newly planed surfaces. They are finished best with two coats of penetrating stain. Two coats of stain on rough surfaces will last up to 10 years.

The second coat of stain should be applied within an hour of the first so that both coats will penetrate. Do *not* allow the first coat to dry because this will act as a sealer, and the second coat will not be able to penetrate. Stain that has not penetrated after an hour should be wiped from the surface. Penetrating stain will "lap" badly if the front edge of stain area is permitted to dry. Stains should be applied to only one or two courses of siding at the time. The course should be completed before painting is stopped.

Because the stain penetrates, there is no coating on the surface that can later separate by peeling and flaking. Penetrating stains are ideal finishes for wood surfaces considered difficult to paint and for those exposed to high-moisture conditions.

MAINTENANCE OF FINISHES

Repainting or Restaining. Hot summer sun, wind-driven rain, hail, dust, and winter snow and ice gradually take a toll on even the best finish. How frequently the finish should be renewed is governed by the rate at which it weathers away. A paint maintenance program is determined by the kind of paint used in the initial paint job. The basic rule of thumb is to paint only after most of the old paint film has weathered away.

Coating thickness builds up dangerously if paint, especially oil base, is applied too frequently. Abnormal behavior spells trouble and possibly costly removal of old paint by blow torch or by paint and varnish remover.

Paint that starts to crack and peel from the wood indicates that a serious moisture problem is involved. It might indicate two conditions:

☐ A primer was used that was sensitive to water and perhaps too porous to provide adequate protection from rain and dew.

☐ Moisture from cold weather condensation or ice dams is excessively wetting the walls and the siding.

Quality latex paints properly applied to old painted surfaces are excellent refinish systems. Latex does not always bond well to chalk surfaces. And because of its porosity, it holds rain and dew. In turn, this water can penetrate the paint film and produce an abnormal peeling problem. When repainting chalky surfaces with exterior latex you should:

☐ Remove the chalk by sanding, scrubbing, or steel wooling.

☐ Apply a new coat of oil-base primer over the chalk.

Penetrating natural stains are easy to renew. Fresh finish is simply applied when the old finish appears to need it. As with the first finishing job, any excess of stain or oil should be wiped off so that formation of a surface coat is prevented.

ELIMINATING PAINT TROUBLES

Paint troubles arise from various causes. Most common are porous finish systems that allow rain and dew to enter the coating, improper first priming of wood with wide summerwood bands, repainting too soon without washing, moisture vapor troubles in tightly built insulated houses that lack vapor barriers, or rain or other water getting behind the siding. Evidence of paint trouble is seen in the form of cracking, blistering, and peeling.

If these problems arise, the probable cause of the trouble should be ascertained before repainting. If it is due to springtime blistering on localized areas on the house in the colder regions of the country, a more effective vapor barrier is needed. This can be obtained by painting the indoor side of the exterior walls. Two coats of aluminum paint plus two coats of decorative paint are best for sand-finish plaster. On smooth plaster, a primer-sealer and at least one coat of semi-gloss paint make a good barrier. Shutting off humidifiers will also help.

Where the trouble is due to water getting inside the walls from the roof, leaks should be found. If the trouble is due to ice damning (Fig. 8-19) the situation can be improved by increasing the insulation in the attic floor to a minimum thickness of 6 inches and by increasing the screened venting area of the attic to 1/225 of the ceiling area. See Chapter 3 for complete details.

If the gutters overflow during heavy rains, additional downspouts might be needed or the gutters might need to be cleaned and rehung with a greater pitch. If paint fails first at ends of boards, water is getting through the joints of the siding, and lap and butt joints should be treated with water-repellent preservatives before repainting. Water-repellent solutions are highly penetrating. They creep well into the joints to seal them against future inroads of rainwater.

"Snowflake" peeling of paint, especially in protected areas, indicates that the old paint surface was not adequately washed before repainting.

Tan-to-brown-discoloration stains on redwood and cedar siding on all sides of the house mean that the paint was too thin and porous. This allowed rain and dew to pass through the coating to dissolve the extractives.

This type of paint condition frequently involves peeling because too much rain and dew penetrate the old paint layers. These failures occur on all sides of a building and on both heated and unheated buildings. Such failures are usually corrected by priming an old paint surface with a good nonporous oil-based primer before the top coat is added. Regardless of the cause of a paint problem you should:

—Find the problem.
—Correct the problem.
—Repaint.

Chapter 9

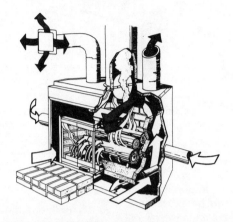

Fireplaces

THE EFFICIENT USE OF FIREPLACES is one way to cut expenses for heating fuels and to conserve energy. What kind of fireplace is most efficient? What wood should be used as fuel? Is it safe? Where can firewood be found? Is it less expensive than other fuels? How should fireplaces be handled by the homeowner?

A fire generates a large flow of air from the hearth and up the chimney. The source of this flow is usually the air in the house that has already been heated by the furnace. While the fire is warming the immediate area with radiant heat, it is also cooling the rest of the house by expelling warm air out through the chimney.

A heat transfer occurs and results in a heat loss if the inside/outside temperature difference is greater than 30 degrees. If your thermostat is set at 68 and the outside temperature is more than 38, a fire in the fireplace will cause your furnace to burn more fuel than it otherwise would. A fireplace designed for producing heat eliminates the problem. A draft supplies the fire with outside air rather than air from within the room.

CHIMNEYS

All fireplaces and fuel-burning equipment, such as stoves and furnaces, require some type of chimney. (Fig. 9-1). The chimney must be designed and built so that it produces sufficient draft to supply an adequate quantity of fresh air to the fire and to expel smoke and gases emitted by the fire or equipment. A chimney located entirely inside a building has better draft than an exterior chimney because the masonry retains heat longer when protected from cold outside air.

A poorly constructed chimney will be a constant source of trouble and create a poor source of heat. The construction of a chimney should be designed to retain as much heat as possible to reduce the cooling of your chimney and also reduce the creosote and condensation buildup. This is especially important when the fire will burn overnight. Good construction also aids in proper draft.

The lining should be smooth, clean, and nonporous so that it is easily cleaned and will not absorb moisture. The size of the liner should not be reduced to a size smaller than the stovepipe connecting the stove to the chimney. Because smoke and heat travel upward in a spiral motion, a round liner is most desirable. A square or rectangular-shaped liner with rounded corners is more efficient than with sharp corners.

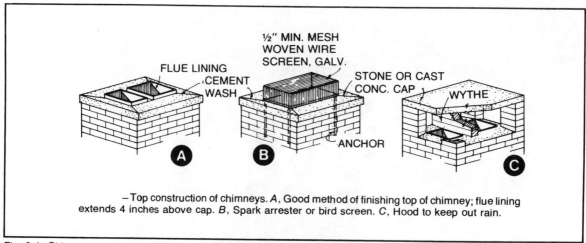

—Top construction of chimneys. *A*, Good method of finishing top of chimney; flue lining extends 4 inches above cap. *B*, Spark arrester or bird screen. *C*, Hood to keep out rain.

Fig. 9-1. Chimney construction.

Any space between the liner and outer wall should be dead air space. It should not be a circulating air space. Dead air will retain heat; circulating air will chill the liner. A chimney can be much too large for the stove to operate in a satisfactory manner, but one is seldom found too high.

The chimney to which your stove is to be attached should be clean, free of obstruction and airtight.

☐ Single-wall pipe will chill rapidly and cause poor drafting and creosote.

☐ A single-brick-wall chimney will also chill rapidly causing poor drafting and creosote problems.

☐ A porous cement block chimney without a good liner will give poor drafting and cause creosote problems. These chimneys are considered to be fire hazards and are not permitted by the NFOA or other codes.

☐ A short, single-wall metal extension on the top of any chimney will chill rapidly and cause creosote.

☐ The flue size, shape, and height of an chimney are equally as important as material used to construct the chimney.

☐ All chimneys should be constructed with a cleanout that will be airtight when closed.

☐ A straight chimney is best. If an offset chimney is unavoidable, it should be gradual—not sharp.

☐ The chimney must terminate at least two feet higher than any portion of the roof that is within 10 feet of the chimney and a minimum of 3 feet above the highest point where it passes through the roof.

☐ All chimneys should have chimney caps to help prevent downdrafts.

FLUE SIZE

The flue is the passage in the chimney through which the air, gases, and smoke travel. Proper construction of the flue is important. Its size, height, shape, tightness, and smoothness determine the effectiveness of the chimney in producing adequate draft and in expelling smoke and gases. Soundness of the flue walls affects safety in the building should a fire occur in the chimney. Overheated or defective flues are one of the chief causes of house fires.

HEIGHT

A chimney should extend at least 3 feet above flat roofs and at least 2 feet above a roof ridge or raised part of a roof within 10 feet of the chimney. A hood (Fig. 9-2) should be provided if a chimney cannot be built high enough above a ridge to prevent trouble from eddies caused by wind being deflected from the roof. The open ends of the hood should be parallel to the ridge.

Low-cost, metal-pipe extensions are sometimes used to increase flue height, but they are not as durable or as attractive as terra-cotta chimney pots or extensions. Metal extensions must be securely anchored against the wind and must have the same cross-sectional area as the flue. They are available with a metal cowl or top that turns with the wind to prevent air from blowing down the flue.

SUPPORT

The chimney is usually the heaviest part of a building and it must rest on a solid foundation to prevent differential settlement in the building. Concrete footings are recommended. They must be designed to distribute the load over an area wide enough to avoid exceeding the safe load-bearing capacity of the soil. They should extend at least 6 inches beyond the chimney on all sides and should be 8 inches thick for one-story houses and 12 inches thick for two-story houses having basements. If there is no basement, pour the footings for an exterior chimney on solid ground below the frostline.

If the house wall is of solid masonry at least 12 inches thick, the chimney can be built integrally with the wall and, instead of being carried down to the ground, it can be offset from the wall enough to provide flue space by corbelling. The offset should not extend more than 6 inches from the face of the wall. Each course should project not more than 1 inch and should be not less than 12 inches high.

Chimneys in frame buildings should be built from the ground up or they can rest on the building foundation or basement walls if the walls are of solid masonry (12 inches thick with adequate footings).

FLUE LINING

Chimneys are sometimes built without flue lining to reduce cost, but those with lined flues are safer and

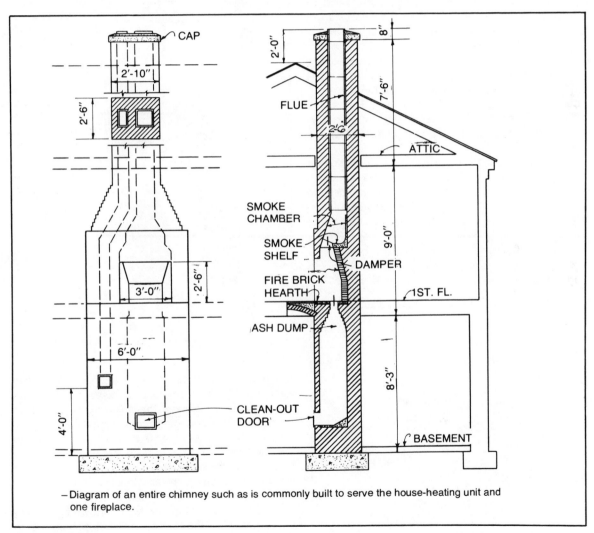

—Diagram of an entire chimney such as is commonly built to serve the house-heating unit and one fireplace.

Fig. 9-2. Height for chimneys.

221

more efficient. Lined flues are definitely recommended for brick chimneys. When the flue is not lined, mortar and bricks directly exposed to the action of flue gases disintegrate. This disintegration, plus that caused by temperature changes, can open cracks in the masonry that will reduce the draft and increase the fire hazard.

Flue lining must withstand rapid fluctuations in temperature and the action of flue gases. Therefore, it should be made of vitrified fire clay at least ⅝ of an inch thick.

Both rectangular and round-shaped linings are available. Rectangular lining is better adapted to brick construction, but round lining is more efficient.

Each length of lining should be placed in position—set in cement mortar with the joint struck smooth on the inside—and then the brick laid around it. If the lining is slipped down after several courses of brick have been laid, the joints cannot be filled and leakage will occur. In masonry chimneys with walls less than 8 inches thick, there should be space between the lining and the chimney walls. This space should not be filled with mortar. Use only enough mortar to make good joints and to hold the lining in position.

Unless it rests on solid masonry at the bottom of the flue, the lower section of lining must be supported on at least three sides by brick courses projecting to the inside surface of the lining. This lining should extend to a point at least 8 inches under the smoke pipe thimble or flue ring. See Fig. 9-3.

Flues should be as nearly vertical as possible. If a change in direction is necessary, the angle should never exceed 45 degrees. An angle of 30 degrees or

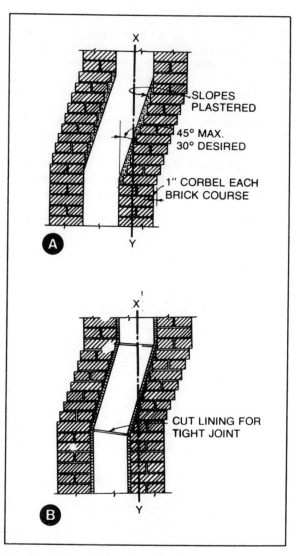

Fig. 9-4. Flue positions.

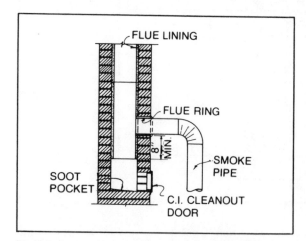

Fig. 9-3. Soot pocket and cleanout for a chimney flue.

less is better because sharp turns set up eddies that affect the motion of smoke and gases. Where a flue does change directions, the lining joints should be made tight by mitering or cutting equally the ends of the adjoining sections. Cut the lining before it is built in the chimney; if cut after, it might break and fall out of place. To cut the lining, stuff a sack of damp sand into it and then tap a sharp chisel with a light hammer along the desired line of cut. See Fig. 9-4.

When laying lining and brick, draw a tight-fitting bag of straw up the flue as the work progresses to catch material that might fall and block the flue.

WALLS

Walls of chimneys with lined flues, and not more than 30 feet high, should be at least 4 inches thick if made of brick or reinforced concrete, and at least 12 inches thick if made of stone. Flue lining is recommended, especially for brick chimneys, but it can be omitted if the chimney walls are made of reinforced concrete at least 6 inches thick or if unreinforced concrete or brick at least 8 inches thick. A minimum thickness of 8 inches is recommended for the outside wall of a chimney exposed to the weather.

Brick chimneys that extend up through the roof may sway enough in heavy winds to open up mortar joints at the roof line. Openings to the flue at that point are dangerous because sparks from the flue could start fires in the woodwork or roofing. A good practice is to make the upper walls 8 inches thick by starting to offset the bricks at least 6 inches below the underside of roof joists or rafters (Fig. 9-5).

Chimneys can contain more than one flue. Building codes generally require a separate flue for each fireplace, furnace, or boiler. If a chimney contains three or more lined flues, each group of two flues must be separated from the other single flue or group of two flues by brick divisions or wythes at least 3 ¾ inches thick. See Fig. 9-3.

SOOT POCKET AND CLEANOUT

A soot pocket and cleanout are recommended for each flue (Fig. 9-3). Deep soot pockets permit the accumulation of an excessive amount of soot that might support a fire. Therefore, the pocket should be only deep enough to permit installation of a cleanout door below the smoke pipe connection. Fill the lower part of the chimney—from the bottom of the soot pocket to the base of the chimney—with solid masonry.

The cleanout door should be made of cast iron. It should fit snugly and be kept tightly closed to keep air out.

A cleanout should serve only one flue. If two or more flues are connected to the same cleanout, air drawn from one to another will affect the draft in all.

Two flues grouped together without a dividing wall should have the lining joints staggered at least 7 inches and the joints must be completely filled with mortar. If a chimney contains two or more unlined flues, the flues must be separated by a well-bonded wythe at least 8 inches thick.

MORTAR

Brickwork around chimney flues and fireplaces should be laid with cement mortar. It is more resistant to the action of heat and flue gases than lime mortar. A good mortar to use in setting flue linings and all chimney masonry, except firebrick, consists of 1 part portland cement, 1 part hydrated lime (or slaked-lime putty), and 6 parts clean sand—measured by volume. Firebrick should be laid with fire clay.

SMOKE-PIPE CONNECTION

No range, stove, fireplace, or other equipment should be connected to the flue for the central heating unit. Each unit should be connected to a separate flue. If there are two or more connections to the same flue, fires could start from sparks passing into one flue opening and out through another.

Smoke pipes from furnaces, stoves, or other equipment must be properly installed and connected to the chimney for safe operation.

A smoke pipe should enter the chimney horizontally and should not extend into the flue (Fig. 9-3). The hole in the chimney wall should be lined with fire clay or metal thimbles should be tightly built into the masonry (metal thimbles or flue rings are available in the follow-

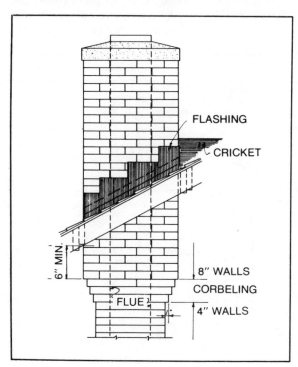

Fig. 9-5. Corbelling a chimney.

223

ing inch diameters: 6, 7, 8, 10 and 12 and in lengths of 4½, 6, 9, and 12 inches). To make an airtight connection where the pipe enters the wall, install a closely fitting collar and apply boiler putty, good cement mortar, or stiff clay.

A smoke pipe should never be closer than 9 inches to woodwork or other combustible material. If it is less than 18 inches from woodwork or other combustible material, cover at least the half of the pipe nearest the woodwork with fire-resistant material. Commercial fireproof pipe covering is available.

If a smoking pipe must pass through a wood partition, the woodwork must be protected. Either cut an opening in the partition and insert a galvanized-iron, double-wall ventilating shield at least 12 inches larger than the pipe or install at least 4 inches of brickwork or other incombustible material around the pipe. See Fig. 9-6.

Smoke pipes should never pass through floors, closets, or concealed spaces or enter the chimney in the attic. Each summer when they are not in use, smoke pipes should be taken down, cleaned, wrapped in paper, and stored in a dry place. When not in use, smoke-pipe holes should be closed with tight-fitting metal flue stops. Do not use paper tin. If a pipe hole is to be abandoned, fill it with bricks laid in good mortar. Such stopping can be readily removed.

SMOKE TEST

Every flue should be tested as follows before being used and preferably before the chimney has been furred, plastered, or otherwise enclosed:

☐ Build a paper, straw, wood, or tarpaper fire at the base of the flue.

☐ When the smoke rises in a dense column, tightly block the outlets at the top of the chimney with a wet blanket.

☐ If smoke escapes through the masonry, it is an indication that the location has leaks.

This test can show bad leaks into adjoining flues, through the walls, or between the lining and the wall. Correct defects before the chimney is used. Because such defects can be hard to correct. You should check the initial construction carefully.

INSULATION

No wood should be in contact with the chimney. Leave a 2-inch space between the chimney walls and all wooden beams or joists unless the walls are of solid masonry 8 inches thick. In that case, the framing can be within ½ inch of the chimney masonry. A plan of chimney showing proper arrangement of three flues. Bond division wall with sidewalls by staggering the joints of successive courses. Wood framing should be

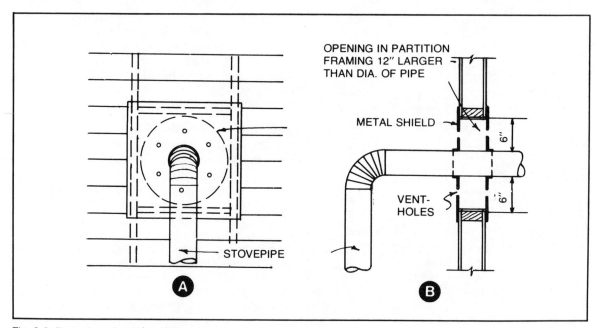

Fig. 9-6. Protection of wood partition.

at least 2 inches from brickwork. See Fig. 9-7.

Fill the space between wall and floor framing with porous, nonmetallic, incombustible material such as loose cinders. Do not use brickwork, mortar or concrete. Place the filling before the floor is laid. This forms a firestop and also prevents the accumulation of shavings or other combustible material.

Flooring and subflooring can be laid within ¾ of an inch of the masonry. Wood studding, furring, or lathing should be set back at least 2 inches from chimney walls. Plaster can be applied directly to the masonry or to metal lath laid over the masonry. But this is not recommended because settlement of the chimney may crack the plaster. A coat of cement plaster should be applied to chimney walls that will be encased by wood partition or other combustible construction.

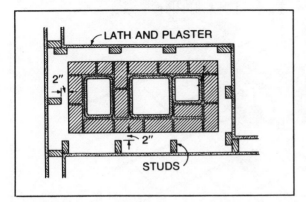

Fig. 9-7. Chimney/flue plan.

If baseboards are fastened to plaster that is in direct contact with the chimney wall, install a layer of fireproof material, such as asbestos, at least ⅛ inch thick between the baseboard and the plaster. See Fig. 9-8.

CONNECTION WITH ROOF

Where the chimney passes through the roof, provide a 2-inch clearance between the wood framing and the masonry for fire protection and to permit expansion due to temperature changes, settlement, and slight movement during heavy winds.

Chimneys must be flashed and counterflashed to make the junction with the roof watertight. See Figs. 9-9 and 9-10. When the chimney is located on the slope of a roof, a cricket (Fig. 9-9) is built high enough to shed water around the chimney. Corrosion-resistant metal, such as copper, zinc, or

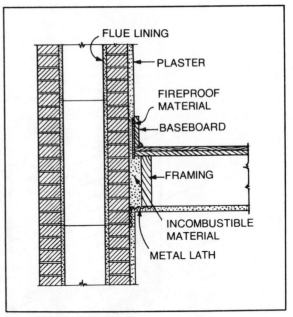

Fig. 9-8. Insulating a chimney.

lead should be used for flashing. Galvanized or tinned sheet steel requires occasional painting.

TOP CONSTRUCTION

Figure 9-1(A) shows a good method of finishing the top of the chimney. The flue lining extends at least 4 inches above the cap or top course of brick and is surrounded by at least 2 inches of cement mortar. The mortar is finished with a straight or concave slope to direct air currents upward at the top of the flue and to drain water from the top of the chimney.

Hoods (C of Fig. 9-1) are used to keep rain out of chimneys and to prevent downdraft due to nearby buildings, trees, or other objects. Common types are the arched brick hood and the flat-stone or cast-concrete cap. If the hood covers more than one flue, it should be divided by wythes so that each flue has a separate section. The area of the hood opening for each flue must be larger than the area of the flue.

Spark arrestors (B of Fig. 9-1) are recommended when you are burning fuels that emit sparks, such as sawdust, or when you are burning paper or other trash. They may be required when chimneys are on or near combustible roofs, woodlands, lumber or other combustible material. They are not recommended when burning soft coal because they can become plugged with soot.

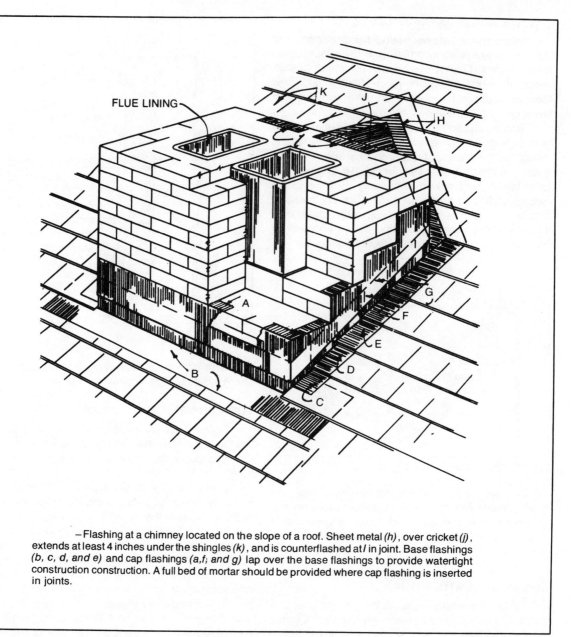

FLUE LINING

—Flashing at a chimney located on the slope of a roof. Sheet metal *(h)*, over cricket *(j)*, extends at least 4 inches under the shingles *(k)*, and is counterflashed at *l* in joint. Base flashings *(b, c, d, and e)* and cap flashings *(a,f, and g)* lap over the base flashings to provide watertight construction construction. A full bed of mortar should be provided where cap flashing is inserted in joints.

Fig. 9-9. Chimney flashing at the roof.

Spark arresters do not entirely eliminate the discharge of sparks, but if properly built and installed, they greatly reduce the hazard. They should be made of rust-resistant material and should have screen openings not larger than 5/8 of an inch nor smaller than 5/16 of an inch. Commercially made screens that generally last for several years are available. They should completely enclose the flue discharge area and must be securely fastened to the top of the chimney. They must be kept adjusted in position and they should be replaced when the screen openings are worn larger than normal size.

MAINTENANCE OF CHIMNEYS

Inspection. Chimneys should be inspected every fall for defects. Check for loose or fallen bricks, cracked or broken flue lining, and excessive soot accumulation by lowering an electric light into the flue. Mortar joints can be tested from the outside by prodding with a knife.

If inspection shows defects that cannot be readily repaired or reached for repair, you should tear the masonry down and rebuild properly. Do not use old bricks that have been impregnated with soot and creosote. They will stain plaster whenever dampness occurs. Soot and creosote stains are almost impossible to remove.

Cleaning. Chimney cleaning is periodically necessary. Vacuuming by a commercial cleaning firm is the best and cleanest method.

Chemical soot remover are not particularly recommended. They are not very effective in removing soot from chimneys and they cause soot to burn (which creates a fire hazard). Common rock salt is not the most effective remover, but it is widely used because it is inexpensive, readily available, and easy to handle. Use 2 or 3 teacupsful per application.

Creosote forms in chimneys, expecially when wood is burned and in cold weather. It is very difficult to remove. The only safe method is to chip it from the masonry with a blade. You must be careful not to knock out mortar joints or damage the flue lining.

FIREPLACE DESIGN

While it is true that a fireplace is not an especially economical, nor the most energy efficient means of heating, a well-designed, properly built fireplace can:

☐ Provide additional heat.

☐ Provide all the heat necessary in mild climates.

☐ Enhance the appearance and comfort of any room in any house in any climate.

☐ Burn as fuel certain combustible materials than otherwise might be wasted. Examples are coke, briquets, and scrap lumber.

Varied fireplace designs are possible. Figure 9-12 is well-designed to fit any decor. But, your fireplace should harmonize in detail and proportion with the specific room in which it is located.

Location of the fireplace within a room depends on the location of the existing chimney or the best location from the standpoint of safe construction for the proposed chimney. A fireplace should not be located near doors.

The most common size for fireplace openings are from 2 to 6 feet wide. The kind of fuel to be burned can suggest a practical width. For example, where cordwood (4 feet long) is cut in half, an opening 30 inches wide is desirable. Where coal is burned, a narrower opening can be used.

The height of the opening can range from 24 inches for an opening 2 feet wide to 40 inches for one that is 6 feet wide. The higher the opening, the more chance of a smokey fireplace!

In general, the wider the opening the greater the depth. A shallow opening throws out relatively more heat than a deep one, but holds smaller pieces of wood. In small fireplaces, a depth of 12 inches might permit good draft, but a minimum depth

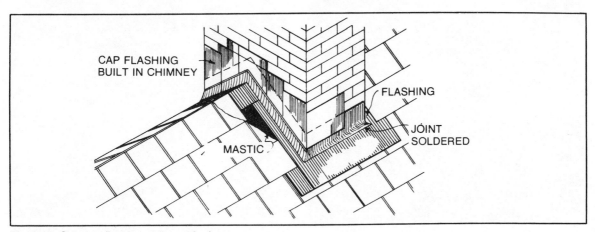

Fig. 9-10. Chimney flashing at the roof edge.

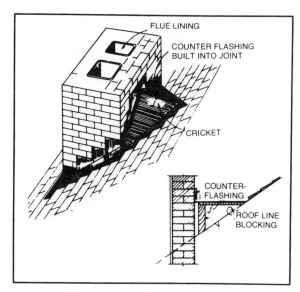

Fig. 9-11. Chimney counterflashing.

of 16 inches is recommended to lessen the danger of brands falling out on the floor.

Suitable screens should be placed in front of all fireplaces to minimize the danger from brands and sparks. Glass enclosures are especially desirable because they are:

—Ideal for safety.
—Attractive.
—Closeable at night. The heat loss that would go

up the chimney from the "cold" fireplace is able to be cut off.

Second-floor fireplaces are usually made smaller than first-floor ones because of the reduced flue height.

FIREPLACE CONSTRUCTION

Fireplace construction is basically the same regardless of design. Figure 9-13 shows construction of a typical fireplace. Table 9-1 provides recommended dimensions for essential parts or areas of fireplaces of various sizes.

FOOTINGS

Foundation and footing construction for chimneys with fireplaces is similar to that for chimneys without fireplaces. Be sure the footings rest on good firm soil below the frostline.

HEARTH

The fireplace hearth should be made of brick,

Fig. 9-12. A well-designed fireplace (courtesy USDA).

Fig. 9-13. A well-designed fireplace (courtesy of Heatilator, Inc).

Table 9-1. Recommended Dimensions for Fireplaces and Size of Flue Lining Required.

Size of fireplace opening		Depth	Minimum width of back wall	Height of vertical back wall	Height of inclined back wall	Size of flue lining required	
Width	Height					Standard rectangular (outside dimensions)	Standard round (inside diameter)
w	h	d	c	a	b		
Inches	Inches	Inches	Inches	Inches	Inches	Inches	Inches
24	24	16–18	14	14	16	8½ x 13	10
28	24	16–18	14	14	16	8½ x 13	10
30	28–30	16–18	16	14	18	8½ x 13	10
36	28–30	16–18	22	14	18	8½ x 13	12
42	28–32	16–18	28	14	18	13 x 13	12
48	32	18–20	32	14	24	13 x 13	15
54	36	18–20	36	14	28	13 x 18	15
60	36	18–20	44	14	28	13 x 18	15
54	40	20–22	36	17	29	13 x 18	15
60	40	20–22	42	17	30	18 x 18	18
66	40	20–22	44	17	30	18 x 18	18
72	40	22–28	51	17	30	18 x 18	18

stone, terra-cotta, or reinforced concrete at least 4 inches thick. It should project at least 20 inches from the chimney breast and should be 24 inches wider than the fireplace opening (12 inches on each side). The lower right-hand drawing in Fig. 9-14 shows an alternate method of supporting the hearth.

In buildings with wooden floors, the hearth in front of the fireplace should be supported by masonry trimmer arches or other fire-resistant construction. Wood centering under the arches used during construction of the hearth and hearth extension should be removed when construction is completed. See Fig. 9-14.

The hearth can be flush with the floor so that sweepings can be brushed into the fireplace or it can be raised. Raising the hearth to various levels and extending in length as preferred is common practice, and especially in contemporary designs (Fig. 9-13). If there is a basement, a convenient ash dump can be built under the back of the hearth. An ashpit for a fireplace should be of tight masonry and should be provided with a tightly fitting iron cleanout door and frame 10 inches high and 12 inches wide. The lefthand drawing in Fig. 9-15 shows a cleanout for a furnace flue.

The recommended method of installing floor framing around the hearth is shown in Fig. 9-16. Where a header is more than 4 feet long, it should be doubled. If it supports more than four tall beams, its ends should be supported in metal joists hangers. The framing may

be placed ½ of an inch from masonry chimney walls 8 inches thick.

A DO-IT-YOURSELF FIREPLACE

There are now many prefabricated models of fireplaces available. For the do-it-yourselfer, summer is the ideal time to enhance the beauty of your home, cut energy costs, and get ready for winter by installing a modern factory-built fireplace. Cost is far less than a masonry unit. Installation is relatively simple.

Factory-built fireplaces, such as a Heatilator's new Advantage unit, can be completely installed and decorated in two week-ends of do-it-yourself work. The imitation brick chase encloses the metal firebox, prefabricated chimney sections, ducts to circulate warm air from the fireplace into the room and piping that brings outside air into the firebox for combustion. See Fig. 9-17.

The Advantage's double-flow heat system draws room air into the firebox from the sides of the fireplace, channels the air over the rear surfaces and the double heat exchanger, and returns the heated air to the room at the top front of the fireplace.

Flush hearth design eliminates cold air entry slots, usually found at the bottom of pre-engineered fireplaces, provides trimmer styling and low profile. The Advantage has complete refractory lined brick-pattern fireboxes fully insulated for safety. The heat-

229

circulating air return features an extra-large screen area for greater efficiency.

Heavy-gauge stainless steel and galvanized steel are used throughout the system, which meets or exceeds all code requirements and the safety standards set by Underwriters Laboratories, Inc.

Features of Heatilator's Advantage fireplace with heat circulation, outside air, and glass doors are shown in Fig. 9-17.

The Advantage fireplace, while offered in two "standard" widths, 28 inches and 36 inches at the opening are really a variety of fireplaces because each is available with options that permit the builder or do-it-yourselfer to tailor the fireplaces to individual needs. Features include:

☐ Bifold tempered-glass doors with solid brass framing, providing a picture-window view of the fire while reducing heat loss up the chimney and preventing both cold air entry and danger from flying sparks. See Fig. 9-18.

☐ Two 6-inch diameter outside combustion air inlets with adjustable, positive-seal shutoffs.

☐ Heat ducts, with adjustable flue damper, as well as circulating fans to carry fireplace heat into other parts of the same or an adjoining room.

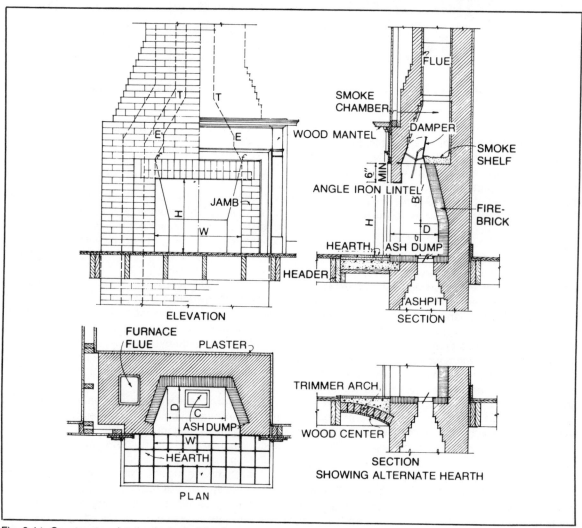

Fig. 9-14. Construction details of a typical fireplace.

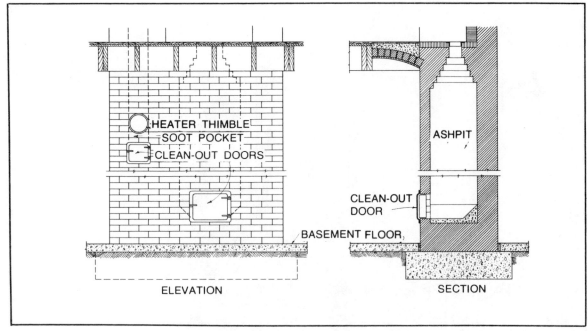

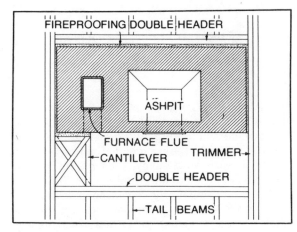

Fig. 9-15. Ashpit (dump).

Along with the Advantage fireplace, Heatilator has introduced a chimney system that features the industry's first thick, blanket-type insulation design. This Heatilator chimney has a 1¼-inch thick blanket of noncombustible mineral wool insulation sandwiched between inner stainless steel wall and outer galvanized steel wall. The design gives the chimney rigid standing strength while maintaining all of the blanket's insulating capability.

Fig. 9-16. Floor framing around hearth.

The chimney is faster and simpler to install than most chimney systems available today because of its Twist-Lock design. Assembly requires fitting two chimney sections together, twisting, and locking. Unlike some air-cooled chimneys, there is no need to separately fasten the inner, middle, and outer walls to make a complete chimney section. See Fig. 9-19.

The chimney system has an 8-inch flue. Heatilator also offers a UL-approved adapter which permits installation of the new fireplace with a 9-inch chimney flue.

The Advantage can be installed on inside or outside walls, in most instances, and because of its low profile can be used in basement, recreation rooms, dining room, living room, den, bedroom, or kitchen.

Installation of the factory-built Advantage fireplace from Heatilator starts by locating the area that enhances the room and allows the roof for chimney pipe. The fireplace can be placed directly on the floor. In most cases, no special bracing or insulation is needed because the unit is much lighter than masonry construction and it is equipped with built-in insulation.

Connect the section of factory-assembled chimney pipe to reach from the fireplace to the roof. Top the pipe with a chimney cap or imitation brick chimney surround. See Fig. 9-20.

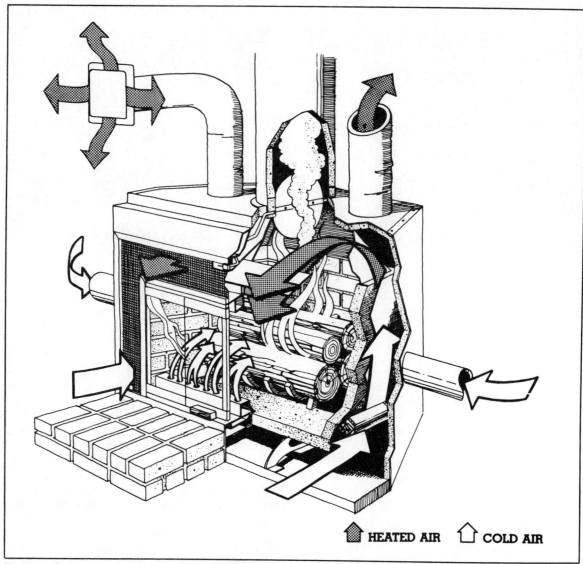

⬆ **HEATED AIR** ⇧ **COLD AIR**

Fig. 9-17. Cutaway drawing of the Advantage (courtesy of Heatilator, Inc.).

Attach the outside air ducts to both sides of the fireplace. These ducts, made of flexible metal, will be covered by the finishing material (Fig. 9-21). Attaching the duct pipe to each side of the firebox allows air to flow from outside the home into the firebox to support combustion for efficient supplementary heating.

Connect heat-circulation ducts from the top of the fireplace to room outlet vents mounted in the wall.

Insulated pipe, behind wood beams, directs warm air from the fireplace heat exchange chamber into the room through vents on the front of the fireplace enclosure. A wood frame temporarily supports the brick fireplace surround (Fig. 9-22). Attractive decorating additions can be incorporated into the fireplace installation such as a sturdy wood mantel, built-in shelves with doors and convenient storage (Fig. 9-13).

Now you can put your decorating skills to work. Build 2- ×-4 framing to hold the wall enclosure that will house the fireplace components. Then select a variety of finishing materials—imitation brick or stone, panel-

232

Fig. 9-18. The Advantage fireplace with glass doors (courtesy of Heatilator, Inc.).

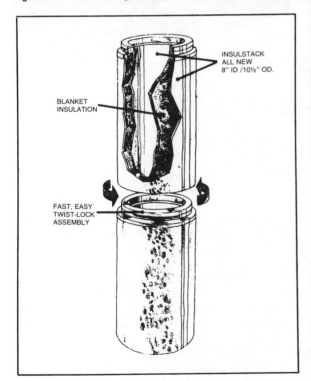

INSULSTACK
ALL NEW
8" ID /10½" OD.

BLANKET
INSULATION

FAST, EASY
TWIST-LOCK
ASSEMBLY

Fig. 9-19. Insulstack chimney pipe (courtesy of Heatilator, Inc.).

Fig. 9-20. Chimney connection (Heatilator, Inc.).

233

Fig. 9-21. Attaching air ducts (courtesy of Heatilator, Inc).

Fig. 9-23. Decorating around installed fireplace (courtesy of Heatilator, Inc.).

Fig. 9-22. Insulated pipe behind wooden beams (courtesy of Heatilator, Inc.).

ing, wallpaper, paint or a combination—to fit the decor of your home. See Fig. 9-23.

CAST-IRON STOVE

For those who are interested in cast-iron stoves, All Nighter Stove Works, Inc., Glastonbury, Connecticut, offers several styles.

The practical design features include airtight craftsmanship, energy efficiency, heat storage capability, heat radiation or circulation, controllability of the burning process, safety, and hot-water heating capability.

The All Nighter's basic stove offers several styles and provides the choice of an in-wall installation or free-standing, wood-burning or coal-burning model. See Figs. 9-24 and 9-25.

Stove Break-in Period

All new stoves require a breaking-in period of at least seven days of continuous burning before they begin to operate at peak efficiency. Many new stove

Fig. 9-24. An in-wall iron stove (courtesy of All Nighter Stove Works).

Fig. 9-25. Jumbo-Mo All Night Cast Iron Stove free-standing model (courtesy of All Nighter Stove Works).

owners are unaware of this and sometimes become dissatisfied with their new stove. Give your stove the opportunity to break-in properly by following these instructions carefully.

A matte black 122° F paint is applied to All Nighter stoves. This requires that your first two or three days of operation should be slow to moderate burning so that you will temper the finish and the construction of the stove. You should also realize that the All Nighter stove door requires a breaking in period. It is recommended that you follow these steps, at the beginning of each season, if you are using the stove on a seasonal basis.

Recommendations

First obtain a building permit from your local building inspector for the installation of your stove.

Use only United States listed chimneys, residential type, and building heating appliance chimney systems for your utmost safety and for proper installation.

All inside stovepipe must be made of 22 ga. or 24 ga. and must *not* go through any combustible material at all.

All Nighter cast-iron stoves are high-efficiency airtight stoves. They are designed to operate with the door closed. Always operate it in this position and you will not have any heat problems and you'll get more usable heat out of your wood.

Always build your wood fire directly on the firebrick. Never build it in an elevation position such as on a grate or andiron.

Parts and Materials

A noncombustible stove mat must be placed under the stove. This mat must be made of noncombustible material at least ⅜" thick. Materials such as asbestos, brick, pumice block or tile may be used. See

Fig. 9-26. An excellent design for a brick stove mat for a free-standing fireplace model (courtesy of All Nighter Stove Works).

Fig. 9-26. This stove mat must extend a minimum of 8 inches out from the sides and back of the stove, and at least 18 inches out from the front door of the stove. See Fig. 9-27.

A section of 22 ga. or 22 ga. 6 inch Stovepipe, U.L. Listed insulated chimney sections, fittings and connections is needed for the type installation you will be doing. All chimney parts must be United States Listed chimneys, residential type and building heating appliance chimney parts.

A drip-tee is needed for ease of clean out and easy elimination of creosote build up in the connection of your stove to either the stovepipe or chimney system. See Figs. 9-28 through 9-30.

Installation of an Insert

1. Remove the existing damper in your fireplace flue. In most cases, this is done by removing a single cotter pin, then reaching up the chimney, grasping the damper flap and twisting slightly so it will drop down through the opening. This *must* be done to prevent accidental blockage of the flex cubes you will install in step 3.

2. Inspect and clean your chimney of all obstructions and creosote. This must be done prior to every heating season or you will risk a possible chimney fire.

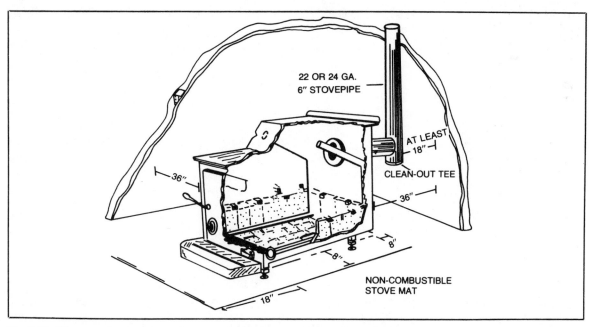

Fig. 9-27. Diagram of a stove mat placement (courtesy of All Nighter Stove Works).

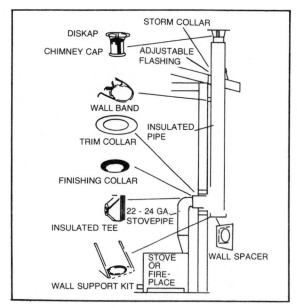

Fig. 9-28. Through an exterior wall (courtesy of All Nighter Stove Works).

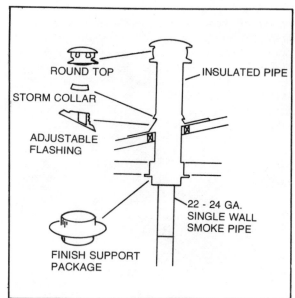

Fig. 9-30. Through a ceiling and a typical-pitched roof (courtesy of All Nighter Stove Works).

3. Set the inset on your fireplace hearth in a "half-in-half-out" position. See Fig. 9-31.

4. With the insert in this position, take one of the flexible tubes provided. Reach in from one side and push the flex tube up through the damper opening into the chimney flue. Place the lower end over one of the round openings on the top of the insert. It will fit loosely over the opening. Repeat this process with the other tube. When completed, the tubes will resemble those shown in Fig. 9-31.

5. With the flex tubes in position, slowly push the insert into the fireplace until there is only about a 1-inch

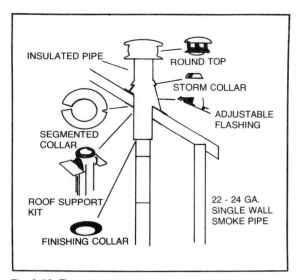

Fig. 9-29. Through a hith-pitch or chalet ceiling (courtesy of All Nighter Stove Works).

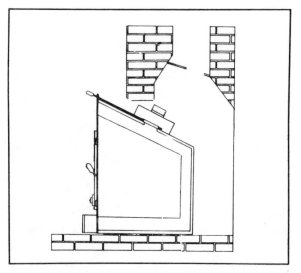

Fig. 9-31. Insert at the half-in, half-out position (courtesy of All Nighter Stove Works).

space between the faceplate of the insert and the fireplace brick. As you push the insert into the fireplace opening, the flex tubes will move up into the chimney flue even further than before.

6. Take the fireplace shroud, lift it up above the insert, and slide it down between the faceplate of the insert and the fireplace brick until it stands on the fireplace hearth. Center the shroud on the opening.

7.Slowly push the insert into the opening as far as it will go. The faceplate will hold the shroud against the brick and create a reasonably tight seal around the unit. In some cases, additional sealing might have to be obtained and installed. This will be necessary where uneven stone or rough brick facing prevent a flush fit.

8. Now attach the blower unit to the insert with the two metal screws provided. Follow the separate instructions packed with the blower unit.

Operating Instructions

Place paper and kindling directly on the floor of the insert. Do *not* use a fireplace grate. The paper will start the kindling as well as help to create a draft in the chimney.

Open the insert damper to the full open position by pulling the damper handle toward you as far as it will go.

Open the draft caps on the door to the "full open" position by turning them to the left as far as they are able to go.

Turn on your blower to the *low* speed. *Never* burn your insert with the blower off. Hot fires could possibly cause high temperature damage to your blow unit.

Ignite the paper. When the kindling is burning, add a small amount of dry wood and gradually build up to a moderate fire.

Always burn a moderate fire for about 20 to 40 minutes before adding larger logs. This important step allows the firebox, walls, and chimney flue to heat up and create a better draft. It prevents smoking and backpuffing into the living area.

Once the fire is burning well, you can adjust the easy-spin draft caps on the door. This reduces air and prolongs burn times. The best setting is with the caps about 1½ inches open. This varies depending upon the height of your chimney and other conditions.

When reloading, open the door about ½ inch and wait a few seconds before fully opening the door. This prevents a sudden rush of air into the stove that could possibly create a dangerous flare-up of the wood fuel.

This also creates a stronger draft that will pull the smoke in the stove up the chimney rather than let it escape into your room.

You must build small to moderate fires only during the first seven days of operations to allow your new insert and the cast-iron door to temper and season properly.

The purpose of flexible flue tubes is to exit the smoke directly into the chimney flue above the damper. This helps prevent creosote formation on the interior walls of the fireplace. In case of a chimney fire, the burning creosote will be confined to the chimney and will be less likely to travel down into the area behind the insert. Do not defeat the purpose by leaving the flex tube off when installing your insert.

After your first fire, it is best to leave a bed of ashes on the floor of the insert and build your fire on the ashes. Some people prefer to put 1 inch of sand on the floor. Either method protects the floor and helps hold and radiate heat to the firebed for a better fire.

Safety Tips

Never burn coal, cannel coal, charcoal, trash, or artificial logs in your All Nighter insert. They create dangerous gases and excessive heat.

Never use kerosene, gasoline, or other liquids as a firestarter.

Never build a huge blazing fire or use oversized logs. A large, hot fire could warp your steel firebox.

WHY YOUR STOVE MIGHT SMOKE

It is imperative that the installation be airtight. This is best accomplished by using furnace cement at each pipe joint, where the stove is joined to the pipe, and where the pipe enters the chimney flue.

The All Nighter Stove is designed to operate on a airtight principle. Any air leak will cause the draft to draw at a point where least resistance is offered. Examples are at joints, where pipe enters the flue, around a loose flue thimble, other flue openings into the chimney, around cleanout doors in the chimney, and where decayed mortar between bricks has fallen out. All permit air to leak into the chimney.

When this occurs, the gases and smoke are not drawn off the stove in proper amounts causing them to build up in the stove. The result is backpuffing. All leaks must be eliminated. Air must enter only through the proper entrance.

There are two main causes for a down-draft. One easily recognized is air currents being deflected down the chimney by nearby objects such as trees, buildings, or land formations. The second—more common, but less readily recognized—is that in many chimneys the flue gases are chilled too quickly as they pass up the chimney. The temperature of the flue gases drops and they become heavy. Then other gases from the wood fire have to push a column of heavy air ahead of them in order to escape up the chimney. This often results in backpuffing, odors in the house, or poor combustion.

Chapter 10

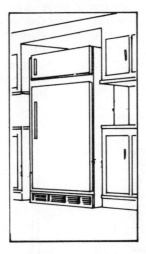

Appliance Care and Repair

EVEN IF YOU ARE NOT A professional electrician, you can do many small electrical jobs around the house. Don't attempt anything that you are unsure of, but don't be afraid to learn how to tackle some of the more simple electrical repair jobs that will help you run a more energy efficient home. By learning some of the simple elements of electrical repair, you will save yourself time and money and conserve energy.

If a piece of equipment has seen its better days, then often the better alternative is to purchase a new appliance. Nevertheless, learning how to do minor repairs on household equipment will add to the efficient operation of the home. Keeping your household equipment in good operating condition not only conserves energy, but it will enable you to make household equipment last as long as possible.

HOME TOOL KIT

The following tools will be helpful in making those simple, money-saving, energy-efficient repairs:

Screwdrivers.
Wrenches.
Utility knife.
Putty knife.
Nails.
Tacks.
Screws.
Pliers.
Hammer.
Ruler.
Brush.
Ice pick.
Flat file.
Whetstone.
Oil can.
Electrical tape.

REFRIGERATORS

Refrigerators and ranges, can, from time to time, have minor problems that the do-it-yourselfer can take care of without having to contact a repairman. This is taken care of with good housekeeping maintenance.

Problem. Motor will not run.

Causes. Fuse blown. Loose connection at wall outlet or motor. Cord or plug needs repair.

Remedy. Inspect and replace or repair fuses, cords, plugs.

Problem. Motor runs too much.

Cause. Condenser dirty.

Remedy. Clean the condenser once or twice a year with a long-handled brush or vacuum cleaner attachment. See Fig. 10-1. The condenser is usually located at the top back or at the bottom of the refrigerator. If necessary, pull the refrigerator out from wall. Always disconnect the refrigerator from the power supply before cleaning the condensers.

Cause. Food containers shake or rattle.

Remedy. Move containers so they do not touch each other or the coiling unit.

Cause. Loose parts.

Remedy. Tighten any loose bolts or screws.

Problem. Motor runs but will not freeze ice.

Cause. Refrigeration unit not operating properly.

Remedy. Call serviceman.

Problem. Freezing unit collects too much frost or

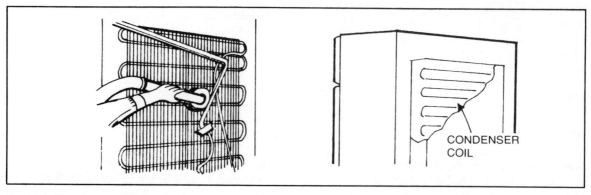

Fig. 10-1. Cleaning a condenser.

Problem. Door leaking air.

Cause. Test by closing the door on a dollar bill or a piece of paper of the same thickness. If you can pull the paper out easily, there is a poor fit at this point. Test at several points around the door.

Remedy. Adjust the door latch. On some models, this might require a serviceman. Doors might need a new gasket. The old gasket usually can be taken off by removing the screws around the door edges.

Cause. Door opened too frequently or allowed to stand open.

Remedy. Have all foods ready to place in the refrigerator before opening the door. Locate the refrigerator so that the door opens conveniently to a nearby work surface. Close the door immediately after the foods are placed inside.

Cause. Refrigerator improperly located.

Remedy. See that refrigerator is not too close to a range or too close to the wall or cabinets. Allow a 12-inch space above the refrigerator and a 4-inch space at the back and sides. See Fig. 10-2.

Problem. Noisy refrigerator.

Cause. Refrigerator not level.

Remedy. Adjust leveling screws or place a thin piece of wood under the legs. Metal discs can be obtained from the dealer or hardware store.

moisture condenses in cabinet.

Cause. Door leaking air.

Remedy. Adjust door latch or replace rubber gasket, if worn.

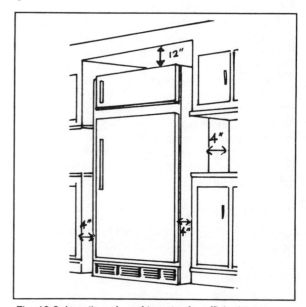

Fig. 10-2. Location of a refrigerator for efficient use.

Cause. Incomplete defrosting.

Remedy. Defrost completely; see the following general care directions.

Cause. Temperature too low in refrigerator.

Remedy. Set temperature control to maintain 35 degrees F to 45 degrees F.

Problem. Foods will not keep.

Cause. Improper storage or too high temperatures.

Remedy. Remove vegetables from packages, discard wilted leaves and spoiled parts, wash thoroughly, drain and store in a covered pan or hydrator in bottom of refrigerator. Unwrap meat, cover with waxed paper, and place in coldest part directly under freezing unit. Keep temperature between 35 to 45 degrees F. Defrost when frost becomes ½-inch thick on freezing unit unless it automatically defrosts.

GENERAL REFRIGERATION CARE

Sealed units require no oiling because oil has been sealed in the unit at the factory.

Defrost whenever the frost on the freezing compartment exceeds ¼ inch unless it automatically defrosts. Do not pry trays or frost loose with a sharp instrument. Melt the frost, by turning control switch to defrosting, or turning off the electricity. The process may be speeded up by leaving the door open while defrosting, by filling pans with hot water, or by directing the air from a fan into the compartment.

After defrosting, clean the entire cabinet interior, including freezing compartment, with a mild solution of warm water and baking soda. Do not use soap on the inside as it might cause an odor. Wipe up spilled foods immediately. Avoid the use of coarse cleaning powder on the inside or outside. If shelves became stained or rusted, clean with fine steel wool. Periodic cleaning is also essential for automatically defrosting refrigerators.

Clean the outside of the cabinet with mild soap and warm water. Light waxing with regular furniture polish helps keep the enamel surface bright (plus providing protection). Nicks and scratches should be painted with touch-up enamel to prevent rust.

Avoid touching the gasket when opening and shutting the door. Grease from hands softens rubber.

After setting the control for fast freezing, and freezing is completed, be sure to turn the control to normal setting.

If you have an ice-maker, completely empty the ice container periodically to avoid buildup of ice cubes.

ELECTRIC RANGES

If all surface units are not heating, see if the range plug is pushed firmly into the receptacle. If this is not the cause, try lights in other parts of the house to see if fuse is blown or if the power is off. Replace the range fuse or main fuses if blown. If the main service panel is the circuit-breaker type, reset the main or range circuit breaker.

Cause. Loose connection or broken wire in the unit.

Remedy. If wire is broken at terminals, clean the end of the wire and make the proper connection. If the wire is broken any place except at terminals, it should be repaired by a serviceman.

Problem. Oven heats improperly.

Cause. Thermostat set wrong or thermostat out of adjustment.

Remedy. Set the thermostat for the preferred cooking temperature. If the temperature is still incorrect, call a serviceman for thermostat readjustment.

Cause. Oven door opened too often while baking.

Remedy. Watch the clock, or set the timer clock to buzz to help you remember, and do not open door until required cooking time is completed.

Problem. Oven browns food unevenly.

Cause. Range not level.

Remedy. Test by placing a level or a large pan of water on an oven rack. To level the range, place wooden blocks under legs or discs can be secured from dealer or hardware store.

Cause. Oven door fits improperly.

Remedy. Check fit with a piece of paper. The door should fit tightly at the top, but have ⅛-inch space at the bottom edge. The adjustment might require a serviceman.

Cause. Utensils placed improperly in oven.

Remedy. Place pans in oven so that air can circulate around them. Stagger pans; do not place one pan directly over another.

Problem. Convenience outlet on range will not operate.

Cause. Fuse probably blown.

Remedy. A plug-type fuse is located in the range. It might be found at the back, in the front, or under a surface unit. It might be necessary to remove the drawer to find fuse.

GENERAL ELECTRIC-STOVE CARE

Clean heating elements by burning off any spilled food and brushing with a soft brush. Never scrape or use water to clean unit.

Keep the Four S's away from the wires of an open unit: salt, soda, soap, and sugar.

Avoid using a higher heat than necessary. The heat should be turned to cover the bottom perimeter of the pan that is set on the burner. Rotate the use of the surface units. Use the largest unit only when using a large pan. Keep the drip pans beneath the surface units clean to prevent burning of wires leading to surface cords. On some models the drip pans come out. If so, wrap these (after cleaning) with aluminum foil to assist in longer life for the drip pans and help keep them clean. For those models where the drip pan cannot be removed, you can still lift them up, wrap the foil around them and set them down.

Clean beneath the drip pan surface by wiping with a sponge with warm, soapy water.

Use utensils with flat bottoms and tight fitting lids. When a large utensil must be used, protect the porcelain enamel, around the surface, with a heavy asbestos sheet larger than the utensil with a hole in the center of the size of the unit. This is especially needed if you do a lot of canning and use extra-large cooking utensils.

Clean the porcelain top after it is cool with warm, soapy water or whiting. Wipe up lemon, vinegar, or other acids immediately.

Be sure the deep-well cooker (in models that still have them) has water in it before you turn on the switch. Always remove the pan and use a rack when baking in a deep-well cooker.

Keep the broiler pan clean and stored in a utensil drawer except when broiling.

GAS RANGES

Problem. Excessive surface temperature.
Cause. Improper fitting of oven door.
Remedy. Adjust the oven door for a proper fit.
Problem. Oven too hot or too cold.
Cause. Burner over or under gases.
Remedy. Adjust burner flame until it is approximately ¾ of an inch maximum flame.
Cause. Thermostat out of calibration.
Remedy. Call serviceman. If the thermostat will not hold calibration, replace the thermostat.
Problem. Gas odors from lighted oven.
Cause. Poorly adjusted burner or pilot.
Remedy. Adjust burner and pilot. If odor persists, call serviceman for possible leaks.
Cause. Stoppage in flue.

Remedy. Check flue for obstructions.
Problem. Top pilot outage.
Cause. Pilot outage can be caused by many mechanical or nonmechanical factors. The location of the range in the kitchen is important because an open window or door can admit a draft that could put out pilot flame.
Cause. Improper adjustment of the top burner. Too much air or too much gas.
Remedy. Readjust top burner so that ignition does not put out pilot flame.
Cause. Lighting jet smothers pilot flame.
Remedy. Clean pilot valve to eliminate dust and dirt particles.
Problem. Top burner fails to light.
Cause. Ignition tubes out of position.
Remedy. Check ignition tubes for proper alignment.
Cause. Ignition tubes might need cleaning.
Remedy. Wash ignition tubes.
Cause. Burner might require air and gas adjustment.
Remedy. Adjust air and gas mixture or call a serviceman.
Problem. Oven pilot outage.
Cause. Oven burner flame putting out pilot.
Remedy. Relocate pilot or call serviceman.
Cause. When oven pilot will not light, safety valve is not holding open.
Remedy. Call serviceman to check safety valve and thermocouple.
Problem. Oven burner failure (match-lit oven).
Cause. Dirty burner pilot.
Remedy. Clean the burner with a wirepipe cleaner or a wire brush.
Cause. Burner might be out of line.
Remedy. Check burner for proper alignment (matchless oven).
Cause. Oven pilot is out.
Remedy. Light the pilot and, in 60 to 90 seconds, the oven should turn on. If this does not work, make sure that the thermocouple fitting adjacent to the pilot light is free from foreign material. This connection should be bright and clean. If the burner still fails to light, call a serviceman to check the safety valve and thermocouples.
Problem. Noisy operation.
Cause. The burner is overrated.
Remedy. Reduce gas input to the oven burner or call a serviceman.

GENERAL CARE OF GAS RANGES

Cool the range before washing. A sudden change in temperature will cause enamel to craze.

If acid-containing food such as tomato juice, lemon juice, onion juice, or milk is spilled on a range, wipe it off with a dry cloth to prevent enamel from getting dull spots.

Use soda to remove any stubborn spots from enamel. Avoid use of harsh, gritty abrasives.

Wash with soap and water, rinse, and dry.

Use chromium or silver polish on chromium.

Surface Burners

Clean porcelain and chromium burners and drip trays with a soap and water or a baking soda solution of 1 tablespoon soda to 1 quart of water. This cuts grease and helps to remove stubborn spots.

Rinse well and then turn burners upside down to drain thoroughly and dry.

Inspect port holes to see if they are open.

Use only a fine wire brush, pipe cleaner, or a wire to clean port holes.

Oven

Wash the inside of the oven with soap and water.

Then rinse and dry. Use a mild abrasive or soda or commercial oven cleaner to remove stubborn spots.

Clean racks with fine steel wool such as soap pads.

If foods run over, let it char before trying to remove it.

Saturate a cloth with household ammonia and allow to stand a few hours or overnight. The fumes will loosen grease and spill-overs. Remove racks and wash with soap and water or soap pads that are fine steel-wooled. Rinse and then dry.

An insulation bottom should not be immersed in water.

Glass windows in an oven door should be cleaned frequently with a weak solution of household ammonia and water or soap and water. Rinse and dry thoroughly.

Broiler

After food is removed, allow the broiler grill and pan to cool 5 to 10 minutes. Sprinkle with soap flakes and fill with hot water. Wash, then rinse dry.

When the broiling compartment is under the oven, the broiler pan should be removed when the oven is in use.

Chapter 11

Appliance Management

ALONG WITH HEATING AND COOLING, the water heater is the third greatest consumer of electricity in the home. The number of people in a home and their habits determine the consumption rate of hot water.

It is important that the size water heater installed meets your family needs. Oversizing wastes energy because you are maintaining a supply of unwanted hot water. A 40-gallon water heater is recommended for the average four-member household. The number of bathrooms adds to the size water heater you should select. Table 11-1 provides an indication of how to size water heaters.

Storage capacity and recovery rate are based on supplying enough hot water for three automatic washer loads of clothing using 25 gallons of water over a 2-hour peak period. An additional 9 gph in either storage capacity, recovery rate, or a combination of the two has been added for each additional bath or two bedrooms.

PURCHASING A WATER HEATER

When purchasing a water heater for a new home or to replace an existing water heater, make energy-efficiency your main criterion. Look at the thickness of

the insulation around the tank. The energy loss during non-use periods can be considerable on a poorly insulated tank.

Gas-fired water heaters with pilot lights also can use a lot of energy keeping the pilot lit. Consider a water heater with an electronic ignition system. Two-inch thick fiberglass insulation wrapped around the outside of a water heater will reduce heat loss and result in considerable energy savings.

Select a water heater that meets your needs as closely as possible. Keeping large quantities of water hot requires a good deal of energy.

Plan on spreading out your hot water needs during the day so that the peak requirements do not occur at the same time.

Locate the water heater as near to the bathrooms and kitchen as possible. This reduces heat loss from long pipes.

If a bathroom is a long way from the kitchen or water heater, consider installing a small water heater just for that bathroom.

Insulate hot water pipes.

Stop faucet leaks as soon as they occur. A faucet that leaks one drop per second wastes 2400 gallons of hot water each year. That is enough water for 160

Table 11-1. Sizing Water Heaters.

Bedrooms		1 BATH Storage (Gallons)	Recovery	2 BATHS Storage (Gallons)	Recovery	3 BATHS Storage (Gallons)	Recovery
		\multicolumn{6}{c}{R-recovery: 100°F temperature rise in one hour = gallons of water}
2	gas	40	30	50	35	50	45
	elec.	66	18	66	28	82	28
3	gas	40	35	40	45	50	63
	elec.	82	18	82	28	82	28
4	gas	50	35	50	45	50	63
	elec.	66	28	82	28	2/66	18
5	gas	40	45	50	63	75	63
	elec.	82	28	82	28	2/66	18

5-minute showers. Besides this, a dripping faucet is a nuisance and it overworks the water heater, can erode valve seats, and often causes unsightly sink drains. Usually this can be fixed by simply installing a new washer. See Fig. 11-1.

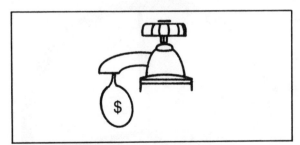

Fig. 11-1. Leaky faucets use excess energy.

HOW A WATER HEATER WORKS

A water heater is part of a system that includes a storage tank, heating elements, thermostats, and a lot of piping to carry the heated water. All of the various parts of this system are important. Many of them are potential areas of waste. To have an economical water-heating system, each part must work to maximum efficiency.

As shown in Fig. 11-2, the heating elements (1) are suspended inside the water tank. They are controlled by thermostats that are set to maintain the desired temperature. Cold water flows into the tank through the dip tube (2). Because warmer water rises,

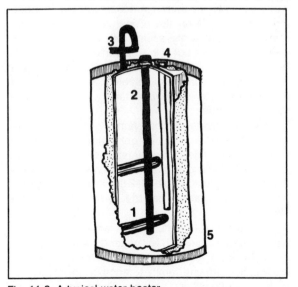

Fig. 11-2. A typical water heater.

247

Table 11-2. Consumption Costs.

Usage	Gallons/hot	Cost to heat
BATHS		
4 inches deep, 100°	7.8	7¢
6 inches deep, 100°	11.7	10¢
SHOWERS		
5 mins, 2gpm, 105°	5.6	5¢
5 mins, 3gpm, 105°	8.3	10¢
DISHWASHING		
Hand, one meal only	5	4¢
Automatic	13	11¢
CLOTHES, WASHING		
Hot wash, warm rinse	31	27¢
Hot wash, cold rinse	25	21¢
Warm wash, warm rinse	22	19¢
Warm wash, cold rinse	11	9¢
MEAL PREPARATION		
Simple meal	2	2¢
Complex meal	3	3¢

the cold water enters at the bottom of the tank to keep mixing with the heater water at a minimum. The cold water activates the thermostat that turns on the heating elements. When the proper temperature is attained, the elements switch off. As hot water is needed, it is drawn out of the top part of the tank via the hot water outlet (3). A water heater also has a temporary/pressure relief valve (4) on top, a layer of insulation all around the water tank, and a drain valve (5) at the bottom.

The average American family uses 26,000 gallons of hot water per year. Larger families might use as much as 50,000 gallons of water a year. As shown in Table 11-2, bathing, laundry and dishwashing are the major usage areas. Table 11-2 illustrates average hot water for each task. The rate used is 5 cents per kilowatt hour.

Certainly, automatic clothes washers and dishwashers have increased hot water consumption rates in recent years. Although hot water consumption varies greatly from one family to another, the best estimate is 26,000 gallons per year. The average annual

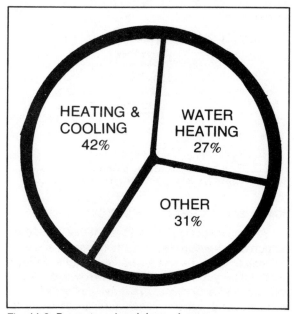

Fig. 11-3. Percentage breakdown of energy use.

248

cost of heating this water for a family of four is approximately $270 (including heat losses).

Figure 11-3 indicates the percentages of water heating use in the average home. Regardless of how old, how new or how well-insulated your house is, your water-heating system is a potential source of saving energy and money. See Fig. 11-4.

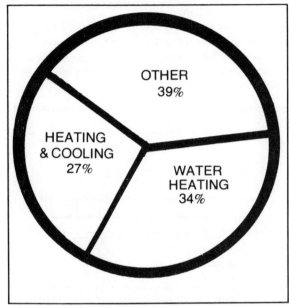

Fig. 11-4. Reduction of energy use.

SOLVING WATER-HEATING PROBLEMS

Hot water consumption in your home is made up of usage for bathing, etc., and energy loss due to an inefficient system. With an inefficient system, as much as 20 cents out of every dollar spent for hot water is consumed by loss. This loss is generally divided into three major areas:

☐ Tank loss (loss of heat only)
☐ Pipe loss (loss of heat only)
☐ Drip loss (loss of heat due to water leak)

Tank Loss

Tank losses are not water losses; they are temperature losses. After the water is heated to a certain temperature—examples used will be the standard 140° F—the heating elements switch off. Immediately the water begins to cool. This cooling is slowed by the insulation. The water will cool to the point where the elements must switch on to reheat the water. This usually happens during late night and early morning, and during the day between breakfast and 4 P.M. when the use of hot water is decreased. There are two major factors which affect the rate at which the water cools:

Tank Insulation. The more insulation around a water tank the less heat is lost to the surrounding air. Compared to 1 inch of fiberglass insulation, 3½ inches of fiberglass cuts tank loss by about 57 percent. Six inches of fiberglass reduces tank heat loss by about 73 percent.

Tank Location. The location of your water heater can affect how quickly the water in the tank cools. Common practice calls for putting the water heater in the garage, on a back porch or in some other unconditioned space. Because you are trying to maintain the water in the tank at a high temperature (140°), this exposure to extreme outdoor temperatures in the winter increases tank losses significantly.

Tank Loss Solutions

When you buy a new water heater, find out how much insulation it has. The amount and type of insulation varies among manufacturers. Although a really well-insulated water heater costs more to purchase, the savings will become apparent.

You can insulate your present (or new) water heater by purchasing a do-it-yourself kit—there are several on the market—that fits over the tank. The average kit costs approximately $20. These generally have an R-value (insulating value) of around R-4.5.

You could use fiberglass blankets purchased through your local insulation supplier. These come in a variety of thicknesses and backings. Although more expensive, do use the foiled-back insulation because of its greater durability. Fiberglass blankets can be purchased only in rolls. Therefore you might want to purchase a roll jointly with some friends. Use any excess insulation to cover water pipes and other exposed systems.

Table 11-3 will help you analyze your hot water requirements to determine whether you might benefit from insulating your water heater tank.

How to Insulate Your Water Heater

With a flexible rule, measure the circumference of your heater and make a note of it. After selecting the thickness of insulation to be used, select the appropriate "add" factor from the chart in Table 11-4. Add this figure to the circumference of the tank to deter-

Table 11-3. Water Heater Insulation and Savings.

Unit of Insulation	Thickness of Added Insulation	Total Cost of Insulation	Monthly Savings
28¢/ft.	2"	$1.46	$2.80
39¢/ft.	3½"	2.19	3.15
48¢/ft.	6"	3.01	3.70
*Note: Cost may vary slightly in various locations			

mine the length necessary to wrap the tank without compressing the insulation. The figures in Table 11-4 include 6 inches for overlap flap.

Measure the height of the heater (from the floor to the top). Note the measurement. Then measure the top of the heater by measuring from the center of the

Table 11-4. Add Factors.

If the insulation is this thick:	1"	2"	3½"	6"
"Add" this to the circumference:	12½"	18½"	28"	44"

top to the edge. Add this figure to your height (you will fold the extra few inches over the top). Example:
    62" height
     6" top
    68" total (see Fig. 11-5)

Cut the blanket to the measurements. Remove the fiberglass from the 6" flap area (see Fig. 11-6).

Wrap the insulation around the water heater (foil-side out). Fold the flap over where the ends meet and fasten with duct tape. Cut a slit opening around the top.

Fold the extra insulation over the top of the heater and tape. If there are any open spots around the pipes, plug them with scraps taken from the flap.

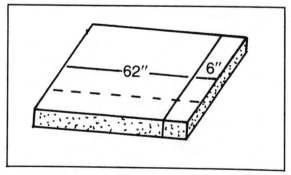

Fig. 11-5. Measure to 68 inches (total).

If you use two layers of insulation, one on top of the other, be sure to remove the foil vapor barrier from the inside blanket. *Note:* If you have a gas heater, be careful not to block the air flow at the bottom. Do not cover the top of the heater.

If you are considering plumbing renovations, think about moving the tank indoors and insulating it. A closet will serve or it can be placed in a convenient corner and partitioned off.

If you are building a new home, have the builder or architect put the water heater inside a conditioned area and ask him to insulate it or use a superinsulated water heater. There are advantages to having your water heater located inside.

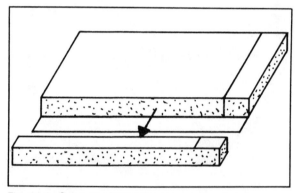

Fig. 11-6. Cut a blanket to the measurement and remove fiberglass foam.

Pipe Loss

Just as water-heater tanks dissipate heat, so water left in pipes quickly cools when the water flow is stopped. You are familiar with having to run the hot tap to let the water warm up. The greater the distance between water heater and usage point, the more heat is lost. Figure 11-7 illustrates how much money is lost each month if you run the cooled water out of a ¾" hot water pipe six times a day. The longer the pipe the more hot water is left to cool—and is wasted.

Solutions to Pipe Loss

Where possible, insulate existing pipes to help retard heat loss. This is especially important for pipes that are outside or in crawl spaces. Here is where you can use the overage of a full roll of insulation.

If you are building a new home, install your water heater close to usage areas. Generally, it is better to have it closest to the kitchen because this is the area with the most frequent number of uses.

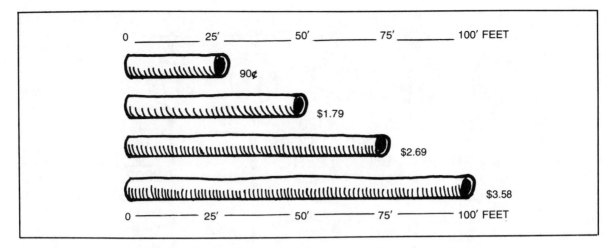

Fig. 11-7. Solution to pipe loss.

Use the smallest-diameter pipe to achieve proper pressure and volume. Larger diameters leave more water in the pipes. The "extra" water cools and this wastes energy.

When renovating an older home, consider moving the water heater inside, closer to usage areas. This reduces the length of piping and is a better location for the heater because it is inside a conditioned area. See the tank location section.

Periodically check pipes in older homes for cracks and general deterioration.

How to Insulate Your Pipes

Measure the length and diameter of your exposed pipes.

Purchase pipe insulation at a hardware or plumbing supply store. Pipe insulation usually comes in the form of flexible rubber tubing in various diameters. It is already slit for ease of installation.

Slip the insulation around the pipes and wrap every 12 inches with any good quality tape: friction, electrical, duct, etc.

Drip Loss

Surprisingly, leaks are a widespread problem in water heating systems. Figure 11-8 shows how much money is wasted each month if the hot water faucet leaks. The solution is usually as simple as the problem is widespread. Most hot water leaks are caused by worn-out washers. Washers are available in any hardware store, cost about a dime, and can be in-

stalled in 10 minutes. More complicated problems might require a plumber.

How to Replace a Faucet Washer

Turn off the water supply below the faucet you are working on. If there isn't one in your home, you will have to turn off your entire water supply at the meter.

Remove the faucet head and carefully extract the stem assembly; keep it in order.

Remove the old washer and install the new one. Make sure that it is properly seated.

Replace all parts in their proper order. Secure the faucet head and turn on the water. See Fig. 11-9.

Other Solutions to Hot Water Losses

Reduction of Tank Water Temperature. Every water heater has a temperature regulating thermostat that generally allows you to set the water temperature anywhere between 120° and 170°. It is usually preset at the factory at about 150° or perhaps higher. For more energy efficiency with your hot water heater lower this setting to a maximum of 140°. You will save energy and money while having water hot enough for all household uses.

Reducing water to 120° creates problems for clothes and dishwashers. If you do not use either of these appliances, you could reduce your setting to 120°. Remember, however, that it will take a greater volume of hot water to provide the same comfort level for showers and baths.

Do You Need Two Water Heaters? Some families that use large amounts of hot water have

251

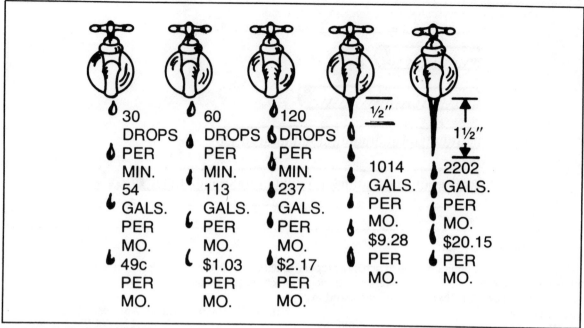

| 30 DROPS PER MIN. 54 GALS. PER MO. 49c PER MO. | 60 DROPS PER MIN. 113 GALS. PER MO. $1.03 PER MO. | 120 DROPS PER MIN. 237 GALS. PER MO. $2.17 PER MO. | ½" 1014 GALS. PER MO. $9.28 PER MO. | 1½" 2202 GALS. PER MO. $20.15 PER MO. |

Fig. 11-8. Drip loss.

found it effective to use two water heaters. One is for the bathrooms (set at 120°) and one is for the kitchen and laundry (set at 140°).

There are several factors that determine whether you should have two water heaters. Your home's floor plan and the distance between usage areas are important. An example is if your home is L-shaped (Fig. 11-10) with the baths at one tip of the L and the laundry and the kitchen at the other tip. Family size and habits

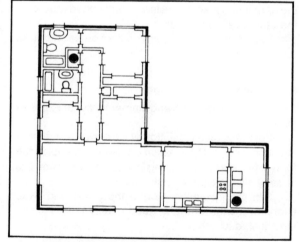

Fig. 11-10. Two water heaters or one?

are also important variables. If you are having difficulty deciding whether to install two water heaters, contact your local electric company. They will assist you in making the right decision.

Tank Timers. A tank timer is simply a clock apparatus that turns off your water heater after your major usage period and then turns it back on prior to

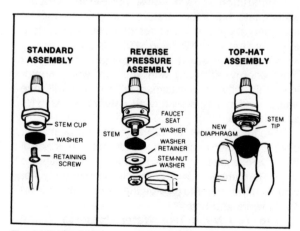

STANDARD ASSEMBLY
STEM CUP
WASHER
RETAINING SCREW

REVERSE PRESSURE ASSEMBLY
STEM
FAUCET SEAT
WASHER
WASHER RETAINER
STEM-NUT WASHER

TOP-HAT ASSEMBLY
NEW DIAPHRAGM
STEM TIP

Fig. 11-9. Replacing a faucet washer.

when you will again require large amounts of hot water. If a family follows fairly consistent habits in food preparation and cleanup, bathing and laundering, a timer is an inexpensive way to conserve electricity by letting the water cool when you don't need it. There are two important points to rememeber when considering the installation of a tank timer:

☐ A timer only saves money when you can leave the water heater off for a minimum of 12 hours each day.

☐ A timer should be used only when it is impossible to insulate your tank (table-top, builtin, or in a similar situation). Timer savings on an insulated tank of R4-5 and better are minimal and probably not worth the expense.

CHANGE YOUR HABITS
AND LOWER YOUR BILLS

Another way to cut water heating costs is by reducing the amount of hot water you use. Often this can be done without any real difference in comfort or service.

For example, take the practice of using cold water to wash your hands. Sometimes you really need hot water, but usually cold water will do perfectly well. How many times have you turned on the hot water and finished washing your hands before the water got hot? All you really do is fill the pipe between the water heater and sink with hot water. This water then cools and is wasted (thus wasting energy).

Some Practical Conservation Measures

Location of the water heater is first and foremost. Locating your hot water heater as close to the point where it is used is a fundamental requirement for minimizing water heater energy requirements. Long pipe runs result in using cold water and waiting for hot water. Therefore, the energy that remains in the hot water pipe is lost through dissipation. It might be true that a greater volume of hot water is used in the bathroom, but the number of withdrawals is the important figure.

Because there are many more withdrawals of hot water at the kitchen sink compared to the bathroom, it is important that the pipe leading to the sink be short. Losses of energy in pipes due to heat dissipation can be minimized by insulating hot water pipes from the source to the point of use.

Do not run hot water needlessly.

Always use cold water when running your disposal.

When shaving, close the sink drain. An average of nearly 20 gallons of water runs down the drain before the last whisker.

If you wash dishes by hand, stopper the sink or use a dishpan. A running water wash of rinse will use about 30 gallons of water per meal. Rinse dishes under cold water.

Equipping your shower with a flow control or regulator will reduce the volume of water to between 2 and 4 gallons per minute while increasing the pressure to a stimulating 30 pounds per square inch. These devices are usually available at your local hardware or plumbing supply store.

Shampoo your hair in the sink instead of the shower and you'll save three times as much hot water.

Do not overheat water for *any* needs. In most cases 140° hot water is a good temperature for any normal house.

Dishwasher manufacturers have long recommended a water temperature ranging from 140° to 160° delivered to the dishwasher. The reasons are that animal fats and tallow, plus everyday food soils, are not soluble below 130°. Not only do they stay on the dishes, but they can be deposited as a waxy film on all items in the machine.

Another reason is that the detergents themselves are not soluble below 115°. Don't think that the heating element in your dishwasher will make up for low water temperature. It is only tended to maintain water temperature.

Some machines do offer a thermostatically controlled delay while the water is brought to the correct temperature. Others have a sanitizing rinse that reduces bacteria count, but has little cleaning effectiveness. For every 10 degrees you raise the temperature above 140° degrees, your hot water costs increase 3 percent. Wait until your dishwasher is full—but not overloaded—before turning it on.

The conservation of hot water in the laundry requires common sense. Obviously, some items need hot water. Combining dissimilar fabrics and soils to make a full load can bring about a disasterous result. Therefore, it is perhaps better to wash smaller loads of similar fabrics and simply use a lower water level.

Although there is a variety of cold water detergents available, greasy soils (including skin oils) will need the hotter 140° water. For many fabrics and soils, warm-water washing is satisfactory and will reduce hot water needs by 30 percent.

Perhaps the best combination overall—when fabrics and soil permit—is a warm-water wash and cold-cold-water rinse. Cold rinse can save about a third of hot-water requirements. Most washers now on the market offer a wide choice of water temperature combinations, water levels, and cycles so that water heating costs can be reduced by programming your washer to suit the load and soil.

LAUNDRY
TECHNIQUES FOR SAVING ENERGY

Eighty percent of the family wash is done in the home laundry. It requires energy for water heating, washing, and drying. Many factors are involved:

—Water temperature.
—Detergents.
—Cleaning agents.
—Varied fabrics and finishes.
—Overall laundering practices.

Water Temperature

The biggest share of energy used for washing clothes, approximately 85 percent, is for heating water. Your washer can run about 50 cycles on the energy needed to heat water for just one hot-water wash. The general rule of thumb is the hotter the water the cleaner the clothes and the colder the water the more difficult the cleaning job. Nevertheless, hot, warm, and cold water all have a place in energy conservation if you learn how to use them.

Standard capacity washers use 16 to 18 gallons (61 to 69 liters) of water per fill (plus spray). Large capacity washers use 22 to 27 gallons (84 to 103 liters) per fill (plus spray). Most washers have two fills and use 2 to 3 gallons (8 to 12 liters) of water for spray. A hot water and warm rinse in a standard capacity washer would use about 25 to 28 gallons (95 to 107 liters) of cold water. Studies have shown that the average washing temperature is between 125° and 135°. Energy consumption can be reduced about 50 percent by using warm water for washing and cold water for rinsing. And you can save even more if you wash and rinse some laundry loads in cold water.

For best results, the most important factors in selecting water temperature are:

—Type of fabric.
—Color of fabric.
—Amount of soil.

Guidelines

Use hot (130° or warmer) water for:

☐ One-hundred percent white and colorfast cottons.
☐ Heavily soiled white or light-colored cottons.
☐ Greasy, oily stains that generally need hot water to melt and remove fats.
☐ Perspiration and deodorant stains.
☐ Diapers.

Use warm (100° to 110°) water for:
☐ Man-made fabrics.
☐ Knits.
☐ Woven fabrics.
☐ Permanent press.
☐ Wash and wear.

All of the preceding require less pressing with warm wash and cold rinse.

Use cold (80° or cooler) water for:

☐ All rinsing. You can use cold water for all rinsing regardless of wash water temperature.
☐ Washable woolens.
☐ Bright or intense colors (unless heavily soiled.
☐ Dark or bright colors that bleed.
☐ Stains such as blood, fruit juices, and milk.
☐ Moderately to heavily soiled items that have been presoaked or pretreated.

Washing

While the typical home washer is designed to wash, rinse and extract water from the clothes without attention, it is essential that the dial settings and other laundry techniques be adhered to for it to do an effective job without wasting energy. Good laundering practices are always important regardless of water temperature, but they become especially important for cold-water washing where the removal of soil is somewhat more difficult to accomplish.

Do it right the first time. Each load is unique. If washing results are not acceptable and clothes have to be rewashed, energy is wasted. If you are cold-water washing, extra steps might be needed for satisfactory results.

Measure the cold water temperature using a candy thermometer or cooking thermometer. (Fig. 11-11). For best results, cold water should be 60° or warmer (preferably 70°). Temperatures below 50° are generally too cold to give good washing results for modern fabrics with today's detergents. Remember,

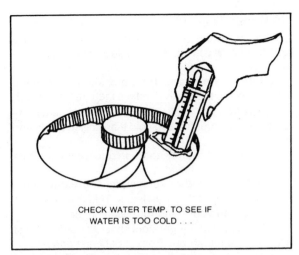

CHECK WATER TEMP. TO SEE IF
WATER IS TOO COLD . . .

Fig. 11-11. Checking water temperature.

cold tap water temperatures change with the seasons and vary according to location.

Use a water softener if your water is hard or if it is medium to hard and you use a nonphosphate detergent. Although soft water means cleaner washes regardless of water temperature, soft water is especially helpful when using cold water.

Pretreat spots, stains, and heavy or greasy soils with your liquid detergent, powdered-detergent paste, or a laundry penetrating aid. Pretreating sprays, spot removers, and grease solvents are needed as substitutes for hot water that is generally used for oily soil removal. See Fig. 11-12.

Use more detergent. The exact quantity of detergent will depend on water hardness, the type of detergent, the amount of soil, the size of the load. As a general rule for cold water wash, use 1½ times the usual amount of detergent.

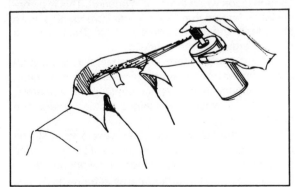

Fig. 11-12. Pretreat spots and stains.

Carefully read and follow directions on your detergents and cleaning agents for the best results as well as for energy conservation.

Fill your washer with cold water, add the detergent in liquid form, then agitate a few minutes before adding clothes.

Wash longer. Select the longest cycle on your washer or add agitation time to a short cycle. For best soil removal, agitate the wash load for 12 to 14 minutes or use a prewash or presoak to give extra washing action.

Have the washer close to the water heater because the water will cool as it travels through the pipes. Generally, the temperatures will drop about 1° per foot of pipe. See Fig. 11-13.

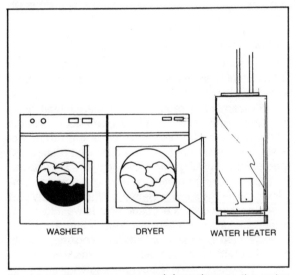

WASHER   DRYER   WATER HEATER

Fig. 11-13. Keep the washer and dryer close to the water heater.

The preceding are just a few energy conservation methods you should be practicing in the laundry. Many more can be practiced after careful thought and consideration.

ENERGY AND THE KITCHEN

The kitchen is an area where meals are prepared, dishes are washed, water and lights are frequently used, and people gather. All of these things consume energy. There are many "hidden" energy-using factors centered in this area of the home. Learning about just a few will help you curtail your energy consumption and expenditures.

255

Microwave Cooking

Microwave cooking has increased in popularity not only because of its speed, but because it is considered energy efficient. Microwave cooking is meant to supplement and compliment conventional cooking. Some foods require longer, slower cooking to develop full flavor and texture. This can be accomplished more satisfactorily with conventional cooking procedures. Nevertheless, you can produce up to 95 percent of your cooked meals with a microwave oven. A tremendous energy saver!

All microwave ovens must meet rigid government standards for safe use. If damaged or misused in a way that will allow microwave energy to escape, a microwave oven might leak energy in small amounts. It is important that the manufacturer's directions on use and care be followed.

Ways to Cut Energy for Cooking

Be sure your range is turned off immediately after use. Establish the habit of turning off the range before removing the utensil.

Frozen foods require more energy than completely thawed foods whether you are cooking in the oven, under the broiler, or on top of the range. For instance, a roast that has been defrosted requires 33 percent less cooking time than one that is still frozen.

Use cooking utensils of the right size to completely cover the surface element. Whenever any part of the cooking coils is exposed heat is wasted. Pressure cookers are excellent for conservation of energy.

Develop the habit of "lids on" cooking. Tightly fitted lids help keep heat within the utensils while permitting the use of lower temperature settings and shorter cooking time.

Reflector pans beneath cook-top heating elements should be used.

For self-cleaning ovens, it means you are using 15 percent less energy than a comparable range not equipped with a self-cleaning oven. This energy savings is made possible by the additional insulation. A study indicates this energy savings offsets the annual energy use of the self-cleaning feature.

Do not peek into the oven as food is cooking. This permits heat to escape and wastes energy. Each time the door is opened, the oven temperature drops 25 to 50 degrees.

When heating or boiling a large quantity of water, start with hot tap water. A major part of the heating has already been done at a more efficient rate.

Cut Energy Costs of Food Preservation

The following are some helpful energy saving hints as to how you can save while storing or preserving food.

Refrigerators and freezers should be filled to the proper capacity that makes them most efficient.

A half-empty appliance uses more energy because air is harder to keep cold than chilled foods and liquids.

Place foods slightly apart on refrigerator shelves for proper air circulation.

Gaskets around the refrigerator and doors should be checked regularly for air leaks. This is easily done by feeling with your hand for escaping air.

Nonfrost-free refrigerators should be defrosted at least twice a month and freezers at least annually. A frost build up of more than ¼ inch makes the cooling unit work harder.

Estimates vary widely on just how much more energy self-defrosting refrigerators use than the older models that require defrosting. Due to the variation in different models and individual usage, it is almost impossible to estimate how much more energy is used. It is true, in general, that they do use more energy. Nevertheless, it also has been shown that, in addition to convenience, a self-defrosting refrigerator can save energy by eliminating the need to defrost.

When conventional units are defrosted, the freezer section must be completely emptied and warmed to room temperature. Then it must be refilled and its motors must work double-duty bringing the temperature back to 0 degrees F.

Chest-type freezers are less likely to lose cold air, when doors are opened, than upright freezers.

Some self-defrosting refrigerators have tiny heaters in the doors to prevent the build up of moisture from condensation when the door is opened. This is a convenience feature that keeps water from running down the sides of the unit and onto the floor. The amount of extra energy required is negligible.

Place refrigerators and freezers in a location away from warm air sources as direct sunlight or heating equipment such as space heaters, water heaters, dishwashers, washing machines, clothes dryers, and ranges.

Keep the lids on liquids as covers in frost-free units. Moisture is drawn into the air from uncovered liquids. This makes your refrigerator work harder.

Set refrigerator temperatures at between 37 and 42 degrees and the freezer set to 0 degrees. Turn the

Table 11-5. General Living Costs.

Function Activity	Estimated (kwh or Th)	Typical Energy Cost
LIGHTING:		
General household	3 kwh per day	15¢ per day
Outdoor gas light single mantle	½ Th per day	15¢ per day
FOOD:		
Broiler, portable, electric	1½ kwh per hour	8¢ per hour
Coffeemaker, electric	¼ kwh per brew	1¼¢ per brew
Dishwasher, electric for normal cycle	1 kwh per load	5¢ per load
Electricity required for hot water	3 kwh per load	15¢ per load
Or gas required for the hot water	1/6Th per load	5¢ per load
Freezer, frostless 15-cu. ft.	5 kwh per day	25¢ per day
Freezer, 15 cu. ft. manual def.	3 kwh per day	15¢ per day
Frying pan, elec.	½ kwh per hour	2½¢ per hour
Microwave Oven (5 mins)	1/10 kwh per use	½¢ per use
Oven, elec-self-cleaning	½ Th per clean	15¢ per clean
Range, electric	1 kw per meal	5¢ per meal
Range, gas, total use	1/10Th per meal	3¢ per meal
Range, pilot light usage (800 BTU per hour)	1/5Th per day	6¢ per day
Refrigeration, frostless 16 cu. ft.	5 kwh per day	25¢ per day
Refrigerator, frostless-20-cu.ft.	5 kwh per day	30¢ per day
Refrigerator, partial automatic, 12 cu. ft.	3 kwh per day	15¢ per day
Refrigerator manual 10 cu. ft.	2 kwh per day	10¢ per day
Toaster (2-slice)	1/20 kwh per use	1¢ per day
Toaster-oven, electric portable	½ kwh per hour	2½¢ per hour
ENTERTAINMENT:		
Radio-phonograph	1/10 kwh per hour	¼¢ per hour
TV, black and white	¼ kwh per hour	1½¢ per hour
TV, color	1/3 kwh per hour	2¢ per hour
TV, Instant-on-Feature	From 4 to 43 kwh per month	20¢ to 2.15 per month
LAUNDRY:		
Clothes dryer, electric	3 kwh per load	15¢ per load
Clothes dryer, gas with elec. ignition	¼ kwh plus 1/6Th per load	6¼¢ per load
Steam iron (hand)	1/3 kwh per hour	1¾¢ per hour
Washing machine, cold water (50 gallons)	¼ kwh per load	1¼¢ per load
electricity used for hot water	6 kwh per load	30¢ per load
or gas required for the hot water	1/3 Th per load	10¢ per load
Water heater, gas (about 62 gals. of water-includes pilot usage of 750 BTU per hour)	1 Th per day	30¢ per day
Water heater, electric	12½ kwh per day	62½¢ per day
COMFORT:		
Air Cond. Central, elec. (36,000 BTU per hr., EER-7)	5 kwh per hour	25¢ per hour
Air Cond. room (12,000 BTU per hr. EER-7)	1½ kwh per hour	7½¢ per hour
Fireplace log, gas	1/3 Th per hour	10¢ per hour
Floor or wall heater, gas-total usage, pilot usage (1,000 BTU per hour)	1/3 Th per hour	10¢ per hour
Furnace, gas, central forced air-total usage (100,000 BTU per hour)	½ kwh plus 1 Th per hr.	32½¢ per hour
Swimming pool heater (250,000 BTU per hr. total usage)	2½ Th per hour	75¢ per hour
pilot usage (1,000 BTU per hour)	¼ Th per day	7½¢ per day
Waterbed heater	4 kwh per night	20¢ per night

refrigerator dial two or three settings warmer when you are away from home longer than two days.

Open and close the refrigerator and freezer doors only when necessary. Several items can be removed at once to reduce loss of cold air.

ESTIMATED HOME ENERGY COSTS

The cost of running the average household will depend upon the individual family. The following (see Table 11-5) are estimated usages and costs. They do not apply to any particular installation or manufacturer's product and they vary depending on individual operation and locale. Climatic conditions play a role in the amount of energy consumed. One kilowatt hour (kwh) is 1000 watts of electricity used for one hour, such as ten 100-watt lamps turned on for one hour, and is equivalent to 3413 Btu of heat energy. One therm (Th) of natural gas when burned will produce 100,000 Btu of heat energy. One Btu is nearly equal to the heat produced by burning one standard kitchen match.

The typical energy costs were computed using 5 cents per kwh and 30 percent per therm, and may be used for evaluating the relative operating cost of various appliances. Water costs vary widely, but a common rate is about 13 gallons per penny. The rule of thumb for air conditioning usages is 500 kwh per year (however wide the variance).

Table 11-6 shows the estimated annual energy use of some of the most used household appliances. With this information, you can figure your approximate energy use and cost for each item listed.

ENERGY-SAVING TIPS

About 8 percent of all the energy used in the United States goes into running electrical home appliances. Appliance use and selection can make a considerable difference in utility costs. Buying energy-efficient appliances might cost a bit more initially, but that expense is more than made up by reducing operating costs over the lifetime of the appliance.

Do try to buy products that will last. More durable products save the energy that would be required to make replacements more often.

Do buy equipment on the basis of initial cost plus operating costs rather than on the basis of purchase price alone.

Do buy products made of recycled materials or those that can be recycled such as steel, aluminum,

257

**Table 11-6. Annual Energy
Requirements of Electric Household Appliances.***

*Source: Edison Electric Institute

MAJOR APPLIANCES	Est. kWh Used Annually
Air Conditioner (room) (based on 1000 hours of operation per year. This figure will vary widely depending on geographic area and specific size of unit)	860
Clothes Dryer	993
Dishwasher including energy used to heat water	2100
Dishwasher only	363
Freezer (16 cu. ft.)	1190
Freezer: frostless (16.5 cu. ft.)	1820
Range with oven	700
Range with self-cleaning oven	730
Refrigerator (12 cu. ft.)	728
Refrigerator: frostless (12 cu. ft.)	1217
Refrigerator/freezer-frostless (17 cu. ft.)	2250
Washing Machine: automatic including energy used to heat water	2500
Washing machine only	103
Washing Machine: nonautomatic (including energy to heat water)	2497
Washing machine only	76
Water Heater	4811

KITCHEN APPLIANCES	
Blender	15
Broiler	100
Carving Knife	8
Coffee Maker	140
Deep Fryer	83
Egg Cooker	14
Frying Pan	186
Hot Plate	90
Mixer	13
Oven, Microwave (only)	190
Roaster	205
Sandwich Grill	33
Toaster	39
Trash Compactor	50
Waffle Iron	22
Waste Disposer	30

HEATING AND COOLING	
Air Cleaner	216
Electric Blanket	147
Dehumidifier	377
Fan (attic)	291
Fan (circulating)	43
Fan (rollaway)	138
Fan (window)	170
Heater (portable)	176
Heating Pad	10
Humidifier	163

LAUNDRY	
Iron (hand)	144

HEALTH AND BEAUTY	
Germicidal Lamp	141
Hair Dryer	14
Heat Lamp (infrared)	13
Shaver	1.8
Sun Lamp	16
Toothbrush	.5
Vibrator	2

HOME ENTERTAINMENT	
Radio	86
Radio/Record Player	108
Television black and white tube type	350
Solid State	120
Television Color Tube Type	660
Solid State	440

HOUSEWARES	
Clock	17
Floor Polisher	15
Sewing Machine	11
Vacuum Cleaner	46

Note: When using these figures for projections, such as factors as the size of the specific appliance, the geographic area of use, and individual use should be taken into consideration.

paper, and glass. More energy is used in the production of products from virgin materials than from recycled or reclaimed materials. For example, producing steel from scrap requires only one-quarter of the energy it would take when using virgin ores. Making a product from recycled aluminum requires less than 10 percent of energy that would be needed for the same product made from the ore.

Do choose fabrics or garments that can be washed in cold water or that require little or no ironing.

Do telephone ahead to various stores when shopping for an unusual item to see if the store has it in stock. If it doesn't you have saved energy and time of traveling there—plus being disappointed.

Do give gifts with year-around benefits. If you have an appliance on your gift list, select long-lasting models that use the least amount of energy and pass your "energy savings know-how" on to friends and relatives.

Do shop wisely and buy the household equipment that's right for you. Using it wisely and taking good care of it can reduce energy costs considerably.

Do comparison shop when buying appliances. Compare energy-use information and operating costs of similar models by the same company and by several manufacturers.

Don't leave your appliances running when they're not in use. It's a total waste of energy. Remember to turn off your radio, television, or record player when you leave the room or the house.

Do keep appliances in good working order so that they will last longer, work more efficiently, and use less energy.

Don't think that bigger is better. Don't buy a larger or more powerful piece of equipment than you need (regardless of what it is from your air conditioner to your cake mixer).

If you purchase a new television set, buy one with the label saying "solid-state." Solid-state designs draw about one-third less current than tube sets. They dissipate less heat and, therefore, put a lighter burden on the cooling system.

When using your dryer, avoid over-drying. This not only represents a waste of energy but, it harms fabrics as well.

Clean the lint filter thoroughly after each complete drying cycle.

Do not overload washers and dryers, but do load them to their carrying capacity.

Locate the dryer in a place vented with fresh, dry air. Circulating humid air through the machine increases drying time and the energy needed to run it. A clothes dryer vented to the outside will operate more efficiently. Because a long vent pipe requires a longer drying time, the vent should be less than 16 feet long and contain no more than two elbow joints.

Buy as many no-iron clothes and household items, such as sheets, as possible to cut down on ironing.

Energy can be saved by ironing large batches of clothes at one time.

Most importantly, do keep all appliances in good working order.

Chapter 12

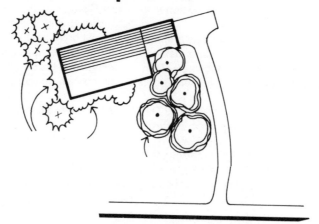

Landscaping for Energy Conservation

WITH PROPER SELECTION AND placement, plants and trees play a major role in decreasing the amount of energy required to keep your home more comfortable during both winter and summer.

Trees, shrubs, vines, and other plants protect your home from intense solar radiation, storms, and high winds. They help reduce fuel consumption, lower dust levels, and reduce noise from highways and other sources. Shrubbery against the outside walls and trees that shade the roof, especially during the afternoon, can reduce the amount of cooling required.

One of the most effective ways to shade your home is to plant deciduous trees and vines adjacent south walls and windows. The foliage screens out the summer sun and the bare branches allow the sun's heat to warm the house during the winter. Retain existing shade trees. Select and position newly purchased trees and plants to block summer sun and admit winter sun.

Take advantage of the landscape for wind protection. Use windbreaks such as evergreens, shrubs, and tall wooden fences. As shown in Fig. 12-1, a wind velocity of 12 mph—hitting an evergreen shrub planted within the immediate vicinity of the house—will be reduced to 3 mph.

Landscaping is used to protect as well as beautify the home. Locate a row of evergreens or a slatted fence a short distance to the north or northwest of the house to serve as a barrier to cold winter winds that increases the heat loss from the building. Shrubs or berms that surround an exposed doorway will help.

If possible, plant tall, deciduous shade trees for the south, west, or east sides to reduce solar heat gain on walls, windows, and roofs in the summer. In the winter, when the leaves have fallen, the trees will not block the roof and walls from the sun's warmth. Put vines and low shrubbery on the south and west side of the house to provide protection from the sun's hot rays. Shade your cooling units (compressor-condenser units) with structures of plantings. Heavy winter winds in extremely cold areas usually come from the north and west. Windbreak trees are generally most useful when planted on those sides. See Figs. 12-2 through 12-4.

USING TREES IN LANDSCAPING

A tree planted on the west side of a house shields a house from the hot summer afternoon sun. A tree

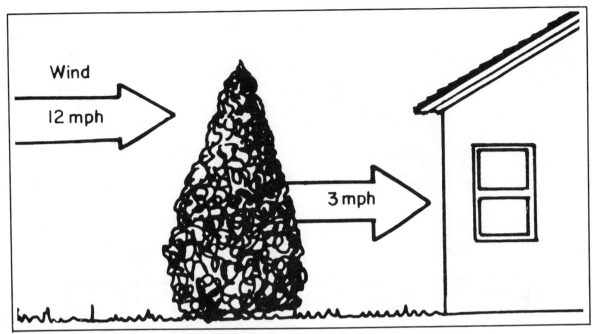

Fig. 12-1. Trees and shrubs cut down wind velocity.

planted on the east side would shade a nearby neighbor's house.

To shade a wall in a one-story house, plant medium to large trees as close as 15 to 20 feet from the side or 12 to 15 feet from the corner of the building. To obtain the maximum amount of shade, allow the canopy of the tree to extend over the roof.

Fig. 12-2. Espaliered wall planting helps insulate a home.

Trees that reach a height of 1½ times the height of the house should be planted at a distance of four to six times their mature height from the house, space permitting. While a single row of trees is adequate, another row is better if space permits. Remember that you aren't trying to build a solid barrier against the wind; you just want to break it up somewhat.

Don't plant trees where their roots can get tangled in water pipes or underground utility lines. Be careful not to plant them where they will grow into overhead electric lines. Avoid planting trees where their limbs will overhang a driveway or where limbs could fall on to the house during high winds. Think before you plant a new tree. Avoid those trees that drop sticky fruits on the ground.

For winter warmth in cold climates, an evergreen vine, such as English Ivy, is effective when grown on a sun-starved north wall. The leaves deflect cold and the stems have an insulating effect (thus an energy savings effect too). Use a wall trellis for your vines, if you have a frame house, in order to prevent clinging ivy from growing in between boards and causing rot.

ESPALIERED PLANTS AND VINES

Espaliered plants (Fig. 12-2) and vines grown on a bare exposed wall acts as a heat control device.

261

Fig. 12-3. Vine-covered walls help insulate your home for energy efficiency (courtesy of John Wahlfeldt).

They insulate walls by absorbing and reflecting the sun's rays before they strike the wall.

There are many varieties of plants that lend themselves to espaliering. Wisteria, a deciduous vine, will shade windows in the summer while permitting sunlight to enter the home in the winter. Pyracanthia, with its pretty red berries in the fall, is excellent.

DEAD-AIR SPACE

A row of evergreen trees placed next to a wall creates an area of dead air between the plants and the wall. This air has much less cooling power than moving air. The temperature differences between the inside of your home and the outside dead-air space is reduced and held relative constant. This greatly de-

Fig. 12-4. Deciduous trees provide shade to your home and they help conserve energy.

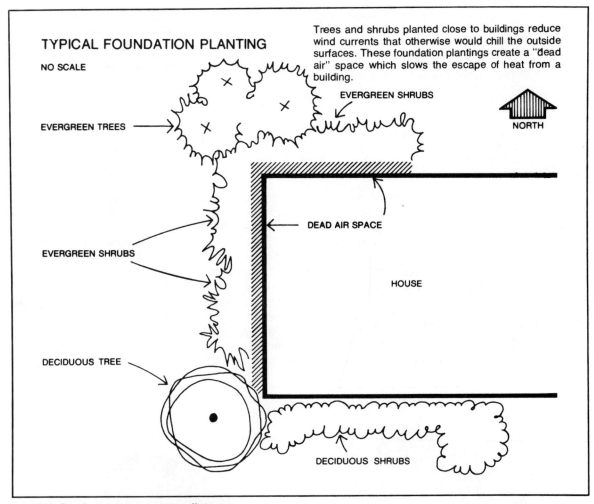

TYPICAL FOUNDATION PLANTING

NO SCALE

Trees and shrubs planted close to buildings reduce wind currents that otherwise would chill the outside surfaces. These foundation plantings create a "dead air" space which slows the escape of heat from a building.

EVERGREEN TREES

EVERGREEN SHRUBS

NORTH

DEAD AIR SPACE

EVERGREEN SHRUBS

HOUSE

DECIDUOUS TREE

DECIDUOUS SHRUBS

Fig. 12-5. Dead-air space is energy efficient.

Fig. 12-6. Evergreens provide a solid wall windbreak (courtesy of John Wahlfeldt).

creases the loss of heat through the walls (Fig. 12-5). In the summer, this dead-air space also insulates your home from hot air and helps reduce your air conditioner's cooling load.

Be sure to plant the evergreens close together because they must be very dense and form a "solid plant wall" for this method of wind protection to function properly. See Fig. 12-6. Studies of windbreaks have shown that they can reduce winter fuel consumption by 10 to 30 percent. The amount of money saved by windbreaks around a home will vary depending on the climate of your area, the position of the home, and what materials were used to build the house. In addition to reducing the force of the wind, windbreaks also can reduce wind chill impact.

263

Table 12-1. Impact of a Three-Row Windbreak of 25-Foot Trees.

Measured wind velocities in miles per hour	5	10	15	20	25	30
Wind chill index at 10°F	7	−9	−18	−24	−29	−33
Velocities in miles per hour, 75 feet in lee of a windbreak	0.5	2	3	5	8	15
Moderated wind chill index at 10°F, 75 feet in lee of a windbreak	9	8	8	7	−2	−18
Difference degree Fahrenheit	2	17	26	31	27	15

Table 12-1 shows that a three-row windbreak, where trees are 25 feet tall, effectively reduces wind velocities and wind chill. Windbreaks can be used to control snow. This reduces the energy required to remove the snow from around the home, other buildings, and roads. Plant windbreaks so that they have the desired effect on drifting snow.

WINDBREAK DESIGN AND COMPOSITION

The height and density of trees determines the amount of protection they will provide. Windbreaks of two to five rows of trees and shrubs generally provide good protection. Even a single row of evergreen trees provides some protection.

Windbreaks reduce wind velocity significantly for a distance of approximately 10 times the height of the trees. The taller the trees, the more the wind velocity is cut down or slowed. For example, windbreaks of 30 feet protect an area extending as far as 300 feet downwind. And some protection is afforded for as far as 30 times the height of the trees. Maximum protection is provided within a distance five times the height of the tree. See Fig. 12-7.

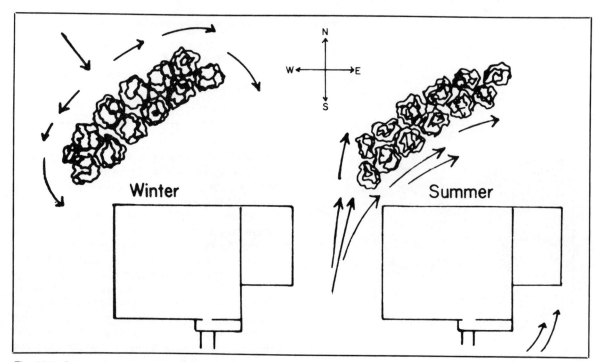

Fig. 12-7. Seasonal windbreak design.

Trees and shrubs act as obstructions and guiding barriers to reduce wind speed. Trees with dense foliage extending to the ground create a solid barrier. Trees with sparse foliage and removed lower branches form an incomplete barrier. Coniferous evergreens that branch to the ground are the most effective year-around plant for wind control. By planting shrubs and trees on the northwest side of the house, you protect it from cold winter winds and you direct summer breezes around it. See Fig. 12-8.

PLANTING FOR SHADE

Maples and other trees with full crowns are best for summer shading. Their high branches permit great visibility and they do not block the flow of cooling summer breezes.

Evergreens have a cone-shaped crown that provides less summer shade on walls and roofs. Their branches often extend to the ground to block visibility and the flow of cooling breezes. Do not plant them in the wrong location; they might shield your house from

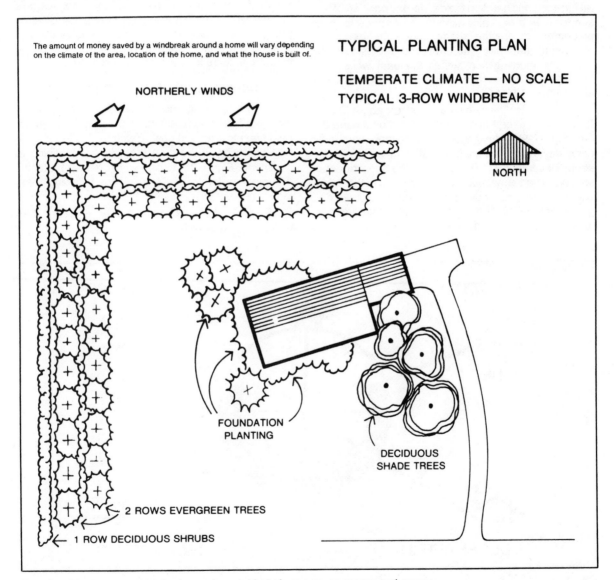

The amount of money saved by a windbreak around a home will vary depending on the climate of the area, location of the home, and what the house is built of.

TYPICAL PLANTING PLAN

TEMPERATE CLIMATE — NO SCALE
TYPICAL 3-ROW WINDBREAK

NORTHERLY WINDS

NORTH

FOUNDATION PLANTING

DECIDUOUS SHADE TREES

2 ROWS EVERGREEN TREES

1 ROW DECIDUOUS SHRUBS

Fig. 12-8. Planting to protect the house from cold winds conserves energy and money.

the sun's warmth in the winter. Trees provide maximum shade when planted in groups beside the house. Studies have shown that an 8° F difference between shaded and unshaded wall surfaces is equivalent to a 30-percent increase in insulating value for the shaded wall.

MOVEMENT OF THE SUN

The major factor to consider when positioning a tree for effective shade is the position of the sun. By taking into consideration the day-to-day position of the sun for your area, calculations can be made for tree placement to provide shade during the period of maximum heat load. The heat load begins to build when the morning sun strikes the east walls of a house. It usually reaches it maximum in the afternoon around 3 to 5 P.M.

The sun is directly over the equator about March 21 and thereafter it appears northward until June 21 (see Fig. 12-9). Then it appears a little more southerly each day and reaches its most southerly position about December 21. The angle of the sun from due south is called an *azimuth*. In the direction of the rising sun, the azimuthal angle is measured in negative degrees (Fig. 12-10). Afternoon the azimuthal angle is measured in positive degrees.

A sun path diagram depicts the path of the sun over a given site (Fig. 12-11). The path is determined by the time of day, season, and latitude. The *altitude* of the sun changes with each season and latitude. Altitude is the angle between the rays of the sun and the horizon.

A tree should be planted at a distance that allows its shadow to reach the wall of the house during periods of peak heat load. Length of a tree shadow at a particular time of day can be determined by multiplying the shade factor by the height of the tree. A tree's shadow will be foreshortened if cast uphill or elongated if cast downhill. Figure 12-12 shows climatic zones of the United States. This will help you determine the latitude in which you are residing.

LOW-MAINTENANCE LANDSCAPES

Proper planning prior to planting will result in an attractive and functional landscape with minimum maintenance time and cost. Begin by making a landscape drawing of the area that you are planning to landscape. Figure 12-13 shows suggested materials to begin your landscape design. The following steps should be kept in mind.

Size. A small, well-kept garden is better than acres of weed growth.

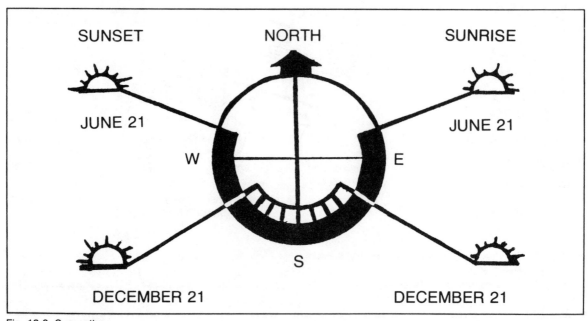

Fig. 12-9. Sun paths.

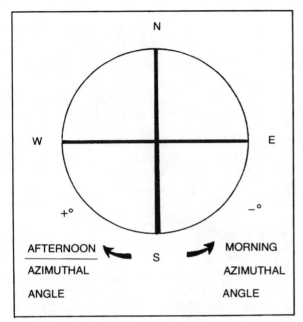

Fig. 12-10. Azimuthal angle of the sun.

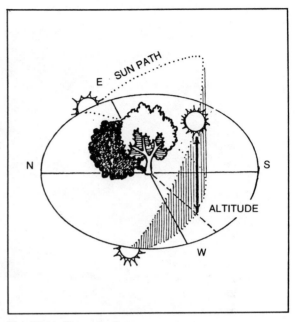

Fig. 12-11. Sun path diagram.

Simplicity. Eliminate frills such as too many flower beds, bird baths, etc. Instead of planting just for the sake of variety, let each plant serve a definite function.

Arrangement. Plant shrubs in masses to cut down on weeding and hand edging. An established, dense shrub border needs little more than watering and pruning and it helps energy conservation.

Gravel Beds. A gravel bed or ground cover around trees eliminates trimming and speeds mowing. Make the beds wide enough so that the person mowing doesn't run into low-hanging tree branches.

Pruning. Prune trees so the wind can move through them without causing damage. Prune lower limbs and thin branches to let more light reach the grass. Pruning equipment needed is minimal (Fig. 12-14).

Hand shears are used to cut twigs, small branches and vines. Cut straight through the wood. If you twist the blade as you cut, the wound will be ragged and take longer to heal. A pruning saw is used to cut branches and stems that are too large for the shears. Purchase a saw with a narrow, curved blade and coarse teeth set wide because it is best for pruning shrubs that have branches growing close together.

Lopping shears have long handles and are useful in reaching high branches and to reach through branches with spiny leaves. As with the hand shears, don't twist the blade when cutting. Small pruning cuts of less than 1 inch usually heal quickly if pruned correctly.

If the prune is over an inch, then it is best to treat the wound to prevent decay, disease and penetration by insects. Use asphalt varnish containing an antiseptic that alleviates the spread of harmful organisms. Swab the wound with alcohol prior to applying the asphalt varnish.

SELECTING SHADE TREES

Shade trees are divided into two main groups: deciduous (leaf losing) and evergreen (retains their leaves year around). Deciduous trees produce new leaves in the spring. These leaves die and drop at the end of the growing season. Evergreen trees hold their leaves for one or more years.

Hardiness against the cold is the primary requirement to consider when you select a shade tree. The coldest area, as shown in the plant hardiness zone map (Fig. 12-12), indicates where each species will normally succeed. Some species are intolerant of high temperatures. By watering, however, you can grow some species in hot, dry climates where they would not otherwise survive. In areas of low rainfall,

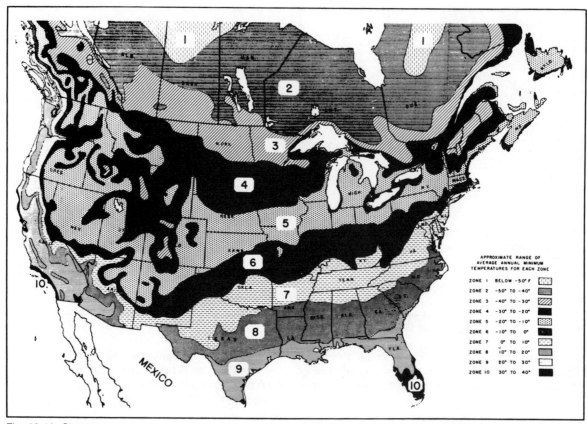

Fig. 12-12. Climatic zone map.

drought-resistant species require less care than trees that must be watered.

On the whole, however, it is far more economical to plant trees that are more conducive to your particular climatic conditions.

Consider the rate of growth of different kinds of trees. Usually, trees that grow rapidly have weak wood that is easily damaged by storms and decay. Slower-growing trees have stronger wood. If you want "quick shade," the use of fast-growing trees is possible.

In selecting the variety of plants for your yard, remember that trees native to the area are not likely to suffer from lack of water during periods of normal rainfall. Trees planted close to the street can never receive their normal share of water. Rain flows off into gutters and storm drains and is carried away. For city planting, select trees that can grow in reasonably dry soil. Then see that they get sufficient water to keep them growing until their root system adjusts to a continuous subnormal soil moisture.

AVOID COMMON PROBLEMS

Try to avoid planting trees such as elms, willows, poplars, and maples close to septic tanks, sewer lines, and drainage pipes. They clog them.

Avoid planting trees beneath telephone lines and power lines. Trees that grow over the roof of a house can fill the gutter with leaves, but these trees also shade the house from the hot summer sun. It is not too difficult to clean leaves out of the gutters once yearly.

Do not select a young tree with a divided lower trunk; it might split at maturity.

Trees such as horsechestnut produce hard, poisonous fruits. The thorny fruits of sweet-gum and other varieties can be a nuisance in lawns.

Fruits of the ginkgo smell bad when they decay. Plant only male ginkgo to avoid producing smelly fruits.

Trees such as Siberian elm, poplar, red maple, and mimosa produce abundant fruits, seeds, and

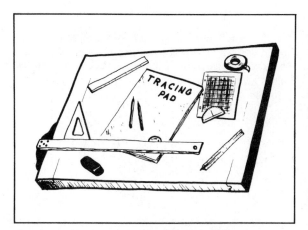

Fig. 12-13. Materials to begin landscape design.

seedlings that can become a nuisance in lawns and gardens.

Dry foliage hanging on palm trees can become a fire hazard.

While it is difficult to find a species with no faults, when selecting your trees balance the faults of the tree against its good qualities in deciding what kind to plant. Learn from your nurseryman all of the individual species' idiocyncracies and remember that your main reason for planting is energy efficiency.

WHEN TO TRANSPLANT

The best time for transplanting deciduous trees and shrubs is when they are still dormant in early spring or after they have become dormant in the fall.

The length of dormancy is dependent upon the climate as well as the kind of plant.

In the spring, deciduous trees and shrubs should be moved before the buds start to grow. In the fall, they should be moved only after their leaves turn color and drop off. Spring is considered the best time to plant in areas where the ground freezes deeply, where strong winds prevail, or where soil moisture is deficient.

In cold regions, needle-leaf evergreens such as pine, spruce, juniper, and arborvitae usually are planted early in the fall or in spring after the ground has thawed. You can plant needle-leaf evergreens that are balled and burlapped or in containers anytime the ground in cold regions is workable. But you must mulch and water them after planting.

In warm regions, plant needle-leaf evergreens anytime. They must be watered regularly after planting. Young needle-leaf evergreens will live in warm regions if planted bare rooted, but large ones will survive better if they are balled and burlapped.

Plant broadleaf evergreens, such as magnolia and holly, in the spring. The best time to plant palms is during warm, wet months, but they may be planted anytime if kept watered. Shading trees for the first few days after replanting will cut down water loss. Cover the tree or shrub with burlap.

You can purchase shade trees with the soil held around their roots by burlap, wire, or plastic. These are known as balled-and-burlapped trees. Trees and shrubs sold in containers are known as container-grown trees and shrubs. Those without soil on the roots are called bare-rooted trees/shrubs.

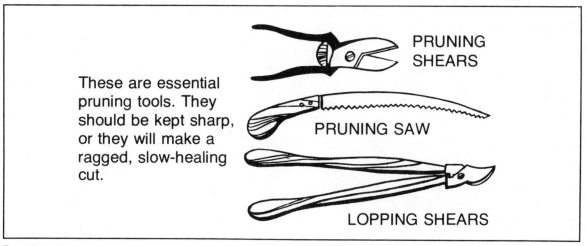

These are essential pruning tools. They should be kept sharp, or they will make a ragged, slow-healing cut.

PRUNING SHEARS

PRUNING SAW

LOPPING SHEARS

Fig. 12-14. Pruning equipment.

Balled-and-burlapped trees and container-grown trees and shrubs have a better survival chance than trees dug from their natural environment—in the woods—and they are easier to handle for the homeowner. Balled-and-burlapped trees should have a root-ball of 1 foot in diameter for each inch of diameter of the tree trunk.

Trees with a trunk diameter of 1¼ to 3 inches can be planted with bare roots and can be purchased this way at your local nursery. Larger trees and shrubs are balled and burlapped to disturb the roots as little as possible.

Glossary

ambient temperature—The temperature of the air surrounding an object or person, such as the temperature inside a room.

arborvitae—Low-growing evergreens.

arcing—Electric flashes.

azimuthal—Angle of the sun.

batts—Pressed mats of mineral wool insulation sold in 4' and 8' lengths.

berm—A bank at the top or bottom of a slope.

blankets—Pressed mats of mineral wool insulation sold in continuous rolls that can be cut to preferred lengths.

brands—Ashes from a fireplace.

British thermal unit (Btu)—A measure of heat quantity in the English system. Equal to the amount of heat necessary to raise the temperature of 1 pound of water 1° F.

cambium—Cells between wood and bark.

Celsius—Centigrade thermometer scale.

char—Burn as when food overruns.

comfort zone—The range of temperatures and humidities in which most people feel comfortable when dressed in typical indoor clothing and engaged in typical indoor activities.

condensation—Formation of water on cold surfaces below the dew point temperature of the surrounding air. It can occur on the surface of a window glass (surface condensation) on a cold inner face of wall sheathing (concealed condensation), or within a material. Excessive condensation, especially in walls, can cause problems that often result in excessive maintenance and increases in heating costs.

coniferous trees—Trees that do not drop their leaves or needles in preparation for cold weather.

convection—Transmit, transfer or remove.

corbel—To arrange (form) stones or brick.

crawl space—A shallow space below the living quarters of a house. It is generally not excavated and can be constructed with a foundation wall or with piers and skirt-board enclosure.

craze—Enamel.

creosote—Oily liquid obtained by burning off wood having a burning odor.

crown—Tops of trees or bushes.

dead-air space—Unventilated space.

deciduous trees—Trees that drop their leaves or needles in preparation for cold weather.

dehydrate—Deprive of water; dry up.

dew point—The temperature at which the water vapor in space becomes saturated and can hold no more moisture. Water vapor cooled below the dew point appears in the atmosphere as fog and on the surface as water or frost.

duct—Tubular passage through which heating or cooling flows.

duff—Dust from a fireplace or from shrubbery.

efflorescence—To bloom (blossom) out; to expose.

energy efficiency ratio(EER)—A measure of the efficiency of an air conditioner or a heat pump expressed as the ratio of output in Btu to the energy input in watts. The minimum EER for food performance is 7.5.

flue—Smoke hole.

fly ash—Fine powdery ash.

heartwood—Inactive wood section of trees.

heat exchanger—A device used to transfer heat from one medium to another (as from water to air).

heat gain—The increase in the amount of heat contained in a home, as a result of sunshine, warm air leakage, warming of the walls and roof, and heat given off by people and equipment.

heat loss—The decrease in the amount of heat contained in a home resulting from heat flow through walls, windows and the roof. Air leakage through many parts of the building envelope.

heat pump—A reversible refrigeration system capable of both heating and cooling. A heat pump always delivers more Btu that are contained in the electrical energy used to operate it.

heat sink—A building component such as a wall or floor that is capable of absorbing heat and reradiating it over a period of many hours.

humidifier—A device designed to discharge water vapor into a confined space for the purpose of increasing or maintaining relative humidity. It can be attached to the central heating plant or consist of small room-size units.

ice dam—Ice forming at the eaves from melting snow on the roof. Melting snow can enter walls and cornice.

impervious—Nonporous.

incandescent—To be hot; to glow.

infiltration—The undesirable flow of air into a building through cracks around doors, windows and other openings in the building envelope. Infiltration is generally accompanied by exfiltration (flow out of the building).

insulation—Normally a low-density material used to reduce heat loss. It is made of wood fiber, cotton fiber, mineral or glass wool or fiber, vermiculite, expanded plastics, and other materials. It is made in several forms including flexible, in blanket or batt form; fill, a loose form that can be poured or blown; rigid, includes insulating board or other materials in sheet or block form. Often used as sheathing materials, as perimeter insulation, etc. Reflective insulation has a polished surface such as aluminum foil that has high reflectivity and low emissivity.

kilowatt—A unit for measuring electrical energy. One kilowatt is equal to 3,413 Btu.

louvers—Air passage, air duct, air shaft, air hole, vent hole, or transom.

lumens—The measure of light.

mansard—A roof with two slopes on all four sides. The lower slope is very steep and the upper one is almost flat.

mildew—A mold or discoloration on wood in areas of excessively warm, humid conditions or in areas of poor air circulation.

perm—A measure of vapor movement through a material. Grains per square foot per hour per inch of mercury difference in vapor pressure at standard test conditions.

permeable—Runny, oozy, leaky.

permeance—Rate of water vapor transmission through a material, measured in perms. The lower the permeance the better the vapor barrier.

phloem—Inner bark of a tree.

plenum—Continuity, uninterrupted, uniform.

radiant heating—A heating system in which only the

heat radiated from panels is effective in providing the heating requirements. The term radiant heating is frequently used to include both panel and radiant heating.

refrigerant—A substance that produces a refrigerating effect by its absorption of heat while expanding or vaporizing.

relative humidity—The amount of water vapor expressed as a percentage of the maximum quantity that could be present in the atmosphere at a given temperature. The actual amount of water vapor that can be held in space increases with the temperature.

roll roofing—Roofing material composed of fiber saturated with asphalt and supplied in 36-inch-wide rolls that cover 100 square feet including a lap seam. It can be obtained in weights of 45 or 90 pounds per roll.

R-value—A measure of a substance's resistance to the transfer of heat. The higher the number the greater the resistance.

sheathing paper—A paper for use between wood board sheathing and the exterior covering to reduce air infiltration. Materials such as 15-pound asphalt felt or red rosin paper with a perm value of 5 or greater is commonly used.

soffit—Air hole, air duct, air passage, air vent.

solar cell—A device that generates an electric current when exposed to solar radiation. Also known as a photovoltaic cell.

space heating—Heating the inside of a building or room.

thermal conductivity (k)—The amount of heat expressed in British thermal units (Btu) that will pass through 1 square foot of uniform material, 1 inch thick, in 1 hour when the temperature difference between surfaces of the material is 1° F. The lower this value the better the material is for insulating purposes.

thermal transmission—The passage of heat through a material.

thermostat—An instrument that responds to changes in temperature and that directly or indirectly controls temperature.

U-value—The number of Btu transmitted in 1 hour through 1 square foot of building section when the temperatures of the two surfaces of the section differ by 1° F.

vapor barrier—A building material that resists the passage of invisible moisture in the air; usually plastic film, metallic foil or asphalt-coated felt.

vapor permeability—The property of a material that allows the passage of water vapor.

ventilation—The process of supplying or removing air, by natural or mechanical means, to or from any space. Such air may or may not have been conditioned.

warm-air heating system—A warm-air heating system where a fan circulates the air. Such a system can include air-cleaning devices.

water vapor—An invisible gas present in varying amounts in the atmosphere. There is a maximum amount that can be held at a given temperature.

watt—The electrical unit of power or rate of doing work. It is analogous to horsepower or foot-pounds-per-minute of mechanical power. One horsepower equals 746 watts.

weather stripping—Foam, metal, or rubber strips to form a seal around windows and doors to reduce air infiltration.

whiting—Calcium carbonate chalk for cleaning metals.

Index

A

Air conditioning, 5, 7, 72
Air leakage, causes of, 87
Air leaks, 87
Air leaks, checklist for, 89
Air leaks, common
    areas for, 88
Appliance care and repair, 241
Appliance management, 246
Appliances, 3
Arborvitae, 271
Arcing, 271
Attic ceiling insulation, 48
Attic gables, 49
Attic insulation, 42
Attic rafters, 49
Attics, 114
Azimuthal, 271

B

Basement insulation, 51
Batts, insulation, 271
Berm, 271
Blanket, insulation, 271
Burners, 80

C

Cambium, 271
Carports, 18
Caulk, 19, 132

Ceilings, 31, 114
Celsius, 271
Char, 271
Chimney cleaning, 80, 227
Chimney construction, 225
Chimney flashing, 226
Chimney flue lining, 221
Chimney flue size, 220
Chimney height, 220
Chimney inspection, 80, 227
Chimney insulation, 224
Chimney maintenance , 227
Chimney mortar, 223
Chimneys, 219
Chimney smoke-pipe
    connection, 223
Chimney smoke test, 224
Chimney soot pocket
    and cleanout, 223
Chimney support, 220
Chimney walls, 223
Coal, 81
Coal-burner controls, 83
Comfort zone, 271
Concrete slabs, 99, 101
Condensation, 94, 122, 271
Condensation, concealed, 96
Condensation, visible, 98
Condensation problems, 96
Cooling, 71, 89

Cooling-system mainte-
    nance, 89
Cooling systems checklist, 73
Corbel, 271
Crawl space, 98, 271
Crawl space covers, 100
Crawl space insulation, 63
Crawl spaces, 51, 52
Crawls spaces, heated, 105
Crawls spaces, unheated, 103
Creosote, 271

D

Dead-air space, 262, 271
Decorative panels,
    installing, 163
Dew point, 272
Doors, 123, 132
Doors, insulated, 142
Doors, patio, 155, 166
Doors, plastic covers for, 129
Doors, storm, 129
Duct, 272
Duct insulation, 69
Duff, 272

E

Efflorescence, 272
Electric heat, 82

Electric heating, 76
Electric ranges, 243
Electric service, 3
Energy, 1, 16, 18, 22, 72,
    142, 254, 256
Energy, alternate sources of, 2
Energy, costs and savings of, 4
Energy, solar, 19
Energy and the kitchen, 255
Energy budget, 5
Energy conservation, 260
Energy costs, estimated, 257
Energy savings, 2
Energy-savings
    comparisons, 6
Energy-saving tips, 257
Espaliered plants
    and vines, 261

F

Fan belt, 91
Fan belts, 84
Finish, for a lasting, 199
Finishes, maintenance of, 217
Finishes, natural, 213
Finishes, wood, 213
Finishes, wood siding, 216
Finishes, wood trim, 216
Fireplace, a do-it-yourself, 119
Fireplace construction, 228
Fireplace design, 227
Fireplaces, 219
Flue, 272
Fly ash, 272
Foamed in place insulation, 41
Food preservation, 256

G

Garages, 18
Gas, 81
Glass, 18, 23, 24
Glass, insulated, 125
Glazing, 17

H

Hearth, 228
Heat exchanger, 272
Heat gain, 272
Heat loss, 272
Heat pump, 78, 79, 272

Heat pump installation, 79
Heat sink, 272
Heat storage, 24
Heating, 5, 7, 20, 21, 22, 71, 89
Heating, area, 74
Heating, central, 74
Heating, electric, 76, 82
Heating, mobile home, 78
Heating, radiant, 272
Heating, space, 273
Heating and cooling,
    checklist for, 92
Heating and cooling,
    general guidelines for, 91
Heating system, warm-air, 273
Heating-system mainte-
    nance, 89
Heating systems, 73
Heating systems, forced-
    hot-water, 76
Home, design tips for
    building a, 18
Home, siting a new, 16
Homes, mobile, 18, 19
Homes, orientation of, 24
Hot-water systems for
    heating, 80
House checks, seasonal, 92
House designs, 25
Humidifier, 272
Humidistat maintenance, 87
Humidistats, 85
Humidity, 87, 273

I

Ice dam, 272
Infiltration, 272
Insulated doors, 142
Insulated glass, 125
Insulate your basement
    walls, 54
Insulate your floors, 53
Insulate your walls, 50
Insulate your water heater, 249
Insulate your wood
    frame walls, 63
Insulation, 39, 44, 94, 272
Insulation, attic, 42
Insulation, batt, 39
Insulation, blanket, 40, 109
Insulation, buying, 41

Insulation, costs and
    savings of, 46
Insulation, do-it-yourself, 63
Insulation, finished attic, 48
Insulation, foamed in place, 41
Insulation, friction, 109
Insulation, heating duct, 69
Insulation, installation of, 58
Insulation, loose fill, 40
Insulation, mobile home, 69
Insulation, reflective, 109
Insulation, rigid board, 40
Insulation, thermal, 100
Insulation, unfinished attic, 43
Insulation and safety, 60
Insulation materials, 60
Insulation preparation and
    installation, 62
Insulation steps, 46
Insulation tools, 60

J

Jalousie windows, 140

K

Knee walls, 113
Kilowatt, 272

L

Landscapes, arrangements
    of, 267
Landscapes, avoid common
    problems with, 268
Landscapes, gravel beds
    for, 267
Landscapes, low-main-
    tenance, 266
Landscapes, simplicity of, 267
Landscaping, 260, 261
Laundry techniques for
    saving energy, 254
Loose fill insulation, 40
Louvers, 272
Lumber, 200
Lumber, certification, 200
Lumber, grades of, 200
Lumber, grading, 200
Lumber, moisture
    content, 200
Lumber, species mark, 200

M

Mansard, 272
Microwave cooking, 256
Mildew, 272
Mildew, removing, 198
Mobile home cooling, 73
Mobile home heating, 78
Mobile home insulation, 69
Mobile homes, 19
Mobile homes and energy, 18
Moisture, 88, 98, 131
Moisture and the house, 212

O

Oil, 1
Oil burner controls, 82
OPEC, 2
Organization of Petroleum
    Exporting Countries, 2

P

Painting, 217
Paint primers, 215
Paints, alkyd, 214
Paints, house, 214
Paints, how many coats
    for, 216
Paints, latex house, 215
Paints, oil-base, 214
Paint troubles,
    eliminating, 218
Patio doors, 155, 166˙
Perm, 272
Permeable, 272
Plants, 261
Plyform, 181
Plywood, 176
Plywood, APA grades, 177
Plywood, care and
    protection of, 195
Plywood, engineered grades
    of, 179
Plywood, exterior, 177, 194
Plywood, interior, 177
Plywood, types of, 177
Plywood floor con-
    struction, 188
Plywood grades, 178, 181
Plywood sheathing, 181
Plywood species groups, 178

Plywood subfloors, 189
Plywood subfloors,
    installing, 191
Plywood underlayment, 192
Porches, 18
Pruning, 267

R

Radiant heating, 272
Ranges, electric, 243
Ranges, gas, 244
Ranges, general care of, 245
Refrigeration care,
    general, 243
Refrigerators, 214
Relative humidity, 273
Rigid board insulation, 40
R-value, 273

S

Screens, sliding, 164
Shade, planting for, 265
Shade trees, selecting, 267
Shading, 24
Shutters, 25
Siding, treatment for, 212
Soffit, 273
Solar cell, 273
Solar energy, 19
Solar heat, 21
Solar heat collector, 32
Solar-heated water, 36
Solar heating, 20, 22, 24
Solar heating ideas, 23
Solar questions and
    answers, 19
Solar water heater, 32
Staining, 197, 217
Staining, surface prepara-
    tion for 197
Stains, 195
Stains, application
    methods for, 196
Stains, semitransparent, 195
Stains, solid color, 196
Storm doors, 129, 141
Storm windows, 126, 140
Stove, cast-iron, 234
Stove break-in period, 234
Stove installation, 236, 237

Stove operating
    instructions, 239
Stove parts and materials, 236
Stove safety tips, 239
Stove smoke, 239
Sun, 16
Sun, movement of the, 266

T

Temperature, ambient, 271
Temperature setting, 85
Thermal conductivity, 273
Thermal insulation, 100
Thermostat, 273
Thermostat control, 6
Thermostat controls, 86
Thermostat maintenance, 87
Thermostat zone control, 86
Thermostats, 85
Tool kit, home, 241
Trees, coniferous, 271
Trees, deciduous, 272
Trees, when to transplant, 269
Trees in landscaping, 260

U

U-value, 273

V

Vapor barrier, 99, 111, 121, 273
Vapor barriers, 100
Vapor permeability, 273
Ventilation, 83, 94, 100, 114,
    115, 116, 117, 120, 273
Ventilators, outlet, 118
Ventilators, ridge outlet, 119
Vines, 261

W

Walls, 109
Walls, knee, 113
Water heater,
    purchasing a, 246
Water heater costs,
    cutting, 253
Water heater insulation, 249
Water heater problems,
    solving, 249
Water heater system, 247

Water usage patterns, 37
Water vapor, 273
Watt, 273
Weather stripping, 19, 132,
    133, 141, 273
Wind, 16

Windbreak design and
    composition, 264
Window installation, 135, 139
Window installation
    safety, 134
Window installation tools, 134

Windows, 18, 123, 132, 133
Windows, plastic covers
    for, 129
Windows, storm, 126
Wood finishes, 213
Wood fuel, 80